Wild Ride

The Rise and Tragic Fall
of Calumet Farm, Inc.,
America's Premier
Racing Dynasty

Henry Holt and Company
New York

Wild Ride

Ann
Hagedorn
Auerbach

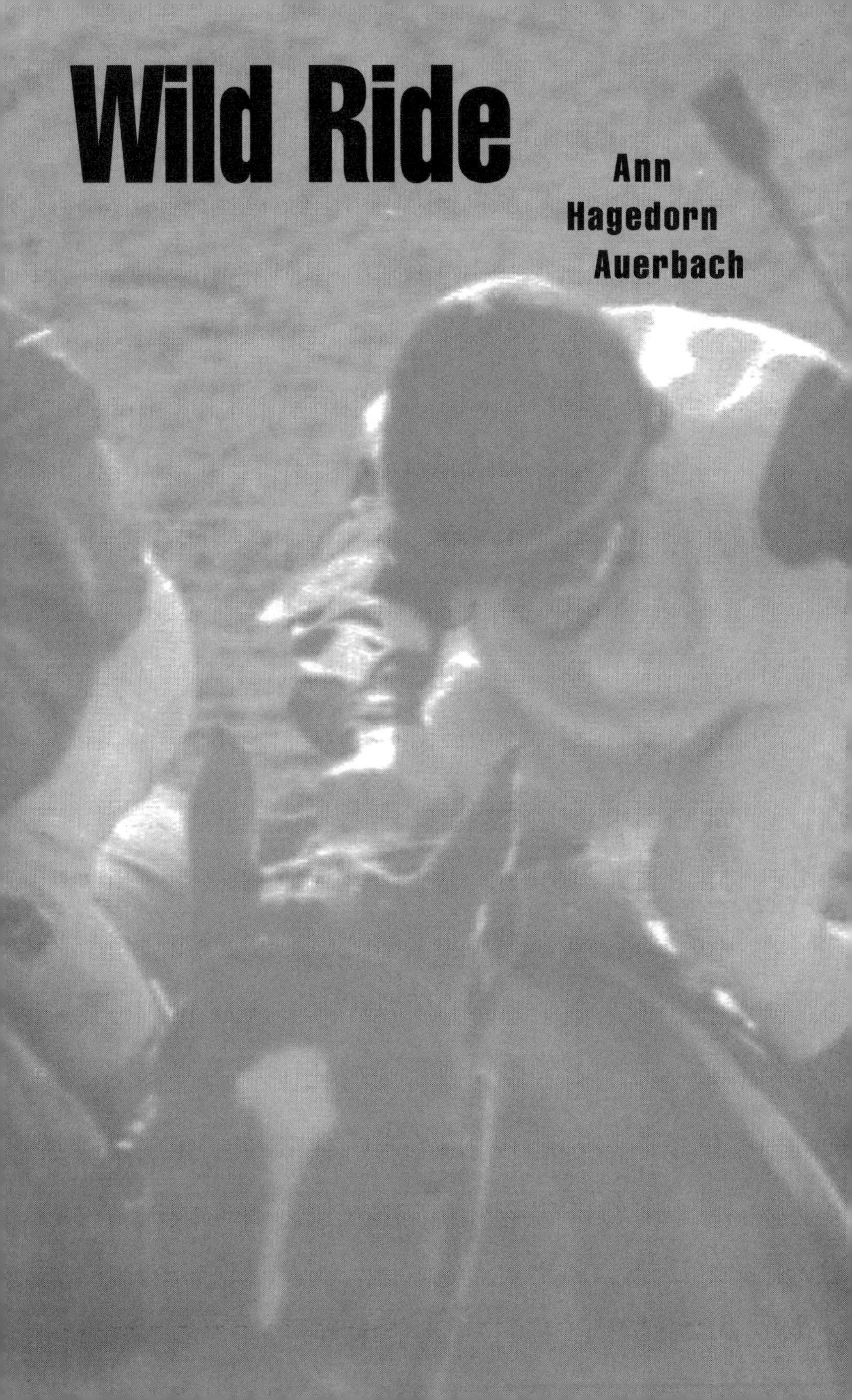

Henry Holt and Company, Inc.
Publishers since 1866
115 West 18th Street
New York, New York 10011

Henry Holt® is a registered
trademark of Henry Holt and Company, Inc.

Library of Congress Cataloging-in-Publication Data
Auerbach, Ann Hagedorn.
    Wild ride : the rise and tragic fall of Calumet Farm, Inc., America's premier
racing dynasty / Ann Hagedorn Auerbach.—1st ed.
        p.   cm.
    Includes bibliographical references and index.
    ISBN 0-8050-2003-9
    1. Calumet Farm—History.   2. Thoroughbred horse—Breeding—Kentucky.
I. Title.
SF290.U6A84   1994
338.7′636132′09769—dc20   94-2321
                                                                CIP

Henry Holt books are available for special
promotions and premiums.
For details contact: Director, Special Markets.

First Edition—1994

Designed by Paula R. Szafranski

Printed in the United States of America
All first editions are printed on acid-free paper.∞

10   9   8   7   6   5   4   3   2

The publisher gratefully acknowledges permission to reprint the following photographs: the title
page photograph of Alydar and Affirmed at Belmont, 1978: Bob Coglianese; the part-title Calumet
photograph and Alydar's grave: Sari Levin, 1991; Warren Wright, Sr., and Warren Wright, Jr.: The
Blood-Horse, Inc.; Lucille Markey (with Prince Aly Khan and Elizabeth Arden), Bertha Cochran
Wright, and Henryk de Kwiatkowski: *Lexington Herald-Leader*; the Markey Christmas card: Melinda
Markey Bena; the main residence at Calumet: Lee Thomas; Margaret B. Glass with Whirlaway:
Margaret B. Glass; Leslie Combs II: Keeneland-Morgan; the aerial photograph of Calumet: William
Strode; the Calumet Farm office: Lee Thomas; John Veitch with Alydar: Dell Hancock; J. T. Lundy
with John Fernung: Louise E. Reinagel; Lyle Robey: Karen Compton; the Keeneland yearling sales:
Anne M. Eberhardt. The photograph of William Monroe Wright is reproduced with permission from
Kraft General Foods, Inc. The photograph of Gene Markey is courtesy of the Academy of Motion
Picture Arts and Sciences. The photograph of Alydar's stall is courtesy of Tom Dixon.

In memory of my father, Dwight

And to John, Elizabeth,
Sarah, Gloria, and Phil

Contents

PART I

MYSTERY

In the vast farmlands of the Bluegrass, night brings a deep and layered darkness that hovers over the land like a heavy fog. Faraway lights on rafters and spires appear closer than they are. Sounds, echoing from distant barns, are difficult to discern and seem to come from nowhere and everywhere at once. The backfiring of a pickup might be mistaken for a gunshot; the simple creaking of a barn door could be confused with an animal's cry.

Alton Stone was accustomed to the terrain of a rural night and felt a certain comfort in the darkness. He had nothing to fear because in his years as a groom and even in his childhood on a farm in western Kentucky, nothing frightening had ever happened. His nerves were solid and his country instincts went well beyond his four years on the job. If there had been a sound that night that could have warned him, he would have known what to do.

But the darkness may have played a trick on Stone. There was nothing extraordinary that he could recall hearing, and no one else would ever come forward to report the wild, unnerving cries that must have emanated from the stallion barn at some point that night. No one would ever say they had heard the first bone crack.

It was a chilly night in mid-November of 1990, and Stone, a groom at Calumet Farm, was filling in for his friend Cowboy Kipp, the regular night watchman. From 6:00 P.M. to 6:00 A.M. he was to drive from barn to barn across the rolling acreage, checking on the welfare of two hundred thoroughbred horses, filling their water buckets, and dropping straw into their stalls. Stone remembered driving his red Ford Bronco slowly and without distraction along narrow, asphalt roads, the truck's headlights punching holes in the darkness ahead.

The routine was menial, but for the young Kentucky native it seemed as much a privilege as a job. Stone was raised on the legends of Whirlaway and Citation, two of Calumet's many Kentucky Derby winners. Just as a boy growing up in New York might know the batting averages of legendary Yankees, boys in the Bluegrass knew the victories, pedigrees, and earnings of the champions who had thrived on Calumet's nine hundred acres over the past sixty years.

There was something reassuring about Calumet, as if its miles and miles of white fences were a monument to some high ideal. No single racing stable had ever won more accolades and trophies. For half a century, Calumet had been the standard by which all achievements were measured in the thoroughbred racing industry. It was the reason the American thoroughbred had become the most sought-after horse in the world.

Just a glimpse of the farm was like a journey to another era, to the 1940s or 1950s, Calumet's glory years and a simpler time in America. The sight of foals and mares grazing in emerald fields between white barns and pristine fences spelled innocence. In the womb of Calumet, adages about a brighter tomorrow always seemed plausible.

Calumet was all about cycles of life. Generations of horses born on the farm were trained there to race. When they retired, they grazed in pastures adjacent to the ones where they had learned to walk at their mother's side and where their offspring would soon take their first wobbly steps. And when they died, they were buried alongside their mothers and fathers, brothers and sisters at the Calumet cemetery.

Stone felt a burst of pride each day when he tipped his hat to the man in the white frame guardhouse at the farm's main entrance. As massive red iron gates inched open and a long avenue of towering sycamores filled his vision, the soft-spoken, blue-eyed groom had a feeling that he was part of something truly great.

And so when Cowboy Kipp told Stone he wanted to take the night off, on Tuesday, November 13, 1990, Stone, though on vacation, agreed to work the shift. The rounds of the night shift required nearly two hours to complete, but every half hour no matter where the groom might be, he was instructed to circle back to the stallion barn. Part of the routine, too, was a break for twenty minutes or so around 9:30 P.M.

On schedule, Stone, after checking the stallion barn at 9:30, steered his Bronco toward a small white building with bright red trim that served as a canteen for the farm's one hundred workers. Inside he chatted with the only other guard on duty that night, a private security officer hired to patrol the perimeter of the vast farm. It must have been about 9:50 P.M., Stone would later say, that he felt a sudden pang in the pit of his stomach, a feeling of panic unfamiliar to him and that he has never quite been able to describe. All he knew at that moment was that he had to go back to the stallion barn.

Abruptly, Stone turned away from his colleague, left the canteen, jumped into the Bronco, and barreled down the winding roads, all the while trying to block out thoughts of Alydar, the thoroughbred industry's preeminent stallion and Calumet's number one money-maker.

Not only was this not Stone's normal job, but guarding the stallions had only recently been added to Cowboy Kipp's duties. In past years the farm had always employed one night guard whose only duty was to oversee the stallions, especially Alydar, who was worth more than the farm itself. For reasons unknown to Stone, Calumet president J. T. Lundy had eliminated the $7.50-an-hour job.

It was a move that puzzled Stone and others who knew the stories of Lundy's obsession with security in past years, especially regarding Alydar. Back in 1983, Lundy had realized that it was possible for a sniper, with the help of a scope on a high-powered rifle, to stand at one particular spot on the balcony of the Eldorado Motel, down the road from the farm, and send a bullet over rolling fields and white fences into Alydar's beautiful head. Lundy moved Alydar to a paddock that was out of the path of destruction.

Around that time, too, the farm was getting letters with words cut out of newspapers and pasted together into such chilling messages as "Your prize horses will be shot" and "We'll start shooting horses," unless the farm handed over $500,000. The FBI eventually apprehended a young woman who worked at a local furniture factory, along with her alleged accomplice, a laid-off truck driver.

After that scare Lundy hired two former soldiers of fortune from eastern Kentucky to guard the farm. They'd worked for some years as strikebreakers in coal country and before that had toured the world looking for trouble that paid well. With pistols strapped to their ankles and shotguns above the dashboard, the men spent their nights touring the farm as if it were a war camp. They'd crouch in bushes, perch in trees, and sometimes linger for hours outside the stallion barn listening for sounds that signaled trouble.

But they were long gone. On this night, it was all Stone's responsibility. The more he thought about the sparse security that November night, the harder he pressed his foot against the accelerator. Farms less prestigious than Calumet had security systems with video monitors in the corridors of stallion complexes and sometimes even in the stalls. Calumet did not. How could Stone or anyone else be expected to guard fifteen barns across hundreds of acres of pastureland and many miles of roads?

To reassure himself, Stone tried to remember how the stallion barn had looked when he had checked on things at the beginning of his shift. Except for a few snorts and the muffled clopping of horseshoes against straw-covered cement floors, the barn had been quiet. Everyone was accounted for: Alydar, in the far stall once occupied by Derby winner Tim Tam; Secreto, valued by one appraiser in 1988 at $75 million; Triple Crown winner Affirmed; Criminal Type, who would soon receive the horse industry's version of an Oscar, the 1990 Horse of the Year award; and four other prized stallions, collectively appraised at $16 million or more.

But Stone couldn't recall seeing or hearing anything unusual. And as he drove up to the barn, he began to wonder whether the extent of his responsibilities that night had given him a case of the jitters.

Getting out of the truck, he pulled open one of the thick, double-wide doors at the end of the barn. He stepped into the warm air, hardly smelling the familiar mix of manure and straw, then walked briskly down a wide red-painted corridor between the stalls and brass nameplates of the champions of the sport. As he looked intently between the bars of the stall windows, into the dimly lit, oak-paneled stalls on both sides of the hall, he heard a faint nickering, a moaning sound that seemed almost human. It was Alydar's stall, the last one on the left, that he anxiously sought. When he reached it and peered through the bars, he saw the source of the eerie sound.

To Stone's horror, the chestnut stallion was nearly black with sweat, his flanks heaving and trembling. In the dim light, he could see Alydar's eyes, white with fear. For long seconds Stone stared, his feet unable to move, as if the horse's eyes were transmitting a paralyzing fear.

Stone snapped himself out of the trance, snatched the two-way radio from his belt, and summoned his boss, Sandy Hatfield.

Hatfield lived only a few hundred yards from the stallion barn. Like most horsemen, she was in bed by 9:30 P.M. and up, at the latest, by 5:00 A.M. It was after 10:00 P.M. by now. From her bed, she spoke into the radio, "What is it, Stonie?"

"It's Aly."

Stone's first instinct, as he would later tell an investigator, was that Alydar was suffering from colic, a painful buildup of gases in the intestinal tract. But he said nothing more to Hatfield. He knew the farm's concerns about privacy and that the local newspapers monitored the two-way radios. Both employees had been told never to talk about sensitive issues on the airwaves. Alydar, no matter what he did, was front-page news in the Bluegrass and on sports pages worldwide. Hatfield asked no questions. She knew that a late-night call on a farm, except during foaling season, could only mean trouble. She said simply, "I'll be right there."

After calling the farm's resident veterinarian, Lynda Rhodes, Stone picked up some carrots from a bag in the corridor and rushed back to Alydar's stall, hoping he hadn't overreacted. He unlatched a brass hook, slid the heavy oak door to the side, and stepped into the sixteen-by-eighteen-foot stall.

Alydar, magnificent even now in his stillness and fear, seemed so alone. Gingerly, the groom approached with his offering of carrots, moving close enough to gently snap a leather shank to the halter. The horse tugged at the strap and glared down at Stone with the look of a conquered king. But instead of kicking his way out of Stone's grip and reclaiming his power, he stared once again into Stone's eyes, which were now stinging with tears and sweat. Alydar allowed the groom to stroke his wet and tangled mane. As Stone felt Alydar's trust, he looked away and, for the first time, spotted specks of dark blood in the straw beneath the horse's hooves. Searching for the source of the dripping blood, Stone saw reason for fear and panic.

Alydar was holding his right rear leg off the ground, the last eight inches or so dangling loosely and a sliver of white bone showing through the dark skin. Several inches of skin lay open on the front of the leg, torn by the jagged edge of the broken bone. It appeared that the lowest portion of Alydar's leg was hanging by tendons alone.

When Hatfield and Rhodes arrived, they told Stone he looked as if he'd seen a ghost. But they too were stunned by what they saw as they entered the stall, now filled with steam from the horse's profuse sweating. They resisted talking about the whys or hows of Alydar's predicament. There was no time to ask questions now. Rhodes, a quiet, efficient woman in her early thirties, pulled a syringe from her bag and injected a powerful painkiller into the horse's jugular vein. She then made two calls: one to the farm's chief vet, William Baker, who lived in another county, and the other to Lundy, the Calumet president. Shuddering at the thought of what lay ahead, she asked Lundy to call the insurance agents.

For now, Rhodes knew the greatest challenge was Alydar himself. Fractious and prone to tantrums, the horse had a reputation for hating vets, even when he wasn't hurt. During a routine checkup, he'd swing his head back and forth and sometimes rear up and kick. If he didn't like something he saw or heard, he'd just pull away and leave, like a celebrity accustomed to his own way. But with an injury like this, rearing up or running off could cause his death.

Alydar's temperament hadn't always been so unpredictable. In 1978, before one of the Triple Crown races, one Alydar groom told a sportswriter, "Alydar doesn't seem excited by events. . . . He's a low-key horse. Whatever you ask him to do, he'll go on and do it."

Alydar's longtime trainer John Veitch described the horse's temperament as "ideal, good around the barn. . . . He wasn't like a kid's saddlehorse or pony, as he was a stallion, but he wasn't difficult." Veitch, who was with the horse every day from 1976 to 1982, used words like "endearing" and "affectionate" to describe the horse. He said Alydar had the best memory he'd ever witnessed in a horse.

"It's like Alydar memorized the sound of your footsteps and the rhythm of your walk," Veitch said. "When he heard a familiar walk, he'd press his head against the window of his stall and snort a sort of welcome. If he didn't recognize the rhythm, he wouldn't bother moving. He was like a friend to me."

But by the mid-1980s, Alydar had the reputation among grooms and vets as a difficult horse determined to get his own way no matter what. Though always spirited and feisty, his personality now had a nasty edge. Every six weeks or so, he'd suddenly throw a fit in his stall, pawing at the stall door or wall, nickering and snorting until he got the attention he felt he deserved. He'd paw and paw with his front hooves or run around the stall as if it were a track, until a groom or the guard who watched the stallion barn would come by and feed him a carrot or two, reminding him that he was still the great Alydar whose racing career no one could ever forget and whose semen was now as prized a commodity as gold or oil.

By most accounts, he seemed bedeviled by something out of his control, but nobody could ever figure out what. A few had the theory that his good nature and charm in past years might have been exaggerated in the effort to create a media superstar. Others said horses sometimes get cranky and aggressive after they retire from the track and start their careers as studs. Still others—mostly critics of Lundy's management practices—were apt to say the horse's temperament was ruined through overbreeding.

As if wallowing in vicarious pleasure, horsemen could talk for hours about the pros and cons of Alydar's hectic sex life. To be kept in a continual state of excitement could cause behavioral problems for an already high-strung animal like a thoroughbred horse, they surmised. Burnout was also a possibility. While stallions normally enjoy their work, there were limits beyond which even the most dynamic studs would lose interest. Lack of exercise was another theory. "Aly was spending too much time breeding and not enough outside running around, not enough exercise," one groom believed.

Alydar was a stud who earned his keep and supported the comfortable lifestyle of several individuals by inseminating dozens of mares each year in the hope of producing sensational racehorses. Alydar's genes and his sexual performance were critical factors in Calumet's prosperity, for the big money in the horse industry during the 1980s was made in the breeding shed, not at the racetrack. Alydar, who had been appraised at values ranging from $40 million to $200 million, appeared to be raking in the cash.

Lundy had sold twenty or so lifetime breeding rights to Alydar for as much as $2.5 million each. Such rights entitled the buyer to breed one mare each year to the stallion and one additional mare every other year during the stallion's life. Usually, pricey stallions like Alydar are owned by a syndicate of forty shareholders, who have the right to breed once a year for every share they own. A share also gives them the authority, through a syndicate agreement and an annual syndicate meeting, to make decisions about the stallion's stud career, such as whether or not he will be bred to more than the shareholders' forty mares, and if so, how many.

What was unique about Lundy's concept was that it gave the farm the benefits and proceeds of syndicating the horse while allowing Calumet to own him and Lundy, as Calumet's president, to manage his career as a stud. Lundy could decide, for example, how many mares were booked to Alydar's breeding schedule each year. If he was in the middle of negotiating a deal to buy a horse, he could sweeten the offer by throwing in an Alydar season. Considering Alydar's status, the arrangement gave Lundy significant power in the world of horse trading. By the mid-1980s, owning a right to breed to Alydar, if only for one season, had achieved high status among the very rich. Even Queen Elizabeth II had sent a mare to Alydar.

Part of the stallion's appeal were his past triumphs at the track and a dashing aura that he projected, whether he lost or won. He was a showman who relished crowds and liked attention. One longtime Calumet worker called him "cock of the walk." He had what horsemen refer to as "heart," a limitless devotion to racing and a will to overcome all obstacles to win. Yet it was three second-place finishes that had secured Alydar's exalted place in racing history. Though he never won the Kentucky Derby, Preakness, or Belmont—the three Triple Crown races—he did become, in 1978, the only horse ever to win second place in all three. For five weeks that spring, Alydar and Affirmed—who now lived in adjacent stalls at Calumet—dazzled the racing world with a head-to-head competition considered the greatest rivalry in the history of American racing.

Both horses were undefeated three-year-olds as they went to the gate that year for the first Triple Crown race, the Derby. Alydar, racing in the devil's-red and blue colors of Calumet, lost by a length. At the Preakness, in a heart-pounding finish, he lost by a neck, and in the Belmont Stakes, the final race of his career, Alydar lost to Affirmed by only a head. Affirmed's trainer Laz Berrera once said, "I think Affirmed is greater than Secretariat or any other Triple Crown winner simply because only Affirmed had to face Alydar."

But what really placed Alydar in the spotlight of history was that the media and the horse industry credited him with bringing Calumet back to the top of American racing, restoring a radiance and glory that Whirlaway had introduced to the farm with his Triple Crown victory of 1941. One columnist called Alydar "the legend of Whirlaway returned to flesh and blood." A 1978 headline on a Red Smith column read "Alydar Born, Calumet Born Again."

By 1990, Alydar was nothing less than a genetic institution in the horse industry. Alydar's progeny would soon give him the lofty title of the industry's number one sire. Seven millionaire racehorses could trace the magic in their blood back to Alydar: Alysheba, Easy Goer, Turkoman, Althea, Miss Oceana, Clabber Girl, and Criminal Type. Derby winner Alysheba was racing's all-time leading money winner at $6.7 million. By 1991, not only would the earnings of Alydar's progeny exceed $35 million, but a son, Strike the Gold, would win the Kentucky Derby—the ninth Derby winner bred at Calumet.

In addition to lifetime breeding rights, Lundy, well aware of Alydar's appeal, sold bushels of seasons, the right to breed a mare to Alydar once in a breeding season, for as much as $350,000 each. He was breeding Alydar to as many as 100 mares a year, far beyond the industry's average of 50 to 60.

Instead of the number of mares in Alydar's schedule decreasing as he got older, his workload was intensifying with each birthday. In 1987, Alydar was bred to 98 mares; in 1988, 97; in 1989, 104; and in 1990, 107.

Alydar's average number of covers per mare—the number of times he literally covered the mare's back with his body during breeding to impregnate her—was less than two. This meant that during the breeding season, typically from mid-February to late June, he was mating with mares at least two hundred times. And that meant a trip to the breeding shed several times a day, at 9:00 A.M., noon, 3:00 P.M., and on some days, at 7:00 P.M., too.

Though Alydar's fertility rate was better than average, by most accounts he was not a zealous breeder, and by 1990 he was approaching his work with occasional disinterest. There were mares he just didn't like, and "Aly," as the grooms called him, would sometimes take his sweet time to get his interest up.

"What horse wouldn't be winding down, considering his schedule?" one Alydar groom asked. "I mean, it might be fine for an eight-year-old [stallion], but for Alydar, at his age, it was more like work. And besides, you just get tired if something's pushed at you all the time like that."

Alydar, at age fifteen, was clearly middle-aged. Rates for equine mortality insurance begin to increase steadily after the horse's thirteenth birthday. Some racehorses live well into their twenties, such as Derby winner Tim Tam, who died at twenty-seven. Whirlaway, on the other hand, died at fifteen of a heart attack, shortly after covering a mare.

Most stallions, however old, show signs of fatigue during the last month of the breeding season. Some take a little longer to be aroused; others lose their concentration altogether and are distracted by people or sounds in the breeding shed. By June, the job of the groom, or "pilot," who guides the stallion's penis into the mare can be challenging. By the end of the season most stallions are ready for the July-to-January holiday when they frolick in their private, three-acre paddocks, roll in the lush bluegrass, and become the objets d'art for tourists. In the fall, breeders and investors visit the farms to examine stallions as prospects for their mares as they plan the mares' matings for the upcoming season.

But Alydar had an unusual schedule. Unlike most American stallions, he was also covering mares in the fall months. Lundy had a special arrangement with an Australian breeder who sent mares to Calumet for breeding each year. Australian mares come into heat according to the climatic rhythms of the Southern Hemisphere; their spring is Kentucky's autumn.

Alydar's breeding schedule was the kind of thing investors during the

1980s as well as bankers and insurers would have liked to know about. This wasn't because they worried about the horse's libido or cared if he was losing interest in his work, wearing down, or developing a bad disposition. No one really knew the effects of so much breeding on a stallion over the course of several years, though anything in such extremes—even sex—naturally raised questions about the animal's welfare.

The real concern among investors in potentially overbreeding the horse was the economic threat. The more Alydar foals there were, the greater the potential for a glut that would lower the demand and the sales prices for Alydar's offspring on the open market. This oversupply would make it more difficult for owners of Alydar seasons to get a return on their expensive investments. Some investors claimed Lundy told them he intended to breed the horse to sixty-six mares a year, at most seventy.

Most Bluegrass breeders who knew what Lundy was doing frowned upon their neighbor for his apparent lack of respect for tradition. His practices were evidence of what they had suspected for years—that Lundy was sacrificing the quality and dignity of a great sports dynasty to make money. Lundy, meanwhile, made no apologies when called to task. To breed so often was sound business, he firmly believed. The more times a horse was bred, the more the chances of creating a superstar. Whereas past generations at Calumet had embraced the philosophy "Breed the best to the best and hope for the best," Lundy's motto was, "They're here to breed, and that's what we're gonna do with them."

Regardless of theories, Lundy appeared to be prospering and bringing more money into the farm than his predecessors would have dreamed possible—at least $20 million a year in revenue from Alydar alone. It wasn't surprising, then, that Alydar was insured by Calumet and the breeding right holders through Lloyd's of London and several other firms, for a total of $36.5 million. If anything happened to Alydar, the mortality claim would be the largest in the history of equine insurance.

What nobody knew in the fall of 1990 was that Alydar would bring only a few million dollars at most into the Calumet coffers in 1991. In one recent year, the stallion had added less than $1 million to Calumet's cash flow. The problem was that Lundy was preselling Alydar seasons, committing them to this and that deal, to the extent that there were very few cash-earning seasons left each year. Alydar and Lundy were caught up in a self-destructive cycle. The more seasons Lundy presold in years prior to a particular breeding season, the more times Alydar had to breed during that season to bring cash into the farm. Alydar was probably the most highly leveraged horse in history, more like a credit card reaching its limit than a legendary racehorse whose trainer had considered him "like a friend."

Within an hour of Stone's call to Hatfield, the stallion barn was bustling with beepers, cellular phones, and chatter. Lundy arrived, followed shortly by his top assistants, Janice Heinz and Susan McGee; then Lundy's sister, Kathy Lundy Jones, who was also Alydar's insurance broker; the vet Dr. Baker; and the insurance adjuster Tom Dixon.

When Dixon arrived at the stallion barn, people were milling about the corridor waiting for the two vets to enter the stall and take their first look at Alydar's injury. Dixon, a tall, sturdy-looking man with thin brown hair pressed into waves, stood for a moment at the entrance to the barn, pulled out a pocket tape recorder, and tested it. Besides participating in the decision making that night, if a claim was later filed, he would be called upon to describe all considerations leading to those decisions. A confident man, he viewed himself as thorough and exceedingly responsible in his duties. Recorder in hand, he marched onto the scene.

But as Dixon entered the barn, something in the corridor caught his eye. On the floor, amid the tanbark and errant clumps of straw, was a large metal bracket, with a metal roller inside. Almost tripping over it, Dixon said in a loud voice, "What the hell is that?" Someone yelled back that the bracket was part of the stall door.

The door to the stall was a solid slab of oak, about eight feet high, three feet wide, and two inches thick. Hanging from a steel track, it slid open to a position flush against an eight-inch-thick wall that separated the stall from the barn's central corridor. The bottom of the door, instead of touching the floor, was held against the wall by a bracket bolted to the floor with two three-eighths-inch iron bolts right next to the stall's entrance. The roller inside the bracket allowed the door to slide back and forth, covering and uncovering the opening to the stall, while firmly anchoring it. When the door was closed, the bracket and a brass hook secured it.

Looking at the bottom of the door, Dixon saw that the bolts that once secured the bracket were sheared off, smoothly and exactly where they entered the floor. Dixon didn't probe further because, he would say later, he thought it was inconsiderate during such an emergency to run around asking questions. But the bracket was never far from his thoughts.

Inside the stall, Baker, a stocky man with gold wire-rimmed glasses and sandy-brown, gray-speckled hair, was telling Lundy that an injury like

Alydar's typically required no treatment—just euthanasia. Horses with compound fractures are almost always humanely destroyed. Poor circulation following the injury often leads to an infection that usually causes the death of the leg. And horses cannot survive lying down, nor can they live standing on three legs without extreme discomfort and recurrent pain.

While Baker was examining the leg, Lundy extended the antenna on his phone and called Dr. Larry Bramlage, renowned as the nation's foremost equine orthopedist. In confident tones, Bramlage said the probability of saving the horse was very slim. "But this is the most productive horse in the industry. . . . We've got to try something," Lundy said.

Within twenty minutes Bramlage had arrived, and, gathering round the ailing horse, the three vets, Rhodes, Baker, and Bramlage, inspected Alydar's leg while he swung it wildly about, trying in vain to gain control of it. The reaction was uniformly somber. Alydar had broken the third metatarsal, or cannon bone, which is the main weight-bearing bone in the back end of a horse's massive body. In a rare decision in the history of equine medicine, they agreed to try to save the horse.

Their long-shot plan was to sedate the horse till dawn, allowing the shock from the accident to wear off. In the morning they'd perform leg-reconstruction surgery, and then Alydar would begin a long, expensive rehabilitation.

Stone stayed until midnight, regularly peeking into the stall to check on the mighty horse. He watched as Hatfield and Rhodes sat on the floor of the stall in the blood-splattered straw, taking turns holding Alydar's head in their laps, caressing his great mane, and calming him when it seemed that hellish visions caused him to thrash about and toss his head. Despite sedation, Alydar struggled against his condition, trying several times to stand up. A horse needs to lift its head to help shift its weight to a standing position; to stop him from standing, the two women had to heave their bodies onto his rising head.

To stabilize the injury, the vets had taped two two-by-fours to the sides of a temporary wraparound cast. The wood, which extended a few inches below the hoof, would serve as a support for the horse, so that when he tried to walk the next morning he would put his weight on the supports, instead of his mangled leg.

That night Lundy remained in the stallion barn with Hatfield and Rhodes. Sitting on a benchlike concrete ledge built into the wall outside the stallion's stall, he burst into occasional exaltations about the sons and daughters of Alydar and the horse's fighting spirit at the track. He'd occasionally roll a piece of hard candy in his mouth, taking it out when he spoke and always, with the nervous anticipation of a chain smoker, popping new ones in before the old ones could possibly be gone. And he'd mumble this or that and then turn up the pitch of his slurred Kentucky accent, as if a constant stream of words could form a wall to hold back his anxiety.

Despite his languid drawl, Lundy was a nervous man, so nervous that by February he would have an ulcer one of his lawyers later described as "bigger than a thumbnail." As he watched Alydar struggle for life, Lundy must have known that Calumet, despite its healthy public image, was also teetering on the brink of ruin.

On Wednesday, November 14, as daylight rolled back the darkness, Drs. Baker and Bramlage arrived at Alydar's stall to begin their effort to save his life. While daylight usually mitigates the intensity of a crisis, this one seemed worse by dawn.

A pungent smell wafted through the stallion barn, a combination of dried sweat and blood from an animal who had struggled for nearly nine hours against the effects of sedation and his own fears. Hatfield and Rhodes still sat on the stall floor where they had spent the night. Lundy milled about the barn's corridor along with a few morning-shift workers who had dropped by to see if what they had heard in the canteen was really true.

Soon the equine ambulance, a white van about the size of a small U-Haul moving truck, pulled up outside. Moments later, with the help of a dozen or more human hands, the 1,200-pound horse lifted himself to his feet and, though unsteady, positioned himself on the makeshift splint, hobbling out of his stall to the ambulance.

Lundy nervously scanned the area. He was more than just a little worried about leaks to the press, to investors, and to certain banks. The absence of Alydar, the farm's greatest asset, was enough to spark rumors. So, before joining Alydar in the ambulance, Lundy told a groom to move another chestnut stallion to Alydar's paddock for the benefit of the press.

The ambulance moved ever so slowly, as if it were carrying a bomb that could explode with the slightest jiggle. Its destination, the farm's veterinary hospital, was only half a mile down the road. The hospital, another white building with bright red trim and the red cupola that stood atop of most Calumet buildings, contained a twenty-four-by-twenty-four-foot operating room, a slightly smaller recovery room, two stalls, and a half-dozen offices and labs. Next door in a circular, glass-enclosed build-

ing was a large equine swimming pool. Equipped with underwater tread-
mills and Jacuzzis, it was used to rehabilitate runners with strains and
injuries. Alydar would be spending many months in that building—if he
survived his operation.

A crew of nearly a dozen employees laid a large red foam cushion on the
floor of the recovery room and walked Alydar next to it. Rhodes, hand
steady as always, gave the horse an injection. The massive animal slowly lost
his balance, falling with the crew's guidance onto the cushion. Then the
workers rolled him over, feet over his head, onto the operating table, which
was wheeled into the large red and white operating room. Hydraulic lifts
moved the table up to a level to accommodate the surgeons.

To isolate Alydar's injured leg and make it accessible to the surgeons, the
crew used a blue-plastic milk crate. Slipped between Alydar's back legs, the
crate served to spread the legs and support the injured one in the air. One
observer would say later that the horse looked like "a dead bird lying on its
side."

Rhodes's job was to give Alydar just enough anesthesia to keep him unconscious. She inserted a tube down his throat and needles into his jugular
vein to carry the various drugs needed to maintain the delicate balance of
Alydar's chemistry. Then she attached monitors all over his body that would
be hooked to digital screens that measured blood pressure, heart rate, and
other vital signs.

Half a dozen anxious faces peered through the glass of the clinic's obser-
vation windows a few feet from the operating table. Conspicuously absent
were the owners of Calumet Farm, the heirs to the fortune of Warren
Wright.

This wasn't surprising; the Wright family rarely visited the barns. Lundy's
wife, Lucille "Cindy" Wright Lundy, one of the owners, spent much of her
time at her $2.5 million home in the Virgin Islands. In a deposition a year
later, Cindy would say that she had bad memories of Calumet and of her
grandmother, Lucille Markey, the grande dame of Calumet, and so chose to
live away from her family home.

After Mrs. Markey's death in 1982, Cindy, her mother, her two brothers,
and her sister had entrusted Calumet's management, including horse sales
and purchases, bank loans, renovations, and breeding rights, to Lundy.
Though he consulted his lawyers and other advisers, Lundy was exceedingly
independent of the Calumet owners—sometimes, it seemed, to the point of
secrecy. Knowing the Wrights understood little about the horse industry and
business in general, he didn't want them to fret over the details of how deals

were structured or which assets served as collateral for which loans or even how much money he paid himself each year from the Calumet coffers. On this day, he informed Bertha Wright, the family matriarch and his mother-in-law, that the horse was injured and would undergo surgery, but he saw no reason to call the owners to the clinic and so didn't.

The surgery would take about two hours and forty minutes. Baker began by extending the cut on Alydar's leg and opening the thick skin to survey the damage. It was as he expected. The bone, about the size of the thin end of a baseball bat, was broken in two, the ends ragged and threatening.

After removing chips of bone from the injured tissue, he guided the two broken ends together and placed a large piece of stainless steel—about five inches by two inches—along the side of the broken bone. Using a power screwdriver, he attached the plate to the bone. To facilitate the reunion of the two halves of the bone, Baker sawed the top layer of bone off Alydar's hip, scooped out the red, spongelike marrow, and packed the marrow around the steel plate, pushing it into the crevices where the bone had been fit together.

Baker then threaded long steel pins through four holes drilled in the cannon bone above the break. To support the pins, which stuck out of the skin several inches, he and Bramlage installed a huge fiberglass cast extending from the bottom of Alydar's hoof to the top of his leg. Finally, Rhodes unhooked the horse from needles and monitors and wheeled him into the recovery room. The vets smiled and shook hands.

"If all goes well, we'll take the pins out in four to six weeks," Bramlage told Lundy. "And then he'll wear a cast until the leg is strong." This meant another four to six weeks, at least.

But about an hour later, Alydar began to stir prematurely from his anesthesia. The vets decided to help him to his feet with a nylon sling that fit beneath his belly and attached to a hydraulic lift on the ceiling.

The first attempt was a disaster, with Alydar fighting all the way. As Dixon would later write in his investigation report, Alydar "was having obvious difficulty adjusting to the sling and could not figure the proper positioning of either of his front or rear legs. On at least two separate occasions, he made a sudden lunge forward, striking the recovery room door."

The vets sedated the horse again, and forty minutes later, with grooms and doctors and others, including Lundy, they pulled his legs into the correct position and Alydar for the first time in about sixteen hours stood on his own.

Lundy moved close enough to Bramlage to ask the vet a few questions.

First he wanted to know if it was possible to predict when Alydar might be ready to breed again.

Bramlage paused before answering, taking a moment to clean his thin-rimmed glasses, all the while looking at Lundy. "I'd say about a year or more . . . the earliest possible, six months from now," Bramlage said. "Alydar's got a long fight ahead."

Alydar, he went on to explain, would have to adjust to a whole new lifestyle. After fifteen years of frolicking and running as he pleased, the horse would have to learn restraint. A carefree kick or an anxious tantrum could reinjure the broken bone, and no horse, not even a fighter like Alydar, could survive that.

But for now there was hope in the air. Alydar had survived an operation that few horses in history had ever undergone. One by one he seemed to conquer the obstacles. Bramlage and Baker were thrilled.

In the afternoon Lundy left the clinic to go to his office and begin the unsettling task of informing investors of Alydar's condition. He would tell them the horse was injured, the operation was a success, and the horse would be able to perform for the 1991 breeding season. At the very worst, Alydar would start the season a little late.

At his office, the phone and fax machine had been ringing all morning. A few television reporters, tipped off by a Calumet employee the night before, had gathered at the gate during the hours before the surgery. The few soon became several. Despite Lundy's efforts, word was spreading like fire in a hay barn.

Several miles down the road from Calumet, at the Keeneland auction house, breeders and bloodstock agents from all over the world had gathered for the fall horse sale. As bidders turned the pages of their catalogs and watched the horses walking into the auction ring, they swapped rumors about Alydar. The gossip centered on how and why the injury had occurred, recollections of the 1978 Triple Crown races, and what his death or inability to breed would do to the value of his progeny. As with works of art after an artist's death, everyone speculated the prices might soar. Then the chatter mellowed into the usual scuttlebutt about what might be going on behind the iron gates at Calumet. Where was Cindy, and why, if she was always gone, didn't she just divorce Lundy? And what was Lundy's relationship with his assistants? Were they simply business associates?

Though Lundy knew the Alydar buzz was reaching a high pitch, both in the United States and abroad, with all those breeders at Keeneland speaking into their cellular phones or the phones in their private planes on nearby landing strips, he refused interviews and imposed a temporary news black-out on the farm. He even declined to confirm reports of Alydar's injury airing on radio stations early Wednesday, the morning after the injury, in Lexington, Louisville, and Frankfort. This enforced silence and suppression of information was a regrettable move, one that among other things would later cast shadows of suspicion over the event.

By mid-afternoon Alydar appeared to be adjusting to the sling and his appetite was back, a sign that the shock had lifted. At that time Lundy finally issued a statement from Calumet Farm, Inc., to the press confirm-ing Alydar's injury and the success of the operation. It said also that "if no complications develop, the horse should be able to stand the 1991 breeding season." The reason given for the horse's injury was that "Alydar kicked his stall door with his right hind leg." While the news releases cir-culated, Lundy allowed one television crew through the gates. Standing outside the clinic doors, a few feet from Alydar's recovery room, Lundy, looking washed out and disheveled, granted an exclusive interview to ABC reporter Kenny Rice. It was brief. The next forty-eight hours, Lundy said, were crucial.

At the same time, Bramlage answered the questions of other reporters. A balding, blue-eyed Kansan with light brown hair and a matching mustache, the vet had a casual, unpretentious style that had a calming effect on all who met him. His reputation in the horse industry was impeccable. The *Lexing-ton Herald-Leader* quoted Bramlage saying, "He's in as good a shape for this type of fracture as he could be at this time. . . . If things are going good in two months we can begin to get optimistic."

But deep into the night it became clear that Alydar was experiencing sharp gas pains in his stomach, much like a horse with colic. The vets believed the tranquilizers had slowed down his digestive tract, causing his intestines to fill with gas and become painfully distended. Horses typically try to relieve such pain by shaking their bodies or rolling on the ground. Alydar was trapped in a medical catch-22, as one of the vets described it. As the anesthesia had worn off, his feisty personality slowly returned and he began to fight what he believed was his enemy: the sling. Tranquilizers were necessary because anxious, abrupt movements, such as a violent attempt to get out of the sling, could be disastrous. Yet the tranquilizers appeared to be causing the painful abdominal distension, which could also provoke him to shake and twist.

Lundy, Hatfield, and Rhodes stayed again with Alydar through a second night, monitoring the horse's every move. By dawn it was clear that Alydar could not endure the confinement of the sling much longer. When the other vets arrived, Lundy discussed the problem with them. Bramlage wanted to slowly wean Alydar out of the sling, leaving it in place until the horse had adjusted to the cast, but the consensus was that the sling must go—immediately.

The room was silent as a groom unhooked the canvas sling and slipped it out from under the great horse's body. Alydar stood still, dropped his head, and began eating. He seemed calm for the first time since Alton Stone had first seen his sweat-soaked body nearly thirty-six hours before.

Everyone who watched was thinking the same thing. Such a quick adjustment was a miracle. Dixon, the insurance man, raised his gray brows, adjusted his silver-rimmed glasses, and with a spring in his step, the sixty-one-year-old man rushed out of the room to send an update to Lloyd's. Bramlage also departed, saying he'd return in the early afternoon to check on things. And Lundy walked over to his office, about half a mile away, to make some calls. There was a general hustle and bustle in the corridor that seemed to say to everyone, life may be normal again soon.

But then something happened—something that caused Alydar to move suddenly. In a jerky, all-too-quick way, he stepped forward, first with his front left leg. Instead of taking his time and moving with the cast, which required a new type of motion, he bolted, expecting the rest of his body to follow in its usual graceful way, as if there were no cast at all. But almost instantly, he stumbled as his left front hoof fell awkwardly onto the floor. Baker was in the stall, folding up the sling, and saw Alydar trying to catch himself, first with his front right leg, then quickly shifting most of his weight onto his back right leg, the injured one. The cast couldn't support him. The horse fell heavily toward his right side, as Baker stared. It was like watching a train tumbling over a cliff, with the cars one by one crashing into ledges and rocks. There was nothing Baker could do to stop the fall.

The snap sounded like a muffled gunshot. As the vet's assistant standing nearby rushed to avoid being crushed by the falling animal, Baker knew it was all over. Unable to get his balance, Alydar had put all his weight on his right hip and had snapped the right femur bone, in the same leg as the first break.

"It felt like someone had stuck a knife in my heart," Rhodes, who was just outside the stall, would later say.

The horse flailed and jerked for a few seconds after collapsing onto the floor. His eyes filled with the same terror Alton Stone had seen two days before. Then suddenly he lay still, staring at the wall ahead, as if he knew the end had finally come.

Though stunned, Rhodes quickly took painkillers from her bag and injected them into Alydar's neck, caressing him as she had done for the past two nights. Baker called Lundy at his office, and Bramlage, who was in his car a few yards from the Calumet gates on his way back to his office. Baker left a message at Dixon's office instructing him to return to Calumet immediately.

When Lundy arrived, he found Alydar lying on the floor, surrounded by the vets and two grooms. An overwhelming sense of loss filled the silent room; it was as if uttering a word would unleash all the pent-up feelings. Lundy dug his teeth into his lower lip, his gaze anchored on Alydar's hip where the bone was pushing against the skin from the inside. For long seconds he stared ahead. When Dixon arrived, he asked if there was anything else that could possibly be done. Bramlage said simply, "Nothing."

Then Dixon, whose straight posture added to the self-assurance in his voice, took a deep breath and said, "Let's do it."

Baker took out a syringe, filled it with a barbiturate, and injected it into Alydar's jugular. His breathing stopped immediately. The horse closed his furious eyes for the last time. Two minutes later, Alydar's mighty heart gave out.

When racehorses die, their hearts, heads, and hooves are usually buried somewhere on the owner's farm. Great horses, like Whirlaway, Citation, and Secretariat, are buried whole. And so it was with Alydar.

On the afternoon of November 15, seven people stood before a huge hole in the middle of the Calumet cemetery, an acre of land studded with century-old pin oaks on the far north side of the farm. Along its winding walkways and beside its old stone benches were the gravestones of Calumet's countless champions. The oldest marker was that of Dustwhirl, Whirlaway's mother, 1926–46.

There was no formal ceremony, and few words were spoken. Standing on one side of the hole were Lundy and three of his business associates from Miami, Toronto, and Fort Lee, New Jersey. Lundy's assistants Janice Heinz and Susan McGee and another partner stood on the other side.

The sun shone brightly, though its angle presaged the coming of winter. Alydar lay on the flatbed of a Calumet devil's-red pickup, covered with a sheet, his long tail hanging over the back edge of the truck and slightly swaying in the light breeze.

"He fought and fought; he was really tough to the end," Lundy said, shifting his weight restlessly from one foot to the other and back again.

No one responded as they watched a groom pull away the sheet and attach the hook of a large tractorlike crane to several strands of thick rope that tied Alydar's ankles tightly together. The cast was still on his right leg, and portions of his coat were matted from hours of sweat—proof of his struggle to survive.

As the crane hoisted the horse by his bound ankles into the air, Heinz and McGee walked away from the graveside to a nearby tree. Looking back, Heinz wiped away tears as she saw the white star on Alydar's forehead catch the sunlight one last time.

A few weeks after Alydar's burial, a New York ad firm selected Calumet Farm as the setting for a multimillion-dollar Ford Motor Company commercial. The idea was to associate Ford with American institutions that reflected a long-standing tradition of excellence. Calumet was the first in a series, and the narration for the ad, which would air in the spring of 1991, began, "When excellence becomes a tradition, there's no end to the greatness."

Calumet was the perfect backdrop for the ad. Alydar's death, after all, didn't affect the physical grandeur of the farm. Its fences gleamed as white as ever, advertising the sheen of prosperity that had made it the crown jewel of an industry. And 1990, except for the bad luck of Alydar's accident, had been one of Calumet's best years ever.

At the track, Calumet horses were winning, again and again, all over the country. Criminal Type, a son of Alydar, won seven big races. An Alydar daughter, 'Tis Juliet, had victories too. Troves of trophies were filling the glass cases at the Calumet office, while the press cheered the stable's success.

But by early 1991, when the camera crews rolled their equipment across the farm's legendary roads, the end to the greatness the commercial would espouse was in sight. Calumet was a house of cards that within days of Alydar's death would begin to slowly tumble. Soon there would be no horses in the training barns, no broodmares to bring to life a fresh crop of wobbly foals, no silver bowls or golden chalices to add to the trophy case. The only signs of life would be nests of hawks and hoot owls high in the oaks and sycamores overlooking Calumet's mist-shrouded fields. And the Calumet coffers, once brimming with hundreds of millions of dollars, would be empty while dozens of creditors, including several large banks, would seek more than $150 million in unpaid bills and notes.

During the fall of 1990, no one—not the media, the banks, the lawyers, the owners of the farm—knew how fragile Calumet had become, and not even Lundy anticipated the impact of Alydar's death. But all too quickly, the secrets of an industry, a dynasty, and a decade would spill out of the Bluegrass and into the courts. An empire with an aura of immortality would die, and the heirs of Warren Wright, the astute, conservative businessman who had built the empire, would sink into a morass of legal disputes and personal despair.

For years the pressure had been building, as if beneath the farm's lush pastures there existed a fault and the death of Alydar was the first tremor. Eventually the tumult would rock banks and insurance companies nationwide, countless investors, and every law firm in the country with an equine specialist. The disaster would touch the lives of hundreds of people, from farmhands and horse trainers to heiresses and horse breeders. Lawyers would be accused of malpractice; bankers, of breaching fiduciary responsibilities. Embezzlement, larceny, and fraud would be alleged against the heirs of Calumet's founder. The scandal would involve jet planes, racecars, priceless works of art, property in the Caribbean and the Florida Keys, a stable called Calumet Australia, and a farm allegedly part of the empire of Mafia kingpin John Gotti.

Within a year of the horse's death, Lundy would be a legend in the Bluegrass, but not as the folk hero the president of Calumet might have hoped to be. Instead, he would become a larger-than-life villain suspected of everything from stealing and hiding millions of dollars to all sorts of fraudulent practices. He would be a defendant in one of the largest lender-liability cases ever brought against a bank. But worst of all he would be suspected of conspiring to kill Alydar for the insurance money.

By the second anniversary of Alydar's death, Lundy would be so elusive that "J.T. sightings" would become the talk of the Bluegrass. From the elegant parlors of Cornelius Vanderbilt Whitney to the local soda fountain with its red-vinyl and chrome stools, everyone had an opinion about where Lundy might be living, what he might have done and why, and exactly how many times Calumet's founder must be turning in his grave. Secretaries at law firms and restaurant waiters would whisper snippets of conversations they'd heard, hoping to piece together clues to the mysteries that had become Lundy's legacy.

Lundy's friends claimed he was a hapless scapegoat for the economic woes of the horse industry and that the federal tax reform of 1986 was the real culprit in the tragedy of Calumet. Besides, they said, whatever Lundy had done was not unusual during an era when thoroughbred horses were treated as commodities like so many bars of gold, when bankers invaded horse country looking for deals, and when horse breeders couldn't find a barn big enough to hold all the money they were making.

Others talked about the meaning of certain Mafia-related ties and claimed the farm was used by someone outside the Bluegrass in a larger scheme, perhaps to launder money. "You know the book *The Firm*?" they'd say. "Well, change the 'i' to 'a' and that's the story here: *The Farm*." Still others saw the saga of Calumet as a morality tale in which everyone involved— bankers, family members, lawyers, trustees, deal makers, and Lundy—had succumbed to greed and everyone was to blame.

The reasons for the tragedy of Calumet, most people agreed, were buried deep in the past of a family that took for granted a legacy of great wealth and awakened to economic realities too late. Weakened by years of rifts, the family failed to adequately guard its treasures, and, when no one was look-ing, predators fed upon the riches.

Soon after Alydar's death, the heavy dew that covered the Calumet fields each dawn seemed less like the blanket of security it had always appeared to be and more like a veneer of evil settling across the land.

PART II

DYNASTY

1 Calumet Farm sits on a high plateau in central Kentucky, a land of rolling savannahs known as the Bluegrass and the world center of the thoroughbred horse industry. Here, partly because of an accident of nature, breeders have produced more champion racehorses than on any other piece of land in the world.

The geological accident occurred more than 450 million years ago. At that time, while the eastern United States was still under water, great collisions on the earth's surface forced the formation of mountains where the Appalachians stand today. Over the next 200 million years, a pattern emerged: the mountains eroded, the collisions resumed, and new mountains rose, only to erode once again. As each range of mountains formed, the impact sent waves of the earth's crust westward. Of the many waves, one grew until it formed a high ground that consisted largely of limestone and measured fifty miles across and several hundred miles long, extending from what is now Ohio to southern Tennessee.

On the surface of this high ground was a dark brown soil, nourished by the limestone beneath it and uncommonly rich in phosphate from millions of deposits of shells and skeletons. The soil also contained an abundance of calcium, but it was the phosphate, normally found at such concentration only on ocean floors, that would dazzle geologists for centuries. The grass that grew from this soil was unique in its ability to nurture strong bones in the animals that grazed upon it. And the greatest concentration of the soil was in a 2,500-square-mile area whose center would someday be Fayette County, Kentucky, the heart of the Bluegrass.

Thousands of years after the first grass grew on the high plateau and many miles away, horse breeders in England began a centuries-long pursuit that would have as much impact on the future of the Bluegrass as geology. Their quest was the search for a new type of horse to take advantage of a new kind of weapon—gunpowder.

Horses were used mainly to transport men, supplies, and weapons until the Normans, in 1066, won the Battle of Hastings with the help of superior horses. For several centuries thereafter, the breeding of a sturdy mount capable of carrying the 350-pound weight of a knight in full armor was a critical part of military strategy. But with the invention of gunpowder in the fourteenth century, armor became obsolete and armies needed fast, agile horses capable of darting quickly out of the range of fire. In the Middle Ages, though, the only light horses in England didn't have the stamina for war, while the strong horses were too slow.

For centuries the English tried, without success, to create the perfect steed. By the sixteenth century, not only armies sought the new breed, but horsemen did, too, because racing was growing in popularity, especially in the royal courts of James I, Charles II, and Queen Anne. For the inventive breeder who could find the right combination of speed and stamina, there were big profits to be made. The breakthrough came in the late seventeenth century when the English began breeding their mares to stallions from North Africa and the Middle East. From these matches came the "invention" of the thoroughbred horse.

Every thoroughbred's male line extends back to one of three sires: the Byerly Turk, the Darley Arabian, and the Godolphin Barb. Captain Richard Byerly captured the first of these, a black warhorse, during a 1688 battle in Turkey, shipping it to England in 1689. Around 1704 the merchant Thomas Darley purchased the second stallion in Syria and sent it to his brother, a breeder in England. By most accounts a North African ruler sent the third stallion, born in Yemen in 1724, as a gift to the king of France. But the king didn't like the looks of the horse and discarded it. A few years later, a Frenchman walking along the streets of Paris noticed a horse with welts on its back and wounds on its legs pulling a cart. He rescued the horse, which was the Yemen stallion, nursed it back to health, and sold it to the second earl of Godolphin, who then took the stallion to his farm in Newmarket, England, to breed with his finest mares.

The new breed ranged in size from fourteen hands—a hand measures four inches—to seventeen hands tall from ground to withers (the point where the base of the neck and top of the shoulder meet), with powerful muscles, especially in its hindquarters, to propel its stride. Bred for speed, it had a high-strung, fiery nature, which gave it the classification, in breeding parlance, of a "hot blood," as opposed to a "cold blood" like the heavy animals used to support the armored knights and the horses that toiled in fields. A lithe, elegant animal with the grace of a gazelle and the endurance of a larger mammal, the thoroughbred was capable of carrying weight while running at high speeds.

During the last half of the eighteenth century hundreds of thoroughbred horses were shipped from England to the New World, where racing was in vogue and the demand for faster and faster horses was high. Horse racing had become so popular on the streets of colonial towns that it was considered a public nuisance. Soon tracks dotted the landscape from New York and Virginia to Maryland and the Carolinas. Even George Washington indulged; a 1772 diary entry shows that he had lost one-sixth of a pound at a track in Annapolis.

Thoroughbreds didn't arrive on Kentucky's high plateau until about 1800, thirty years after Daniel Boone's first expedition to what was then the untamed sector of Virginia. It was Boone, on his 1769 trip, who might have brought the first horses to the region, though they were probably only pack animals. Still, it was Boone's splendorous tales that lured others with better horses to the lush rolling savannas. Accounts of his two-year trip gushed with descriptions of a land covered with dark soil that grew an abundance of herbs, wild rye, and wild lettuce and that fed a bountiful supply of game, including turkey, deer, bear, and buffalo. There were walnut trees, blue ash, buckeyes, and the biggest oak trees he had ever seen.

Soon a rush of settlers from the Carolinas, Maryland, Virginia, and Pennsylvania crossed mountains and coal-filled valleys to settle on the high plateau. Most were from Virginia, where horsemen were by far the best among the New World's breeders, a skill they took to the new land. And although none knew of the events of 450 million years before or were aware of the unique composition of the soil and grass, early annals show they did acknowledge the weather as a significant factor in raising their horses. Similar to parts of England and Ireland, the high plateau was temperate. Foals and yearlings were spared the harsh cold of the North and the even harsher heat of the South. And the new grass of spring came in as early as mid-March, at least a month before what most of the settlers were accustomed to. This meant the grass was edible by late March or early April, giving newborn foals early nourishment, a head start for building strong bones.

The first time on record that the grass was referred to as "the Bluegrass" was apparently in a 1795 ad in the *Kentucky Gazette,* selling a plantation "rich with the Bluegrass." Though the phosphate-rich soil gave the grass unique qualities and the term "Bluegrass" would help to market sales of the land and its products for centuries to come, the strain of grass itself was probably not indigenous to the high plateau, and it was not all that blue.

The grass was part of the Gramineae family and the genus *Poa.* In Kentucky the strain was *Poa pratensis,* which means literally meadow grass. It is unclear how it ended up in Kentucky; filling the gaps of historical fact is a mountain of folklore about its origins. Some say the grass came from England during the last twenty-five years of the eighteenth century. In one story, an Englishman who accompanied Boone to Kentucky brought the seed. Another tale claims a settler carried the seeds in a thimble from England. Yet another credits a man named Blue who supposedly migrated from Pennsylvania, spotted the grass already growing in Kentucky, and named it after himself. Another account attributes the label Bluegrass to a simple mix-up of names. A strain of the same genus, *Poa compressa,* found in parts of Canada does in fact have a discernible blue tint.

The grass in Kentucky is remarkably thick and lush, growing eighteen inches to twenty-four inches tall and rippling in the wind in the same memorable way as a field of wheat in Kansas. Its deep green hue in springtime is startling in its intensity, especially on a sunny day. And in the early morning light, as the sun's rays reflect off dewy blades of grass, its tint is slightly mauve, which might be why some nineteenth-century landscape artists in Kentucky painted the grass in tones of pink. Just how blue it is differs from one account to another. Some locals say they've never seen the blue. Others were told as children they could see blue grass on the night of a full moon if they stood in a field, bent over, and looked upside down between their legs. Still others say that the grass, when producing its tiny seeds and in full bloom, really does appear slightly blue usually for a week or ten days in late May or early June.

By the late eighteenth century, the first families of the Bluegrass—the

Alexanders, the Dukes, the Warfields, the Clays—were planting their roots deep in Kentucky soil. Most who made the journey were English, Irish, Scottish, or Scotch-Irish. It was a group that stuck together in a remarkable way, living, working, loving, marrying, and begetting among themselves generation after generation.

The families came largely from Virginia. They were often wellborn, headed by the second and third sons of wealthy landowners who knew their older brothers would inherit the family land and so wanted their own manors and estates. They replicated the Doric-columned mansions of their homeland, bringing with them a band of servants and a repertoire of patrician tastes and habits. For them, breeding horses was already a third-generation pursuit. And because of them, the social and political institutions of the high plateau, including slavery, would always be firmly grounded in Virginia, though Kentucky severed its legal ties in 1792 and became a state. Together, the clannish, cultured Virginian and the independent, hard-bitten settler generated a new breed of American, the Kentucky gentry.

Breeding horses quickly became a lucrative business and so popular that laws were passed to restrain ambitious horsemen from breeding their stallions in public squares. The region's reputation for producing good racehorses soon reached the nation's capital, where the government ordered the U.S. Army in 1792 to buy its horses only from Kentucky breeders. And in 1797, newspaper ads of the period indicate the first thoroughbred stallion arrived in the Bluegrass. Blaze, a dark chestnut born in England, was shipped to Virginia in 1793 and four years later to Kentucky, where his stud fee was twelve dollars.

To be the best of the breeders, the Bluegrass needed an edge over its competitors in Virginia, Maryland, New York, and the Carolinas. That meant bringing in money from outside the region, luring investors out of their homeland and into Kentucky. Then, as now, that meant publicity.

In 1839, in a clever marketing scheme, a Louisville man named Yelverton Oliver promoted a racing series that would give Kentucky the attention it needed. At a Louisville track, two of the nation's champion racehorses, Kentucky-bred Grey Eagle and New York–bred Wagner, would compete in four one-mile races. Posters advertising the event were plastered on lampposts and trees from Chicago to New York. Spectators included half the population of Louisville and scores of visitors such as William T. Porter, the editor of a New York paper, *Spirit of the Times*.

Wagner won the series by a neck, and the races were so gripping, so popular, and so profitable that Oliver arranged another series, of three races, two days later. Even more people pressed against the rails and placed their bets. Grey Eagle won the first race; Wagner won the second. The crowd went wild when in the last race, the horses were running neck and neck. Then suddenly, Grey Eagle broke his leg. Though the Kentucky-bred horse would never race again, the event, with the help of Porter and other journalists, led the Bluegrass out of obscurity.

But what secured the future of the Bluegrass as the horse capital of the nation and then the world were three much bigger events, the first being the panic of 1837.

During the 1830s speculative fever had reached a high point, not unlike that in America in the 1980s. Prices of everything from land to horses to sewing machines soared, and money poured into every business from the burgeoning coffers of individual investors and from banks. Horse breeders, mainly in Virginia, Maryland, New York, and North Carolina, were no exception. They borrowed heavily from the banks and the investors to expand their acreage and stables, and they brought in so much money from selling each crop of horses that every year they doubled and tripled the number of foals they produced.

Kentucky breeders, meanwhile, abstained from such indulgences. Competitors called them "stodgy," "self-centered," and "backward," but the Bluegrass farmers continued the practice of breeding the same numbers of stallions every year to the same mares owned by the same families with whom they'd done business for generations. Their operations remained self-sufficient.

When the economy collapsed in 1837, breeders in other states were stuck with an oversupply of a product no longer in demand. Prices plummeted, and the horse industry took a dive—except in the Bluegrass, where greed had not overwhelmed common sense.

With the Kentucky breeders riding high, the success of a horse named Lexington—the second big event—brought them further renown. A foal of 1850, Lexington won six of seven big races and earned nearly $57,000, making him third among the nation's leading money winners. But it was in the breeding shed that Lexington, who for many years of his stud career was blind, would make history. No stallion before or since would sire as many winners as Lexington had, though some, like Bull Lea, Northern Dancer, and Alydar, would come close. Between 1865 and 1880, the sons and daughters of Lexington accounted for 50 percent of the winnings of all races in this country. So important was he to the history of the American thoroughbred that his skeleton, standing erect, was placed on permanent display at the Smithsonian Institution.

The other event was the Civil War. Though fierce battles were fought throughout Kentucky, the state was officially neutral, and the devastation it suffered was far less than in the Carolinas and the rest of the South. The breeding industry remained intact in the Bluegrass and even improved, owing to the presence of Lexington. Breeders across the South, where racing was temporarily defunct, shipped their finest stallions to the Bluegrass for breeding. At the same time, the Kentucky breeders who had joined the cavalry returned home in their uniforms and their heavy boots. They would soon be known as "Kentucky hardboots"—horse traders who drove hard bargains, drank hard whiskey, and sold the finest horses in the nation.

Soon the high plateau of central Kentucky became the undisputed thoroughbred breeding mecca of the New World—a solid position until the aftermath of the 1980s when many horsemen succumbed to the temptations their ancestors in the 1830s had resisted. For nearly 150 years, however, Bluegrass breeders would dodge the bullets of cyclical downturns in the nation's economy, banding together in hard times and, in good times, astutely managing their crops of horses to keep the quality high and the production low enough to maintain strong demand in worldwide markets.

By the 1940s, more than half the nation's champion racehorses would come from the Bluegrass, but what would bring the greatest recognition to Kentucky-bred horses, spurring global demand beyond anyone's expectations, were the champions of Calumet Farm. These were the crops of Warren Wright, whose father migrated to the Bluegrass country in 1924.

2

William Monroe Wright, a newcomer from Chicago, was something of an outcast in the Bluegrass of the 1920s. This was a region that brimmed with Old World expectations, where it still mattered how the fathers of the up-and-coming had made a living and how much land, if any, their grandfathers had owned. Genealogical identity as a way of looking at the world was likely the influence of the Virginia gentry, but it was also a by-product of the horse business. Breeders sized up their horses by pedigrees, and the habit, it appeared, had inspired a way of looking at neighbors, especially newcomers. "Who's your daddy?" followed quickly after "Pleased to meet you."

Despite past achievements and a sizable fortune, Wright and his newly purchased 407 acres were at first nonentities in the Bluegrass. During his first year in Lexington, his wife asked the wife of a prominent horseman to go for a spin in Wright's sparkling new Rolls-Royce. The woman responded icily, "No thank you, I have one of my own."

Not even Wright's additional acquisition of Balgowan Farm, a prestigious homestead that he purchased from the grandchildren of Kentucky's favorite son, statesman Henry Clay, earned him the acceptance he felt he deserved. Nor did his prominent visitors, such as William Wrigley, Jr., the chewing gum magnate and Chicago Cubs owner, give him status. No matter who Wright knew or how many Rolls-Royces he owned, the crisp sound of new money kept the Kentucky gentry at bay.

In a clubby society renowned for its rigid rites of passage, the absence of a fancy pedigree wasn't Wright's only obstacle. He was a northerner, and in the Bluegrass the scars of the Civil War were still visible. There was also his age.

Wright was seventy-three years old when he moved to Kentucky, and when he spoke of his plans to make Fayette County the world center for the breeding of trotters and harness racing, he wasn't taken seriously. A local publication quoted a trainer saying that Wright's "lofty aspirations" as a breeder were viewed universally as "an old man's plaything."

Wright countered the skeptics by saying he wasn't in the Bluegrass to impress anyone. It was the land he had come for, not a place in society. He was there to do a job, to breed horses and to do it better than anyone ever had.

His land was decent enough, though the Calumet acreage was his second choice and, as was the case throughout much Bluegrass property, caves beneath its lush pastures posed the threat of sinkholes. He had first agreed to purchase the estate across the road, but a few days after signing a sales contract, the owner would not allow the servant Wright sent to pick some apples to carry his filled basket off the property.

"They are not your apples yet!" the owner told Wright, who came to retrieve the abandoned basket. Wright battled briefly, then simply marched across the road to buy Fairland Farm, the future Calumet.

In 1924 Wright's arrival seemed about as significant as another blade of grass growing on the high plateau, but his impact would ripple through the

Bluegrass like a torrential wind for almost seventy years. What Wright and his son brought to Kentucky was far more impressive than Roman numerals following a name. Both men possessed the hard-driving middle-class attitude of making it on their own. Neither the elder Wright nor his son, who would move to Lexington in the 1930s, had ever depended on luck or family fortunes. Theirs was a legacy of sweat and ingenuity, dogged determination and devotion. Their way was simply to aim for things they wanted and never stop until they got them.

As a boy in the Ohio towns of Dayton and Xenia, William Wright had watched his father, a common miller, work twelve-hour days year after year just to get by. From the time Wright was ten years old until his sixteenth year when his father moved the family up the road to Springfield, he worked nights and weekends at his father's side. Springfield was only thirty miles away, but Wright's friends and dreams were firmly rooted in Dayton, his birthplace. He planned to return there and start his own mill, but in February of 1874, Wright's father died. Wright was twenty-two years old. A few months later he met Clara Lee Morrison, a New Yorker who was visiting relatives in Springfield. Morrison, a willowy woman who towered over the portly Wright, had an unusual asset for a woman in nineteenth-century America: a college degree. In 1875, they married.

These were intense days for the young Wright. His marriage followed quickly after his father's death, and in the same year, 1875, he and Clara had a son, Warren. The following spring, his mother died, leaving him little money and little reason to stay in Springfield. So with a large steamer trunk, some canvas grips, two horses, and a simple carriage, Wright took his wife and year-old son to Indianapolis to peddle the then-popular "Dr. Price" baking powder. Two years later they moved again, this time to Chicago, where the commissions and the customers were worth much more. Soon after the move Wright took a job as a traveling salesman for the Royal Baking Powder Company, the nation's number one maker of a product then as integral to the American lifestyle as microwave ovens are today. During an era when breads and pastries were baked at home, Royal competed with at least twenty other brands.

By the mid-1880s young Wright had earned a reputation as "the best salesman to ever carry a grip," and he advanced quickly up the corporate ladder at Royal, through sales and advertising to a management post. But his restless, independent spirit, perfectly suited to the life of a traveling salesman, was not a smart fit for the executive suite. He longed for his own business.

So in 1888, at the age of thirty-seven, Wright embarked on his life's work. Moving his family to a small apartment on Chicago's west side, he launched his own baking powder enterprise in a four-hundred-square-foot room in the corner of a downtown loft. He spent days and nights devising a formula for a baking powder that he hoped would bury existing companies. Half of the room was his dimly lit office, furnished with a desk made out of a barrel and a board and boxes used as makeshift file cabinets. The other half, beyond a curtain partition, was a poorly ventilated factory. After experimenting for nearly a year, putting his family on an austerity plan, and sinking his entire savings of $3,500 into the project, he came up with a product that he believed would capture the burgeoning market of American housewives.

The idea was simple. He added a small quantity of dried egg whites to the baking powder formula. This ingredient was something completely new, and, advertisements boasted, it gave the product "double leavening action."

With a staff of six, Wright started his new enterprise in late 1889, making the powder at night and selling it during the day. While he and three men tended to the factory and sales promotions, the other two men were always on the road peddling the new product, which he called Calumet Baking Powder.

"Calumet" was the name the French had given to the peace pipe that the Indians offered to Père Marquette when he explored the Chicago territory in 1675. From then on, the long reed pipe, with feathers dangling from its red stone bowl, became a symbol of peace, used for welcoming strangers. And the trademark for the new baking powder company, displayed on baking powder cans, was the profile of an Indian in full headdress. As the company became more successful, a story evolved that Wright had chosen the name because of its familiarity to the homemakers in Wright's target market, Chicago, home of the Calumet River, Calumet Lake, and Calumet Harbor. Wright, in addition to inventing a supposedly better baking powder, was a man with astute marketing instincts. But there was possibly another explanation for his choice. Wright had a brother, four years his junior, who had died years before and whose name was listed two ways in genealogical records, as "C. F. Wright" and "Calumet Wright." If his brother did have such a name, Wright clearly named the company for that reason, but he likely was also aware of the power of name recognition in using "Calumet" in the Chicago area.

In June 1892, Calumet was incorporated in the state of Illinois. During the same year, Clara Lee Morrison, Wright's wife, died. He absorbed himself in work, moving his operations to a 2,800-square-foot building with three stories and a basement on Chicago's west side. Five years later, he married a Chicago woman, Georgia Daniel, who grew up in Tennessee and who loved horses.

With surging sales and a thousand workers at two Calumet factories, Wright, during the first decade of the new century, began to loosen his hold on the corporate reins, placing them in the competent hands of his son, Warren. Always looking for new challenges, Wright found his interest lagging as the company became more and more successful. In 1910, he started a new venture, a farm in Libertyville, Illinois, then the nation's center for training trotting horses. He called it Calumet Farm.

While Wright poured his spirit and money into the risky business of breeding horses, his son, with the regularity of a pendulum, moved the company along, patiently conquering one sales territory after the other, buying ever-larger factories, and inching toward national sales records. In 1912, the company built a 160,000-square-foot factory—four hundred times the size of the little room Wright had rented twenty-four years before. A few years later the elder Wright retired, passing the leadership mantle to his son.

Warren, much more than his father, was cut out for corporate life. The elder Wright had mourned the slavish routine of his own father's life as a common miller and had dreamed of the independence of running his own enterprise. Young Warren took for granted the independence; what he wanted was money and power.

While the elder Wright was a classic late bloomer who began his life's work in his late thirties, Warren had an acute case of early achievement. As a boy, he had no patience with school and restlessly looked for other ways to engage his quick mind. He even worked briefly as an assistant cowhand at a Texas ranch owned by a friend of his parents. Upon his return—at his mother's request—he took a more sedate job as a newspaper delivery boy, but Warren soon discovered a way to manage his time so that he could double the deliveries per hour on the list his supervisor gave him and use the excess time to generate new customers. He leapt onto horse-drawn buses between stops and peddled the papers to riders. Eventually, his mother caught him, and because of the hazards involved in jumping onto moving vehicles and not paying a fare, she made him quit.

Next Warren worked as a bill collector for a wholesale grocer in downtown Chicago while taking classes at the nearby Bryant and Stratton business school. He was a shy, soft-spoken teen, but he had the tenacity of a Doberman and his persistence got him thrown out of more than one office.

Finally, on the eve of his fifteenth birthday, his father hired him to collect bills for Calumet. By the time he was twenty-four, in 1899, he had taken over the management of Calumet's central office and soon had the title of president.

Warren was a short, stout man whose neat, precise appearance spelled efficiency and control. Throughout his life magazine and newspaper writers would refer to him variously as Napoleonic or as "the little giant." He was a great champion of the ordered life. At his father's company, he created expense forms to accompany receipts salesmen typically submitted in a pile stapled together with a tally scribbled on the top. He ordered an office boy to spend a day once a month pulling forms randomly and making calls to check the honesty of the salesmen. He established sales quotas and staff evaluations. A former Calumet salesman told a reporter in 1948, "The old man would be sitting there kidding with everyone in the office, then Warren would walk in and you could hear a pin drop. Warren was always raising hell with the salesmen over their expense accounts."

Battles in the Calumet executive suite were common, at least until Warren took the post of Calumet chairman in 1914. The central issue appeared to be what to do with the growing profits. Warren, a stubborn man with a firm mouth to match his temperament, wanted to expand the company into more plants and subsidiary enterprises. He had some ideas, too, about squelching the competition through more aggressive advertising. The elder Wright, perhaps preoccupied now with his new passion for breeding and racing trotters, wanted to sustain the status quo.

Warren was apparently irked that his father, although resourceful and creative at making money, didn't seem to care as much about keeping it. In the largest enterprises like Calumet as well as the smallest deals, Wright came up with an idea, sacrificed all to execute it, and then, satisfied when it worked, moved on to the next challenge. He had a serendipitous nature and was not always practical, especially when it came to money.

One mid-November night in 1909, hunting dogs at the Wrights' summer home sixty miles north of Chicago on Lake Michigan broke into a barn and killed fifty chickens. Learning of the incident, Wright beckoned a worker to the front yard of the estate and asked him to quickly bundle up the chickens, take them into the city, and try to sell them. If there were questions about the slaughter of the chickens, the worker was to simply shrug his shoulders. If necessary, he could say that the dogs carried no diseases. Back at midnight, the employee was met at the gate of the great house by Wright, in his nightshirt, anxiously asking about the success of the venture. Satisfied with the results, Wright walked back to the house, forgetting about the proceeds from the sale. The employee ran after him with the money, but Wright waved him away.

To the father, life was about process; to the son, it was about goals, about winning. When the sparks flew in Wright's office, secretaries and office boys listened at the door. By most accounts, the elder Wright started the rows inadvertently by overwhelming his son with the details of his latest horse purchases or adventures at the Grand Circuit, a big national race held in Libertyville.

"Warren was always fighting the old man about his extravagance with the horses," an employee once told the *Saturday Evening Post*. "The old man would draw some money and go off to the races. When he'd come back he'd be broke. Warren couldn't see any point to this."

And Wright couldn't see the point of worrying. There was enough money for both father and son to have their way. Wright, whose purchases of the best mares had seemed extravagant, ended up breeding the world's fastest trotter, a horse named Peter Manning, on his Illinois farm. And Warren continued to expand the Wright empire, buying larger and larger factories, a chemical plant, a printing plant, and even a factory for making the tin cans in which the powder was sold.

By the 1920s, Calumet Baking Powder had become a household word, and every pantry in middle-class America stocked the bright red cylindrical container with the trademark profile of an Indian in full headdress. A 1922 ad in *Country Gentleman* magazine showed rosy-cheeked children sitting around a table, each holding a thick piece of chocolate cake, with the headline "Cake Properly Leavened Is a Great Body Builder for Children."

In 1924, *Liberty* magazine ran an ad calling Calumet "The World's Greatest Baking Powder." There's "nothing better for the growing child than Graham muffins. . . . But do not interfere with the body-building elements of wheat by using an inferior leavener. Employ Calumet and know that your bakings are raised to their fullest nutritional value. Its use always results in pure, uniform, and economical bakings which go a long way towards health."

Warren's mark was all over the company, from its money-saving policies in the management and sales departments to its airtight efficiency standards and monitoring systems in the factories. And the Calumet salesmen, like an army of evangelists, were everywhere.

In groceries, hotel lobbies, restaurants, college and high school home economics classes, and department stores, salesmen held demonstrations to show how fast acting the Calumet powder was in comparison with others. At the same time, canvassers traveled in crews of twenty or twenty-five to the kitchens of America's homemakers. With a crew leader, the salesmen marched into a territory with orders to call upon at least 90 percent of all housewives in the area homes.

The company also deployed checkers to compile reports on the salesmen, ringing doorbells the day after the salesman was to arrive at a particular address and making sure he had done his job. The watchdogs would ask the housewives which baking powder they were using, whether they were swayed by the salesman's pitch, and if not, why. A month later the housewives were visited again, by yet another Calumet employee, and interviewed about their baking habits and the products they used. All this information was organized and studied back at headquarters in Chicago, a mammoth task in the precomputer era. If a territory was consistently weak in sales or sales had dropped during a twelve-month period, the salesmen had to re-canvass the area at their own expense or lose their jobs.

Calumet's ability to topple the best companies in an already well-established product line was remarkable—perhaps too much so. At the pinnacle of the company's success came trouble.

Beginning about 1915, the company launched a secret campaign to sully the image of its competitors. While the ads bearing a Calumet label showed wholesome children with happy housewives eating healthy Calumet-leavened cakes, the company was also sponsoring books, articles, and ads with information about allegedly unhealthy and even dangerous ingredients in competitive products, especially a new product that threatened all baking powder companies: self-rising flour.

Calumet paid a Dr. Thomas G. Atkinson to write the 1915 book *Domestic Science Text Book, Baking Powder, a Healthful Leavening Agent,* which the company distributed to home economics teachers in high schools and colleges. The book didn't tout Calumet, or even mention it, but it did caution consumers about an "acid ingredient" that was added, without any controls or purity tests, to all self-rising flour. Another book with a similar message, entitled *Twenty Lessons in Domestic Science* and written by a Calumet employee, went through twelve editions between 1917 and 1922.

In 1917, housewives and schoolteachers nationwide received reprints of anonymous articles, supposedly from journals of medical associations, suggesting there was a link between self-rising flour and a disease known as pellagra, a gastrointestinal disorder caused in part by a deficiency in niacin and protein. The articles also said that the flour contained calcium sulfate, which is a gypsum popularly known as plaster of paris. One article noted that cheap baking powder and this new type of flour both consisted of as much as 25 percent plaster of paris.

It was a brilliant campaign, bearing the earmarks of the younger Wright's unrelenting determination, though he never publicly took credit for it. Within five years, Calumet moved from fourth in sales among makers of baking products to number one.

Its competitors—especially the makers of self-rising flour—were angry enough to kill. Some counterattacked by hiring detectives to check the credentials of authors and the authenticity of articles. They sent their findings to the Federal Trade Commission. And soon, the government began to investigate.

From the earliest indication of the FTC's interest in Calumet's sales practices, competitors smelled blood, and the game got dirty. Sometime during 1923, Calumet hired four men in the sales promotion division to work as demonstrators of the Calumet product. The new salesmen learned their jobs well, asking more than the usual how-to questions and earning impressive points on Warren's report card of performance. Unknown to Calumet, they worked for the William J. Burns International Detective Agency. Their client was a law firm retained by the Royal Baking Powder Company, Calumet's biggest competitor. Their job was to obtain evidence to shatter the credibility of Calumet's "water-glass test," a test Wright's hard-working salesmen were instructed to use to demonstrate the superiority of the Calumet product.

The test involved mixing a small quantity of Calumet baking powder with cold water in a glass and doing the same with two or three competing products. The mixture in the Calumet glass always foamed and effervesced impressively to the top, whereas the other brands became pasty, soggy, and any foam fell quickly to the bottom of the glass. This, the salesmen told consumers, was a clear indication of the leavening strength of the respective powders. What Calumet had that other baking powders didn't, they said, was a novel ingredient, .015 percent of the white of eggs.

In 1924, the FTC, armed with complaints from the Royal Baking Powder Company and the Jaques Company of Chicago, makers of K-C baking powder, charged Calumet with unfair sales practices designed to deceive "countless housewives and others of the consuming public who purchased its said powder." It claimed that the water-glass test was not an indication of what the powder could do in an oven and was therefore a misleading demonstration of the product's value.

As the hearings regarding these charges began, the government, in another case involving Calumet's ad campaign, accused the company of "unfair methods of competition," through a "practice of publishing to the purchasing public, adverse, disparaging, and derogatory opinions." In 1926 Calumet signed a cease-and-desist order, agreeing to stop these practices the same year.

One year later, Calumet finally discovered the identity of its eager new workers and brought charges of industrial espionage against several manufacturers. But by then, the damage was done. About three hundred witnesses, including housewives, trade representatives, scientists, home economics teachers, and the four bogus demonstrators, had testified, many against Calumet, at FTC hearings held in cities nationwide. Never before had a product's effectiveness been so thoroughly analyzed.

The four detectives who had posed as Calumet workers testified that Calumet was well aware that the egg albumen did nothing for the cakes and cookies in America's ovens. Housewives were deluding themselves if they believed their cakes were rising faster, the detectives said. A home economics graduate who conducted a study of 109 housewives baking with Calumet told the commission that in ten out of eleven cases, cakes baked with Calumet powder were "inferior."

The elder Wright was devastated that the company he had founded and the new and better baking powder he had concocted were called to task. Executives he had known through his many years in the baking industry were clawing at the integrity of the Wright leadership. He responded by investing his soul and money ever deeper into the horse industry and his new stable in Lexington, Kentucky, which he named Calumet Farm.

Warren, meanwhile, fought back, first by hiring his own detectives, who had uncovered the spies hired by the competitors' attorneys. Next, he began talking with lawyers and associates about the possibility of a merger or a buyout.

His promotions staff assured him that Calumet was a habit American housewives were unlikely to break. There was little press coverage of the probes; Chicago papers didn't even report it. Still, Warren was smart enough to distrust the booming economy of the 1920s, and he knew the FTC eventually might ban the water-glass test. Warren also happened to have met some executives from a New York company, Postum.

Postum, soon to be called General Foods, was on the move, snatching up

America's premier companies in every food group, from Minute Tapioca, Jell-O, and Swans Down Cake Flour in 1926 to Franklin Baker's Premium Shred Coconut and Log Cabin Syrup in 1927. On November 1, 1928, it bought the assets of the Cheek-Neal Coffee Company, whose chief products were Maxwell House coffee and tea. From Postum's view, Calumet was a perfect fit.

Wright apparently never knew about his son's negotiations with Postum until lawyers had drawn up the sales agreement and the papers were ready to be signed. The deal, coming at the peak of the 1920s boom, was irresistible. Postum would buy out Calumet's stock for about $32 million. Warren could stay on as president and be a Postum director. But when Warren went to Kentucky to tell his father about the plan, the elder Wright responded quickly and to the point. He refused to make a deal. To give up the company was a humiliating, unthinkable step for him. Warren later told friends that the biggest challenge of his career had been to persuade his father to let go of Calumet. After a week-long standoff, Wright capitulated.

There's no record of any fanfare as Wright departed forever from the $32 million company he had founded with only $3,500. He had already left the office years before, and though his son would continue as Calumet Baking's president until 1931, Wright now asked for his few remaining possessions, including a large oil portrait of himself that hung in a meeting room and that his second wife wanted for the house in Lexington.

In the summer of 1929, the FTC, after years of hearings, issued an order against Calumet to stop the water-glass test and all related advertising, thus putting an end to at least fifteen years of aggressive promotions that had made Calumet shine in the spectrum of American business and had given the Wright family a heritage of privilege. The Calumet deal was one of the biggest mergers of the era and a prescient financial move on the part of Warren Wright. Barely half a year later, the speculation bubble of the 1920s exploded in the crash of 1929. The Wrights would enter the Depression among the wealthiest families in America.

3 Despite his public image as "the baking powder king" and his title as Calumet's president, Warren Wright had little to do with the company after December 1928. While his father spent most of the year in Kentucky tending to the horse business, Warren, now in his fifties, was to have one more career before his own forays into horse country: politics.

For years the ruddy-faced, white-haired Warren Wright, with his homburg hat and rimless glasses, had traveled in powerful, monied circles. John Hertz, one of Chicago's wealthiest businessmen, was a close friend. Wright was an early backer of Hertz's Yellow Cab Company. And Hertz and Wright, with a few other investors, bought Arlington Park racetrack in the late 1920s at the request of the Illinois governor, who was concerned that a potentially mob-controlled syndicate of investors was scheming to do so.

Wright owned office buildings and apartment complexes around Chicago, and he was a director of General Foods, on the board of two big Chicago banks, the chairman of the National Realty and Investment Company, president of Warren Wright, Inc., a financing company, and a member of the Chicago Yacht Club and five prestigious country clubs. Most important, perhaps, he was a big contributor to the Republican party. Though on first impression a reticent man whose fastidious style made him seem austere and aloof, he could be charismatic. His piercing gray-green eyes made him engaging when he chose to be, and he had a great ability to listen to people, even if he disagreed with them. He clearly had the makings of a politician.

It was fitting, then, that in 1930 Governor Louis L. Emmerson, a Republican, appointed Wright to be president of the board of the Lincoln Park commissioners, a post that often led to higher offices. The appointment naturally gave rise to speculation that Wright was his party's pick for the upcoming mayoral election—a rumor the state party chairman never denied in news reports. A *Chicago Tribune* headline in December 1930 read, "From Office Boy to President Is Wright's Record. Head of Lincoln Park Board Mentioned as Mayor Possibility."

Other articles featured extensive interviews with Wright, mainly about his political ideas. He was outspoken about his plans for getting the mob out of Chicago. Concerning his remedies for organized crime, he told one reporter,

"The police department must be divorced from politics . . . the mayor must be fit morally."

Always the businessman and an efficiency expert long before time management was trendy, Wright attacked the commission with his usual missionary zeal, proceeding to straighten out the finances of an urban operation that had wallowed in red ink for more than a decade. Within six months of assuming his new post, the commission had cut its expenses and was out of the red. It had saved $410,000 in operating costs by December 1930— apparently a first for Chicago's massive parks administration. By 1932 the operating budget was nearly $1 million less than it had been in 1931. Wright appeared to have turned around one of the biggest burdens to the Chicago budget. He did so without curtailing any of the park's city-funded events and during a year when taxes for the park system were cut 17 percent. The commission even retired a $163,000 bond, and in July 1932 a headline read "Retire Lincoln Park Bond Issue: Finances Excellent."

Though seemingly heroic, Wright was not exactly politically astute. Part of his strategy was to curb the spending habits of the commissioners in much the same way he had cracked down on the Calumet salesmen years before; he even initiated a system of reports of each commissioner's expenses. Commissioners were no longer allowed to drive city-owned vehicles, a privilege Wright believed they had abused. Such extravagance, he told the press, took money out of the hands of the citizenry. He also announced that each year tax dollars were thrown away on excess office supplies. After taking a detailed inventory, he banned purchases and refused to take receipts until the stored pens, paper, staplers, and notebooks were put to use.

But his most controversial tactic was to slash the payroll literally in half, cutting about $20,000 from the monthly budget. Wright told a *Chicago Tribune* reporter in September 1932 that the cuts not only helped the bottom line but also inadvertently boosted park attendance. "This has been one of the biggest years in our history, with unemployment adding thousands daily to the number of park visitors," he said. Around the same time, he issued a press release saying, "Idle and unnecessary employees have been eliminated from the payroll."

This was not a popular move, though he apparently realized the political errors of his ways. In 1932 there were news stories in the Chicago and Miami papers about his plans to build a $350,000 home in Miami to help the unemployment problem. The home was a palatial estate, with swimming pool, guest lodge, patios, walks, and carefully landscaped gardens on Collins Avenue, then the millionaires' row of Miami Beach.

"I did not expect to build for a year or two," a press release read, "but then I thought that now, in response to President Hoover's plea to build homes, would be the opportune time to release the money and put men to work. My home will keep quite a few men employed until next January [1933] at least."

By January, Chicago's park system had been groaning with efficiency for three years and Illinois had a new governor, a Democrat. Some of the city's aldermen and commissioners apparently were counting the days until Wright might leave. One *Chicago Tribune* article described Wright as "the despair of certain politicians" because he had cut the payroll "with outrageous disregard for the political affiliations of those who were dropped."

Two aldermen took it upon themselves "as friends of the [new] governor" to launch their own unofficial investigation into the workings of the Lincoln Park board. Within days of the induction of Democratic governor Henry Horner, a minor scandal erupted in Chicago. The aldermen released to the press "preliminary findings" that Warren's board was short $400,000. They alleged that the board was able to appear solvent and efficient only by taking funds from other, less visible accounts under its jurisdiction. The self-appointed investigators said the board "had switched cash from fund to fund in such a manner that auditors will have difficulty in untangling the transactions."

The aldermen said publicly that no criminal charges would be brought. The mere mention of that possibility was enough to ruin the credibility of Warren and his staff. Victims of an apparent political trap, they resigned three days after the news story. In his letter, Warren said, "I will appreciate your relieving me as early as possible as I am arranging to go south. I also have some business matters which are going to take a great deal of my time."

Once again fate had pushed Warren Wright closer to the Bluegrass. With his hopes for a political career dashed, he would focus his energy and zeal on creating the world's best racing empire. And in this venture, he would be a spectacular success.

4 By 1933, Warren Wright had been married for four-teen years, had a thirteen-year-old son, Warren Wright, Jr., and possessed one of the largest fortunes in America. His father, who passed away in 1931, had left an estate of $60 million. His stepmother received a $1 million trust fund, enough to provide her a $70,000 annual income for the rest of her life, plus a grand home in Highland Park, Illinois, $100,000 in cash, and lifetime tenancy at Calumet Farm. After the estate was settled and bequests totaling nearly $350,000 were sent to friends and relatives, the rest of the millions, including Calumet Farm, went to Warren.

Unlike his father at the same age, Warren Wright, now fifty-eight, had a station in life. He was the second generation of a monied family. His money, though not yet "old," had lost its crispness, and his life was graced with the symbols of the upper classes. He had titles in prestigious clubs and associa-tions. He had trust funds, drivers, butlers, and maids. He had a palatial estate on Collins Avenue in Miami Beach, another home called El Contento outside Chicago, a posh apartment on Chicago's Gold Coast, and lots and lots of land.

Wright was described time and again in news stories as "the son of a rich man." No one in the Bluegrass knew about the federal probe of Calumet's sales practices or about Wright's disappointments in the political arena. None of these details apparently were reported in the Kentucky newspapers. Besides, what mattered in the horse industry were things like his knowledge of horses, his money, and his father's achievements as a breeder.

The elder Wright, within five years of buying his first four hundred acres in the Bluegrass, had achieved a great deal. He was the world's premier breeder of trotters—horses trained for harness racing—and as a result, he brought the hub of the sport of harness racing to Kentucky. In 1931, at eighty years old, as he lay in a coma at the old brick farmhouse at Calumet, his horse Calumet Butler won the Hambletonian Stakes, the Kentucky Derby of harness racing and the sport's highest honor. He had finally achieved what he said he would do seven years before, with Calumet Butler as the proof of his superior instincts as a breeder of champions. Sadly, he died without knowledge of his accomplishment.

The eulogies and obituaries mentioned his age—once an issue to those who doubted his abilities—only in the context of his undaunting spirit.

Wright's rags-to-riches story became local legend. In the end he was a sort of hero in the Bluegrass, particularly to those who believed that standard-bred horses, a breed developed for racing in harness at a trotting gait, were the best, even better than thoroughbreds.

To his descendants, he was especially heroic. Despite his penchant for spending, he left a legacy and a bankroll that could allow generations of Wrights to live comfortably on only the interest from millions of dollars' worth of trust funds. It would take a great deal of irresponsibility or wrong-doing to undo all that the elder Wright had achieved.

In 1933, Warren Wright could easily have rested on the laurels of his father's glory, but despite the acclaim Calumet already had attained, this was not enough for him. Just as he was critical of the management of the baking powder company when he first arrived, he had problems accepting Calumet Farm as he found it.

In the world of sports Calumet Farm and William Monroe Wright had fared well. But in the business world, Wright saw both the father and the farm as disappointments. While his father was alive, Calumet was not a money-making operation. The elder Wright's investment in the 1,200-acre farm—initially $2 million—totaled nearly $10 million, including the blood-stock, land, facilities, and trainers. But Wright never came close to recoup-ing even a small percentage of his investment. Warren once told reporters that the farm under his father's management had always frustrated him be-cause it wasn't run like a business. "The setup in harness racing is such that you can't make it pay. . . . My father did better than anyone else, but except for enjoyment, he was just throwing money away."

For one thing, harness racing didn't pay well; the purse for the top race, the Hambletonian, was then only $60,000. With low purses, it was hard to get good prices in trading and breeding trotters.

Besides the money, Wright had no interest in standardbreds or in harness racing. The sport was simply too slow for him. He preferred the fast pace of thoroughbred racing, the sound of thundering hooves on the track, the adrenaline rush of the finish line, and the potential for big money. Within a few years of inheriting Calumet, Wright swept away all that his father had built. By the time he was ready to redirect his energy from Chicago to the horse industry, he had sold all but one of his father's 550 trotters. The one he kept, a thirty-four-year-old mare, was his father's favorite horse.

Wright's goal was to repeat his father's success in the higher-stakes and more glamorous world of thoroughbred breeding and racing, about which he knew virtually nothing. But he was unabashed about his ignorance. He believed that what he knew about running a big business would give him an edge over breeders who had spent their lives watching horses rather than finances. His first step was to buy the world's finest thoroughbred blood-lines—mainly mares—that money could buy. For the man who once told the *Chicago Tribune* and the *Saturday Evening Post* that he had "made a fortune saving money," spending thousands upon thousands of dollars on horses was a new experience. Perhaps to justify it, he created a theory, one his father would have endorsed: "The person who puts in the most money deserves to win the most races." As a businessman, he also recognized that the horse who wins the most races brings the highest stud fees when it retires to the breeding shed.

As he tore apart his father's empire and built his own, Wright slowly began to appreciate the elder Wright's accomplishments and indulgences. Wright's mission was to turn Calumet into a bustling, assembly line–style breeding operation, hell-bent on producing winner after winner. Breeding a champion seemed a rather logical procedure that could be achieved with enough money to buy thoroughbreds whose family trees were full of champions. Then it was a matter of matching a male and female with superior traits, such as good temperament, strong shoulders, long elegant neck, sturdy bones, and muscular hindquarters, to produce a foal with the best of both. But he would quickly learn that the challenge of mating just the right mare with the right stallion, breeding the best to the best to create a thoroughbred superstar, was a money-eating proposition with no surefire formula for success. It was also an addiction as intense as betting.

Producing a racehorse wasn't like manufacturing baking powder. It was as much a matter of luck, a sort of genetic lottery, as it was a science or an art. The industry's past was filled with instances of horses with lousy pedigrees turning out to be winners and horses from the best lines unable to win a single race. Even the moment of conception wasn't that simple to orchestrate. To determine whether a mare was ready to mate, the farm used a teaser, a horse whose job was to tease the mares in any number of ways, including unconsummated humping, flirting, or nuzzling across a paddock fence. If the mare appeared to be ready, she was brought into a room about the size of a squash court. Her rear legs were hobbled in case she tried to kick the stallion; her tail was wrapped in gauze bandages to prevent the tough strands of her tail from cutting the stallion's penis; attached to her upper lip was a cord affixed to the handle of an ax that could be tightened if she began to act up. The mare's genitals were washed while she waited for the stallion to be led into the breeding shed, and the stallion's penis, too, was washed with a mild solution from a bucket bearing his name and used only for this purpose. Two or three grooms held the mare, while another groom led the stallion to her. When the stallion's tail swooshed up, the grooms knew the horse had completed his job.

But after all this effort, the mare didn't always become pregnant, and the process was sometimes repeated three times without success. Even if the mare did conceive, she might abort, or the foal could be stillborn. The percentage of mares bred each year who actually produced healthy foals was about 55 percent. And even if the foal lived, the product off the assembly line was quite unpredictable.

Unlike other types of livestock such as cattle or pigs, horses have to be trained to perform and must do well to bring money back to the farm that owns them. No amount of efficiency charts or evaluation reports can guarantee the quality of the merchandise. A live foal, though otherwise fit, may have a hoof problem or a tiny abnormality, like knock-knees, that prevents it from ever racing. The horse might make it through training and set impressive times during its practice runs around the track, but then only moments before the gates open for a first race, it could develop a hoof infection. Or, off to a good start, it could in the midst of the race stumble, break a leg, and be "put down" minutes later. Years of hope, determination, and money are sometimes washed away in a moment.

Wright was also learning what almost anyone who spends time with horses knows: that horses, with their mystical beauty, grace, and power, have a seductive quality alluring enough to distract breeders from the folly in their hopes and risks as they pour millions of dollars into a dream. "There is something about the outside of a horse that is good for the inside of a man," one of Wright's staffers once told him.

In addition to buying the world's best bloodlines, Wright spent thousands of dollars rebuilding the farm's dozens of barns and residences, painting them all bright white and trimming them in the red of Calumet's "devil's-red and blue" racing colors. His father already had built a $50,000 stud barn, considered the best of its kind on any farm in the United States, as well as new roads, new fences, and new residences. The elder Wright had also expanded the estate to more than 1,000 acres. His son wanted to build and to expand even more. The only part of the past he seemed to retain, besides the portrait of his father mounted prominently in the library of the farm's main house and the thirty-four-year-old mare, was his father's manager, Dick McMahon.

The new Calumet's first victory came in June 1932 when a horse called

Warren Jr., after Wright's son, won by a nose and earned $850 at Arlington Park in Chicago. By the end of 1932, Calumet had earned $1,150, from one win, one place, and two shows, all achieved by the stable's first three year-lings.

The farm's first big year was 1933, with earnings of $22,000 from nine-teen wins. This was a considerable gain over the previous year, though Wright, who estimated it would take at least $200,000 in annual earnings to break even, was disappointed. That year, Wright, who seemed to go through trainers like a hot knife through butter, hired a new trainer, bought more horses, and ordered farm manager McMahon to put everyone on a more rigorous schedule. Daily training sessions were extended, and workers had to submit reports showing track times and exercise regimens for each horse.

Unlike many horse farm owners, who in those days were typically absen-tee landlords, Wright not only lived on the farm but made frequent trips to the barns and to the Calumet racetrack, checking on the progress of horses in training. "I made up my mind that I'd run this farm like a business and use the same principles," he told a reporter during the 1940s, as he sat in his office, his father's portrait hanging above his head. "There isn't a thing going on here that I don't know about."

But Calumet horses weren't winning enough races to satisfy Warren Wright. Although in 1934 his horses won five more races than the year before and earned $88,060, the next year earnings were down by almost 50 percent. "He wanted home runs from the first day he walked in the door of a barn," said trainer Jimmy Jones years later.

Soon Wright and McMahon hired detectives to check out the jockeys. Wright fired another trainer, and McMahon intensified the workouts even more. Finally, the Calumet horses, one by one, broke down, with everything from sprains and infections to intestinal disorders.

Never one to despair, Wright kept trying. "Whenever I go into anything, I go into it to make a success of it," he once said. While Wright was learning some tough lessons about the horse business, the Bluegrass was getting a strong injection of Wright's theory that what dictates whether a man or even a horse succeeds is the "will to win." This time his dictum was put to the test.

The new trainer, Frank Kearns, brought in nearly $100,000 with sixty-one victories in his first year, 1936; sixty-three wins and $104,113 in 1937; and $100,320 for fifty-eight wins in 1938. Wright was winning, and his stable was gaining recognition. "Warren Wright Stable Headed for No. 1 Ranking: Chicagoan Draws Interest of Turf World," read a *Chicago Tribune*

headline in 1938. The article referred to Calumet as a "gigantic turf empire—one that overshadows the Whitneys, the Vanderbilts, the Wideners in
this country, that towers above Baron de Rothschild's in France, and that
ranks with the Aga Khan's in England."

But Wright still didn't have what he wanted—a Kentucky Derby victory.
Late in the 1930s, he began casually interviewing local breeders about their
methods, jotting down the bits of wisdom sometimes handed down through
generations of thoroughbred owners. He also subscribed to horse and livestock journals, looking for tips about horse vitamins and new ideas for
protein supplements to the basic diet of grass, hay, and oats. Soon his horses
were getting seven or eight pills a day to nurture sturdier bones and stronger
hearts and to prevent infection. Wright had become the Adelle Davis of the
breeding industry.

Despite Wright's hopes, his horses, though improving, were not sweeping
in the first-place trophies, and 1939 was an especially disappointing year.
Earnings were in the five figures with only thirty-nine wins, down from
fifty-eight the year before. Worst of all, he still hadn't won the Derby. It had
been seven years since he had begun his campaign to be the best; in his
father's seventh year as a breeder, Calumet had won harness racing's biggest
race.

One day in early 1939, according to one account, Wright, who often
made daily rounds through the barns, confessed his feelings of failure to an
employee. The man was unabashed in speaking with Calumet's owner and
told Wright outright what, in his humble opinion, was wrong. It was all so
simple. Everything the farm was doing, from the physical layout of barns
and shelters and paddocks, to the training regimens of the horses, was designed for standardbred horses, the breed that Wright's father had raised on
a farm that had been managed by the same man now managing the new
Calumet. Wright's horses didn't have the stamina to win a race, the man told
him, partly because they spent the winter outside and, despite their fancy
vitamin regimen, they weren't fed enough. Thoroughbreds were too fragile
for snow and frost and in winter needed more food than they could get from
the feeding troughs placed in the fields.

Over the next few days, Wright checked out the opinion, calling on the
wisdom of fellow breeders and old friends. When he decided the man was
right, Wright was full of fury. As his anger intensified, his head beneath his
white hair turned crimson red. By the time he found manager McMahon, his
head looked like a beet. McMahon, as stubborn and scrappy as his boss,
resigned after the discussion. But there were no hard feelings; Wright, never

one to hold a grudge, allowed McMahon to live on the farm in retirement until his death six years later.

Soon the farm was transformed. Single shelters in the fields were torn down; clusters of shelters were converted into barns. Come the next winter, every horse would spend the night indoors.

Filled with hope once again, Wright sought yet another trainer. The trainer's importance was one thing Wright clearly understood. It was the trainer who decided how long individual horses should work out each morning, how often they should race and at what distance, and when they should not race. A good trainer, he knew, had to have an instinct about each horse's abilities and potential, much like a parent feels for a child.

This time Wright targeted a man who was so close to the souls of the horses he trained that he was sometimes described as "half-horse." He had trained the 1938 Derby winner, Lawrin, for Kansas City millionaire Herbert Woolf. His name was Benjamin Allyn Jones.

Jones, a tall man with chubby jowls, had the earnest, rough-hewn style of a gunslinger from the Old West. Though he bore the nickname "Plain Ben," supposedly because he was hardworking and unpretentious, he was not a plain man. His presence, from his white Stetson hat to his leather boots, was intimidating, and he had the toughness to validate it. Some said he was a man who knew how to live by his fists. He could clean out a barroom in seconds, they said, but he had chosen to live by his wits instead, using his wild instincts to understand the same in the animals he trained. Training horses is all about harnessing energy and wildness, teaching discipline while preserving spirit. And Jones understood horses, some would say, better than any trainer in history.

So in the summer of 1939, when Jones quit Woolf's stable, Wright wasted barely a millisecond in offering him the post of Calumet trainer. Jones, who had never considered training for Calumet, flew home to Parnell, Missouri, to think about it.

From the trainer's point of view, Calumet was no prize. Wright had a reputation for being difficult and for firing trainers in the tick of a stopwatch. The farm was beautiful and the bloodlines were scintillating, but so far the fancy pedigrees had not produced any truly extraordinary racehorses. It wasn't exactly a move up for Jones, who had just trained a Derby winner.

Wright, renowned for his tightness, upped the ante for Jones, eventually doubling his initial offer to $15,000 and the percentage of the horses' winnings to 10 percent. He also agreed to hire Jones's son, Jimmy, as assistant trainer. He flew Jones to Chicago to discuss terms. Jones in his cowboy hat towered over Wright in his Homburg hat as they walked into the Drake Hotel for their meeting. A few hours later, Jones accepted the post.

Wright now believed he had a winning combination—the best pedigrees, a top-notch trainer, and, of course, the best vitamins. But his insistence on the "Wright way" curtailed any chance of bliss.

Jones said Wright's regimen of vitamin supplements had to go. "He threw the vitamins into the manure box," Jimmy Jones said of his father. "He believed in a little alfalfa, hay, and grazing, that's all." Wright, who had spent thousands of dollars on concoctions to supplement sunshine and grass, refused to stop ordering the vitamins. With mulish rebellion, he launched a campaign to prove Jones wrong. Among other tactics, he asked consultants to send letters to Jones endorsing the pills and farm managers to write brief notes thanking the farm for introducing them to such effective supplements. Jones finally blew up and told one such consultant, who delivered his message personally, to get out of his barn. Wright, it seemed, had finally met his match.

Jones also balked at what Wright called "our experiment." Wright had delayed the training of five of Calumet's best yearlings until they were three years old. "We think horses might be racing too soon, too early, and we are trying this method," Wright told Jones. Thoroughbred training typically begins no later than age two, but Wright had been willing to try anything to produce a winner.

Eventually Wright backed down on almost all issues. Perhaps he sensed that Jones had the brains and talent to rescue him from obscurity and from the frustrations of the past decade, so he loosened the reins. He even gave Jones the right to bring in his own cadre of trusted grooms, stable hands, and exercise boys, who came to be known as the "Jones gang."

In 1940, the stable was looking far better with seventy-six victories, forty-eight seconds, fifty-two thirds, and earnings of $155,110—closer to Wright's $200,000 break-even mark. That year Calumet ranked third on the list of the nation's leading stables.

In October of Jones's first year, Tom Piatt, the president of the Thoroughbred Club of America, and Kentucky's governor Keen Johnson honored Wright as the "Man of the Year" in American racing and lauded him for his many contributions to the efforts of American breeders to produce the world's finest horses.

It was a memorable night for Wright because he was beginning to get the recognition he so persistently sought. And in the history of Calumet it would turn out to be a night of irony, one that future generations would recall with a how-strange-life-is fascination. Piatt was a landowner, with acres and acres of tobacco fields in Fayette County and Scott County, mostly worked by tenant farmers. In Scott County the man who worked his land, giving crops to Piatt in exchange for living on the land, was a salt-of-the-earth fellow by the name of John Lundy. A few months after Piatt gave the award to Calumet's dynamic leader, Lundy had a son, John Thomas Lundy, who would someday take over Calumet Farm.

In 1941, Calumet was on the threshold of an era of glory and power that the sport of racing had never seen before and would never see again. While the elder Wright had made Calumet well-known in the horse industry and the Bluegrass, his son would make the farm internationally famous.

Wright's earlier moves started to pay off in 1941, especially his stallion purchases. In 1936, Wright had spent $14,000 at the Saratoga yearling sales for a brown colt with four white legs whose sire was Bull Dog and whose mother was Rose Leaves. Mrs. Wright named him Bull Lea. The colt wasn't a big favorite at the Keeneland sales that year, and other bidders chided Wright about the probability that the horse might bring bad luck because he had four white feet.

In such a luck-obsessed business, superstitions—some sillier than others—were and still are rampant. Changing the name of a horse is considered bad luck, as is killing a cricket in a stall, drawing the thirteenth post position in a race, and hanging a horseshoe with the open end down, supposedly allowing the luck to run out. Some jockeys think it's unlucky to have their pictures taken before a race. And while a horse with one white foot, or "stocking," is considered good luck, a horse with four white feet bears bad, at least back in Warren Wright's day.

Wright scoffed at such caveats and followed his instincts. Only one other person bid against him in what would someday be one of racing's most lauded purchases.

That same year he also bought a quarter interest, for $62,000, in an English stallion, Blenheim II, considered the most successful sire in Europe. Among other victories, the stallion had won the 1930 Epsom Derby, England's greatest race. Wright's neighbor, Arthur Hancock, a blueblood breeder who owned Claiborne Farm, had purchased the horse from the Islamic leader Aga Khan.

Wright bred Dustwhirl, a prize mare, to Blenheim II the next year, and the result, in 1938, was a feisty chestnut colt with one of the longest tails any horseman had ever set eyes on. His tail came within an inch of the ground. Wright's wife named him Whirlaway, though he was often referred to as "Mr. Longtail" or "Whirly."

By the time Ben Jones and his son moved to the farm, Whirlaway was a yearling and ready for training. From the start, he was fast and temperamental, the reason for another of his nicknames, "Wacky Whirly." One groom described him as "the next thing to a savage." Though he won his first race in 1940, his record by Derby Day 1941 was only ten wins in twenty-three starts. Jones had tried seven jockeys in his efforts to control the horse's flyaway spirit, but for most jockeys, Whirlaway was just too wild and strong. He had a dangerous tendency to bolt to the far outside area of the racetrack no matter what his post position.

Jones, unyielding in his belief in Whirlaway's capabilities, made two crucial moves right before the Derby. He called jockey Eddie Arcaro, who had ridden Jones's only Derby winner in 1938, to ride his mount. Arcaro knew the horse's reputation for bolting and wasn't thrilled with the offer, but Jones told him Whirlaway was the fastest horse in America and that with Arcaro in the saddle, the horse was sure to win the Derby. Also, Jones outfitted Whirlaway with a unique contraption—a one-eyed blinker partially covering the right eye, to discourage the horse from running to the outside, and completely open on the left, to keep the horse's attention on the inner part of the track. To test it, Jones sat on a horse several feet from the rail and asked Arcaro to ride Whirlaway through the narrow gap—a test that took tremendous courage for both men. The heart-pounding second when Whirlaway ran smoothly through the opening would become part of the lore of racing.

After nine years of trying everything but witchcraft, Wright got what he wanted in May 1941. As Whirlaway, with his billowing tail streaming out behind him, thundered round the bend toward the finish line at Churchill Downs, the race announcer blurted out: "We've a throng in the throes of frenzy as Whirlaway, number 4, smashes the Derby track record in the time of two minutes, one and two-fifths seconds. Kentucky's heartthrob riding to gold and glory."

A clocker for the race told Arcaro, "That horse did something I never thought a horse could do. He ran an eighth of a mile in a little over ten seconds." And in the jockey's room after the race, Arcaro said, "He was the runningest son of a bitch I ever sat on."

In the next few weeks, a time when most Americans were preoccupied with the mounting fear of war, the sport of racing provided a few exciting, upbeat moments for the nation. A week after the Derby, Whirlaway, charging up from last position in the final moments of the race, won the Preakness by five and a half lengths. He won the Belmont, the last race of the Triple Crown, the following month.

Whirlaway's record time at the Derby would be unmatched for twenty-one years, but what happened next at Calumet would never be matched in racing or in any sport. Sports columnist Red Smith wrote that the team of the Jones boys—Ben and son Jimmy—and Calumet "laid it over the competition like ice cream over spinach."

In addition to winning the Triple Crown, racing's highest achievement, Whirlaway was named Horse of the Year in 1941, and Calumet was the nation's leading stable in earnings from both racing ($475,091), and breeding ($528,211)—far exceeding Wright's desire for the stable to break even. The next year, Whirlaway was again the Horse of the Year, and Calumet was again the nation's leading stable in 1943, as it would be in 1944 and every year of the decade except 1945. For seventeen years in the era from 1941 to 1961, Calumet was either one, two, or three in the ranking of America's top thoroughbred racing stables—twelve times as number one. Calumet's Twilight Tear became the first filly to win Horse of the Year, in 1944, the same year the stable scored its second Derby win with Pensive, who also won the Preakness that year. Three years later, Calumet horses earned a record $1.4 million.

Bull Lea, Wright's 1936 purchase with the unlucky four white stockings, was by 1947 the first sire in racing history whose progeny earned more than $1 million in purses during one season. In all, Bull Lea sired twenty-eight six-figure earners and was leading sire in five of seven years from 1947 to 1953. His stud fee soared to $5,000, up from $250 in his early years. Among his star progeny were Citation, Hill Gail, Armed, Iron Liege, and Two Lea, a daughter who produced Tim Tam—all Derby or Triple Crown winners.

In 1948, Citation, a quiet, even-tempered horse lacking Whirlaway's flair, became Calumet's second Triple Crown winner. Though he had a peculiar habit of not giving his full attention to the race, occasionally even gazing up at a tree as he rounded the turn, he was fast and determined. Trained by Ben Jones's son, Jimmy, Citation was a true champion. Jimmy, who also trained Iron Liege and Tim Tam, said in later years, "He could beat a sprinter and also beat a two-mile runner; he could beat 'em in the mud or on a dry track. He was the most determined horse I've ever seen."

By 1951 Citation was the first horse in history to earn $1 million. Then in rapid succession Ponder, a son of Pensive, won the Derby in 1949; in 1952, Hill Gail ran the race a fifth of a second short of Whirlaway's record; Iron Liege won by a nose in 1957; and Tim Tam, whose graceful, rhythmical strides made him appear to be floating rather than running, came home first in 1958. Calumet had beaten the record for a single farm, that of Idle Hour Farm's four Derby winners, the last of which raced to victory in 1933.

It wasn't just that the Calumet horses won first place; they were bringing in trophies for first and second in the same race, a stunning feat considering that barely half of each year's crop of foals ever wins a single race and only about 3 percent of those win a stakes race, the most competitive races run by the sport's top athletes. When Citation won the Kentucky Derby in 1948, his stablemate Coaltown came in second. And in 1951, when Citation won the Hollywood Gold Cup race, which put his earnings over $1 million, his stablemate Bewitch took second in the same race and became the leading mare of all time.

Once at Chicago's Arlington Park, Calumet won first, second, and third place. As Ben Jones emerged from the winner's circle, weighted down with a big silver trophy and silver mint julep cups, a spectator, referring to the ducks in the lake at the center of the track, yelled, "Why didn't you take the ducks, too?"

Calumet indeed monopolized the sport. By the end of the decade, Wright's empire overshadowed that of any other American breeder and ranked even better than the baron de Rothschild's world-renowned stable in France or the Aga Khan's in England. Sports commentators were spellbound by the unprecedented dominance in both racing and breeding. The farm became so famous that by 1950 it was one of Kentucky's top tourist attractions, flaunted as "the jewel of the Bluegrass."

More than 1,000 visitors a day paraded through its spotless barns and gazed over white fences at the stars of the nation's number one spectator sport. As they walked along the farm's winding roads, they might catch a glimpse of a white-haired man neatly dressed in a tailored suit touring the grounds on a motor scooter. This was Warren Wright, as careful as ever to monitor the progress of his dream.

But as the end of the 1940s drew near, Wright began to falter. A seemingly spry seventy-four-year-old, his heart was weakening. Though he told no one at the time, in early 1949 he was beginning to have minor heart seizures. This may have been what happened in May that year at Churchill Downs when Wright couldn't find his way to the winner's circle to accept the gold trophy for Calumet's fourth Derby winner, Ponder. There was only one entrance to the track from the boxes at Churchill Downs, and Wright later told reporters he was led by a guard into a dead end. By the time he got in, the ceremonies were finished and Wright had missed his last chance to hold the Derby winner's coveted cup in front of a cheering crowd.

After suffering a heart attack in the late summer of 1949, Wright spent the fall and most of the winter in a New York hospital, returning to Miami in February 1950 and to Lexington in the spring. At his seventy-fifth birthday celebration on September 25 at Calumet, he told Margaret Glass, his assistant of many years, "I am feeling fine; in fact, I feel 57 instead of 75."

Three months later, on December 28, Warren Wright died in Miami.

Among the hundreds of eulogies and obituaries in letters and news stories, one commentator wrote, "His rimless glasses and gray homburg hat, as familiar to U.S. racegoers as the omnipresent devil's-red racing silks, were the emblems of a driving ambition the like of which a happy-go-lucky institution like racing had seldom felt."

5 Warren Wright's estate was smaller than that of his father, a man whose generous, almost spendthrift ways had agitated the son. Wright left $20 million in assets, including stocks and bonds valued at $11.1 million, $4 million in oil and gas properties in seven states, the mansion in Miami, $1.4 million in cash in Chicago banks, and, of course, Calumet Farm.

To relatives, servants, and longtime farm employees, he distributed $126,000 in stipends ranging from $5,000 to $25,000. To his son, Warren Wright, Jr., then thirty years old, he left $1 million in two separate $500,000 trusts and all his jewelry, including an emerald and diamond ring that his father had bequeathed to him.

About $742,500 was spent on legal fees to settle the estate and on the funeral; there were $198,000 in debts to be paid; and $10 million was paid in estate taxes. What remained were the farm, then valued at $2.2 million, and approximately $6.5 million in oil and gas leases and securities. Under his will, Calumet Farm and 28.01 percent of those investments (worth about $1.8 million) were placed in a trust—the Warren Wright Residuary Trust—a total value of about $4 million. From this trust, Warren Wright's widow, Lucille Parker Wright, would draw a monthly income for the rest of her life. The remaining $4.7 million, or 71.99 percent of the investments, went into another trust for his widow.

Wright was as precise and controlling from the grave as he had been in life. In his twenty-three-page will, he established several trusts "to provide for financial security of the beneficiaries and protect them from any contingencies, including their own improvidence." His chief concern appeared to be what his wife, now a very wealthy widow and an attractive prospect for anyone, including fortune seekers, might do with Calumet, his greatest legacy. Mrs. Wright had assured her husband that she would maintain his standards of excellence at Calumet, and there was nothing in Wright's will that would stop her from fulfilling that promise. But if by some chance what she had said wasn't true, or if she changed her mind down the road, the stipulations of the will discouraged the sale of the farm. If she chose to sell it, she would no longer have the glory of Calumet nor would she have the outright proceeds from the sale. The latter, under her husband's will, would go into the Residuary Trust, the principal of which her son, Warren Jr., would inherit upon his mother's death.

If Mrs. Wright died before her son did, he would receive all the assets of the trust outright, including Calumet. But if Warren Jr. were to die first, his will, according to his father's instructions, must designate a beneficiary for 50 percent of whatever remained in the trust by the time his mother died. Another 30 percent of the trust would be divided evenly among his grandchildren, and 20 percent would be given to charity.

The will, which Wright amended and signed for the last time on July 11, 1950, sent a message of confidence to his son. But the principal message was that Warren Wright wanted the farm to be kept in his family, handed down from generation to generation, just as his father had done. No matter what his widow decided to do, whether or not she remarried, the farm, through his son, had a secure spot in the Wright lineage.

Mrs. Wright, meanwhile, had the right to live at Calumet for the rest of her life and to manage it. She also had plenty of money. Depending on the terms of the various oil leases and the price of oil, which would fluctuate wildly in the years ahead, Mrs. Wright's income would range from $200,000 a year in the early 1950s to nearly $3 million a month by the late 1970s.

Wright's death had a profound effect on his widow, changing her life dramatically for the better, though on the surface the life of Warren Wright's wife had always seemed enviable.

Wright, who was divorced from his first wife when he met Lucille Parker, plucked her from her working-class existence in Chicago and deposited her securely, for the rest of her life, into the fairy tale–like world of a multimillionaire. This was quite a leap from her hardscrabble past. The youngest of seven children, Lucille was born in Lewis County, Kentucky, in the small town of Tollesboro on December 11, 1888. Her mother, crippled with arthritis, was in a wheelchair when Lucille was a toddler, and so Lucille's oldest sister raised her. She spent most of her childhood in Westin, Missouri, where her family moved shortly after her fourth birthday. By most accounts, her father was a livery stable operator, though some county records refer to him as a schoolteacher.

When she returned to Kentucky in the 1930s with Warren Wright, she told her new friends that her ancestors were the Parkers of Maysville, a very prominent family that had large tobacco holdings and a successful warehouse business. A local author writing about the bluebloods of Fayette County in 1938 reported that the "exceptionally well-bred" Lucille Wright was part of a line of Parkers who were among the early settlers of Kentucky, who had erected the first brick house in Lexington, and who were related to Mary Todd Lincoln.

The new heritage fit her new life. During most of the Wrights' years together they lived for six months and one day each year at the estate in Miami Beach, with its gardens and pools and servants. (The one extra day allowed them to declare Florida their legal residence.) Then it was Calumet during the spring and part of the summer. While the servants at one house were putting the silver away and throwing sheets over velvet settees to keep the dust off until the Wrights returned, the servants at the other were filling the vases in every room with fresh flowers and making certain that no one forgot Mrs. Wright's favorite item, a Lowestoft bowl filled with floating flowers. Somewhere in between, the Wrights were flying in their private jet while their staff followed in a caravan of cars jammed with steamer trunks and supplies. And when not in Lexington or Miami, they followed the fashionable trail of the racing circuit—Saratoga Springs and the Gideon Putnam Hotel, New York City and the Ritz Carlton, Chicago and the Drake Hotel.

But Warren Wright, as daring as he might have been in business ventures, was personally not very exciting, nor was he particularly romantic or affectionate. Regardless of appearances and despite the endless luxuries, life with Warren was no fairy tale.

Mrs. Wright was never invited into the winner's circle with her husband. It wasn't even a matter of discussion—she stayed strictly in the background. Her only publicized role at Calumet was in naming the horses.

She also remained in his shadow socially. If they were sitting with another couple in a car or at a party, she was typically silent, and if she began talking he'd soon tell her to be quiet, much to the embarrassment of their companions. In Miami, Warren was a frequent visitor to the trendy Biscayne Club. If Mrs. Wright joined him, she would sit at one end of the table while Warren, at the other end, slipped money to the showgirls who surrounded him and occasionally sat on his lap. A relative would say years later, "His theory was work hard when you work and play hard when you play." In Kentucky, he and Mrs. Wright had an arrangement. He went out one night a week with the boys, no questions asked. Sometimes he'd accompany his friend Leslie Combs II, also a breeder, to a nightclub called the Lookout House, in Covington, Kentucky, whose owner raced horses and treated Wright and Combs like kings. The club had a floor show with dancing girls, and there was gambling in the back room. Warren wasn't so interested in the gambling. He went to look at the pretty girls, though by most accounts he never fooled around. One Saturday night he and Combs went to the club and brought back all the Lookout girls to Calumet. Halfway down the long road to the main house Warren had second thoughts about the escapade, stopped the car, halted the caravan of cars behind him, and told Combs to take the girls to his own house.

In Lexington, Lucille and Warren rarely entertained, though by the late 1930s they were typically invited to the best of the Bluegrass bashes. She had no social identity other than that of Warren Wright's wife, and in her efforts to fit in with the local gentry, she began to add a few broad "a's" to her speech. As one Fayette County resident put it, "I used to tell her an aaauuuunt is your uncle's wife, not an insect, and that if she was going to talk like that, to do it right."

A few years after they married, Mrs. Wright became a Christian Scientist and regularly had a reader come to her home. She also took up needlepoint, almost obsessively making rugs and covering chairs, settees, divans, and pillows in her own upholstery. And she collected eagles, which according to Bluegrass folklore were supposed to bring good luck. Every room had an eagle, in brass or glass or wood or pottery, some with wings spread and some at rest.

About a year after Warren Wright's death, Mrs. Wright began to emerge from the shadows, creating a new life that barely resembled the old. Her

friends noticed her hemlines shortening and necklines lowering. Dior origi-
nals now filled her closets. She had a face-lift in Europe, though her friends
back home said it pulled her face too tightly. She even altered her age.
When she married Warren Wright in 1919, she was almost thirty-one years
old; when he died, she was sixty-two. But two years later in September 1952
when she married her second husband, who was born in 1895, she was
fifty-six again. Not one to even discuss age, she was able to keep her secret
for the last thirty years of her life. The false birthdate December 11, 1896, is
etched on her mausoleum.

Soon after Wright's death, her picture began appearing in magazine articles and in the major dailies of towns with big racetracks like Chicago,
Miami, Los Angeles, and New York. A January 1951 article in the *Chicago
Tribune* announced, "The newest entry in sportdom's most glamorous field
[racing] is Mrs. Warren Wright."

Comfortable in the spotlight, she proudly marched to the winner's circle
many times after her husband's death for dozens of stakes victories across
the country. Calumet horses won the Kentucky Derby four times during
Wright's lifetime—with Whirlaway, Pensive, Citation, and Ponder; under his
widow's reign, there would also be four Derby winners—Hill Gail, Iron
Liege, Tim Tam, and Forward Pass. Mrs. Wright would maintain the
Calumet excellence, and, capitalizing on her husband's success, she would
give herself and Calumet a new image. While William Monroe Wright made
Calumet Farm prominent in the Bluegrass and Warren Wright gave it international acclaim in the horse industry, Lucille Wright, with the help of a
new, young bon vivant husband, would give the farm a touch of glitter,
expanding its presence beyond the sports pages to society columns and
lifestyle magazines.

Shortly after her husband's death, Mrs. Wright sold the estate in Miami
Beach and bought a stucco Spanish-style mansion with winding staircases
and palatial balconies draped in red roses in the Bel-Air district of Los Angeles. It was in Hollywood that she met the man who really turned her life
into a fairy tale: Gene Markey.

6

Gene Markey was everything that Warren Wright was not. During the years Wright was building an empire of money and success, Markey was gadding about the world establishing a lifelong reputation as the most charming man on earth.

Markey never had the dogged determination, will-to-win concentration, or the officious standards to achieve what Warren Wright did in the business world. Yet he did have a ribald wit and a zest for adventure and for fun that most people found irresistible. He also could make anyone he talked to feel like the center of the world, listening with rapt attention as if he treasured each word and every moment.

Movie star Myrna Loy wrote in her autobiography that Markey "could make a scrubwoman think she was a queen and a queen think she was the queen of queens." He could entice the birds off the trees, she said, "though birds were never his particular quarry—women were, the richer and more beautiful the better, and I never knew one who could resist him."

Loy knew because she was Markey's third wife, from 1946 to 1950, following actress Joan Bennett, 1932 to 1937, and actress Hedy Lamarr, 1939 to 1940.

A 1946 article in the *Washington Times Herald* that carried the headline "Other Men Say: What's Gene Markey Got That We Haven't Got?" showed a photo of Rudolph Valentino with a caption: "NOT SO HOT—By comparison. Though all American womanhood swooned over him in his day, Rudolph Valentino was no Markey." The writer reported that soon after arriving in Hollywood in 1929, Markey "became the most sought after unattached man in the cinema firmament, so sprinkled with far handsomer, richer male stars."

About five feet, eleven inches tall, Markey didn't appear to be the swoonworthy type. His only striking and memorable physical trait was his eyebrows, which were thick, dark, and bushy, accentuating large hazel eyes. The far right corner of his right brow turned abruptly upward, giving him a mischievous, Pan-like expression.

Born in Jackson, Michigan, Markey grew up in Battle Creek, where his father ran a factory that made printing presses. A graduate of Dartmouth College, class of 1918, Markey, a caricaturist and writer, attended the Art

Institute of Chicago in 1919 and 1920, worked as a journalist for two Chicago newspapers and for magazines such as *Photoplay,* and wrote several novels about the jazz age before arriving in Hollywood in 1929. There, at the beginning of talking pictures, he worked as a screenwriter for Twentieth Century-Fox.

Markey was probably best known for producing Shirley Temple's *Wee Willie Winkie* in 1937, but he also wrote or produced such movies as *As You Desire Me, The Great Lover, Close Harmony,* and *Lucky in Love.* There were *King of Burlesque* and *Girls' Dormitory* in 1936 and *On the Avenue* starring Dick Powell and Alice Faye in 1937. One of his greatest screen successes was *Sally, Irene and Mary,* for which he was associate producer in 1938. The same year he was associate producer for a saga set in the Bluegrass, called *Kentucky.* Between 1929 and 1941, he wrote or produced twenty-four motion pictures.

Then World War II came, and his life changed. His yacht, the *Melinda,* named for his daughter by Joan Bennett, was taken over by the navy and converted into a submarine chaser. As a member of the U.S. Navy Reserve, he was sent to Balboa in Central America in late August of 1941 as Lieutenant Commander Markey.

In the same space of time that Warren Wright, twenty-one years Markey's senior, won four Kentucky Derbys and two Triple Crowns, Markey made a name for himself in the Navy. He won the Bronze Star, the Legion of Merit, and a Commendation Medal. Italy gave him a Star of Solidarity, and from France he received the Legion of Honor.

As a commander he served as assistant intelligence officer on Admiral William F. "Bull" Halsey's Third Fleet staff in Guadalcanal, and in 1955, when he officially retired from the military, he was promoted to rear admiral. Forever after, he would insist on being called "the admiral" or "Admiral Markey," rarely Gene, and never "Mr." Markey. His pride in his title was so intense that if he received mail that wasn't addressed to Admiral Markey, he threw it in the wastebasket.

After the war, he returned to Hollywood and immediately moved in with Myrna Loy. This was an era when military heroes were as high on the celebrity scale as movie stars. No Hollywood party was complete without its share of admirals and majors. Markey, with his indefatigable social skills, limitless energy for parties, and gift for accumulating the most important and glittering personalities of the era, was in his realm.

In January 1946, he married Loy at a full-dress naval affair on Roosevelt Navy Base at San Pedro, with Admiral Halsey as best man. John Ford, one of

Hollywood's most revered film directors, gave her away, and looking on were two of Hollywood's leading men, Douglas Fairbanks, Jr., and Robert Montgomery.

Four years later Loy, like Hedy Lamarr before her, claimed mental cruelty when she filed for divorce from Markey, but in her autobiography she tempered the claim by saying that he was far from a cruel man and he was in fact deeply involved with her. The problem was he was involved with other women also. At one point he and Loy were on location for her role in Alexander Korda's film *The Case of Lady Brooke,* living in places like a villa in Capri and a medieval castle in the English countryside. Markey apparently couldn't resist the duchesses and countesses he was meeting. One night in the Claridge Hotel, Loy wrote, "his well-tipped sentries weren't quick enough" in picking up the phone to warn him Loy was in the lobby walking toward the elevator bank and to their suite where he was not alone. Shortly thereafter, they separated. But, she wrote, Markey's "international version of open marriage persisted during our eight-month separation. A born courtier—witty companion, skilled lover, dynamic partner—he simply found it impossible to concentrate on one woman."

The divorce was final in August 1950. Markey moved back to Hollywood, buying a modest home in Bel-Air where less than a year later Warren Wright's widow bought her new estate. It's unclear when and how they met, though by most accounts her friends asked him to escort her to a dinner for the cardinal of Los Angeles. Talking to an old friend of Mrs. Wright's, Gene learned that night that Mrs. Wright's childhood nickname was "Zookie." On their second date, after dinner, as they were leaving a friend's home in Bel-Air, Gene put his arm around her and whispered in her ear, "What now, Zookie?" He supposedly won her heart from that moment on. Soon gossip columnists Louella Parsons, Hedda Hopper, and Eleanor Page were buzzing about the couple.

What Markey and Mrs. Wright had in common was an appreciation for Old World grace, a taste for the finest things in life, and timing. She wanted to race away from the past, and so did he. After three failed marriages to glamour girls and with his sixtieth birthday close at hand, he apparently was ready to settle down. And to the amazement of all who had known Markey, that's exactly what he did.

In the plush, comfortable environs of an heiress and in the womblike security of Calumet, Markey eased into a role that he seemed born to assume. No outsider had ever assimilated so completely to the ways of the Kentucky gentry.

7   When Gene Markey arrived at Calumet, it was like a
cabaret moving into a mausoleum. The once-silent dining room was filled
with laughter and warmth many mornings as Markey, who loved to write
limericks and love poems, read his own works or those of his favorite authors to his new wife over breakfast. The butler, Charles Rankin, was soon
routinely carrying the bags of celebrities up the wide staircase. Among them
were Douglas Fairbanks, Jr., John Wayne, and actress Patricia Neal; such
business heavyweights as John S. Knight, of Knight (now Knight-Ridder)
Newspapers; and international playboy and billionaire Prince Aly Khan.

Markey filled the wine cellar with the finest of wines, like Romanee-
Conti, a famous Burgundy selling even in the 1950s for $300 or $400 a
bottle. Once a month he would don his red satin robe with the black trim
and the little sterling cup dangling from the lapel and taste the wines.

Shortly after his arrival, Markey instructed Rankin and his wife, Christine, to carry the stable's hundreds of gold and silver trophies up from the
basement vault, shine them to perfection, and place them on shelves near
windows to sparkle in the sunlight.

New traditions like Easter egg hunts for Warren Jr.'s children brought
festive sounds and scenes to a house that now, with a more human dimen-
sion, seemed smaller, perhaps less stately than before. Markey even had the
design of the cold, barny dining room changed. He didn't like the idea of
the two of them eating breakfast alone at a huge, long table, so he insisted
on the addition of a bay window. In the cozy space with the splendorous
view, the Markeys placed a small table that allowed them to sit closer to
each other and to the out-of-doors. And right outside the window were new
birdhouses, which Markey erected because they both loved to watch and
listen to the birds each morning.

Most memorable perhaps was Markey's "love potion." Rankin was often
relieved of his duty to mix cocktails before dinner and at parties because
Markey took over with his notorious concoction of Puerto Rican rum, another darker rum, pineapple juice, bourbon, and perhaps a third, white
rum. Markey boasted that he used the brew as a way to see into people's
souls. No one could walk after their second drink, but if it was a Markey
party, no one had to leave at any particular time. The parties sometimes
lasted all night.

While Warren Wright knew how to accumulate wealth, Gene Markey knew best how to enjoy it. He loved fine clothes and accessories, collecting bowlers, panamas, fur caps to match his fur coats, and, later in life, canes tipped in silver and gold.

Markey also had an easier time than either of the Wrights fitting into Bluegrass society. Though his background lacked the social antiquing of his new blueblood neighbors, Markey was soon the favorite guest of Fayette County's elite.

"He was everything you'd expect a Kentuckian not to like; and yet everyone loved him," according to Dr. Thornton Scott, the Markeys' physician for a number of years. "He was a member of café society, told off-color stories, came from Hollywood, had been married three times before. It was a recipe for rejection and disdain from the gentry here, but they embraced him."

One key to his popularity was that he very astutely made friends with the men before he became acquainted with their wives, who he knew from experience would like him. With the male bonds firmly in place, Markey was confident the husbands would tolerate the wives' occasional crushes on the charming new neighbor from Hollywood.

Markey, with his sartorial elegance and penchant for storytelling, eased onto the roster at the Idle Hour Country Club, whose highbrow membership he referred to as "a bunch of crumbs held together by their dough." And he quickly became friends with one of Fayette County's highfliers, Leslie Combs II, the owner of Spendthrift Farm.

Warren Wright, too, had been friends with Combs, but Markey and Combs had far more in common—mainly parties. Markey's arrival in the Bluegrass coincided with Combs's agenda for turning up the intensity of the social life in horse country to lure new investors. Though Combs wasn't forcing down the doors that had allowed the Bluegrass to be such a closed society for so many years, he was loosening the hinges. Among his tactics were lavish dinner parties and lots of publicity. Combs wanted Markey, with his Hollywood friends, to fit into the Bluegrass social whirl perhaps as much as Markey did.

Through Combs, Markey broadened his circle to include cosmetics magnate Elizabeth Arden; "Sonny" Whitney, who had coproduced *Gone With the Wind*; and Sonny's fourth wife, socialite Marylou Whitney.

The Whitneys and Markeys, by the late 1950s, were particularly close because of the Hollywood connection and a penchant for drama. Sonny and Gene were infatuated with limericks, the book *The Spell of the Yukon* by Robert Service, and a poem entitled "The Ballad of Yukon Jake," by Edward

E. Paramore, Jr. After dinner, at the Whitneys' estate in Saratoga Springs, the
two men would read and dramatize parts of the ballad, taking turns reciting,
three pages at a time. It began:

> Oh, the North Countree is a hard countree
> That mothers a bloody brood;
> And its icy arms hold hidden charms
> For the greedy, the sinful and lewd.
> And strong men rust, from the gold and lust
> That sears the Northland soul,
> But the wickedest born from the Pole to the Horn
> Is the Hermet of Shark Tooth Shoal!

After hearing Marylou Whitney's accounts of her years as an actress, Markey promised her that if one of his books were made into a movie he
wanted her to play a part. But Markey didn't cling to his Hollywood identity, nor did he use his past glories to impress the Kentucky gentry. In fact,
he seemed to take to Kentucky with the swift devotion and enthusiasm of a
modern-day Daniel Boone. He once told a reporter for the *Los Angeles Times,*
"I cannot restrain my ardor for the place and its people. . . . No duck ever
took to water as I have taken to Kentucky."

Shortly after moving to Calumet, Markey decided to write a book—his
eighth novel—about life in Lexington in the post–Civil War era. His wife, to
show her support for the project, decided in early 1953 to have a log cabin
built for his writing studio not far from Calumet's main residence. With the
help of Leslie Combs II, she found an authentic cabin in western Kentucky
and had it dismantled and moved for $20,000. One by one, the logs, some
of white oak and some ash, the old shake shingles, and even the fireplace
came to Calumet.

The two-room retreat was filled with period furniture and pioneer accou-
trements such as a butter churn, a bed warmer, a big kettle hanging in the
fireplace, gourds for drinking, old jugs, a model of a gin still, and Markey's
collection of old Kentucky rifles, pistols, and powder horns. Outside the
door, for effect, were half a dozen chickens and a rooster.

About once a week in the late spring and early summer Markey would
dress up in overalls, tie a red bandanna around his neck, don a straw hat,
and call to Christine and Charles, the maid and butler, "We're going to the
cabin tonight, so bake that apple pie and put the steaks on." Then when he
and Mrs. Markey were ready to eat, they'd ring a big cowbell to alert the

servants that it was time to cart the food from the main house down the driveway to the hideaway.

The cabin, however, was first and foremost Markey's writing room. There, sitting at an old pine desk, with an antique map of Fayette County on the log wall behind him and a copy of the seal of the Confederacy above the fireplace mantel, he wrote, in longhand, *Kentucky Pride,* a Civil War novel published by Random House; *That Far Paradise,* about the trek of a plantation family from Virginia to Kentucky in the eighteenth century; and a comic novel, *Women, Women Everywhere.* For *That Far Paradise,* he and Mrs. Markey retraced the route that his characters followed, from Culpeper County, Virginia, to Parkersburg, West Virginia, and from there by boat down the Ohio to Louisville. He loved every aspect of writing, from the adventure of the research to the discipline of shaping a story. Once, in filling out a questionnaire for a Saratoga Springs newspaper that included the question "If retired, when did you retire?" Markey crossed out the last four words and wrote above them, "If retired, from writing" and then filled in the blank to read "No! Never!"

He also wrote "The Kentucky Jug," a twenty-page tribute to Kentucky bourbon. With his usual drawing-room wit, his writing brought everybody in Lexington into the fun, quoting local pharmacists, doctors, and friends, and he dedicated it "To the Lady of Calumet—'I raise my glass!'"

"As to its medicinal advantages, I have attempted no survey beyond asking Dr. Thornton Scott, a distinguished Kentuckian, what he thought of bourbon. The good doctor, known for the brevity as well as the soundness of his opinions, snapped: 'I prefer it.' "

Throughout the booklet he praised Kentuckians for their excellent instincts in creating such a fine product as bourbon. "The great forgotten man in our commonwealth's history is Reverend Elijah Craig, a Baptist preacher who distilled the first bourbon in 1789. For his immeasurable contribution to the well-being of mankind, a statue of this godly pioneer should stand in every city park and village square throughout Kentucky."

He devoted a page to mint juleps, with a full-page photo of his butler, Charles Rankin, and an interview on Rankin's seven-minute formula for the perfect julep. He also tells a story:

One May morning the farm office telephoned that the commanding general of Fort Knox had brought some visiting Panamanian Air Force officers over to see the horses. Now, Mrs. Markey and I like generals generally, we like Panama, and we are crazy about Fort Knox—so we invited the general to bring his guests to the house for a drink. Where-upon I set out a bottle of Bourbon with a few julep cups and sent Charles down the hill to our little spring to pick mint leaves. When the general—a highly agreeable fellow—arrived, I was staggered to see behind him a whole phalanx of Panamanians. Twenty-three of them, their eyes feverish with thirst! All had heard of the Kentucky julep—and all wanted to try it. Including the general they were twenty-four and I raised the total to twenty-five. My mind sought to grapple with the problem: twenty-five juleps at seven minutes each. . . . But I was committed. And, Kentucky hospitality being what it is, nobody may have just one julep. For the next several hours I worked harder than a bartender at a Tammany picnic—while Charles, bearing baskets of mint, scurried up and down hill like a Sherpa guide.

Markey even concocted his own bourbons: "Old Commodore," with a label displaying a horse's head against the backdrop of the main house at Calumet; and "Old Calumet Cabin" bourbon, with a picture of the log cabin on the label.

Even more memorable were the couple's tongue-in-cheek Christmas cards. One pictured Markey, wearing a beret, on a motorbike in front of a quaint tavern in Paris. Sitting behind him was Mrs. Markey, looking like Cupid had just struck. In another, they dressed up like Kentucky settlers and sat on the front stoop of the Calumet log cabin. The most memorable of all and the one that recipients would someday search their attics to find showed a lemonade stand at the front gates to the farm with a sign across the front of the table reading "Calumet must survive." The Markeys sat behind the table, and Charles, the butler, held an umbrella over them.

Markey knew little about horses when he came to Calumet, but as with everything else in his new life he eagerly adopted the jargon and the habits of a racehorse owner. At dawn each day, dressed in a morning coat and an ascot, he would walk down to the track to watch the morning workout, sharing observations with his trainer, who for several years was Ben Jones.

At times, he was overbearing to those who knew that he didn't know as much about breeding as he thought he did. According to former Calumet secretary Margaret Glass, "While Mr. Wright did things the 'Wright way,' the admiral did them the 'Navy way,' and both ways you had to stand to atten-tion and take orders. The difference was that Warren Wright had spent a decade learning the business." The "Navy way" was Markey's style in the house as well as at the track. The servants, for example, weren't especially enthusiastic about his Christmas ritual of ordering them to line up every morning of the twelve days before Christmas, each holding a little silver bell, to sing "The Twelve Days of Christmas."

While Mrs. Markey continued to name the horses as she always had done, her new husband soon learned to appreciate the creative challenge and joined the game. The trick was—and is—to find new names never before recorded at the Jockey Club, the social register or "blue book" for thoroughbred racehorses. With thousands and thousands of thoroughbred foals born every year, this task isn't easy. It was Markey who named Alydar. On their frequent visits to see Prince Aly Khan in France, the prince would throw dinner parties for them, and at the parties one woman always made her entrance by nearly shouting "Aly Daawling, how lovely to see you." Markey relished any chance to imitate her, repeating her chant in a high-pitched voice as he leaned back, rolled his eyes, moved his right arm in the air, and collapsed his wrist. One day in the midst of such an imitation, he realized "Alydarling" was the perfect name for a horse, and so anointed Alydar.

Guests still praised Mrs. Markey for the beauty of her needlepoint, displayed graciously throughout Calumet's main residence, but she rarely, if ever, picked it up after 1950. There was no time in her life for it now. As always, she was on the racing circuit, following the Calumet horses to the tracks where they were racing. This meant summering in New York, at Saratoga Springs, and wintering in Florida, at their new home in La Gorce Island, a tiny island of one hundred or so residents adjacent to Miami Beach. But, in a dramatic departure from her past, she had no time to sit, in Saratoga Springs or Miami—there were parties to attend. And there were many trips to Europe, where she and Warren had gone only once, during the first ten months of her marriage. Every autumn the Markeys would go to Baden-Baden and in summer to the Ritz Hotel in Paris.

Nor did she need the attention of Christian Science readers. She once told a reporter for the *Lexington Herald-Leader,* "I never knew what love was until I married [Markey]."

For Markey, a man who had infuriated women because of his inability to concentrate on one at a time and the tireless twinkle in his wandering eye, his relationship with Lucille Parker was nothing less than remarkable. By all accounts he was loyal throughout their twenty-eight years together, and he rarely, if ever, even mentioned Bennett, Lamarr, or Loy. Once at a Calumet party, the couple was sitting at the foot of the front staircase drinking Markey-style rum specials when Markey raised his glass to Mrs. Markey, saying,

"You are the most wonderful and gorgeous woman I've ever known, and that includes those other three women whose names I can't remember."

He enjoyed her money and her adulation of him, and she was enthralled with the glamorous and exciting world he had opened to her. But regardless of her efforts to invent a new life, there were parts of the past that she could never escape and that would affect the future of Calumet.

8 Every family has its secrets, some more troubling than others, and as pieces of the truth disappear into the graves of each passing generation, some secrets become mysteries. It's the mysteries that have the power to destroy the very soul of a family, especially if, over time, they become impossible to solve.

In the Wright family, there was the relatively innocent secret of Mrs. Markey's age. For her to conceal her true age was a harmless game, which only drained some drama from her public persona. When she made her last public appearance as Calumet's matriarch to watch Alydar win the Blue Grass Stakes in 1978, she was hobbled with arthritis and nearly blind, and the sports pages applauded her spirit at age eighty-one. If the public had known she was only a few months from her ninetieth birthday as she grasped the trackside railing with frail, white-gloved hands, cheering on her mighty Alydar, Calumet's grande dame might have engaged the crowds even more. Her secret merely deprived Calumet fans and the press of a piece of trivia.

But there was also the matter of Warren Wright, Jr., in which secrecy led to a deeper deprivation. The only child of Warren and Lucille Wright and the heir to Calumet Farm, young Warren never knew the truth about his origins. The question was more complicated than that of an adopted child seeking his real parents. Warren's problem was that he was not able to determine whether he was adopted or Lucille and Warren were his natural parents.

They told him he was born in Chicago in 1920, on January 11, but he never saw his birth certificate. And when, in the 1940s, he asked an aunt in Chicago to retrieve a copy of his birth certificate for a passport, she told him the courthouse records didn't go back that far because a fire had destroyed them in the 1920s. Warren's lawyer helped him get the passport, but no one helped him find his identity.

In press stories young Warren was referred to as simply "the son of Warren Wright." Wright was apparently insistent that his son, rather than his wife, inherit the farm, which was the heart of his empire, and the will as well as all probate matters never mentioned the word "adopted." After Wright's death, the words "adopted son" began to appear occasionally in newspaper stories featuring the farm and family. The change could be attributed to a more accepting attitude in society about adoption, to a more open style on the part of Wright's widow, or to Lucille's desire to distance herself publicly from a son who did not fit into her new image.

Throughout Warren's life the messages were mixed. As he was growing up, people commented on how he looked like his father, especially in the hips and shoulders. From the back, both men had the same flat and wide shape, though in later life Warren Jr. was much heavier than his father. They also shared eye problems. Warren Sr. was very nearsighted; so was Warren Jr., though his case was far more severe.

At some point, the aunt in Chicago informed him that he was adopted, but neither parent ever devoted a moment to clear up the matter. What's worse is that throughout the last twenty-five years or so of his life, the Bluegrass buzzed with this and that story, each with a different twist, about the origins of the heir to Calumet.

Some locals firmly believed, and barely questioned, that Warren Jr. was a "backyard baby." A southern term, emanating from plantation days, it means he was the illegitimate son of the master of the house and a maidservant, conceived figuratively in the backyard. There were also stories that he was the son of Warren Sr. and Lucille's sister. Some said they knew he was "a wood's colt" or "a woodpussied baby"—synonyms for backyard baby—of a union between William Monroe Wright and a maidservant. They attested to Warren Jr.'s body type being closer to his grandfather's than to Warren Sr.'s. Because William Monroe Wright had been sixty-nine years old when the child was born in 1920, the theory went, he had asked Warren Sr. and his bride to adopt and raise the child.

A college friend of Warren Jr.'s believed the stories were red herrings to distract the public from the truth and to distance the parents from a son who was an embarrassment. Warren Sr. and Lucille Parker were Warren's natural parents, the friend firmly believed: "He was from the loins of Lucille." Supporting this view were not only the physical similarities between father and son but the mysterious wedding date and the timing of the son's birth.

Warren and Lucille were married in 1919. Though they celebrated their anniversary each year on February 19—the date they told friends—they were really married on March 25. Later that spring, they went to France to live until 1920. When they returned, friends learned there were two new-comers at their Lakeshore Drive home: a nanny and a baby.

An oil portrait of Warren Jr. as a toddler, smiling in his mother's arms, was displayed prominently in the living room at the Calumet main resi-dence, but the truth of his origins would die with his parents. His wife, Bertha, has said he longed to know whether Mrs. Markey was his mother. "Maybe he just didn't know whether he should be mad at her for the way she was with him or thankful that she had adopted him. . . . He wanted to know and so did I, for the sake of our children."

Even Margaret Glass, who worked for the family for nearly forty-three years and was close to Mrs. Markey, never knew the truth. Years after they had all died she would say, "To let it rest, I've concluded that she was pregnant when they were married and they went overseas to have the child."

For Warren Jr., the mystery was like a fishhook stuck in his heart throughout his life, and he wore his pain for all to see.

Warren Jr. personified the phrase "poor little rich boy." An old Lexington friend said, "Warren was the spittin' image of his father, but he didn't have the personality and brains to be a big shot. He wanted to be a big deal, if for no other reason than to earn his parents' love."

As a boy, Warren had little contact with his mother and less with his father; he spent more time with nannies and farm managers. He was eleven years old when his father began spending more time in the Bluegrass than in Chicago. Young Warren rarely tagged along, but his father's spirit was al-ways present in the form of expectations and demands and the same set of standards that had pushed the baking powder company and the farm to the top of their respective industries. While Warren Sr.'s work-ethic methods may have succeeded in the workplace, they seemed to fail miserably at home.

From Warren Jr.'s early teens on, he wallowed in a sense of inadequacy. He just couldn't measure up. Part of his problem was physical. He had terrible eyesight and from a young age wore glasses with lenses as thick as the bottom of a bottle of Kentucky bourbon, which exaggerated the size of his eyes. Even with these aids, he had to hold objects close to the lens to identify them. To read, he had to move the paper back and forth across his nose and as close to his lenses as possible. The problem hobbled his social life; classmates sometimes taunted him for his bug-eyed looks.

In 1932, when he was in the seventh grade, his parents sent him to the Riverside Military Academy in Georgia, where he seemed to keep to himself and was considered a very shy youngster. At first he was an excellent student, good enough to skip the eighth grade, going straight to the ninth in the fall of 1933, where he enjoyed another good year of grades averaging in the low- to mid-nineties. But during the next fall, the beginning of his sophomore year, his grades took a sharp dip to the low seventies. Then suddenly, in the second term of that year, he left the school and returned to Chicago, where he finished the second and third terms with a tutor. Though his grades picked up a little, he never again saw the success he had achieved in the seventh and ninth grades. And he never returned to the academy, apparently because his eyesight had worsened enough to require special attention. He was also humiliated by his inability to see the blackboard from his classroom seat. Still, with the help of Chicago tutors, he was able to graduate.

By the time Warren Jr. went to college, he had lost interest in schoolwork. A large part of the problem was his eyesight, but part, too, was his father. Warren Wright never perhaps intended to hurt his son, but he was a perfectionist who believed frailties were a test to make people stronger. Warren Jr., in the face of challenge, seemed to weaken instead. And, desperate for his parents' love, he tried to satisfy their expectations. So in the late 1930s, Warren Jr. entered Northwestern University, a top-rated Big Ten school of his father's choosing, where he majored in liberal arts. Basically a loner, he never joined a club or fraternity and lived in a single room in a dormitory in Evanston, only a few miles from one of the Calumet offices on LaSalle Street in Chicago. By spring of his first year it was clear that Warren couldn't make the grade. Though his student photo showed him without glasses, his eyesight problems were noted on his transcript. For his second year he transferred to the University of Denver, majoring in geology. Three years later he graduated with a bachelor's degree. It was during those three years that he discovered an all-consuming interest, the student radio station, and vowed to someday have his own.

In 1941, he graduated from college, one of the biggest events of his life, though it was considerably overshadowed by Calumet's first Derby victory. Warren was the first college graduate in his family; Whirlaway was Calumet's first Kentucky Derby winner. His father and mother did attend his graduation ceremony, but the talk of the day was Whirlaway.

Shortly after graduation, Warren Sr. arranged for his son to work in Washington, D.C., in a clerical job at the Pentagon, in lieu of being drafted. There Warren met and fell in love with Bertha Cochran. Bertha, who was from a middle-class family in Alexandria, Virginia, worked in a clerical position for John L. Lewis, president of the United Mine Workers. Her father was a dentist, and her great-great-grandfather was U.S. Supreme Court Chief Justice John Marshall. Bertha had no problems passing the strict inspection that Warren Sr. ordered when he heard about Warren's intention to marry. Though she would never flaunt it and few would ever know it, Bertha had a pedigree that far surpassed her future mother-in-law's.

For once, Warren Jr. got what he wanted. In late November 1944 he and his bride moved home to Lexington. The next August, after Wright's former manager Dick McMahon died, the couple moved into the beautiful old farmhouse, the original homestead, at Calumet Farm.

It was an idyllic setting, and for a while it seemed life was good. When Bertha had their first child, she named it after Mrs. Markey, though to avoid confusion they called the child Cindy. Mrs. Markey seemed to soften at the sight of the little girl, and Warren Sr., too, took an interest in his granddaughter, insisting that the milk she drank come from Calumet's own dairy cows; the water, from the Calumet springs; and the vegetables, fresh from Calumet's fields. By most accounts, these were Warren Jr.'s happiest days. The drinking he had begun at the University of Denver all but disappeared as a sort of familial comfort and sense of security set in. He became one of three of Lexington's peace officers, appointed from the ranks of the local gentry, with the dignified-sounding title of deputy constable.

After returning to the Bluegrass, Warren Jr. began learning the insurance business with the help of his father. In early 1945, Leslie Combs II, Warren Wright Sr., and another friend spent $5,000 each to buy out the owner of the Kentucky Insurance Agency, which performed the then-unique service of writing mortality insurance for horses. The premiums, because of the great risk involved, were outrageously high. Still, by the late 1940s Combs and Wright brought in a vast array of wealthy horse owners as clients, including movie mogul Louis B. Mayer as well as Elizabeth Arden. In Wright's estimation, this was a steady occupation for Warren Jr.

Wright never attempted to groom his son to take over the farm, though his greatest hope for posterity was that the Calumet tradition be carried on by generations of Wrights. Wright apparently was convinced that nothing the boy had ever done demonstrated he could direct the farm after his father's death.

Warren Wright's will is perhaps the strongest tangible argument for believing that Warren Jr. was his natural son. If the son had been adopted, Warren Sr., a stalwart traditionalist, might have used his son's frailties and failures as an excuse to exclude him. Incompetent or not, his own son, not his wife, would inherit Calumet Farm.

By the time Wright died, in late 1950, Warren Jr. was the father of two children and was reporting to the insurance offices daily. By most accounts, he was deeply saddened by the death of his father, despite the apparent distance between them. But while his mother's life changed for the better after his father's death, Warren Jr.'s was filled with the same struggles as before. He seemed to be trying harder than ever to be the man his father had wanted him to be.

He invested some of his inheritance in a new Combs venture called Temulac—"Temulac" was "Calumet" spelled backward—which dabbled in real estate, including the construction of a new building for the Kentucky Insurance Agency. And he bought an interest in United Underwriters, another insurance venture.

But more exciting to Warren Jr. was his own company, the Associated Dispatch Corporation, which he launched in May 1951. Harking back to his college days and his love of radios, the company operated a two-way communications system for private subscribers. Its headquarters was in town, while the repair and installation work was done in Warren Jr.'s garage at Calumet. "He loved the radios because this was his thing," his wife would say years later. "He had done it all by himself; it was his baby. He was not an insurance man."

Most days Warren arrived at his office at the insurance company in late morning, took a long lunch, and returned for a few hours in the late afternoon. The rest of his time, at least during these years, was spent at the radio shop.

In the spring of 1954, it appeared that Warren had gotten a big break. Associated Dispatch won a contract for the maintenance of the county patrol radio system, beating out Radio Engineering and Maintenance Corporation which not only had won the contract for sixteen consecutive years but also was credited with installing the county's first two-way radio system in 1938, one of the nation's first county systems. The county couldn't resist Warren's bid of $108.50 a month, as opposed to Radio Engineering's $115.

Warren was elated, announcing that he would be spending most of his time building up his no-longer-fledgling radio company. Soon he had more clients such as vets, who found his twenty-four-hour service indispensable.

He and Bertha also communicated through the system, using their "handle"-like numbers; his was "fifty," hers "twenty-five." But the business didn't grow as quickly as he wanted it to, especially to cover the costs of the seven operators and two technicians. After five years of losses, he was forced to close it.

His fascination with radios and gadgets continued. Warren Jr. was the first in town, and almost anywhere else in the country, to have a mobile telephone in his car. Installed in 1960, the system, made by Motorola, cost about $8,000, and the receiver and transmitter took up the entire trunk of his car. He'd use it to call his office to tell someone that he was on the way to work. On rainy days he'd call a janitor to meet him at the door with an umbrella.

The "electric eyes" he had installed in the doorways of his home allowed him to walk into a room, wave his hand, and have the lights come on. He seemed more fascinated with the inner workings of his Minox camera than with the art of photography. "You've been Minoxed," he would say as he shot photos of the family. And at Christmastime, decorations at the Wright household included a rotating Christmas tree. With an electric motor at its base, the tree would make a complete circle every few minutes.

He had other hobbies, such as building model trains and listening at night to the local police-band scanner. If there was an accident anywhere along the many miles of roads that bordered Calumet, Warren Jr. would know about it. Policemen knew him well. On many a rainy night when drivers were more apt to veer off the road onto a muddy shoulder or into a fence post, the police, looking over the white fences toward the farm, might see a heavy figure carrying a lantern walking toward them and asking, "Is there anything I can do here?"

But Warren Jr. would never be remembered for these interests—even his stint as classical music DJ on a local radio station would be forgotten—for his problems and inadequacies seemed to upstage his virtues. By the mid-1950s, his relationship with his mother had begun to deteriorate, though Gene Markey, for a few years after his arrival, attempted to bring the family closer. Gene organized Sunday lunches with the entire family at a restaurant in the nearby Campbell House hotel, and Warren adored Gene, whose playfulness, energy, and storytelling made him seem more like a brother than a father. But not even Markey could rebuild the bonds the past had destroyed.

Mrs. Markey was increasingly agitated that her son was spending money as fast as he got his hands on it. She knew, too, he sometimes drank more than he should have, though by most accounts he rarely drank during the day. And she knew about his parties. He loved parties, especially the ones he hosted at his cottage on a lake thirty miles outside Lexington.

But most upsetting perhaps was his habit of ignoring his bills. It was common knowledge around his office that he opened his mail only once a year. When he called a secretary into his office and asked that she spend the entire day with him, everyone knew the big day had come. Together they would open and sort mounds of envelopes containing bills, checks, cards, letters, and ads. Because of this idiosyncrasy, his mother all too frequently received calls from town merchants telling her Warren Jr. hadn't paid this or that overdue balance. Then she would call him to the main house, lecture him, shake a finger, and plead with him to do better. He would walk away, shaken, hurt, the old wound of rejection reopened.

The final blow came in 1955. For months, rumors were racing through the Bluegrass that Warren Jr.'s wife had found a lover and wanted to leave Warren. When the vicious tales, which described dozens of scenarios, reached Mrs. Markey, she called a meeting at Calumet, with Warren, Harry Sutter, her lawyer from Chicago, and Bertha. She confronted the couple with what she had heard and asked for the truth.

Bertha, who told friends she only wanted the best for her children, said simply that she would like to leave her husband. She had an arrangement in town with her "friend" that would give her three children—Cindy, Courtenay, and Warren III—a comfortable, though humbler, lifestyle. Mrs. Markey, horrified and humiliated, gave Warren a choice: leave his wife, or move out of the old Calumet farmhouse and never return home. Warren chose to stay with his wife, and Bertha, too, decided to stay. Though the Wrights would have to cope with rumors and the stigma of the exodus from the farm, in some ways it was a relief for the couple to live a distance from the Calumet matriarch.

In 1956 Warren Jr. moved his family from the farm he would someday inherit to a modest $25,000 house with two tiny bathrooms. When his fourth child was born the same year, Warren Jr. was so self-conscious about the rumors regarding Bertha and so tormented by the mystery of his own origins that when he visited friends to show off his new baby, he obsessively pointed out every feature of his son's little face that could possibly be construed as looking like his own. In fact, the child bore no resemblance to him, which intensified the rumors. "It just looked like any other baby, not like him or anyone else for that matter, but he had to make a big deal out of it and that only made matters worse for him," an old friend said years later.

Warren's children, though the heirs and heiresses of racing's finest dynasty, would not grow up among horses and would have almost no interest in thoroughbred racing. Only his grandchildren, who didn't associate the racing stable with rejection and pain, would begin to bring horses back into the family. By then it would be too late.

The rift between mother and son was not at first as pronounced as it seemed or as the local gossip depicted it. For a few years, he stored his steaks and meat in the freezer at the main house and would call from his car to tell Christine and Charles—the maid and the butler—that he was on his way. He would still see his mother, though typically about his unpaid bills or something he had done that agitated her. And when Cindy Wright decided to marry J. T. Lundy, Warren and his mother apparently talked more than usual. He confided to a friend, "Mother's in an awful snit."

During the 1960s the imperious Mrs. Markey was in the habit of calling merchants—instead of waiting for them to call her—to check on Warren Jr. One Mother's Day, she dropped by a local florist that Warren Jr. had used in the past and said, in front of two customers standing at the counter, "If that son of mine calls up to buy me a Mother's Day plant, please refuse the order. I don't want to pay the bill."

From the point of view of Mrs. Markey's friends, Warren Jr. was an embarrassment, and her tolerance for so many years was admirable, far beyond the call of duty. They liked to recall what a stately, honorable woman Mrs. Markey was and how tragic it was that she was plagued with such an albatross. This was a woman who graciously told the press in 1954, a down year for the farm, "This year hasn't been as fortunate for Calumet as others. But we can't complain. We've had more than our share of good fortune and we can take our share of misfortune."

Bertha tried to minimize the rift, telling folks it wasn't as bad as it appeared to be. In later years she said, "[Mrs. Markey] thought she was doing right. She thought if she was stern he would shape up. She worried a lot about the drinking."

Warren Jr.'s friends, meanwhile, described his mother as "tougher than a three-year-old steak." The list of complaints was long. Near the top was her edict that he had to make appointments to see her, and that for a few years Warren Jr.'s children had to leave Christmas presents for their grandmother on the front porch at Calumet. "Warren didn't have a mean bone in his body," an old friend said. "But she, she was born mean."

There were other instances that demonstrated her glacial side. Shortly after Wright died, she ended an employees' benefit that staffers had cherished. Wright had allowed all Calumet employees to have $5 worth of goods from the farm each week. Considering that the farm was producing milk, eggs, and a bounty of vegetables, this was a wonderful treat, one that had helped some workers' families survive the war years. They were stunned by Mrs. Wright's decision. This was a benefit that couldn't mean as much to the farm's bottom line as it did to the budgets of employees whose salaries were already low.

Shortly after banishing her son from his home, she caused a stir again when she asked Paul Ebelhardt, her farm manager of fifteen years, to resign without a pension. It was a tradition on the Bluegrass farms to take care of the older employees, and most farm owners provided pensions. Ebelhardt, whom Wright hired in 1945, was struck by lightning while playing golf, and he was still at home recovering when she decided to let him go, with a paycheck through the following year. While the accident's impact was debilitating and he likely would not have returned to the same post, friends were stunned that she cut him off. Warren Wright, they bristled, would never have done such a thing. He was domineering and tight, but he was not unkind.

Though Warren Jr. continued to check in at the insurance agency, he did so without any regularity. His co-workers liked him but vacillated between compassion for him and frustration over his erratic behavior. Evelyn Stewart, whose desk was near Warren's, was always amazed that his mother went to a dentist whose office was right across the hall from young Warren's for ten years but never once stopped to visit with her son. At least his father had called, in the early years of the company, every day, sometimes twice, to check on when Warren Jr. had come to work, how long his lunch hour had been, and what he was doing at that moment. And high on the wall across from Warren's desk was a portrait of his father looking down on him.

Tom Dixon, the insurance adjuster who would later stand watch over Alydar, worked with Warren Jr. in the 1960s and described him as "a wonderful person . . . but he didn't have the best smarts in the world." He recalled Warren's generosity with his time and his money. Every February when car owners were required to get new plates, Warren would gather everyone's driver's license in the Temulac office, drive downtown to the courthouse, and stand for hours in a line that wrapped around the building. Toward the end of the day, he'd return to the office with new plates for all.

When Warren didn't show up for work, there was always concern at Temulac partly because he was a heavy drinker. Once, when this happened and Dixon couldn't reach Warren by phone, he was worried enough to go to

Warren's house. There he found Warren sitting on the floor of a two-car garage surrounded by the dozens of pieces of a dismantled air-conditioning unit. Warren was holding pieces up to his eyes to identify them and then bending over almost to the floor to fit them together. The air conditioner had broken in the night, and since dawn Warren had been trying to fix it, which he eventually did. "I felt so sorry for him. Here was the son of one of the richest people, I kept thinking, and the family . . . just forgot about him," said Dixon years later.

In the 1960s, Warren's habit of pitching his mail into a desk drawer for a year caused greater problems. Not only was he failing to pay bills, but when April 15 rolled around in 1967, 1968, and 1969, he failed to file his federal income taxes. On November 6, 1970, in U.S. District Court in Louisville, the Internal Revenue Service indicted Warren Wright, Jr., charging him with three counts of failing to file returns reporting a gross income of $46,250.94 for 1966, $42,788.24 for 1967, and $53,924.93 for 1968.

Dixon said, years later, "He wasn't trying to beat Uncle Sam. He was just kind of an absentminded-professor type . . . no common sense."

On March 16, 1971, Warren pleaded not guilty to all three counts, because, having completely forgotten about his taxes, he truly believed he wasn't guilty. The judge scheduled a trial for April 15, 1971, but when Warren arrived at court the day of the trial, he changed his plea. The judge sentenced him to three months on each of the three counts, to run concurrently, and fined him $15,000. On April 29 Warren surrendered to the U.S. marshal in Louisville and the next morning reported to the federal prison camp at Maxwell Air Force Base in Montgomery, Alabama.

His mother, more distant than ever, never wrote to him in jail. But Margaret Glass, Calumet's longtime office manager, exchanged letters and sent him a booklet of facts and figures she had compiled called "The Calumet Story." Warren was thrilled and asked for several copies for the prison library, which he ran during his incarceration. When he returned home, he told an old friend, Evelyn Stewart, that he was very proud of the work he had done for the prison library and loved it more than any other job he had had. "He wanted to stay in jail because he had found a position where people really looked up to him," said his friend Kent Hollingsworth.

Warren had little contact with his mother during the years after prison. She had instituted the rule that he should call for an appointment before coming to see her, and though he never said a nasty word about her to his friends and never talked about his problems, his drinking escalated. "He wasn't a vindictive person at all; he just turned the other cheek," said an old friend.

In 1976, the insurance agency was sold. It's unclear who decided to sell it, but Warren had neglected the business since his return from Alabama. That same year, the Markeys came home to Lexington in the spring, and Gene was diagnosed with colon cancer. Lucille was at the hospital from 8:30 A.M. to dusk every day for weeks and weeks. Warren called a few times at the house to ask if he might help, but he never reached his mother. The maid, sensitive to his desire to connect, told Warren that his mother was too exhausted to call back.

By 1978 Gene had recovered enough that in late April the Markeys were chauffeured to the Keeneland Race Course to watch Alydar run in the prestigious pre-Derby race, the Blue Grass Stakes. This event marked the beginning of a whirlwind of press coverage surrounding the rising star of the racing world. Article upon article discussed how Alydar was breathing new life into Calumet and how the hope of having a superstar once again was adding years to Lucille Markey's life. No horse since Whirlaway had won so many hearts; everyone who worked with Alydar loved the horse, but no one as much as Lucille Markey.

Gene and Lucille, both too frail to stand more than a few moments at the rail, sat out most of the race in a station wagon, he in his houndstooth cap, beige tweed suit, and red scarf and she in a blue dress with her trademark white gloves. Alydar was the seventh and last horse to walk to the starting gate, because his jockey veered toward the rail for a few moments, trying to get close enough for the Markeys to see their star.

For much of the race Alydar trailed. But as he turned for the homestretch and began to pass, one by one, each of the other horses, Lucille and Gene were helped out of the car and taken to the rail, where they watched Alydar win the race by thirteen lengths. As his victory was confirmed and announced, Lucille moved slowly toward her husband and pressed her cheek against his.

After John Veitch, the trainer, received the trophy for Calumet in the winner's circle, the Kentucky governor Julian Carroll, Veitch, Alydar's jockey Jorge Velasquez, and a flock of reporters and photographers rushed across the track to a secluded lawn where the Markeys sat in their car. The governor leaned down to the level of the car window and handed Lucille Calumet's trophy. With failing eyesight, she could barely see the faces of her fans, just as the devil's-red and blue colors had been a blur across the track moments before. Nor could she recognize the reporters who moved close to the car and peered into the windows trying to catch a glimpse of the grandest lady the sport of racing had ever known.

But she recognized the significance of the moment, and as her white gloves clutched the heavy chalice, she smiled as she heard the din of clicking cameras. For long moments the Markeys seemed to stare ahead as if floating through a maze of past images, uninterrupted by the harsh realities of illness, infirmity, and family problems. Then, from among the fans hovering near the car, a figure moved closer. Gene, who was sitting in the front seat, saw quickly that it was Warren Jr.'s wife. Lucille was sitting in the back, next to Melinda Bena, Gene's daughter by actress Joan Bennett. Bertha approached the car and leaned into the window. Knowing Lucille couldn't see well, Bertha said, "It's me, Lucille, it's your daughter." Lucille responded curtly, "I have only one daughter, and she is sitting next to me in this car."

As Calumet and the racing world were gearing up for Alydar's run for the Derby roses, Warren, who suffered from liver problems, became so ill he was hospitalized. On May 6, as Warren lay in a Lexington hospital, a splashy article about the splendor and beauty of Calumet ran in the local paper. It quoted his mother about the excitement of perhaps another Derby trophy and about her many years of happiness with Gene Markey. This was when she told the world, "I never knew what love was until I married him," and added she would do anything to prevent her son from inheriting the farm. "I didn't leave it to him, but my former husband did," she told the paper. "He left in his will if anything happened to me, it should go to this boy, but . . . he doesn't know a darn thing about horses."

Alydar lost the Derby to his arch rival Affirmed. Warren grew progressively worse. On the morning after the Derby, Evelyn Stewart, Warren's co-worker and friend from the insurance agency, visited him in the hospital. Warren didn't know the results of the Derby; his mother had not visited him since his hospitalization. But Warren's chief concern that day was apparently his daughter Cindy and her education.

Evelyn, a thin woman in her fifties with petite, refined features, pulled a chair close to Warren, whose eyesight seemed worse than ever. He told Evelyn how Cindy had dropped out of high school many years before to marry J. T. Lundy and how he wanted her to finish her education. After getting her GED, she was now taking college courses, and he hoped he could live to see the day she received a degree. Cindy would feel good about herself, Warren told Evelyn, and he knew that to be important, maybe the most important thing.

Two weeks later, on May 20, the day of the Preakness and Alydar's next chance to beat Affirmed, a banner headline ran across the top of the local newspaper: "Preakness Renews Old Rivalry." In that same paper on page 8, six short paragraphs announced the death of Warren Wright, Jr.

9

The morning after Warren Jr. died, Lucille and Gene Markey sat in their twin wheelchairs at Calumet eagerly awaiting the start of the Preakness. Both too frail to travel to Maryland for the race, they planned to watch at home on television.

But throughout the farm and at the Calumet office, employees talked among themselves about the sadness of Warren Jr.'s early demise and the troubles he had caused his mother through the years. They talked, too, of who might run the farm after Lucille Markey's death, though most everyone knew it would be her son-in-law, J. T. Lundy.

The next morning the talk of the farm was back to Alydar, how he had once more finished second, this time by a neck, to Affirmed, and whether, after losing both the Derby and the Preakness, he would be sent to New York to run in the Belmont Stakes. In the afternoon Gene Markey, at Lucille's urging, called the Calumet office and announced that neither he nor Lucille would attend the funeral of her son. According to Calumet secretary Margaret Glass, "The message was clear that no one on the Calumet staff was to attend the funeral for Warren."

The edict from the admiral created a tough situation for Calumet workers. While employees respected Mrs. Markey, who treated them with some dignity, they also had felt compassion for Warren and knew how adamant and how tight his mother could be. Although their loyalties, by necessity perhaps, were clearly in Mrs. Markey's camp, their souls were divided.

Christine and Charles Rankin, who had known Warren Jr. for twenty-six years, attended the visitation. So did Margaret, who explained to Bertha why there would likely be no one from Calumet at the funeral the next day.

The funeral was a muted affair. Warren Jr.'s pallbearers were a distinguished group of local horsemen and members of the board of Keeneland Race Course. An old college friend flew in from the West Coast. Leslie Combs II and his wife attended, as did various other members of the Kentucky gentry. Also paying their respects were Warren's friends in the Bombay Bicycle Club, a group of men who met regularly to drink together. For each drink they bought, they made a donation to a local charity.

Those who did mention the conspicuous absence of Warren's mother explained it away by saying she must have been too weak to attend. Perhaps her extreme effort to attend the Blue Grass Stakes earlier that year to watch Alydar run had been too exhausting. She was an invalid, clinging to the last moments with her beloved admiral, who was slipping faster than she.

Warren Jr.'s nineteen-page will also was modest, especially in comparison with his father's estate of $20 million. To his wife, Bertha, he left a little over $1.1 million in personal property, which included a general personal estate of $770,000; $270,464 in a trust estate at the Second National Bank and Trust Company, in Lexington; twelve shares of Monsanto stock valued at $600; 702 shares of Texaco stock valued at $16,848; and interests in oil royalties worth about $30,000. To his son, Warren Wright III, he bequeathed the emerald ring with two diamonds that had been handed down from his grandfather.

There were millions and millions more that Warren Jr.'s father had left to him, but this money was sealed in a trust. Warren Sr.'s will granted Warren Jr. the power of appointment (meaning the authority to allocate), for 50 percent of this treasure, which was called the Warren Wright Residuary Trust. It included Calumet Farm and a portion of the father's extensive oil and gas investments as well as miscellaneous securities. The father's will further instructed that 30 percent of the trust be divided among his grandchildren and the remaining 20 percent be given to various charities.

Warren Jr. used his power of appointment to name Second National Bank to manage his 50 percent of the trust—to be called the Warren Wright, Jr., Trust—for the benefit of his wife, Bertha, providing income for her for the rest of her life. But the assets in the Residuary Trust could not be distributed as long as Mrs. Markey, whose income came from that trust, was alive. The wait would not be long. By the summer of 1978, the Markeys were both weak with age and infirmities. They had arthritis, and Mrs. Markey's glaucoma and cataracts rendered her nearly blind.

The Markeys returned to Calumet from their La Gorce Island home in the spring of 1979, but for only a few months. Before returning to Florida, Mrs. Markey asked to be taken to Alydar's stall. For years the media had shown Mrs. Markey in the winner's circle or at the barns nuzzling noses with one of her champions. These poses were never contrived. She may have been tough with her family, but she had an uncanny ability to connect with horses. She was the only one who could get close to Bull Lea without getting nipped. The mare Twosy would whinny when Mrs. Markey entered the barn, and when she moved close to the open, though roped-off, stall, the horse would try to nudge her into it. "They knew me and knew my voice. They were like children to me. . . . I loved every one of them," she once told a reporter.

That final day, in 1979, she couldn't see Alydar well. She caressed his nose and imagined the white star on his face. She visited Tim Tam, 1958 winner of both the Derby and the Preakness, whom Mrs. Markey had named after Timmy Tammy, the little Yorkshire terrier she carried under her right arm everywhere she went from 1953 until the dog's death in 1970. Now Tim Tam was the oldest of the stallions. Mrs. Markey had known him the longest.

It was a time of endings. In August, after the Markeys drove past the eagle-topped columns for the last time, the farm manager called demolition experts to raze the original Calumet residence. This was the roomy brick house near the front gate where William Monroe Wright had lived until his death in 1931 and his widow, Georgia Daniel Wright, resided until she died of heart disease during the autumn of 1936. This was where Warren Jr. had brought his bride and where Cindy Wright Lundy had spent the first twelve years of her life. After Warren and Bertha moved away in the mid-1950s, Mrs. Markey ordered that the house be rented.

It was a large, rambling structure. A wide entrance hall flanked by bay windows and window seats led to a drawing room, a library, a living room with an open-beamed ceiling, a dining room, a pantry, and a kitchen. Upstairs were spacious bedroom suites, each with a dressing room and bath. Adjoining William Monroe Wright's bedroom was a sun-room he used as a breakfast area. Servants' quarters were at the back over a large attached garage.

The house also had numerous entrances, so many that it was a problem. With the building so close to the main road, these entrances, including a cellar door, two side doors, a back door, and the main entrance, seemed like magnets for burglars. In early 1979, the house was vacant and the farm was negotiating with a local company interested in using it as a corporate guest-house, but at the last minute the woman representing the company backed out because, she told Calumet's lawyer, of certain disturbing discoveries. From one visit to the next, she claimed, furniture, paintings, and knick-knacks would be in different places. For example, the portrait of William

Monroe Wright, which was always over the mantel in the library, was turning up in the bedroom with the sunroom. If moved downstairs, it would
end up back on the second floor. She called a friend of hers in California,
she told the lawyer, who warned her that this was the work of poltergeists.

Farm manager Melvin Cinnamon never believed there were ghosts, but
he firmly believed the house was becoming a burden. When the Markeys
were out of town, this house and the farm's main residence, with its millions
of dollars' worth of trophies, were empty. To guard both and to find tenants
for one was time-consuming, so despite its beauty and age, the house would
have to be razed. Cinnamon reluctantly brought up the subject with Mrs.
Markey, though he never told her about the elder Wright's portrait. Out of
respect, the staff waited until she left the farm before bringing in the wreck-
ing balls.

Nine months later, on May Day 1980, the admiral died of cancer in
Miami Beach at the age of eighty-four. The funeral, in Lexington, was a
naval ceremony with rifles borrowed from a nearby Marine base. His daughter, Melinda, and her family attended. Ralph Wilson, the owner of the Buffalo Bills football team, was the only old friend who was there. Irving Berlin
sent a telegram, as did Douglas Fairbanks, Jr. Markey had been the god-
father to Fairbanks's daughter; she sent a large arrangement of flowers. Mrs.
Markey, who never believed she would outlive her beloved husband, was
too ill to travel the distance from Miami Beach to Lexington for the funeral.

Mrs. Markey's health slipped further in the months following Markey's
death. The Rankins, her loyal maid and butler, the cook Mary Woods, and
Virgil Smith, the Markeys' longtime chauffeur, remained with her at La
Gorce Island. But, unable to walk, almost completely blind, and without her
companion of nearly thirty years, she led a desolate life. In early 1982,
Margaret Glass, Calumet's office manager for four decades, took her yearly
trip to Miami to visit Mrs. Markey. Though it was Margaret's vacation, Mrs.
Markey always had chores and errands for Margaret to tend to. This year
was different.

From the moment she walked into the house, Margaret felt the change.
Mrs. Markey was sitting as still as a corpse in a wicker chair on the back
porch looking out over Biscayne Bay. Margaret greeted her and sat down.
Mrs. Markey continued to stare straight ahead without moving even an eye-
lid. Margaret began a monologue, giving Mrs. Markey a full report of life
back in Lexington, reciting the status of horses in training, the latest news
about the staff and their families, Lexington gossip, and even the condition

of the fences. It was as if Margaret felt a barrage of words might stave off the
reality of Mrs. Markey's condition. Quickly and hardly taking a breath, she
continued until she ran out of words.

With a sigh, Margaret placed her hand on the right arm of the wheelchair, stared into Mrs. Markey's blank gaze, and said, "What can I do for
you this time?"

After a long pause, Mrs. Markey moved her fingers, in a drumming fashion, one after the other, on the same arm of the chair, as if deliberating what
Margaret should do. Then, still staring ahead, she moved her right hand
toward Margaret's hand, stretching her fingers in search of Margaret's. When
they finally touched, she answered, "Just love me, I guess."

Six months later on July 24, 1982, Lucille Markey died of bronchial
pneumonia at the Miami Heart Institute at the age of ninety-three.

10

The death of Lucille Markey meant different things to
many people. For the sport of thoroughbred racing and for Calumet, it
meant the end of an era that had begun more than fifty years before.

Calumet, though it would always be the champion of a sport with an
unprecedented record of victories, was by 1982 a throwback to another
time. Unlike most thoroughbred operations, Calumet still bred its own
racehorses; it rarely, if ever, bought or sold a horse at a public sale or
entered into horse partnerships; and, having never borrowed money from
a bank, it was debt free. Mrs. Markey, in her white gloves, with her husband who looked like a 1930s-style ascotted movie director, symbolized a
way of life filled with glory and elegance that was quickly disappearing.
Ogden Phipps, the chairman of the New York Racing Association and a
fourth-generation breeder, told *The New York Times,* "She was an inspiration to everybody associated with the game. She exemplified the finest
ideals in racing."

Trainer John Veitch praised her as a great and understanding horsewoman and manager. "She was the last of those great owners who understood that you can't rush things in this business, and that there is good luck
as well as bad." He lauded her sportsmanship, saying, "When I took over

the stable in 1976 and we had the worst year in Calumet history, I tried to apologize but she stopped me and apologized for the quality of the horses."

Other papers ran stories with headlines calling her "The Lady of Calumet," "The Grande Dame of Racing," "The First Lady of American Racing." The press glowed about her style, her grace, and the tough will to win she had learned from her first husband, Warren Wright. An editorial in Louisville's *Courier-Journal* said Mrs. Markey had "greatly enhanced the luster that surrounds Kentucky's name as an international center of Thoroughbred racing" and had clearly added new laurels to a tradition of excellence that was to racing what the Yankees were to baseball.

Reporters who were at Keeneland in April 1978 recalled the scene of Lucille and Gene Markey watching Alydar win the Blue Grass Stakes. Longtime turf writer Joe Hirsch told also about a day in early 1978 when a Calumet horse, Our Mims, was voted the 1977 Champion Three-Year-Old Filly at the Eclipse Awards dinner in Miami. Mrs. Markey was wheeled into the Omni Hotel, and when the trophy was presented, she pushed against the arms of her wheelchair, stood up, and, Hirsch wrote, "with the indomitable will, she waved to the crowd of more than 1,200 which responded with a thunderous ovation.

"They were applauding a great and courageous lady, an exemplar of all we admire in racing and the men and women who are the pillars of the turf. She was one of a kind. The sport is so fortunate to have had her for so long."

For the family of her late son, Lucille Markey's death meant that at long last the assets of Warren Wright, Sr., held in trust since 1950, would be theirs. It was as if a treasure chest, buried thirty-two years before, now would be unlocked. Only Mrs. Markey and the lawyers for the Warren Wright Residuary Trust in Chicago and Miami had known the full value of the assets all those years, though J. T. Lundy and his lawyer, Lyle Robey, had tried to get this information during the last years of her life.

This was effectively the final step in the execution of Warren Wright, Sr.'s will and the distribution of his assets. At least for a while it appeared that his wishes, mainly the continuity of his fortune and farm through future generations of Wrights, had been fulfilled. Although his wife did remarry, as he had suspected she would, she had kept the farm, caring for it and continuing the traditions he had begun, so that Calumet could, as Warren Wright desired, be passed on to the next generation intact and debt free. So, too, had he intended for his wife to have a sizable income for the rest of her life. He had given his son the right to the assets outright if he survived his mother, and, if not, he gave Warren Jr. power of appointment over 50 percent of the assets of the Warren Wright Residuary Trust. Now those assets, including Calumet Farm, could be distributed.

What Warren Wright could never have anticipated was that the assets he had bottled in trusts from the time of his death to that of his wife had increased in value by no less than 4,000 percent.

In 1950 Warren Wright left a $20 million estate. After bequests, taxes, and debts were paid, what remained were Calumet, valued at $2.2 million, and about $6.5 million in oil and gas leases and securities. Of that, $4 million, including Calumet, went into the Warren Wright Residuary Trust, and the rest went into another trust for Lucille Markey.

By 1982, land values in the Bluegrass and boom times in the horse industry had pushed the farm's value to about $37 million: $13.5 million for the land and $23.6 million for the horses. The securities in the Residuary Trust, once totaling nearly $750,000, were now worth $14.46 million. And the $1 million or so in oil and gas interests had a fair market value of about $40 million.

Part of the reason for the huge increase in value was the astute management of the trust by the First National Bank of Chicago and its lawyers such as Harry Sutter and his son, William. But there was also a peculiar set of circumstances, in fact unprecedented, that caused the gas and oil interests to explode in value twenty-five years after Warren Wright's death.

The origins of the windfall began in the late 1930s when Warren Wright had the good sense to start buying portions of oil fields in several states, mainly Texas. By 1940, he owned a 30 percent stake in one-eighth of the oil gushing from a field known as Waddell Ranch, located beneath the sandy hills of Crane County, about fifty miles southwest of Odessa. The arrangement, typical in oil leases, was that the oil company with a lease to drill the field—in this case Gulf Oil—paid all the costs and took seven-eighths of the proceeds, while the property owners reaped one-eighth of the proceeds. If the costs exceeded the proceeds and the company had no profit, the owners still received their percentage of the proceeds.

World War II boosted the value of all Wright's oil investments so that by 1950, the year he died, he received annual royalties of several hundred thousand dollars. But the need for cash to pay the $10 million in taxes on his estate required that most of the oil properties be sold in 1951. After a careful assessment, the estate lawyers concluded that most of these properties, except perhaps Waddell Ranch, had little potential in terms of future drilling, so they advised selling everything but Waddell Ranch. By 1975, this would appear to be a brilliant decision.

Waddell Ranch may be the most controversial oil patch in history, and the Warren Wright trust was smack in the middle of the fray. In 1925, a lawyer at the Gulf office in Pittsburgh decided to put a term on some of the company's big drilling leases. Oil companies almost always have leases that hold the property for as long as the wells are productive, but the Gulf lawyer was worried about the possibility of someday losing the lease unless a fixed term was set. As a result, at least two big Gulf leases, including the lease on the Waddell Ranch fields, were changed from perpetuity to a fifty-year term.

Unfortunately for Gulf, the Waddell Ranch lease expired in 1975, just after the first oil embargo and the beginning of a wild surge in oil prices. At that time there were an estimated 100 million barrels of recoverable oil still lying beneath the Waddell fields. With so much at stake, Gulf took the owners to court to have the lease extended.

Wright, with his 30 percent stake, was the second-largest owner of the Waddell fields. Another 30 percent was shared by Exxon, Mobil, a Dallas oil family by the name of Penn, and several small holders. The largest owner was Southland Royalty Company, a big Fort Worth–based company.

Together, lawyers for the Warren Wright trust in Chicago, along with a battery of lawyers representing Southland, went up against Gulf, taking the case to the Texas Supreme Court twice. In the end Gulf lost, and Lucille Markey, as well as the Wright heirs, won in a big, big way.

The original lease had given a royalty of one-eighth of the proceeds to the owners. While Gulf kept seven-eighths, the only royalty on the gas was $100 a year for each well. Under a new lease, resulting from the litigation, the owners received a royalty on 100 percent of gas profits and 100 percent of oil for seven years and then 70 percent of oil profits until the wells dried up.

Lucille Markey's income from the oil and gas investments increased between 1950 and 1975 from $100,000 a year to about $100,000 a month, largely because of a proliferation of wells and increased drilling at Waddell Ranch. Under the new lease, her oil and gas income soared to almost $3 million a month. In the last year of her life, it decreased again, due to a decline in oil prices, leveling off at about $1 million a month by the time she died.

By 1982, the assets of the Warren Wright Residuary Trust, including Calumet, the securities, and the original oil and gas properties, were worth

$93 million. The liabilities were only $264,146, including $185,000 in expenses and bills of Calumet. There was no debt.

The family, at the suggestion of their lawyer, Lyle Robey, decided to keep the oil and gas investments, so they bequeathed the securities to fulfill the "20 percent to charities" obligation in Warren Sr.'s will. The ownership split for the oil and gas and for Calumet Farm then became 62.5 percent and 37.5 percent. The 62.5 percent, or $46.5 million, at the bequest of Warren Wright, Jr., became the Warren Wright, Jr., Trust. The funds were to be moved from First National Bank of Chicago to the Second National Bank, in Lexington, where trustees were instructed to manage the investments in the trust in a prudent way, allowing Bertha Wright an income for the rest of her life, in the range of $5 million a year. Among the assets in the trust was Bertha's 62.5 percent stake in Calumet Farm.

Each of Warren Jr.'s four children, Warren Wright III, Thomas Cochran Wright, Courtenay Wright Lancaster, and Lucille Wright Lundy, received outright about $7 million in assets, including their 9.375 percent stake in Calumet Farm.

Unlike his mother, who designated trustees she had known for years to handle her bequests, Warren Wright, Jr., entrusted his inherited wealth to strangers, stipulating only that Second National should supervise the trust for the benefit of his wife while she was alive. When she died, whatever remained would be distributed among her children. But Warren Jr. did take one precautionary step to preserve the funds. He created a spendthrift clause, which legally prevented anyone from invading the principal—or so he thought.

11

While Lucille Markey's death allowed millions of dollars to spill out of Warren Wright's estate into the coffers of his heirs, Mrs. Markey left none of her own assets to the Wrights—not a cent of her accrued $300 million; not her Saratoga Springs estate, which she left to the Catholic church; nothing from her safe-deposit box brimming with ruby, sapphire, and diamond necklaces and bracelets; not one of the 520 solid-gold, silver, crystal, and diamond-studded trophies; not a piece of the 250-

year-old sterling silver table service; not even her gold hairbrush sprinkled with diamonds.

In her will, she wrote, "Because they have been amply provided for in the will of my deceased husband, Warren Wright, I make no provision in this will for my son, Warren Wright, Jr., nor for his descendants." And she said that "in no event" should her son be appointed an executor or coexecutor of her estate.

This gesture was in keeping with the memory some would always have of Lucille Markey, whom one former staffer described as "tighter than a head-band." Salaries, for example, were lower during her regime than they were when Warren Wright ran the farm, and they were considered low even then. Once during the early 1950s, she asked office manager Margaret Glass to send an accounting of the salaries for her staff in California. Account number 96 showed she was paying $10,000 a year altogether for five full-time workers. She immediately contacted Glass and asked if there had been some mistake; she thought the $10,000 figure was too high.

She was more than a little miffed when in the early 1970s the city decided to build a highway around Lexington that would slice through a far corner of Calumet, chopping off nearly thirty-six acres and leaving a chunk of pastures marooned on the other side of the highway. She didn't think it was possible for such a thing to happen. When the city announced the plan, she at first ignored it, but when the project didn't go away, she sought advice from Kentucky governor Happy Chandler. "Don't worry, Lucille, honey," he said. "I'll take care of you and this little problem."

When the bulldozers arrived at the white fences of Calumet, she told everyone she would never give a cent to the town again. Her neighbors, always respectful to her face, whispered among themselves at the empty threat. Compared with the Whitneys and other wealthy landholders, who gave millions locally each year, Mrs. Markey's charity at home was minimal for most of her life.

In later years, she loosened up slightly. She donated thousands for the construction of a large residence for underprivileged and neglected boys called the Bluegrass Boys Ranch. Then during the late 1970s, she opened her wallet wider than ever before. This was in part due to the influence of Gene Markey, but during the last years of her life, by most accounts, her own suffering in old age had increased her sensitivity to the importance of medical research.

When Dr. Ben Roach first approached Lucille Markey in the late 1970s for a contribution toward the construction of a cancer center on the campus of the University of Kentucky, she said graciously, "Of course, Ben, we'll help. We'll give you $1,000."

In response, Gene Markey chimed in, "Dear, he doesn't want a thousand dollars; he wants a million." The next morning Mrs. Markey called Dr. Roach and said, "We're going to give you one million in cash for your center."

Once she got the hang of giving, she did so frequently, mainly for cancer research. While she was alive she gave $5.25 million to the Ephraim Mc-Dowell Research Foundation to build the cancer center at the University of Kentucky, and she bequeathed $8 million more. The center, which eventually became one of the nation's best for magnetic resonance imaging, could not have been built without her help. Everyone connected with the project said that her enthusiasm spread to others in Lexington, which led to the completion of a three-building complex, including a hospital for cancer research and treatment.

In the annals of medical research her name would be mentioned on a par with Howard Hughes, whose medical institute is the world's largest philanthropy. She left most of her $300 million to the Lucille P. Markey Charitable Trust, whose mission is to give away its entire principal and interest by the year 1997 to medical research at hospitals, universities, and technological institutes nationwide. Of the nation's largest foundations, the Markey trust is the only one with a time limit. She limited the time period so that the money would be given out during the lifetime of the trustees she had chosen to do the job, including Calumet office manager Margaret Glass and her lawyers of many years, William Sutter and Louis Hector. She didn't trust strangers to dole out the millions.

In Lucille Markey's name, Wright money would be used to fund scientists who'd go on to win the Nobel Prize for work on cholesterol, to create the department of developmental biology at Stanford University, and, at various universities, to search for a cure for AIDS.

A *Miami Herald* story with the headline "Mrs. Markey's Money," written a few years after her death, began, "Even among America's gleaming pantheon of racing families—the Galbreaths, Vanderbilts, Wideners, Mellons, Whitneys and Phippses—Lucille Markey stood out." While the name Markey is not as well-known as Rockefeller, the Markey trust will have given away nearly $450 million in grants—the $300 million plus interest—by 1997—nearly as much as the $530 million John D. Rockefeller left to charity.

Back home, Mrs. Markey left a trust that would award $100,000 each year to the Bluegrass Boys Ranch. She left $150,000 each to her loyal workers, the butler and maid, Charles and Christine Rankin, who had followed her each year from Calumet to Saratoga Springs to Miami Beach; $150,000 to her chauffeur Virgil; $75,000 to Mary, the cook; $75,000 to another maid; $10,000 to all employees of the farm on the job for more than ten years; $100,000 to farm manager Melvin Cinnamon; and $150,000 to Margaret Glass.

Half a dozen other employees and friends were remembered with gifts of $10,000 to $150,000. She left most of her jewelry, her 1961 Rolls-Royce Silver Cloud II, the contents of three houses—in Lexington, Saratoga Springs, and La Gorce Island—including furniture, needlepoint rugs, all the silver and crystal, and some of the paintings, as well as $1 million in trust— to Melinda Bena, her stepdaughter and Gene Markey's child.

In the end, these bequests would help to erase the memory of her years as a miser and to encourage those closest to her to talk kindly of her, despite what they might remember.

12

Mrs. Markey's funeral was a simple, Christian Science service that lasted thirty minutes. A member of the local Church of Christ Scientist read passages from the Bible and from the works of Mary Baker Eddy.

Dr. Ben Roach delivered the eulogy, extolling Mrs. Markey's generosity in giving millions to the cancer center. He explained that her charitable side was less visible than that of other Bluegrass philanthropists because she "liked to work quietly" and she was "not one to shout from the housetops." He recalled, too, her love for horses and how Whirlaway had been her favorite "until Alydar came along."

About 150 people attended. They talked among themselves about the greatness of Calumet, about their concerns over the fate of what was truly the showplace of the Bluegrass, and about Tim Tam, the 1958 Derby winner and one of Lucille Markey's favorite horses, who had suffered a heart attack the day after Mrs. Markey died.

Across the front row sat Warren Wright, Jr.'s widow, Bertha, Melinda

Markey Bena, her husband, and their two children. Behind them were three of Warren Jr.'s children. Cindy Wright Lundy, who in the 1940s had been the pride and joy of Lucille Wright, did not attend. Her husband, J. T. Lundy, did.

Lucille Markey had adored her stepdaughter, Melinda "Mims" Bena, for whom she named one of Calumet's finest fillies, Our Mims. An attractive, petite woman with the good fortune of looks to match her movie star mother's and a personality as charming as her father's, Melinda and her family had often been invited to Saratoga Springs, to La Gorce Island, even to France with the Markeys. This honor was not shared by any of the Wright heirs. For Melinda, Mrs. Markey's funeral was like reliving her father's, but as she was grieving in the moments between Dr. Roach's words, she heard Lundy say in a whisper loud enough for her and her husband to hear, "Tomorrow it'll be mine."

Years later, recalling the scene, she wasn't sure whether he was trying to taunt her or to say something rude out of disrespect for Mrs. Markey. "I guess I knew what he meant, and all I could think was that it was bad enough for him to say it but to say it so that I could hear was something I never forgave him for."

After the funeral, Mrs. Markey's casket was taken to the Lexington Cemetery, 170 acres on the outskirts of town that until the mid-nineteenth century was the site of Lexington's first thoroughbred racetrack. There across from a small lake, amid dogwoods, magnolias, and pines, the casket was placed in a granite mausoleum next to her second husband. Etched on her side of the mausoleum was the name Lucille Parker Markey. The name Wright was nowhere near. In the same cemetery, about half a mile away, lay her son beneath a four-foot white cross.

13

The morning after the funeral, Margaret Glass awakened as usual at 7:00 A.M., emerged from the first-floor bedroom of her bungalow-style stone house, walked across the living room where tiny crystal figurines neatly arranged on the mantel twinkled in the early morning light, and entered the kitchen. As usual, nothing was out of place in Margaret's life. She had had the same routine since her first day of working for Warren Wright more than forty-two years ago, and she wasn't about to change it now. Her efficient, bustling style left no room for maudlin moments. But as she moved about the kitchen that morning, Margaret had an unfamiliar feeling, reminding her that her world was about to change in ways beyond her control.

When Margaret had received the phone call informing her that Mrs. Markey had died, she was at the farm managers' annual picnic at Hamburg Place, a 2,000-acre farm east of town. It was about 8:00 P.M. on Saturday night, and from that moment through the funeral she hadn't had a second to think about the implications of the death of her longtime employer. At J. T. Lundy's request, she had planned every detail of the funeral, from the choice of pallbearers to the wording of the press releases.

"Well, Margaret, you might as well handle this. You seem to have done everything else," Lundy told her. She agreed to do so, but only as a favor to Mrs. Markey.

Margaret, whose petite physique and cherubic face belied her tough, demanding ways, was willing to do what she knew was a thankless, exhausting task partly out of respect for Mrs. Markey and partly because she didn't trust the Wright heirs to do the job in a way Mrs. Markey would have approved. More than J. T. Lundy or anyone else in the Wright family, Margaret felt she knew best the do's and don'ts of highbrow funerals. She had orchestrated the admiral's, following to the letter three pages of instructions handwritten on legal-size paper he left explicitly for Margaret. Mrs. Markey's funeral was more of a challenge, for she wasn't as organized as the admiral; the only realities of death that had occurred to her had to do with money. The event itself seemed only a remote possibility as long as Gene Markey was alive, and after his death she was too depressed and feeble to care about who might escort her casket to its resting place.

It was logical that Margaret do this one last chore for Mrs. Markey. For years, Margaret had been the behind-the-scenes powerhouse, the wizard behind the curtain at Calumet. She was business manager, accountant, secretary, pedigree consultant, bookkeeper, office manager, historian, and public relations agent all rolled into one. The daughter of a professor of English at the University of Kentucky, Margaret had come to the farm in April 1940 at age nineteen for a secretarial job. Two years later, with the farm's business manager off to war, Margaret assumed his duties, and as soon as Wright realized he had found a kindred spirit in his nearly obsessive quest for perfection, her duties expanded, although her title never changed. Wright, a stickler for tradition, insisted she remain the "secretary" of Calumet because it was "more ladylike."

Still, no employee ever got along so well with Wright as Margaret. His businesslike manner, sky-high expectations, and rigidity didn't intimidate her. He wanted everything documented, and so did she. There were files upon files filled with business transactions, minutely detailed journals of each horse's progress in training and racing, reports on the conditions of barns and fences, and personnel records going back forty or more years.

As Calumet became Kentucky's showcase in the 1940s and thousands of tourists inundated the farm each spring, lining up day after day, bumper to bumper as if some great event were occurring beyond the white fences, Margaret handled the challenge, making sure that children stayed out of pastures, cars were parked in designated areas, and the business of the farm was uninterrupted despite the hands reaching through fence slats and faces pressed against stall doors.

It was Margaret who made certain that the books balanced "to the penny" at the end of every month and that there were no outstanding debts on September 30, the end of Calumet's fiscal year. It was Margaret who set up the schedules each year for the 150 or so mares that would visit the farm to breed to Calumet's superior studs. And as the stallions' books for the coming season filled, it was Margaret who filed a reservation card with the amount due on the stud fee. With Margaret in attendance, no one doing business with Calumet felt the need for a legal contract. This was what Margaret called the "Wright way" of doing business. It was efficient and honest; it was what she had learned from Wright and what she continued long after his death.

In a family where tensions were deep and rifts long-lasting, Margaret seemed to get along reasonably well with everyone. It was Margaret whom Warren Jr. called when his mother exploded over Cindy's marriage to J. T. Lundy. "Mother's in an awful snit about Cindy. . . . She's fit to be tied," he had said. "I'm not sure what to do." It was Margaret who made sure a dozen or so fresh flowers were floating in the fine Lowestoft china bowl near the front door of the main house on the day each spring when the Markeys moved from Miami to Lexington; Margaret who, before the Markeys arrived, arranged each year for a new batch of chickens to be delivered to the log cabin to set the stage for country living that the admiral so adored; Margaret who ran her finger across windowsills, the tops of gilt frames, and dark mahogany banisters checking for dust in the minutes before Mrs. Markey was scheduled to arrive; and Margaret who typed the hundreds of handwritten pages of Gene Markey's manuscripts.

Margaret's loyalty to the farm was unquestionable; she was the keeper of family secrets. She knew Mrs. Markey's real age but never told anyone, and she knew why Warren Jr. had to move his wife and children out of the old Calumet residence. Long after Mrs. Markey died, Margaret would defend her employer's decision to reject her son, saying that a mother can be expected to put up with only so much grief, embarrassment, and disappointment. Mrs. Markey had helped him out of more financial scrapes than most people knew, Margaret said. "She had every right to be put out with him."

Margaret even designed dresses and pants suits for herself in the Calumet colors. Resembling the farm's racing silks, the outfits were devil's-red with bands of blue around the arms, blue Nehru-style collars, and big blue buttons down the front. And for at least twenty years, in her address book under "C," Margaret carried with her two out of the thousands of Calumet fan letters she had read—and answered. One, from a South Carolina breeder, commented on the "considerate ways, sense of humor, and impeccable reputation" of the farm; the other, from an Oregon breeder, remarked on the farm's "honesty, dedication, and the ultimate in class."

Margaret's devotion and pride came at little cost to Calumet. Her salary was low, and though she was sometimes aggravated at Mrs. Markey for being stingy, the anger was usually directed at some aspect of the farm's management. Much to Margaret's disapproval, for example, Mrs. Markey refused to finance the production of a shiny new brochure for the farm after Mr. Wright's death. Margaret, who ended up writing and distributing "The Calumet Story" on her own, had felt it was a critical move to stay on top of the competition at a time when other stables were publishing glossy brochures.

Margaret was as direct and focused as a hawk attacking a chicken in her response to anyone overly critical of the Wrights or Markeys. She was especially protective of Warren Wright, Sr., and was more than a little irritated when Mrs. Markey in her agreement with the University of Kentucky's McDowell Cancer Foundation stipulated that the facility bear the name Lucille Parker Markey, not Lucille Parker Wright Markey. Because the money for the center had emanated from the hard work of Warren Wright, Sr., and his father, Margaret fervently believed his name should be connected to the donation. After Mrs. Markey's death Margaret asked that the name be added, and the president of the university agreed to name another new medical building, across the street from the Markey Center, after Warren Wright.

Margaret's rewards were mostly intangible. There was the adoring attention of the press through the years, quoting her periodically as "the glamorous Miss Glass," and describing her as "the unsung heroine of Calumet Farm," "one of the few top-drawer femme executives in the world of sports," and "a familiar figure on the racing scene." Her good looks inspired some professional photographers to ask Margaret to pose with Whirlaway on several occasions, as well as with Citation.

Mrs. Markey also included Margaret at parties and luncheons. She named a horse Miss Glass, another Margot Verre. She even fought occasionally with Gene about Margaret, whose "Wright ways" sometimes conflicted with his own stubborn "Navy perfect" demands. And Mrs. Markey always remembered the anniversary of Margaret's first day at Calumet with a card or note.

On April 30, 1960, she sent a card saying, "Holy Heaven—Imagine us being able to stand each other 20 years!!—Doesn't seem possible—Seriously—it all has been wonderful. And I can't think of how much I would miss you were you not here—I too feel you are a part of Calumet."

On April 29, 1979, her last such remembrance, she wrote, "Margaret dearest, Thirty-nine years is a long-long time, but not long enough!—Love, Lucille."

In the tradition of the Old South where staff members put their employers on pedestals sometimes undeserved, Margaret felt it was a privilege to work for the Wrights and then the Markeys, to drive to work each day along the great avenue of sycamores planted by William Monroe Wright, to mingle with such greatness. She was proud of every tree, every fence post, and every foal that nuzzled its mama each spring.

On that day in late July 1982 after the burial, Margaret had no idea that she was soon to inherit $150,000 from Lucille Markey's estate and to be appointed a lifetime trustee in the Lucille P. Markey Charitable Trust, a post that would pay her annually three times what she had made each year at Calumet. She didn't expect such things, and though she wondered how Mrs. Markey might remember her, her thoughts were focused almost entirely on her job, what to do on this day, and how to get along with the man she knew would be running the show: J. T. Lundy.

Margaret's opinion of Lundy was not too different from Lucille Markey's. She agreed with Mrs. Markey that he lacked class, a quick way of saying he had failed to learn the basic social niceties that were standard operating procedure among the Bluegrass gentry. But that, to Margaret, was forgivable.

What she resented were his pushy ways, his persistent efforts to tighten his grasp on the Wright family treasures while Mrs. Markey was still alive. As Mrs. Markey's life was consumed more and more with arthritis, Lundy was beginning to flex his muscles. For the last two years of Mrs. Markey's life Lundy seemed to be breathing down her neck, Margaret thought, trying every conceivable tactic to move in on what he somehow felt Lucille Markey owed him. In Margaret's mind Lundy was like a child who saw the countless pounds of candy in the glass display case but, unlike other children, refused to earn the money to pay for it. Instead, he would break the glass and grab the candy as fast as he could.

Margaret knew about the letters Lundy's lawyer, Lyle Robey, had written in the past two years to Mrs. Markey's lawyers in Chicago. The first of many was dated May 1, 1980, the day the admiral died. Right on schedule, in Margaret's estimation.

A few months before the admiral's death, Mrs. Markey, knowing her own health was slipping, had set up a Revocable Trust to manage her affairs, including Calumet Farm. The trustees included William Sutter, a Chicago attorney whose father, Harry Sutter, had represented Warren Wright, Sr., and then Lucille Markey; Louis Hector, the Markeys' Florida attorney for many years; Ms. Laurette Heraty, a secretary in Wright's Chicago office since 1937; and Margaret Glass.

For Lundy, this trust meant that the control of Calumet was effectively out of the hands of someone who refused to allow him on the grounds, and in the hands of a group of people who might be swayed to his way of thinking, especially with the help of his sidekick, Robey. A short, rotund man, with a ruddy complexion, small piercing eyes, and a confident, Napoleonic-style swagger, Robey was smart and very tough. At first glance, Robey was a good old boy with a southern drawl and a penchant for storytelling and punchy one-liners. Even the name Lyle seemed to conjure up images of the Old South. He played the piano and wrote poetry, but he also had a darker side that emerged occasionally in the sharp, abrupt way his mood could change from jocular to sinister or in his habit of drinking during the day or in the telling sweat on his palms as he shook hands. Robey's style seemed almost contrived, a strange mix between a *Dragnet* investigator on the case and an on-the-run hoodlum out of a 1940s B movie. He had the sophistication and brains of a big-time prosecutor, but his manner sent a different kind of message, as if he still, at age forty-one, might not have decided which side of the law he was on.

Robey and Lundy grew up together in Scott County, went to the local high school, raced cars down the same county roads, and shared the dream of getting more from life than a small town could offer. After high school, Robey, whose father was a sales rep for an air-conditioning company, left Kentucky to attend the U.S. Military Academy at West Point. Though he returned for Lundy's wedding in 1962, he rarely spoke with his old friend until his permanent return to the Bluegrass in the late 1960s.

After West Point, Robey spent several years in the U.S. Army, in Texas, Georgia, and then Vietnam. A Green Beret captain, he was decorated for bravery in the Vietnam War, a fact that Lundy loved to tell people who had just met Robey.

Robey returned home after the army and went to law school at the University of Kentucky. Then for twelve years he practiced at one of the finest law firms in the state, Stoll, Keenon, and Park, whose specialists in equine-related legal matters were the nation's best. Robey's own specialties ranged from antitrust litigation to First Amendment law, including a libel case that went all the way to the U.S. Supreme Court. Among his clients were the Lundys.

From May Day 1980 on, Lundy or Robey or both of them contacted at least one of the trustees, typically Chicago attorney Sutter, twice a week either by letter or by phone. Lundy's quest was apparently to wrest control of any part of the farm that he could persuade the trustees to let go of while Mrs. Markey was still alive. He was particularly concerned, if not obsessed, with the subject of managing Alydar. Robey's goal was to serve his client's needs and to reserve a rather large place for himself in Lundy's blueprint for the future Calumet.

The May Day letter reiterated details of a meeting Robey had had in Dallas with Mrs. Markey's Texas lawyers about the oil and gas investments of Warren Wright, Sr., which would fall to the heirs upon Mrs. Markey's death. He assured the trustees that Warren Wright's heirs intended to continue the farm's operations after Mrs. Markey's death and that his own plan, as their lawyer, was to ease the transition and to become informed enough to help them operate it.

In September that year, Lundy and Robey met with Sutter in Chicago to discuss the farm's operations. They complained that Alydar's stud fee of $40,000 was too low. Lundy was particularly critical about the quality of the mares being bred to Alydar in the 1980 breeding season. He claimed the mares whose owners had requested an Alydar season that year had not been "properly screened" for the highest quality, and he asked if he could have the right to breed mares to Alydar. Both Lundy and Robey expressed concern that the trustees might be allowing farm manager Melvin Cinnamon, Margaret, and the farm trainer, John Veitch, to make too many decisions, especially regarding Alydar.

In the late 1970s, Mrs. Markey instructed the farm manager to prohibit Lundy from breeding mares to any of the Calumet stallions, a ban that extended to Alydar when he began his stud career a few years later. Following Alydar's first season at stud in 1980, shortly after the Revocable Trust became effective and before the September meeting in Chicago, Robey had written a letter to Sutter reiterating Lundy's request to breed to Alydar. Most letters and meetings from then on would at least mention Alydar if not focus on him.

The year ended with a few sharp exchanges between Robey, who repeatedly expressed his mission to represent Warren Wright's heirs and to watch out for the dissipation of assets that were rightfully theirs, and Sutter, who believed Robey and Lundy were overstepping their rights while Mrs. Markey was still alive.

By early 1981, Robey and Sutter, in typical gentlemanly style, had smoothed out their immediate differences, but by the spring, Lundy was back with his loyal comrade, suggesting that they begin to oversee all horse sales and the contracting of all stud services. Once again they were critical of the stud fees the farm was charging and of the horses chosen for Alydar's breedings. This time Lundy was very outspoken about how Melvin's choices for Alydar's mares might be weakening the bloodlines of the sire's progeny. He and Robey expressed deep concern in letters and in meetings that Melvin Cinnamon and possibly Margaret Glass could not be trusted to run the farm responsibly or even honestly. Both repeatedly stated their desire to run Calumet to protect the Wrights' assets. Among other documents, they wanted a complete list of mares bred to the Calumet stallions.

Though the letters increased in frequency and the tone seemed to toughen, the trustees didn't give in. They were unwilling to produce the mare list because the owners of these horses were Calumet's longtime clients with whom the farm had had no problems. But by mid-1981 there were veiled hints that if the trustees did not comply with Robey's requests, the Wright heirs might file suit against the trustees. In the fall they wrote to Sutter saying they would like to hire a new trainer because it was their understanding that John Veitch was planning to resign. Veitch, as it turned out, had no intention of stepping down from his prestigious post and leaving Alydar.

By February 1982, the pressure on the trustees was unrelenting. Robey and Lundy wrote one letter accusing Melvin and Margaret of picking friends for stallion seasons and offering the pricey services at a discount. The charge was ironic because Margaret and Melvin had done Lundy a favor by giving him the right to breed to the Calumet stallions including Alydar for the 1981 season without Mrs. Markey's knowledge. They hoped that Lundy would quit complaining about the screening process if they gave him the right to be among the elite breeders. And by spring, the veil was off earlier implied threats. Lundy and Robey were now saying outright that if the trustees did not do what they wanted, they, on behalf of the Wright heirs, would sue. They even cited a case for legal precedent.

The trustees yielded to one request. They released financial records related to both the oil and gas investments and to Calumet. Soon, however, Lundy and Robey pressed for more. At a meeting with one of the Chicago lawyers, Robey said that Lundy needed to begin to get acquainted with the employees on the farm, a top priority for a smooth transition in the event of Mrs. Markey's death. And, he said, Bertha Wright would like to move into the main house as soon as possible. They wanted also to begin the installation of tennis courts and a swimming pool.

Requests for information continued, but while the trustees continued sending reports on this or that asset, they never permitted Robey and Lundy to oversee the farm. They refused to send the breeding registry—and they did not approve the men's request for the swimming pool. Mrs. Markey had a thing about swimming pools. She did not like them and had even had a rather large one filled in years before at her house in Saratoga Springs. The trustees felt it was disrespectful to approve such a request while she was alive.

But Warren Jr.'s widow did move into the main house. The mansion had been vacant since 1979 and had had two recent break-ins. Considering the millions of dollars in silver and gold trophies again stored in the basement, the trustees decided Bertha's occupancy was beneficial for everyone. The moving vans arrived in the big circular drive shortly after Independence Day 1982.

Now, three weeks later, Margaret drove along the winding roads from her home to the farm, crossing the University of Kentucky campus, passing the Campbell House hotel, and moving along the shady lane leading to Versailles Road. She knew her value to the farm was no less than it had ever been. Her knowledge of the pedigrees and breeding records of Calumet's superior bloodstock, her impeccable reputation among the elite breeding establishments of the Bluegrass, and her ability to balance the books year after year were indispensable skills, useful at the very least for the farm's successful transition to new leadership.

Turning into the main entrance, she motored quickly down the sycamore-lined lane toward the Calumet office, breathing the timeless scent of freshly cut grass and reviewing her plans for the day, as she had always done at the first glimpse of her white and red office building. Two hours later, while she was sitting at her desk, she looked up and saw Lundy, from the waist up, standing at the half-opened Dutch door that led to her office. No words were exchanged. Margaret inadvertently began drumming the fingers of her right hand, as if remembering her last conversation with Mrs. Markey and wanting to connect once again.

In the coming weeks, Margaret would start a brand-new tome in her multi-volume set of Calumet scrapbooks. This one, covering the period from Mrs. Markey's death forward, would include obituaries and eulogies, photos from the funeral, and articles about the new regime. On the cover in black letters, Margaret wrote: "July 24, 1982, Armageddon."

14 In the summer of 1982, Armageddon was the last thing on anyone's mind in the Bluegrass, and Margaret Glass's instincts about events rolling toward an inevitable conflict between good and evil seemed sorely out of place. These were high times, and everyone was too busy rolling in clover to fret about the future.

Shortly after Lucille Markey's death and around the time J. T. Lundy announced his new position as president of Calumet Farm, the stock market began its unprecedented rise. By then the horse industry was in the midst of its own giddy climb to unimagined levels of prosperity. What was about to happen in Wall Street's bull market could only intensify the speculative mania that had been escalating for several years in horse country.

From 1960 to 1980, the average price of yearlings sold at the July auctions at Keeneland Race Course in Lexington, considered the industry's equivalent to the Dow Jones Industrial Average, had soared nearly 1,700 percent, from $11,844 to $200,425, while the DJIA had increased by 33 percent during the same period. And whereas the top price at the July 1960 sale was $75,000, by 1982 it was nearly $5 million, and three years later a single yearling—an untested athlete who had never set foot on a racetrack—would bring $13.1 million.

There were more than 550 horse farms in Kentucky by 1980, with an estimated collective value of $2 billion, compared with about 175 farms in the 1950s valued at $300 million. At least 400 of the farms were thorough-bred breeding operations, and 300 of those were situated in the six counties of prime acreage comprising the inner Bluegrass. In 1980, land in Fayette County was selling for as much as $12,000 an acre, up from $1,000 an acre only a decade before.

By 1982, what would later be known as the Bluegrass Bubble was already transforming the stodgy, rarefied world that Warren Wright had entered fifty years before to a fast-track, high-stakes marketplace filled with lawyers, bankers, brokers, and speculators.

The monopoly of old-line breeders—the landowners accustomed to mak-ing deals privately among themselves with bloodlines as familiar to them as their own genealogies—was deteriorating. Their business partners were tra-ditionally their neighbors, and, like their fathers, they had taught their sons to breed the best of the family's bloodstock to the best of their neighbors', all dreaming the same glorious dream of standing in the winner's circle at the Kentucky Derby with a homebred champion.

Even the dream was changing. It was no longer just the glory of winning the Derby or earning the Derby purse of several hundred thousand dollars that mattered. Now the incentive was the million-plus price tag that a top Derby performer and its progeny might bring in the marketplace for breed-ing and for syndication. Yearlings were selling for at least twice what the leading racehorses were making at the track. The focus of the business was moving away from the race at the track to the race to get the best track performers to the breeding shed—sometimes cutting short their racing ca-reers—so they could produce horses to be sold at the annual yearling sales. Slowly and subtly, from the early 1970s on, the notion of the horse as an object of hope and beauty was giving way to a new image, of the horse as a commodity for investment, speculation, and hype.

New players and new money were rushing into the Bluegrass, as if oil were gushing out of its limestone layers and bursting through the surface of the serene savannas of central Kentucky. Wildcatters came from Texas, coal barons from eastern Kentucky, and foreigners—many, many foreigners—

from Japan, Great Britain, and Saudi Arabia. Each year their pursuit of more and more horses, more and more land, pushed prices higher and higher.

New money began to trickle into the U.S. horse business after World War II when a few American war profiteers needed an inconspicuous place to spend their earnings, though "launder" might be the word used in more recent times. The biggest impetus, however, was the shift of the internationally recognized hub of thoroughbred breeding from England to the Bluegrass.

Since the very creation of the thoroughbred, Europe had been the world leader in both the racing and breeding of this sleek, fast animal. The United States became number one largely because the power of the post–World War II dollar enabled American breeders to buy the best bloodlines of Europe. Calumet's stunning succession of victories in the 1940s and its own superb bloodstock helped also to draw international attention to American racing and breeding.

Despite this lead and a few new investors, the horse business was relatively slow during the postwar years. The industry desperately needed to expand its financial base far beyond the small, clubby group that had always controlled it. Many breeders realized this, but only a few had the enterprise or the gall to go out and beat the drum for new players and new money. Among those few was Gene Markey's friend Leslie Combs II.

Combs was a man of many talents, at once a horse breeder, storyteller, scalawag, entertainer, and notorious flirt. Most of all, perhaps, the blue-eyed southerner was a businessman. In later years, his office wall bore a framed caricature of himself as a factory worker on an assembly line cranking out racehorses that farther down the line turned into piles of money.

In the early 1950s, Combs, with the help of his wealthy wife, began to focus his talents on teaching his elite neighbors not to fret about the color of money flowing into the horse business. Pushing a sort of cosmopolitan populace onto the provincial high plateau, he helped transform the business of horse trading into a high-profile industry as tough and competitive as any other American enterprise.

Combs understood that one of the big deterrents to potential investors, then as always, was the huge financial risk involved in owning an animal that, unlike other kinds of livestock, doesn't make money for investors just by eating, growing up, and being sold, slaughtered, and transformed into a product with a ready market. The success of investing in a racehorse depends on whether the animal performs well at the track and whether its genes in combination with another horse's genes create yet another animal who performs well. It's an investment in the hope and the dream of producing a superstar athlete. But the odds of breeding a Kentucky Derby winner or even a stakes winner are only one in many, many thousands each year—quite an expensive roll of the dice for even the gutsiest and wealthiest of gamblers.

It wasn't too surprising, then, that the horse business was known as the sport of kings and cast in the public mold as simply an expensive hobby. Buying horses was what wealthy people did when they couldn't figure out how else to spend their money. From Combs's point of view, bringing in new investors required a change in that image, but the only way to do that was to broaden the range of investors. Combs saw two solutions: lessen investors' fears of losing big money, and enhance the dreamy, romantic part of the investment.

To meet the first challenge, Combs, in the late 1940s, began to popularize a technique known as syndication. Others before him had had two or more partners in horse ownership in what could be termed syndications, but Combs's idea was to bring numerous investors into the ownership, thus distributing the financial risk.

In 1946 when Louis B. Mayer, the movie mogul, wanted Combs to buy his spectacular stallion Beau Pere for $100,000, then an outrageous price, Combs put together a syndicate. During the course of several months he found twenty horsemen willing to share the horse at a cost of $5,000 each. The horse, which was uninsured, happened to die soon after the April 1947 deal was completed, but Combs had brought to the equine world a way not only to minimize the financial risk of the breeding business but also to encourage investors outside the industry to own a piece of a horse. After putting together one or two similar deals, in 1955 he syndicated the three-year-old Derby winner Nashua, owned by the Woodward family in New York, for a stunning $1,251,000, then a record.

Just as he used syndication as a way of luring outsiders with their fresh cash, he also saw the potential in using the entire Bluegrass, including the dream of the Derby, as a sort of sales strategy.

Combs knew that everything about the Bluegrass setting, from the white-pillared mansions with their century-old oaks and voluptuous gardens to the gracious manners and melodious southern drawls, bespoke wealth, privilege, and aristocracy. The Bluegrass was dripping with the symbols of old money, like so much moss hanging from the trees on the lawns of southern plantations. Riding with guests along the winding roads that bordered Calumet, Combs, in his seersucker suit and straw "boater" hat, could point to the bright white fences and the white barns topped with the red cupolas while telling stories about Warren Wright's successes and Lucille Wright's new husband, Gene Markey, whose glitzy past meshed so well with Combs's exciting portrayals of life in horse country. Combs knew all this was an irresistible lure for the nouveau riche.

Through Markey and other friends such as Elizabeth Arden and Louis B. Mayer, Combs brought an impressive mix of old and mostly new money from the nation's roster of millionaires to his plantation-style galas. Combs became, as longtime Bluegrass writer Mary Jane Gallaher put it, "the pied piper of new money."

Among his guests on any evening might be Markey's college buddy Jack (John S.) Knight, the newspaper magnate; movie mogul Harry M. Warner; the glamorous "Miss" Arden; the Markeys and their friend Aly Khan; Mayer and his lawyer, Neil McCarthy; Dolly Green, a billionaire oil heiress from California; Eugene Constantin, a Texas wildcatter; Fred Astaire; and the Whitneys.

With his followers lost in a maze of mint juleps and money, Combs went one step beyond Derby bashes and dinner parties. He organized what local breeders called the "traveling country club." After the Derby in May, Combs and his guests would drive or fly to New York to parties on the eve of the Belmont Stakes; then return to Lexington for the summer yearling sales at Keeneland Race Course in July; then to Saratoga Springs, in upstate New York, for a grand old time for most of the month of August; back to Lexington for the fall horse sales; home, wherever that was, for the holiday season; and then to Florida and Hialeah for the winter. By the late 1950s Combs had initiated the custom, now a common practice in the Bluegrass, of busing his guests to the Derby after a dinner party in Lexington on Derby eve. He called the bus the "Blue Goose."

Combs's style of breaking through the icy surface of blueblood society sometimes seemed more like shock therapy than business strategy. A renowned lecher whose many mottoes included "A tough old cat needs a tender young mouse," and whose wooden cane was topped with the varnished penis of a bull, Combs alone was enough to shake the staid local society. His eccentricity and penchant for vitriol and sarcasm, aimed often at the Bluegrass establishment, kept his critics at a distance, while his charm and class gave him a cultlike following. Whether they feared Combs or revered him, society accepted just about anyone who walked into a party on his arm. Knowing this, Combs reveled in stretching the standards of social acceptance to the limit. One of his frequent guests in the 1950s was Emile

Denmark, a Chicago businessman who boarded his horses with Combs. Combs and his wife, Dorothy, took a liking to Denmark and his wife, despite side-glances from their peers: Denmark, who later poured millions of dollars into the horse industry, was Al Capone's brother-in-law. This was enough in the pre-Combs era to have stopped the man at the Fayette County border, but the stigma was no deterrent to Combs or his wife, a gracious hostess who, as writer Gallaher said, "would have treated Capone himself like the Prince of Wales."

A more typical example of a Combs initiate was Elizabeth Nightingale Arden, one of his first inductees. Arden came from a poor farming family in Canada and, after achieving great wealth in her cosmetics empire, wanted symbols for her achievements: good racehorses and connections to people like the Vanderbilts and Whitneys. Combs could offer his wisdom about racehorses and his social contacts, while Arden provided him with money. By the 1950s, she had invested millions in horse country. A small graceful woman who worked hard to learn the ways of the upper classes, Arden became one of the props in Combs's gala dramas, easily blending in with the sixth-generation Virginians and grandsons of industrial-revolution magnates and useful for bringing even more cash into the industry.

As Combs's movable fetes became social rituals in the Bluegrass, some local horsemen bristled about modern-day carpetbaggers invading their world. There was hand-wringing about the collapse of their monopoly, about newcomers lacking class, about the possibility that outsiders might be using the horse business to hide hot money, and about the flight of superior bloodstock to foreign countries. They feared a Trojan horse was grazing on the pastures of central Kentucky.

Several took their complaints to Frankfort, the state capital, where legislation was proposed to limit foreign ownership of land to ten-acre holdings. The most that ever passed was a foreign-ownership land registration act. With the demand for Kentucky bloodstock far exceeding the supply and rising prices pumping up the value of everyone's assets, xenophobic causes fell largely on deaf ears. Most breeders eventually came to terms with the economic importance of outsiders' cash. They also saw the hypocrisy of boasting about the international dimensions of their industry while shutting out foreigners. And they recognized that the land deals would help stave off an urban sprawl that had long threatened horse country.

During the 1960s and 1970s, newcomers stampeded across the limestone-rich lands of central Kentucky. Among them was Charles W. Engelhard, the metals mogul who was supposedly the inspiration for Ian

Fleming's villain in the novel *Goldfinger.* Engelhard, an acquaintance of Fleming's in the late 1940s, was an international financier who traded in precious metals and had multimillion-dollar interests in gold, platinum, and diamond mines, chemical companies, and timberlands, a large percentage of which were in South Africa. He sat on the boards of nearly twenty companies, and, as one of the largest contributors to the Democratic party, he hobnobbed with the Kennedy family and at least once hosted President Johnson and Lady Bird at one of his numerous vacation homes. Most of his wealth was believed to come from the South African gold investments, and with an estimated investment of $30 million in South Africa, he was the target of much controversy. At one point he tried to dodge international trade restrictions on the sale of bullion by shipping gold out of South Africa in the form of dishes, bracelets, and other items. But in the horse business what mattered was the thickness of his wallet. Horsemen credit Engelhard with ushering in the period during which, for the first time, six-figure sales prices were seen at the summer yearling auctions, sometimes referred to as the Engelhard Era.

Engelhard was a walking advertisement for investing in thoroughbreds, though he didn't walk too fast. He was a large, heavy man who ceaselessly drank Coca-Colas in the days before diet Coke and could fill an ashtray with candy wrappers in the time it took someone else to smoke a cigarette. At the Saratoga Springs auctions in 1960 he bought his first three yearlings in the United States, just "to have a little fun," according to journalist Whitney Tower. By the end of the decade, he had purchased $10 million worth of American-bred horses, had them racing on three continents, and was making big, big profits, mostly through syndication. He paid $84,000 for Nijinsky II, a son of Kentucky Derby winner Northern Dancer, and the horse won all of its first eleven races, including the English Triple Crown. Engelhard syndicated the horse into thirty-two shares, worth $170,000 each, for the record-breaking price of $5.4 million, keeping twelve shares for himself and selling the other twenty.

The new wave of foreign investors included Mario Crespo, a Cuban-born businessman who made his fortune in San Juan, Puerto Rico, in the wholesale dry-goods business. A hardworking man who recognized the importance of marketing, Crespo distinguished himself in 1972 when he gently jolted the staid Keeneland sales rituals by hiring eight leggy women in hot pants to walk his horses around for prospective buyers. In the same wave came Zenya Yoshida, a second-generation horseman and Japan's largest breeder, who at that time spoke no English and wore a cowboy hat turned up on one side with a flourish not unlike his lavish bids. Among others were a psychiatrist from San Juan, Dr. A. E. Maldonado, who bought a 727-acre farm in Fayette County in 1971; the German countess Margit Batthyany, who added an 87-acre farm to her list of estates in eight countries; and from the Texas oil boom Nelson Bunker Hunt, one of the early comers, who bought more than 7,000 acres in the Bluegrass including the farm with the apple orchards across the road from Calumet that was William Monroe Wright's first choice back in 1924.

Combs had started a movement that by the 1970s was speeding along by itself. Foreign investors were spurred on by the strengthening of their own currencies against the ever-weakening dollar and by the triumphs of American-bred horses in European races, such as Engelhard's Nijinsky II in 1970. And at home, regions rich with oil were spewing out new millionaires who, as Combs had so well understood, wanted the symbols of old money to add an aristocratic finish to their shiny new images. After they bought their Mercedes and private jet, acquired a fourth home and a second or third wife, they looked to the Bluegrass for the final touch.

At the same time, there was a more subtle force helping to inflate the Bluegrass Bubble, the force of technology.

15

If a single event could be identified as the start of the horse industry's boom years—more significant perhaps than the inaugural tour of Combs's "Blue Goose" or Engelhard's first $100,000 horse purchase—it would likely be the keynote speech at the thirty-first annual dinner of the Thoroughbred Club of America in October 1962. That year the guest of honor and speaker was Joe Estes, the editor-in-chief of a highly respected trade journal, *The Blood-Horse*. Estes, standing at the front of a room filled with breeders and owners, equine specialists such as vets and geneticists, bankers and lawyers, and local politicians, began: "Racing in the United States is now so big an operation that it may be endangered by its own size. It sprawls and grows bigger and bigger, and there is no possibility of intelligent centralized control of its growth or of its lesser problems. The challenge now is to make possible, through access to information, intelligent decisions at state and local levels. With adequate knowledge at hand, we should be able to salvage the best of our traditions and discard the worst of them. The folklore of yesterday is not a sound basis for the racing of tomorrow. This is the age of automation, and the time has come for automation in racing."

The thin, bespectacled journalist, whose frail appearance belied his towering intellect and strong personality, gently scolded his audience for being stuck in time, abiding by methods and ideas based in the Stone Age or at best, he said, the Bronze Age. Other sports were becoming more popular than racing, partly because of the public's accessibility to information. "Why is the population of this country so fascinated by baseball? Because it knows baseball, and it knows baseball because organized information is always available."

Estes called for an automated data center for the thoroughbred breeding and racing industry. Enlisting his audience in the cause of modernization, he concluded, "We all agree that racing is a wonderful sport, a hazardous business, and a fascinating adventure. Perhaps we shall have the opportunity to join hands in making it a still better sport, a little less hazardous, and even more fascinating."

A year later the Jockey Club launched a national statistical bureau and announced plans for a data base with "the most exhaustive data on the thoroughbred, including not only racing performance but breeding performance too." It was a move that would effectively catapult a business steeped in superstitions and centuries-old customs into an episode of *Star Trek*.

The data base eventually would include the performance and earnings of nearly one million thoroughbred racehorses, going back as far as the late nineteenth century, and every vital statistic regarding their careers at the track and in the breeding shed, top speeds, endurance, owners, purchase prices, and sales figures.

Only a horse's temperament and conformation could not be quantified and entered. Conformation is the horse's physical makeup, how it looks and moves, the brawn of its shoulders, the strength of its forearms, the size of its hindquarters, the angle of its front pasterns, or "wrists."

For horse traders skeptical of quantifying the mystical art of assessing the value of a horse, the exclusion of conformation and temperament discredited the entire notion of bringing computers into the business. Some horsemen believe, for example, that a large rear is critical because the horse's power to propel itself as it runs emanates from the strength of the muscles in the back half of its body. Others believe that horses with heart, that is, a strong will-to-win temperament, are by far the best.

Still, the data base was a breeder's dream. It could accomplish in minutes tasks that once took breeders hours and hours, such as generating a genealogy for a yearling about to go to market or showing the track performances of its ancestors. Using the data base, anyone, with or without a knowledge of horses, could assess the potential value of a horse's pedigree, whether for the purpose of mating stallions and broodmares or for establishing sales and purchase prices of yearlings in the marketplace. This meant that bloodstock brokers and investors would be willing to pay for access to the data base, much as a stockbroker or investor in stocks and bonds might subscribe to the many Dow Jones data bases or to Dun and Bradstreet.

Suddenly knowledge that had been handed down for generations in the closed society of the Bluegrass was available to anyone who could and would pay the price. And just as suddenly, it seemed, bloodstock agencies and consultants, aware of the commercial uses for the data beyond the needs of the Jockey Club's membership, were snatching up the Jockey Club tapes and creating services for subscribers worldwide.

In a business and sport whose fans love statistics, the capabilities of computer manipulation had a broad appeal. Soon there were all sorts of computer indexes for assessing the value of any given horse. One index gave the horse a rating based on average earnings per race; another, a rating for how well a stallion's foals performed; another for broodmares showing how well the broodmare's father had performed as a sire. The lists went on and on. Then all the ratings could be rolled together for a final assessment of the stallion or mare individually and then as a pair, for a profile of the potential performance of their offspring if the mating did occur.

Automated systems answered questions that breeders had long debated, such as whether inbreeding was beneficial in certain bloodlines. Inbreeding, which is the repetition of an ancestor in a pedigree line, was practiced without question for many years until it appeared to a few breeders that some of the best families were producing temperamental progeny with an increased incidence of physical problems. New blood, it seemed, tended to improve a breed. But through statistics, it was possible to prove that some bloodlines benefited from inbreeding. For example, the best-performing foals of Northern Dancer's daughters were sired by Northern Dancer's sons.

More than anything, computerization bolstered the belief that the quest for a winner, for the match that would produce an equine superstar with the ability to thrust its owners and investors into the winner's circle, was perhaps more of a science than an art, more about research and data processing than a game of chance. The advent of computers had the effect of diminish-

ing the image of risk and pushing the thoroughbred industry, with its third-
and fourth-generation breeders hell-bent on doing things as their granddad-
dies had, into even more changes. By the mid-1970s, the industry, from the
stud barns to the auction houses, was experiencing a technological revolu-
tion that appeared to be taking a lot of the "ifs" out of a very iffy enterprise.
The risks in breeding were increasingly less visible, as though hastily swept
into a dark corner of a distant barn.

Some breeders installed sophisticated lighting systems in barns to increase the number of daylight hours in order to fool their mares into thinking it was April in mid-February and to induce the mares into heat as early
in the breeding season as possible. With a gestation period of 336 days, or
about eleven months, the idea is to have as many foals as possible early in
the year because regardless of when the foal is born it will celebrate its first
birthday, as all thoroughbred colts and fillies do, on January first of the
following year. At that time, no matter what its actual birthdate, the foal
becomes a yearling and is either put up for sale or taken to its owner's
trainer. If sold publicly, the yearling will be brought to market at one of
several yearling auctions the following summer. Regardless, it will be introduced to the rigors of training during its first year with the hope of making
its racing debut sometime during its second year. So breeding in the first
half of the season, preferably mid-February to mid-April, gives the foals a
jump in growth on their rivals conceived later in the same season. In theory
an early conception should be easy to schedule—just bring the mare to the
stallion and let nature take over. But mares are fussy about temperature and
seasons, and most prefer to mate in the warmer weather of spring.

If a foal is conceived too late in the spring or in early summer, say June, it
likely won't be able to compete at the track until it's a three-year-old. This
means there's a delay in discovering whether the horse is a good racehorse
and in getting any return on the considerable investment before the horse's
first performance at the track. The costs up to the first race include the stud
fee, the care of the mare and foal, and the training of the yearling. If the
horse doesn't begin to compete at the track until its third year, the chances
of breaking even diminish considerably. Earlier matings allow breeders to
assure investors of a quicker return on their money.

There were also new drugs available to induce mares to ovulate, and
improved ways of determining whether a mare was in heat. The traditional
method for revealing a mare's readiness for the stallion was to use a teaser.
While teasing remained useful, new tests were introduced in the late 1970s
that used smears from the tissue of the uterus to determine whether a mare

was ovulating at the time of a scheduled breeding. Then immediately after the coupling, in a small lab adjacent to the breeding arena, the stallion's semen was tested for fertility.

Lending an even greater sense of certainty to a risky enterprise was the introduction of ultrasound. Until ultrasound, the teasers also were used to establish whether the mare had actually gotten pregnant; if the mares responded to the teasers, they were not pregnant but once again in heat. Using ultrasound, breeders could find out fourteen days after insemination whether the coupling had succeeded. By eliminating a lot of the guesswork, most breeders could be certain for the first time that a decent percentage of their mares would be pregnant each season, barring an unrelated physical problem or illness. And they were able to decrease the average number of covers—the times the stallion must mount the mare to impregnate her—from 3.0 during the 1950s and 1960s to 2.5 in the 1970s and to 2.0 and even 1.6 at some farms by the 1980s.

Though a subtle change, the reduction of the average covers was revolutionary from a financial point of view. With fewer covers, the stallion's bookings could increase, and with the ability to take on more mares each year, the horse could earn more money for the same amount of effort.

Unlike Leslie Combs II's first syndicates in the 1950s, which often involved twenty shareholders, later syndicates were divided into forty shares. Each year shareholders have the option to breed a mare to the stallion or to sell the season. Whether the season is used for one of their mares or someone else's, the investors are gambling that the offspring of the match will sell well at one of the yearling sales or win big at the track. If so, the value of the stallion increases, justifying a higher stud fee and facilitating bigger bank loans using the horse as collateral. And while the shareholders, as owners of a piece of property, wait for success at the auctions or the track, they earn a cut of the sale of the stallion's services to other breeders and from the sale of the foals that result from those services.

When the average number of times a stallion covered a mare was three, a stallion with forty shareholders would go to the breeding barn about 120 times in a season. When the average dropped from three to two, the forty shareholders could sell an extra twenty seasons in a stallion, splitting the profits among themselves, and still not put any extra pressure on the horse. For a horse with seasons selling for $150,000, this meant a $3 million increase in revenue. Selling forty extra seasons added $6 million to the syndicate's income.

Syndication and new technologies were improving the odds that an ordinary investor would make money in the horse market. The doors were opening wide, and with more investors than ever before the demand for the product was pushing up prices and expanding what was once a simple business. By the late 1970s, brokers were acting as middlemen to buy and sell horses, collect commissions, and sometimes guarantee a profit. Soon there were bankers willing to loan millions secured by horses, shares in horses, and even stallion seasons. The bankers would require insurance on their collateral; prices would become so high that investors would feel a need for even more insurance; and battalions of lawyers would be called in to monitor the buying and selling, the borrowing and lending, and the division of the horse into so many pieces.

As opportunity and money rushed in, so did euphoria, like a drug that seemed to impair the judgment of local horsemen and skew their perceptions of reality. The problem was that the rush to invest in the thoroughbred market was not based entirely on an increasing level of confidence in the industry and in its product as much as some horsemen wanted to believe. Rather, it was based on a smoke-and-mirrors illusion, common in pyramid investment schemes, that there would always be someone down the line willing to pay far more than the original buyer had invested for the yearling, the stallion season, or the broodmare. The risk was passed on and on, always to the next investor, as prices and appraised values of bloodstock edged ever upward, allowing everyone connected with the business, from blacksmiths and vets to real estate agents and barn builders, to profit—for a while.

As long as there was more and more new money, no one could lose. But if the money dried up and the new investors lost interest, the game would change, from blackjack, where the probabilities are clear, to Russian roulette.

16

It was the Bluegrass Bubble, some horsemen would say a decade later, that had caused things to happen the way they did at Calumet. No one, neither the bankers nor the lawyers, the breeders nor the investors, appeared to believe that the cash would ever stop flowing from the rich veins of the Bluegrass. Speculative fever simply got the best of them all. If J. T. Lundy didn't have the fever before the summer of 1982, he certainly caught it at the sales that July, most likely on the second day. While the results of the yearling auctions were economic indicators for the entire industry, what happened at Keeneland that day particularly affected Calumet.

The best barometer for high times in horse country, better than land sales or the proliferation of manored estates, was the horse auctions. The business of horse sales, more than the spectacle of the races or the horses or the farms, was what gave Lexington its reputation as the horse capital of the world, and the preeminent sale, the bellwether for the entire thoroughbred industry, was the July yearling sale at Keeneland Race Course.

Built in the mid-1930s, Keeneland is on 907 acres bordered on one side by three-foot-high ivy-covered stone walls. Billboards and signs of any kind are prohibited on the grounds, adding to the old-fashioned, elite aura. With its stately limestone buildings, Keeneland opened first as a nonprofit race-track run for the benefit of breeders within a fifteen-to-twenty-mile radius of the grounds. An upscale operation from its inception, it was called the Keeneland Race Course, not racetrack, to put it more in a league with the Europeans—who call their tracks courses—than the sometimes tawdry lot of the American racetrack. Also setting it apart is the fact that it is the only major track in the world without a public address system. Spectators are supposed to be sophisticated enough to identify horses, riders, and silks without the help of a commentator.

During World War II, Keeneland expanded into the auction business. The war had upped the cost and difficulty of transporting yearlings, typically sent by railcar, to the August auctions in Saratoga Springs, New York, so in the summer of 1943, Combs and a few friends pitched a tent on Keeneland's grounds and sold horses. They later incorporated, becoming the sales division of Keeneland, whose international draw and average sales price soon surpassed the sales at Saratoga Springs conducted each year by the nation's oldest horse auctioneers, the Fasig-Tipton Company.

Part of what makes the Keeneland sales exclusive is the screening process. To ensure that the sale horses are top-drawer, a pedigree selection commit-tee and two vets spend months before the July sale culling the best of each year's equine harvest, like a panel of judges for a nationwide beauty pageant. It's a tough procedure because the horses' talents are untested; the commit-tee members are horsemen who can't always be impartial; and there are far more entrants each year than available slots. Every breeder "thinks his geese are all swans," as one horseman put it, until they prove otherwise, so the selection process can be contentious. Based on pedigree and on conformation, only about a third of the yearlings shown to the committee are accepted. Meanwhile, the screening of patrons for the 795 assigned seats is based on bank accounts, available credit, connections, and past performances on auction night.

The atmosphere at a Keeneland sale is more like that of a casino than an auction. From moment to moment, as the auctioneer slams his gavel and the next horse is led into the ring, fortunes are made or lost. The success or failure of a breeder's work for an entire year can be decided in a three-hour session one summer night at Keeneland.

Yet in the early 1980s there seemed to be no losers at Keeneland. Sellers watched their $100,000 investments walk into the sales ring and minutes later, at the sound of the gavel's rap, reap a 100 percent or even 300 percent profit.

While the transactions of most auctions are repetitive and humdrum, the suspense of the horse sales during these years was high entertainment. For spectators, it was titillating to watch some of the wealthiest people in the world spend money. For sellers, there was the possibility of doubling and tripling investments. And for the bidders, there was the intoxicating sensation of mingling with power, of being part of a select club whose members owned the finest racehorses in the world.

As the auctioneers announced the arrival of each yearling to the ring, all eyes transfixed on the chestnut or brown or black beauty with its sleek body and blue-ribbon bloodline. Accustomed to pastures, freedom, and few human beings, the yearlings became nervous, sometimes rearing to break free and often depositing large, smelly piles of manure near the cast-iron posts and rope fences that separated them from the audience. But the spectators, the ones right next to the odiferous clumps, never seemed to wince at the strong scent wafting through the air. In the 1980s, it was as though the smell of horse manure was a kind of expensive perfume that everyone loved or at least pretended to like. By the time the bidding was done, the horse was no longer the center of attention as spectators shook their heads in disbelief and gazed at the six-figure, seven-figure, and eventually eight-figure prices flashing on the electronic board high above the sales ring.

Each year the private jets landing on the Keeneland grounds hours before the sales seemed to increase in size and number. BMWs, Mercedes, and chauffeured town cars slowly began crowding out pickup trucks and station wagons. Hotels ran out of posh suites, as the number of millionaires wanting space almost tripled from year to year. And each year the social events preceding the sales were more extravagant, more outrageous than the year before, rivaling the region's acclaimed Derby galas.

On the Sunday night before the opening session of the 1980 sales, one local breeder threw a party under a gigantic tent with numerous booths featuring an array of international foods and a comedy act by Bob Hope as well as rides in hot-air balloons. Scattered throughout the tent were lions and tigers in cages, and outside in designated pastures there were rides on elephants and camels. At a party the following year, the entertainment was the trio Sergio Mendes and Brasil '66 and helicopter rides over the undulating acres of the inner Bluegrass.

That year, while the helicopters flew overhead, a colt by Northern Dancer, the 1964 Kentucky Derby winner, sold for $1.4 million on the first night of the Keeneland auction. The next day another Northern Dancer colt sold for $1.25 million.

These prices were stunning, yet spectators were disappointed that the previous year's record, a $1.6 million purchase by Japanese industrialist Kazuo Nakamura, wasn't broken. The crowds, as if viewing some Olympian contest, had learned to expect records. Each year since 1974, when the record was set at $625,000 for a colt of Raise A Native, the top annual sales price had surpassed that of the previous year. In 1975, the record was $715,000; in 1976, it leapt to $1.5 million for a Secretariat colt consigned by Bunker Hunt and bought by three Canadians. Toward the end of the sale in 1980 came the moment everyone had awaited. Stavros Niarchos, the Greek shipping magnate, bought a grandson of Northern Dancer for $1.7 million, a new record.

To talk of caveats or bad deals or putting on the brakes during boom times is taboo, so not much thought was given to the million-dollar yearlings from prior sales that didn't turn out the way their investors had hoped. No one mentioned the star yearling of the 1974 sale—the $625,000 record—who won only $5,950 at the track and not much more in the breeding shed. Or Elegant Prince, the Raise A Native colt who stole the spotlight in 1975 but never raced. Or the $1.5 million son of Secretariat who also was a flop.

Looking ahead was the fashionable attitude. What keeps the good times rolling is the constant hope that things can only get better and that every new deal, no matter what the cost, could be the deal of all deals. The bloodstock brokers who lured investors nationwide into the horse industry during those years were more apt to regale their clients with stories about horses like Wajima, who after selling for a record $600,000 at Keeneland's 1973 summer sale was later syndicated for more than $7 million. Or perhaps the best success story of all: Warren Wright's Bull Lea. Purchased at the Fasig-Tipton sales in Saratoga Springs during August 1936 for $14,000, Bull Lea earned nearly seven times his purchase price at the track, and he sired twenty-eight six-figure earners; the first million-dollar racehorse, Citation; and two other Derby winners.

By 1982 the average price was $337,734, a giant leap from the $5,231 average at the first Keeneland sale during the 1940s, and nearly 120 percent higher than just three years before. The highest 1982 price, and the most glaring example to date of this bullish market, was a record-breaking $4.25 million, for a dark bay colt who was a son of Nijinsky II and a grandson of Northern Dancer. Soon the cost of mating a mare to Northern Dancer, the industry's number one sire since 1978, would soar to as much as $700,000. His initial stud fee had been $10,000.

A big percentage of the new money pushing prices skyward in the early 1980s came from the competition between Robert Sangster, a British soccer-pools magnate, and four petrol-rich Arab brothers from the ruling family of Dubai. A Persian Gulf sheikdom, Dubai is one of the seven states of the United Arab Emirates and about the size of Vermont. Its famous brothers were Sheik Mohammed bin Rashid al Maktoum, the Dubai minister of defense; Sheik Maktoum al Maktoum, the deputy prime minister; Sheik Hamdan al Maktoum, the minister of finance and industry; and Ahmed al Maktoum, the youngest.

Sangster, who controlled the $30 million Vernon Pools bookmaking company in England, bought his first American yearlings in 1972. An ambitious man who had the habit of looking over the shoulder of the person with whom he was talking just to see who might be entering the room, Sangster was particularly interested in buying up the progeny of Northern Dancer, each year raising the price he was willing to pay and soon creating a feverish demand for the Northern Dancer line. Some breeders say the Bluegrass boom began with Sangster's aggressive bidding in the mid-1970s. He headed a group of investors who came to be known as "Sangster's gangsters," and by the early 1980s, his partners included a Los Angeles attorney, several European horsemen, and the Greek shipping magnate Niarchos, who had fought Sangster for several years and then decided it was smarter to join forces with him.

Besides wanting the best American pedigrees, Sangster bought with the hope that if one of his pricey buys turned out to be a star, he could sell it back to the Kentucky breeders for even more. "It used to be thought that buying an expensive horse was a ludicrous hobby or a rich man's whim or fancy," he told sportswriter Billy Reed in 1982. "We have actually proved that we could sell them back to the Americans for fifty times what we bought them for."

The Maktoums, too, had a plan: to reclaim what they felt was their heritage, the best steeds in the world. They first appeared in the Kentucky marketplace in 1980, flying to Lexington in their private Boeing 727 and walking into the sales pavilion with an entourage of Arab bodyguards marching at a distance behind them. They instantly acquired nicknames like "the Doobie brothers" or "the boys from Dubai," though there also was private, racist talk describing them as "sand niggers." That year the brothers spent a mere $4.6 million at the summer yearling sales; in 1981, they came back and spent $10.7 million. Within several years the Maktoums would spend nearly half a billion dollars on American bloodstock, largely Kentucky bred. With that kind of money coming into the region, even the most bigoted of individuals quickly swallowed their epithets.

The 1981 summer sales showed the impact of the Arabs' challenge to Sangster's power. A shocking thirteen yearlings each sold for more than $1 million, topping the previous record of four in 1979. Three of the 1981 yearlings were Northern Dancer colts that brought bids of $2.95 million, $3.3 million, and $3.5 million, after heated competition between the Britisher and the Arabs. The high-flying Sangster and his group won two of the three fashionable progeny.

Whatever the reasons for these men's obsessive buying, their bidding wars brought as many breathless moments to the sales pavilion at Keeneland as the Kentucky Derby brought to Churchill Downs. In combination with the earlier forces of syndication and technology, they were helping to transform the economics of an entire industry. By pushing the high end of the market eventually into eight figures for a single horse, they affected pricing at all levels of the horse business. Their willingness to pay so much to beat each other allowed American breeders to charge higher and higher stud fees based on the hope of producing a horse that a Maktoum or Sangster would purchase.

In the summer of 1982, the Maktoum brothers spent a total of $16.6 million at the Keeneland sale; Sheik Mohammed bin Rashid al Maktoum, the eldest, alone bought nineteen yearlings for $12.8 million, or 12 percent of the week-long sale's total expenditures. The top buyer, paying $4.25 million for a grandson of Northern Dancer, was Sangster. Twenty yearlings brought more than $1 million each.

But it wasn't Sangster's bid or the progeny of Northern Dancer that caught the attention of Lyle Robey and J. T. Lundy. During the second day a son of Alydar walked out of the sales ring as the big price board above the horse's head flashed seven numbers: 2-2-0-0-0-0-0. For those connected with Calumet, the sight was electrifying.

The sales, which took place the week before Lucille Markey died, included the first crop of Alydar's offspring. Though Calumet did not own these particular yearlings, they were the sons and daughters that would prove the stallion's worth as a sire. These sales were Alydar's initiation into the big time. His life would never be the same, and neither would Calumet's.

The $2.2 million paid by Sheik Mohammed bin Rashid al Maktoum for an Alydar colt was the second-highest price that year for a yearling. Another Alydar colt sold for $1.7 million. The average price for Alydar's colts and fillies was $827,132, far greater than the $442,500 average for Affirmed's offspring that summer. Alydar was the second-leading sire for that sale, after Northern Dancer, while Affirmed ranked seventh.

It was cruel irony that Lucille Markey didn't see her beloved Alydar finally beat his lifelong rival Affirmed. Just as William Monroe Wright was in a coma when he finally achieved his dream of breeding a winner of the most prestigious contest in harness racing, Lucille Markey was semiconscious the day Alydar made his debut as a pricey sire at the Keeneland sales.

But that day few spectators thought of the past, especially Lundy and Robey, who were busy planning the future. As Robey watched the Alydar colt walk out of the ring, he scribbled some numbers on a pad. He'd write those trustees in Chicago a letter first thing in the morning. On the basis of these sales, Alydar's stud fee, currently a mere $40,000, should at least be doubled. This horse, everyone now knew, was nothing less than gold. And if just one or two of the yearlings that sold that July performed well at the track, Alydar would be in the running for best sire and next year's crop would bring even more money. If the old lady didn't die soon, they'd have to take legal action to gain control of that horse.

Four days later Lucille Markey was dead.

PART III

KING OF CALUMET

1 Lucille "Cindy" Wright Lundy wanted nothing to do with Calumet Farm and the expectations connected with it. In the summer of 1982, Mrs. Markey's granddaughter and namesake could already feel the walls of convention closing in on her and her family.

The gentry whispered among themselves about the coming of the Wright heirs to Calumet, describing the event as nothing less than the local version of *The Beverly Hillbillies*. It wasn't a kind comparison, but it also wasn't surprising. The Bluegrass, despite its lush and gentle appearance, is a tough place. There's a steely quality beneath the soft southern hospitality and languid drawls, attributable, the locals like to say, to the impact of generations making their livelihoods from Kentucky's three industries: gambling, liquor, and cigarettes.

With the privileges of old money came expectations about conduct, education, and style. Warren Wright, Jr.'s children were, after all, the fourth generation of a very wealthy family and heirs to the nation's premier racing dynasty. But the new Wrights had no college degrees, no experience with giving or attending fashionable parties, and, worst of all perhaps, they didn't know anything about the business of breeding, trading, or racing thorough-bred horses. They had been in exile from the farm since the mid-1950s, but now the regional aristocracy expected them to act, dress, party, and breed horses like rich people running a world-renowned stable.

As long as the family was linked to Calumet Farm, the gentry's expectations and the shadow of Mrs. Markey would hover over them. No matter who attended their parties, who spoke at their benefits, and who sat in their box at the Derby, Mrs. Markey's judgments depicting them as classless and inferior would haunt them. Cindy felt this rejection and declined to play a role in the revamping of the farm, the resurrection of Calumet's glory, or the continuation of the legend.

"We don't know how to run it, and we'll end up falling out over it," Cindy said at a family gathering in 1982. But no one seemed to listen; the rest of the family stayed in Kentucky.

Then thirty-six years old, Cindy Lundy acted on her convictions and left town. After months of traveling and exploring possible new homes, she lived for a while in Scotland, then purchased an estate on St. Thomas in the Virgin Islands and invested in a dive shop there. Years later she would say, "I thought we should work on and have Lundy Farm. But—I don't know; I just—let's put it this way: I have known my grandmother better than any of the other grandchildren, and I lived there, and I have bad memories of the place, and I just didn't like it. I did not like Calumet Farm. . . . Childhood memories do not make it a pleasant place for me."

Bertha Wright had moved into Calumet's main residence about two weeks before Mrs. Markey died, though Mrs. Markey never knew. Mrs. Markey's trustees approved the move at the behest of fellow trustee Margaret Glass, who believed the vacant house was a magnet for vandals. It was a large house with four spacious bedrooms on the second floor, quarters for seven servants on the third floor, and a cellar full of silver and gold trophies worth millions of dollars. The last time Bertha had stayed in the house was nearly forty years before when Warren Jr. brought her home to meet Mr. and Mrs. Wright.

Now she was Mrs. Wright of Calumet, a station in life that was in stark contrast to her recent past. A small woman with a seemingly frail disposition and a frustrating habit of leaving sentences unfinished, Mrs. Wright was a true survivor and much tougher than she appeared to be. A few years after Warren Jr.'s untimely death in 1978, she was diagnosed with cancer. By the summer of 1982, at the age of sixty-two, she was a cancer survivor, a widow, and a very wealthy woman.

She busied herself now with the challenge of redoing the big house, adding rooms and redecorating others. She ripped up the carpet that Mrs. Markey had installed in the 1950s when wall-to-wall carpet was fashionable, and she had the random-width ash floorboards buffed. Along the forty-foot wall of the trophy room, she hung new paintings, including a large portrait of Warren Jr. that she placed next to the one of his father. The only obvious reminder of the past was the portrait of Mrs. Markey holding the toddler Warren. The new Mrs. Wright left the portrait on the wall of the front hall.

The children, meanwhile, began looking into investments of their own. Besides Cindy, they were Courtenay Wright Lancaster, born in 1950; Warren Wright III, born in 1951; and Thomas Cochran Wright, born in 1956.

Warren III's instinct to distance himself from the farm was similar to Cindy's, but he didn't leave the Bluegrass or Fayette County. Instead he bought one hundred acres valued at $250,000 to $300,000 along the western banks of the Kentucky River and built an earth-shelter house. He also began to pursue a lifelong interest in collecting rare coins.

Warren III, who closely resembled his father, had dropped out of high school, later obtaining a GED. He spent a summer semester at Transylvania University, in Lexington, and earned a degree from the Central Kentucky Area Vocational School, where he had specialized in the printing trade. His exposure to the farm had been minimal, though while Mrs. Markey was still alive, farm manager Melvin Cinnamon had arranged for Warren and his brother, Tommy, to spend a summer doing odd jobs around the farm. Cinnamon never asked for Mrs. Markey's permission, knowing she'd refuse. Cinnamon thought it was only right to give the boys a chance, but the boys didn't seem to take to the farm. They lasted half the summer, and one of them took to riding his motorcycle around the farm.

Warren III wasn't interested in the horse business or any other business, for that matter. In trial testimony years later, he would say he had never looked at a Calumet financial statement and that even if he had, he "wouldn't know what it said."

Tommy, the youngest, was not as wide and stocky as Warren III and didn't look at all like his father. A 1975 high school grad, Tommy had attended college at Indiana State University for one year. Until 1982, he had worked a few odd jobs—as a bellman at the Ramada Inn and as an assistant at a photo lab—but never kept one for more than a year. He initially showed some interest in the farm and moved in with his mother at the main residence, but his attention waned after a few months. He stayed on at the big house and soon busied himself with buying cars, taking flying lessons, riding his motorcycle, and looking into various businesses.

Courtenay, a short, brown-haired woman with thick glasses and a wide smile, was a devoted mother and a regular churchgoer. She was the type of person who thought about loyalty and doing the right thing. It pained her that she didn't know the true identities of her paternal grandparents. She once told a friend she was convinced Warren Wright, Sr., was her grandfather, but she wasn't at all sure that Lucille Markey was her grandmother.

She had a high school degree, class of 1969, and here and there had picked up college credits, half a semester in 1970 at Eastern Kentucky University and a full semester at the University of Kentucky in 1984. She and her husband, James, had three children when they received her inheritance, giving them an annual income in the range of $30,000. They lived in an unattractive subdivision of small, single-story brick houses, mostly with two bedrooms, postage-stamp lawns, and carports. James had worked at the Rand McNally factory in Versailles assembling road atlases.

As soon as the estate was settled, their income soared to more than $50,000 a month. With great excitement they moved to an $850,000, ten-acre estate with a big colonial house and a swimming pool along a road dotted with prestigious estates and farms, including one owned by William "Captain Kirk" Shatner of *Star Trek* fame.

At the same time, Courtenay began shopping for businesses. Despite her homemaker image, she wanted to be an entrepreneur, to have the respect that running her own business could bring, and to rise above the hateful stereotype that her lack of education and the Markey stigma might have caused.

Moving quickly into their new lives, Bertha and her children put on blinders to local prejudice and chose to ignore the ghosts of Calumet's past. With inherited wealth of more than $90 million and several million dollars flowing in annually from the gas and oil interests, the Wright heirs appeared to have it made. Memos from the period show that the children each would have a yearly income of about $700,000 from the oil and gas holdings alone; Bertha's income would be as much as $5 million a year from the same source. Keeping the farm couldn't possibly be a risk with all that money coming in, and from now on Alydar, the number two sire at the recent July sales, would surely bring in truckloads of cash.

Besides, there was Cindy's husband, J. T. Lundy. The heirs didn't need to know how to run the farm because Lundy did. It was that simple.

2

J. T. Lundy's sudden leap to prominence was enough to cause the bluebloods to whip out the dainty, hand-painted fans of their parlor-sitting ancestors. "He's drinking champagne, but he can't even spell the word," they said among themselves. In an industry and a region where people seem to know more about one another than they do about themselves, Lundy was a curiosity. Everything about him seemed to send the Bluegrass elite spiraling into expletives. He was simply a gray smudge against the glitter of their world.

A stoutish man, Lundy had the awkward gait and inarticulate manner associated with farmhands, not with the president of Calumet Farm. At social gatherings, he was typically taciturn, which in the effusive aristocracy of Fayette County made him immediately suspect. When he did speak, he often mumbled, and when audible, he was just as often crude; "fuck it" or "fuck 'em" were favored phrases. He typically wore open-necked shirts, corduroy pants, and sneakers or Top-Siders to events where other horsemen wore ties and jackets and freshly polished leather shoes. He once wore a Hawaiian shirt to a meeting with some New York bankers.

He was the kind of guy who ate ice cream out of the carton instead of the Venetian sherbet glasses Warren Wright and Gene Markey would have used. Among his favorite local restaurants were the Cracker Barrel, the luncheon bar at Kroger's, and Wilson's Supermarket where he regularly ordered spaghetti chili.

Lundy loved to eat and had the unusual habit of sending his office staff out to several different restaurants to bring in his favorite fast food for a lunchtime feast. On one of the private jets Calumet would lease over the next few years, Lundy sometimes cooked hot dogs for his friends as they flew to exotic places. "Chips, soda, franks and condiments again today" read the diary entry of a friend during a trip abroad with Lundy.

Self-conscious about the effects of food on his portly physique, he would in the next few years try to eliminate fat by having liposuction. And in an interview with a Louisville reporter he once shrugged off some horsemen's criticisms of him, saying, "If they weren't picking on me, they'd be picking on someone else. Fat people are easy targets."

Lundy's friends found his unconventionality endearing and his unpretentious tastes interesting. They swapped stories about Lundy's crudeness on this and that occasion and chuckled about some of his unusual habits, such as carefully and smoothly sawing off the metal ornaments on the hoods of his cars or leaving the dinner table at a luxurious restaurant or private party the minute he was done eating.

Lundy was a plainspoken country boy with a down-home, bumbling style that was often mistaken for stupidity. Nonetheless Lundy was smart, "country smart," some people called it. Lyle Robey once said, "He appears to be unsophisticated and kind of dumb, you'd have to say. But that's a façade; it's an act, maybe to keep distance."

Although the force of new money had pried open minds in the Bluegrass, they weren't open enough to accept someone with both a style and a pedigree that went hard against the aristocratic mold. Lundy's father, after all, had been a tobacco tenant farmer in Scott County—a far cry from owning an estate in adjacent Fayette County.

For the son of a Scott County sharecropper to cross the county line was no mean achievement in the 1940s and 1950s, Lundy's boyhood years. The land was supposedly more fertile in Fayette County, the farms more bountiful, and the inhabitants were among the richest in the world. Fayette County was like an oasis of manors and aristocrats in the midst of rural America. To work there, or even to date a girl who lived in one of the pillared mansions with dozens of rooms and Tara-like staircases, was exciting for a farmboy from a neighboring county. But "John Thomas" went beyond that.

"J.T.," as Lundy called himself after leaving Scott County, appeared to be luckier than most. As a boy he had "already begun to dream of Calumet," according to his childhood friend Robey. Other old friends said he literally "plotted" to meet and marry Lucille "Cindy" Wright, Warren Wright's granddaughter. When he was twenty-one, he married sixteen-year-old Cindy, an heiress to a fortune that included Calumet Farm.

Nothing could stop Lundy from gaining control of Calumet—not Mrs. Markey, not her lawyers, not the intimidating looks of the bluebloods, not his exclusion from highbrow circles. He even took up jogging in the late 1970s, telling his friends that he wanted to stay in shape to make certain he outlived Mrs. Markey.

When Mrs. Markey did die, Lundy was only forty-one years old. He had won the competition, and the prize was the farm. For years after her funeral, Lundy's closest friends would tell the story of his personal farewell to Calumet's grande dame. Long after the crowds had left the cemetery, friends recalled him saying, Lundy claimed he had ventured back and urinated on the wall of the mausoleum where she was laid to rest.

Those who knew about the farewell message agreed that he could have pissed a river and still not eliminated his resentment toward Mrs. Markey. When Lundy first met her, all he knew were tractors, cows, and tobacco. After marrying her granddaughter, he rented a small farm in Fayette County where he had a few mares and one racehorse. Lundy then set his mind on learning the thoroughbred business, and by the 1970s he was connecting with horse traders nationwide, all of whom were very impressed when he told them he would someday run Calumet. Mrs. Markey, meanwhile, would not allow Lundy to breed mares to Calumet stallions, nor did she want him visiting the farm. He would never forget the indignation in her eyes on the day at Hialeah in the mid-1970s when he was asked to explain his ability to buy his new farm. As palm trees swayed in a gentle breeze, offering relief from the tepid, midday atmosphere of a Miami heat wave, the Markeys and Lundy nestled into wicker chairs, silently moving cloth napkins to their laps. The conversation began abruptly with Mrs. Markey's comment about Lundy's recent purchase.

"How could you afford to buy a farm?" she said.

Lundy, looking up from his menu, retorted, "I don't have to worry about that, do I? After you're gone, Cindy'll have plenty of money."

Shortly after that Mrs. Markey told her advisers she wanted to sell the farm as soon as possible and they entered negotiations with Will Farish, a Texas real estate magnate and close friend of Texas politician George Bush. But just before the papers were drawn up, Mrs. Markey balked. She was willing to sell the farm, but the deal included the racing stock as well as the real estate. She could not part with the horses. And so her only plan to block Lundy's takeover failed.

Mrs. Markey's rejection of Lundy only intensified his determination to one day be the ruler of her kingdom. But whether his ardor was fueled by his resentment for her or by a passionate desire to show the world how powerful and capable he could be, how he could outshine even the queen of Calumet, wasn't clear in the summer of 1982.

Whatever his state of mind, Lundy was now, by virtue of his marriage to Cindy Wright, a multimillionaire. The mantle that Warren Wright, Sr., had so carefully guarded, the right he protected in every word and stipulation of his will, the greatest of all the Wright treasures, fell, by default, to Lundy.

He wasted no time celebrating his good fortune. As the sun rose above the red-trimmed cupolas on the morning after Mrs. Markey's death, Lundy quietly took control. He was the Wright family's designated spokesman, and it was his job to calm the nerves of his Bluegrass neighbors who feared a family with so little interest in the horse business might sell the animals and the land and divvy up the proceeds. There was much hand-wringing about the showplace of the region and the jewel of the horse industry falling into the hands of developers.

Lundy must have spoken to a dozen newspapers that first day, giving them all similar, if not the same, quotes: "Calumet will stay in business and might even get bigger than ever." To one he added, "There's no way this place is going to be houses."

He told *The New York Times*: "Business will continue as usual and John Veitch will stay on as the Calumet trainer. The heirs all want to stay in the business together and keep Calumet the first-class operation it's always been. They feel a strong sense of tradition, and they're very serious about it."

In response to questions about who would run Calumet, he was unabashed about saying he would oversee it for the family. Though he hadn't previously played an active role in the farm's management, he'd had plenty of experience on his own 318-acre spread in an adjacent county, he told one reporter, and added, "I've been watching it [Calumet] ever since I've been in the family."

Setting up back-to-back meetings with lawyers, architects, vets, farm workers, and old friends he now could hire, he began a pattern of frenetic activity that would characterize his rule. It was as though he were playing a catch-up game, making up for lost time or competing with his own past.

One of his early decisions, consistent with his nearly obsessive concern for privacy and security, was to reinstall fifteen-foot-high black iron gates across the main entrance to the farm. There had been gates in the 1930s, but Warren Wright, Sr., felt they were unnecessary and had them taken down. Lundy, hearing they were still somewhere on the farm, found them stored in a hayloft in one of the barns and ordered them restored, erected, and painted a glistening devil's red. The gates extended about twenty feet, from one large white brick post to the other. Atop the brick columns were two black iron eagles with widespread wings—signs of good luck—which Lundy also had refurbished.

To the left of the gates, there would soon be a guardhouse. Down the road a quarter of a mile or so he would install new black iron gates across the entrance to the long winding drive up to the main house. He ordered the construction of two new residences at remote corners of the farm, supposedly for security purposes. When Calumet employee Pam Michul asked him when he planned to dig the moat and bring in the alligators, Lundy didn't laugh.

He doubled Alydar's stud fee; purchased a private jet plane for about $1.6 million; ordered a $30,000 switchboard to replace the two rotary dial phones in the office and dozens of Calumet devil's-red warm-up jackets with a blue collar and two blue hoops on the sleeves for employees and tourists; lined up an ad firm to design the first big, booklet-style brochure, with glossy color photos, since 1950; and called in computer consultants to select the best system for Calumet's record keeping.

High on the list of tasks was a complete renovation of the Calumet office. The old one was a simple single-story building with two spacious pine-paneled rooms, one on the left side of a large entry hall and the other, which had a fireplace, on the right. With its white pillars and red trim, the building was a miniature version of the main residence. While the façade and the bright red trim that characterized all forty buildings on the Calumet property would remain, Lundy wanted the structure to have much more drama. His plan expanded the building to two stories, with a sweeping staircase curving its way to a second-floor suite of offices. And though the new layout would triple the amount of space available, there would be no room for Margaret Glass or anyone else who had worked for Lucille Markey.

3 The first official week of the new regime began the day after Mrs. Markey's funeral. Lundy moved into the office across the wide hall from Margaret's, but they rarely spoke. She worked with the door open, and he, characteristic of his penchant for secrecy, kept the door on his side closed. Only occasionally did he saunter to her side of the building.

One day, Lundy stormed into Margaret's office and announced, as he was walking, "That son of a bitch wants $200,000 a year, and I'm not going to pay it."

Though startled by the outburst, Margaret responded calmly, "Who, J.T.?"

"That Lyle Robey," he said, shaking his head. When he didn't get any apparent sympathy from Margaret, he left the room, muttering to himself, and returned to his side of the building, never again mentioning Robey's salary.

With a business-as-usual attitude, Margaret busied herself with the stallion bookings for the upcoming breeding season. August was the month for bookings, and every phone call she took and every file she touched reminded Margaret of how much she knew about the inner workings of the farm. But what Margaret viewed as her greatest strengths, Lundy saw as the very reasons for her dispensability. The biggest strike against her was a decades-long link with Calumet's past. She seemed more a Wright than the Wright heirs themselves. Worst of all, she was Mrs. Markey's representative from the grave. Whatever came from Margaret's mind or mouth, Lundy figured, was really coming from Mrs. Markey.

With almost military-like efficiency Margaret had kept Calumet at moral attention for more than forty years. Her impeccable memory about how things had always been done and her insistence that they continue to be done the "Wright way" was nothing less than abhorrent to someone trying to launch a new regime. She could never be a loyal soldier to Lundy.

Like a dictator wishing to rewrite the past, Lundy wanted to believe that the history of Calumet Farm began on July 24, 1982. The Lundy way was the way from now on, and anyone who refused to go along or whom Lundy perceived as any less than 100 percent true to his cause was out.

What's more, in Lundy's estimation Margaret's ways of doing things were antediluvian. He was frustrated with the files of reservation cards for breedings kept in file boxes neatly labeled year after year and stacked evenly in storage rooms. While the rest of the Bluegrass was leaping into the world of high finance, computers, international deals, and Wall Street, Calumet was not. Lundy intended to change all that. Margaret and her old-fashioned "Wright ways" had no place in his or Robey's vision for the new Calumet.

Lundy's first week ended with the death of twenty-seven-year-old Tim Tam, Calumet's 1958 Derby winner. One of Mrs. Markey's favorites, Tim Tam never recovered from the heart attack he suffered the day of Mrs. Markey's death.

On Monday morning of the second week, Lundy called a meeting in his office with Robey, Margaret, and Melvin Cinnamon, the farm manager of twenty-five years. Robey did all the talking.

By now Robey had left his position as partner at the Lexington law firm where he had worked for more than a decade. In a few days he would be officially the general counsel for Calumet and for Wright Enterprises, a family partnership he and Lundy were devising to manage the heirs' oil and gas holdings and other investments. The partners were Bertha Wright, her children, and Lundy, who was the managing partner. Income from Bertha's trust, from the oil business, and from other family assets would flow into the partnership. Robey would reinvest the money, pay bills, and distribute funds to family members.

As managing officer of Wright Enterprises, Robey drew a salary of $125,000 a year—not the $200,000 Lundy had grumbled about to Margaret. But the lawyer's pot was greatly sweetened in another way. He also received one-half of one percent of all gross receipts from all operations, investments, and businesses belonging to the Wright heirs, including the oil and gas properties, Calumet, and Wright Enterprises. This commission came out of the Calumet account. Theoretically, if $1 million came out of the Wright treasury to buy an oil lease or a horse or a small plot of land and the purchase decreased in value and could be sold for only $500,000, Robey would make his percentage on the $500,000 sale, though the farm didn't profit at all. So while Robey's job was partly to oversee investments for the family—a commitment he frequently affirmed —he didn't have a financial incentive to ensure the family and the farm made money on every investment. If the gross receipts were greater than the profits, he would still profit.

Robey respected Calumet's reputation and understood the farm's importance as the standard for an industry. He was proud of his new post, but he wasted no time feeling sentimental about the land, the horses, racing's white-gloved first lady, or her loyal servants. Robey once said, "You know it's just a piece of land with a lot of sinkholes."

Looking at Melvin and Margaret that day in 1982, he began, "You two just don't fit into our plans." Margaret barely heard the rest. She didn't have to. There was just one clear message: He wanted them to go, *now*. After the meeting, Margaret excused herself and went back to her side of the building to call Bill Sutter, Mrs. Markey's Chicago lawyer and a trustee of Mrs. Markey's Revocable Trust. He advised her to stay until the end of the fiscal year, September 30, at which time the Markey trustees would officially turn over the estate, including Calumet, to the Wright heirs.

Lundy accepted this delay but would not allow Margaret to do the stallion bookings for the next season. Lundy had his own list of preferred clients, and he didn't want anything to do with certain people from the farm's traditional roster of clients. To them he would say, "Book's full. Sorry, can't accommodate you."

Still, he had plenty of work for Margaret. As if the Wright money were burning a hole in his pocket, Lundy had plan after plan for what he told everyone was the return to the glory of the 1940s and 1950s. He mapped out a major expansion of the farm, which already had forty racehorses in training, three valuable stallions, forty-one broodmares, and fifty-three yearlings and weanlings. By early 1983, Lundy wanted not only to bring in new bloodlines for breeding purposes, but also to have no less than sixty horses in training. He then wanted to split the training operation into three divisions, sending some racehorses to New York and to California, while keeping others in Kentucky.

He intended to employ one of the nation's top trainers, Frank Whiteley, Jr., to manage all three divisions. Whiteley was originally from Maryland, where he was known as the "Fox of Laurel." He had had enough winners through the years to earn his way into racing's Hall of Fame in 1973. A tough, taciturn man with a stern style and a firm devotion to his horses, Whiteley had trained 1967 Horse of the Year Damascus and Ruffian, one of the most powerful and beautiful fillies in the history of racing.

When Lundy called with his offer, Whiteley was training for several well-respected stables. He and Lundy had known each other since the mid-1970s when they had a partnership that involved boarding other people's mares. Although trainers are typically paid per diem, Lundy offered him a good salary plus all expenses paid. Whiteley was also wooed by the aura of Calumet, so much that he was willing to drop everything and move to Lexington.

Lundy's plan caused a stir mainly because it bumped Calumet's current trainer, John Veitch, to the position of running only one division, the New York training operation. This was hardly a just reward for the man who had resurrected the racing stable and ushered in a new era of success beginning with Alydar.

While the Calumet legend had never faded from the hearts and minds of horsemen, during the 1960s the farm lost money for four consecutive years, including one year when it failed to win a single stakes race. The bad years were partly due to the death of Ben Jones in 1961, the death of the stable's superstar sire Bull Lea in 1964, and the resignation of Jimmy Jones the same year. Mrs. Markey, too, was to blame. Her poor decision to sell so many broodmares severely diminished the farm's capacity to breed. She also was unwilling to bring in new stallions after it was clear that Whirlaway, Citation, and Coaltown, the stable's racing stars of the 1940s, were abysmal failures at stud. Following in the traditions of the industry, Mrs. Markey insisted on using her homebred stallions.

"I told her we've gotta heat it up again, get some new, hot blood," said Jimmy Jones. "But she said we had plenty of horses and didn't need more. This was the main reason I left."

Though the farm rebounded for a while and even won the Derby in 1968, with Forward Pass, it slipped again in the early 1970s, this time because the admiral and Mrs. Markey were both ill and had less and less to do with the farm's operations.

By 1976, it appeared that racing had seen the last of Calumet's glory and that its scintillating, still-unmatched record of victories was no longer the chatter of the grandstands but rather the stuff of history books. That year the farm's earnings slipped to a terrible low of $87,725—which was very little considering that its annual expenses ranged between $1.5 million and $2 million during these years. But that year, too, Mrs. Markey authorized the hiring of a new trainer, the thirty-year-old Veitch.

Veitch, a small, muscular man with bright eyes and a shiny bald head, seemed to work miracles. In 1977, the farm's track earnings rose to $633,647, the highest since 1971, and by 1978 the farm was back in the running again, with a million-dollar year, Alydar trying for the Triple Crown, and three horses—Our Mims, Davona Dale, and Before Dawn—winning Eclipse Awards, racing's highest honor. By 1979, Calumet was firmly back in the big time. The Calumet financials brimmed with good news:

YEAR	INCOME	EXPENSES	PROFIT
1978	$1.7 million	$1.65 million	$50,000
1979	$2.1 million	$1.8 million	$300,000
1980	$2.95 million	$2.15 million	$800,000
1981	$3.9 million	$2.5 million	$1.4 million

A stable that seemed always to be competing more with its own glorious past than with any other farm would now have Derby entries on a regular basis, getting closer and closer to its old status where a Derby without Calumet was news. Mrs. Markey put Veitch on a pedestal as high as any she had ever erected for a Calumet trainer. If Bull Lea and Ben Jones were the twin stars of yesteryear, it was now Alydar and Veitch.

But on September 24, 1982, the trainer resigned. Though quitting was one of the toughest decisions in Veitch's life, Lundy didn't balk. Sentimentality had no place in the new Calumet. When Lundy received Veitch's letter of resignation, Margaret heard him across the hall making a quick phone call, to one of his new advisers, possibly Robey. "He's done it; I've got the letter," he said.

Veitch, as if stripped of medals, was told when he left that the farm would not allow him to use his breeding right to Alydar, a right that Mrs. Markey had given to him every year and a right that, in addition to its financial benefits, allowed him to remain connected with the horse he had known for six years. Lundy publicly shifted the blame to Mrs. Markey, telling the press that the breeding right was good only while Mrs. Markey was alive and that she had not mentioned the continuation of the right in her will. As if lamenting this neglected detail, he told a reporter, "Mrs. Markey should have given him the service, for the good job he did training the horse, but she was the kind of woman who wouldn't give anybody anything."

After his departure, Veitch learned that the horse named for him, John the Bald, had a new name. Lundy renamed the horse Foyt after his close friend, racecar driver A. J. Foyt.

The press lashed out at Lundy for his treatment of Veitch, whose self-deprecating wit and humble manner had made him popular through the years, both at the track and in the newsroom. A columnist with the *Miami News* called the move "quintessential small-mindedness" and suggested that if the idea was to rename a horse after a racecar driver, the name Petty, after the famed driver Richard Petty, would have been more appropriate. Veitch, masking his pain in his usual sardonic style, announced to the press that he, too, might change his name—to Foyt.

Ironically, as Veitch walked out the door of the Calumet office for the last time that September day, his first sight was a carhaul with Texas plates loaded with new orange Chevrolets—from Foyt's Houston dealership. Standing out among the rest of the Calumet farm vehicles, which were painted the stable's colors, devil's-red with blue trim, the orange vehicles were soon a familiar sight at the farm. Foyt would provide Chevy trucks for the farm during much of Lundy's reign, though even Lundy disliked their color, officially called "Coyote orange."

"He [Foyt] must have gotten a real good buy on some bad paint," Lundy once said.

Margaret's own last days were relatively uneventful, "pleasant enough," she would say years later. Clashes between Margaret's "Wright ways" and

Lundy's new ones were rare, but when they did occur they were intense contests of wills, especially concerning sales taxes. When Lundy's friend Foyt came to the farm to buy a colt, after Lundy told her the cost was $6,000, Margaret asked whether Foyt intended to race the horse in Kentucky. The answer was yes. "In that case," said Margaret, "the cost is $6,300, not $6,000." The $300 was the 5 percent sales tax required if he bought the horse in Kentucky and raced it there.

Lundy argued that Foyt was assured a certain price and did not have to pay this tax, but Margaret stood her ground. With Lundy in front of her desk glaring down at her and Foyt nearby, she called the Kentucky State Tax Department and asked them to confirm the law. Foyt paid the tax.

4   Although Lundy seemed to resent the clubby behavior of the Bluegrass bluebloods, he was no different. But requirements for joining Lundy's crowd had nothing to do with what your daddy had done for a living, how much land your granddaddy had owned, or how many generations your family had dreamed of the winner's circle at Churchill Downs. Most members of his crowd were not part of the Bluegrass elite and rarely had connections with Mrs. Markey's regime. First and foremost, they had to be smart or at least appear to be. And they had to make Lundy feel even smarter.

Lundy, who had a habit of speaking in sentence fragments, seemed to gravitate toward articulate people. The ability to speak forcefully and educational credentials such as law degrees were as seductive for Lundy as the neon lights of Las Vegas to a craps player. Intelligence and cleverness, even more than money or power, seemed to seduce Lundy into friendships and financial deals.

Lundy's only experience with college was the 1962 spring semester at Georgetown College, in Georgetown, Kentucky, but he wished he had attended a longer time. In a deposition a lawyer once asked him about his educational background:

"Well, I went three years to Georgetown College," he responded.

The lawyer said, "So you've got a high school degree?"

Lundy said, "And I went to Georgetown."

The lawyer asked for the name of the high school, and Lundy told him, and then the lawyer said, "And then you went three years—"

Lundy broke in, "Two and a half years to Georgetown."

To dissemble about college in testimony under oath showed the importance of such things to Lundy, who gravitated toward people who could give him a feeling of having things he wished he had. He also seemed drawn to wild and tough personalities in the same way a teenager might be fascinated by the Hells Angels. He liked rough-and-tumble, self-made men with hardscrabble pasts. One of his closest allies was Robey, whom Lundy relied upon to lay the legal foundation for the new Calumet. While it might have been Robey's high-flying educational background that won over Lundy, Robey's service in Vietnam and his seemingly dangerous side were equally enticing. Lundy liked to play up the image that Robey, once a Green Beret, was tough and might hurt people if they rubbed him the wrong way or that Robey could snap his fingers and get somebody hurt.

One day after a meeting of the new staff members at Calumet, Lundy pulled one of his staffers aside and said, "Whatdoyathink of Robey? You never want to cross him, you know. You never want to use that lip of yours to cross Robey." After a short pause, he looked the manager straight in the eye. "I mean it. He was in My Lai. And you know about that, don't you? Don't ever mess with Robey."

Robey was undoubtedly tough, but because of his ribald sense of humor and his habit of lightheartedly goading friends, his brutish side was sometimes mistaken as joking. He might be kidding around, and then suddenly it would be clear that he was more than just a little bit serious about the subject. At a dinner one spring night with several friends in Ocala, Florida, the subject turned to the Vietnam War, and one of Robey's friends chided another for avoiding the war through a mental discharge while still receiving benefits. Robey chuckled with everyone else, for a few seconds. Then, still with a smile on his face, he said, "You've got to give the money back." Everyone continued to laugh except Robey. "I said you've got to give the money back," he repeated, without a smile. He stood up, pushed his chair away, and leaned into the table to get as close to his friend's face as he could. "Damn it, I'm going to kill you, or you give the money back," he shouted. No murders or repayments resulted from the comment.

A. J. Foyt was another spirited character. He owned a horse ranch about thirty-five miles outside Houston and had met Lundy in the course of buying horses at the Keeneland summer sales during the 1970s. His son, A. J. "Tony" Foyt III, was a horse trainer who would now, thanks to the Lundy connection, have the opportunity to train at Calumet. And thanks to the prestige of his new position and Calumet's money, Lundy was able to fulfill a dream: to sponsor a car on the team of the greatest American racecar driver.

Even before Lundy set his gaze on Calumet, he had, as a boy, wanted to race cars. Now he could do the next best thing. Soon car mechanics wearing Calumet devil's-red and blue badges on their overalls were as common a sight at the tracks on the Indy Car circuit as the Coyote orange cars at Calumet. With Foyt's son training Calumet horses and Calumet sponsoring Foyt's cars, the two men shared a fantasy of winning the Kentucky Derby and the Indianapolis 500 in the same year.

Some days they'd sit in the Calumet office, with Lundy's hound dog Daisy lying nearby, and swap stories from the backstages of both sports. Calumet was the greatest legend in horse racing, and Foyt, with his four Indy 500 victories, was the same in car racing. Lundy admired Foyt's hard-charging, sometimes intimidating, and testy spirit. While Foyt never did anything foolish on the racetrack, he was notorious for his zany off-track personality. Foyt was a storyteller, but he was also, as Robey described it, a "storymaker . . . He did those things people tell stories about." And Lundy couldn't get enough of the action. Foyt and Lundy were "country crazy," according to Robey. "You know, they're the kind of guys who would drive a car through a fence and see how many times and at what rpms they'd have to ram the post before it came down."

Another Calumet newcomer was Peter Brant, a Connecticut breeder, polo player, publisher, and one of the nation's largest manufacturers of newsprint. Brant, whose publications included *Art in America* and *Antiques* magazines, moved in artsy New York circles. Among his friends was Andy Warhol, from whom Brant and his wife had purchased the avant-garde monthly magazine *Interview* in the early 1970s, later selling it back to Warhol.

Lundy had met Brant in the 1970s when Brant hired a partner of Lundy's to train his horses. Brant's style and Lundy's were about as different as an Armani suit and a pair of Oshkosh overalls, but this was all excusable to Lundy. The tall, slender Brant, with his White Birch Farms in Connecticut, appeared to care as much about horses as he did about art. Plus he had lots and lots of money and the toys that came with it. One of the earliest memories Calumet neighbors would have of the Lundy years was the new regime's jet plane, purchased from Brant in August 1982.

Dan Lasater, the whiz kid who came up with the idea for a fast-steak restaurant modeled after McDonald's—Ponderosa Steak House—was also a Lundy chum. Lasater grew up in a trailer park in Indiana but was a millionaire by his midtwenties. Lundy put Lasater, who was clearly a business genius and a wild sort of guy, on a high pedestal. Soon after retiring at age twenty-eight, Lasater had entered racing, and for several years in the 1970s, his stable earned more at the track than any other in the nation. During this time, Lundy and Lasater were partners with several others in a Florida horse partnership called Seaside Syndicate. By 1982 when Lundy took over Calumet, Lasater was among the nation's top-ten thoroughbred breeders, one of Arkansas governor Bill Clinton's biggest backers, and circulated in a crowd that included the governor's brother. He had a reputation for throwing extravagant, wild parties and for giving horses lewd names, all of which amused Lundy. Among other deals, Lundy would purchase another jet from Lasater—one that the Arkansas governor had used on occasion.

A close Lundy associate for many years was Harry Ranier, a newcomer to the Bluegrass from the eastern Kentucky town of Prestonsburg. Ranier was part of a traditional migration among the upper classes in Kentucky. The local lore is that the mountain folk—the very few, that is, who are rich—in Prestonsburg and other mining communities dream of coming down from the mountains to the lush savannahs of the inner Bluegrass to build manors, breed horses, and live like lords and ladies. It wasn't surprising then that the coal boom of the early 1970s brought the now very rich coal operators out of the mountains and into horse country.

Ranier and his father, an Italian immigrant, were well positioned to profit from the new demands for tonnage in the mid-1970s. By the time the coal boom was over, the profits of their Triple Elkhorn Mining Company had catapulted the Raniers from the realms of the rich to the superrich. With his fortune of more than $30 million, Ranier underwrote Grand National stock car teams headed by top-notch drivers like Cale Yarborough; purchased television evangelist Jim Bakker a $300,000 home in Charlotte, North Carolina; and swept up real estate, including a golf course and oceanside condos, in South Carolina. But much of his fortune he spent in horse country.

In the mid-1970s he and another investor purchased a 521-acre farm in the inner Bluegrass which they called Shadowlawn Farm. Ranier soon bought out his partner, and by 1981 he was pouring his millions into creating a spectacular showplace, replete with twenty-one miles of Calumet-style white plank fences, several new barns, and a red-brick mansion whose floor plan was a duplicate of the Governor's Palace in Williamsburg, Virginia. The final product, with its 20,000 or so square feet including ten bedrooms, each with a bath and a walk-in cedar closet, would make Tara seem like a cabin.

Still, Ranier never quite fit into Bluegrass society. It could have been the crisp sound of his new money, though clearly the region was accustomed to that by now. But some said it was because he razed the estate's landmark residence to build his modern palace. Though he meant no harm and benefited the region by bringing truckloads of cash into the local economy, demolishing a landmark had broken a sacred, unwritten rule. Lundy, who had met Ranier through a mutual friend in eastern Kentucky, as always disregarded the prevailing social attitudes. Passions for fast cars and fast horses, a penchant for making big money, a gambler's boldness, and defiance of social convention seemed to be the requirements for connecting to Calumet's new regime.

After forty-two and a half years at Calumet, Margaret Glass departed, on schedule, at the end of September. She left behind the last of the Markey loyalists, Pam Michul.

A trim, peppy woman with blond hair and a full smile, Michul had been with the farm for six years. What allowed her to keep her job was her understanding of computers. Lundy desperately needed her to convert the Calumet records to the new IBM computer system. Michul's instincts were to leave, but she decided if she could get exactly what she wanted, she would do the job. She asked for a one-year contract, a car, and a considerable salary increase. Lundy said okay.

When she waved good-bye to Veitch, to Cinnamon, to Glass, and the others, Michul felt as though she had been left behind in enemy territory. This perception was exaggerated by Lundy's penchant for drama and his "with me or against me" view of the world, which created an atmosphere of secrecy and distrust. Lundy rarely spoke with Michul, always sending his orders through his operatives Heinz and McGee.

Michul was told she would have nothing to do with the stallion bookings, originally part of her job; they were to be handled exclusively by Lundy's lieutenants. Occasionally she'd answer the phone, and the call would be an inquiry about a particular booking. She'd look at the official records, but there would be no appointment for that client. The client would insist the farm had agreed to accommodate the client's mare to a Calumet stallion. Protecting the farm, Michul would state there was no record of such an agreement. But this was a special arrangement with Lundy, the client would insist; perhaps that was why the season was not in the books. When Michul would inquire of Lundy, she was told to refer all such calls to Heinz.

On other occasions, Michul might be alone in the office when a client came to pay a bill. The bill, according to Michul's calculations, included sales tax, but the client believed the total was more than it should be. If she pressed the matter, the client would insist that Lundy had quoted a lower price. Worried about the farm, Michul mentioned to Lundy her concerns about clients not paying taxes. Lundy, who already seemed unhappy about Michul's continued relationship with Margaret Glass and her occasional conversations with the farm's former trustees in Chicago, apparently was unimpressed with Michul's knowledge of state tax laws. Six months before the end of Michul's contract, Robey fired her. He told her that Lundy was unsure of her loyalty.

5 The Wright heirs were more than pleased that Lundy had moved right in, like a bulldozer, pushing people and money around, and promising to make the farm better than ever. They seemed impressed with his sophisticated advisers such as Robey and his ideas for modernizing the farm and brightening the spotlight that Veitch had brought back to the stable. They understood why he wasn't able to keep them informed of every little decision. The Wrights felt so lucky to have Lundy that their tolerance for any oversights on his part was high.

But in the rush of change, as workers poured cement for the swimming pool, carpenters secured the office's sweeping staircase, businessmen visited the hallowed grounds for the first time, and Warren Jr.'s widow, with the enthusiasm of a schoolgirl, redecorated the main house, events of a purely legal nature slipped by, unnoticed and soon forgotten, like pieces of paper slowly floating into a fire.

In the fall of 1982, Lundy and Robey created a new corporation in the state of Kentucky and called it Calumet Farm, Inc.—a move that would affect Calumet's future perhaps more than any other.

Lundy soon asked members of the Wright family to ratify several documents that would define the farm's new power structure. One, signed by the four children of Warren Wright, Jr., and Second National Bank, on behalf of the trust left for Bertha, conveyed their entire interest in the farm to the new corporation. In return, the bank received 62.5 percent of the common capital voting stock of Calumet Farm, Inc. Each of the children received 9.375 percent of the stock.

Lundy became the president of the new corporation. Management of the farm fell to a board of directors: Lundy, Lyle Robey, Bertha Wright, her four children, and at least one representative of the bank. The board then agreed to form an executive committee that consisted of Lundy, Robey, and a bank representative.

Warren Jr.'s will had directed the bank to "hold, manage and control" his assets and to pay the net income from the assets to his widow for as long as she lived. But in agreeing to the executive committee, the bank, despite its status as the majority shareholder, assumed a minority position in the body now created to control those assets. The committee had the power to promote or veto actions affecting the day-to-day operations and the viability of Calumet. In short, Lundy and Robey were now in control. Soon their power would be even greater owing to another document—one that Bertha alone would sign.

Trustees at Second National apparently were not convinced that Lundy was the man to fill Mrs. Markey's shoes. If Warren Jr., who knew of Lundy's ambitions, had wanted Lundy to run the farm, some lawyers reasoned, he would have specified so in his will. At the very least he would have said publicly that he wanted Lundy to take over. He would not have left majority control in the hands of the bank trustees. Before approving the new leadership, the bank apparently felt it needed some sort of assurance that it wouldn't be held liable if things didn't work out for the best.

Thus on October 1, 1982, Bertha signed what is officially called a release-and-indemnity agreement. Its purpose was "to indemnify and hold the trustee harmless against any and all loss, damage, claims, suits and attorneys' fees in defending claims, suits or demands which in any way or manner arise out of or result from the retention of Calumet Farm or any interest therein and the operation thereof as an asset of the trust."

Warren Jr. had created a trust for his wife's welfare in part because he did not believe she was capable of handling a multimillion-dollar fortune. She had no knowledge of money management, no business experience. To accommodate his wishes, his lawyers added the spendthrift provision, which effectively put a lock on the trust by prohibiting anyone from invading the principal. This made it harder to pillage than a regular trust. He specified one particular bank to administer the trust, but now Bertha had signed a document, perhaps unwittingly, that released the bank from responsibility for whatever might happen to the trust, effectively saying that if anyone was adept enough to pick the lock on Bertha's treasure, the bank wasn't liable for the consequences.

Colloquially referred to as a "hold-harmless agreement," this document undermined a trust that the Wrights, father and son, had established to try to control from their graves the fate of their dynasty, to ensure immortality of the Wright legacy and continuity through the generations for the Wright fortune. Bertha, who would sign other lethal documents during the next several years, would someday understand all too well the damage that was done during those autumn days of 1982. But as long as there was plenty of money, no one would question these and other legal papers, nor would the corporate directors' responsibilities be an issue.

At first, it was all a sort of game, one in which each player was given a title and a role and money. If the money ever ran out, there would be the perplexing legal and moral questions of who had been responsible for preserving the assets in this trust and who was the keeper of Calumet. Was it the bank Warren Jr. named in his will to oversee Bertha's assets? Was it Bertha, who willingly and routinely signed documents apparently without understanding their significance, including one indemnifying the bank? Was it lawyer Robey, who typically advised the Wright heirs to sign papers and who laid the legal foundation of the new Calumet Farm, Inc.? Or was it Bertha's son-in-law, who would take full advantage of the power entrusted to him?

One of the first acts of Calumet's new ruling body was to authorize the Calumet president to borrow substantial funds in the name of Calumet Farm, Inc., as much as $10 million at a time from any bank, without prior approval by the board. This meant that as long as the farm had enough assets to pledge as collateral and its name was powerful enough to entice bankers, the opportunity existed to use the farm to siphon millions of dollars out of the American banking community and to bleed the Wright legacy of all its worth.

The era of Calumet Farm, Inc., had begun.

6 The excitement of life beginning again that comes in spring is greater and more convincing in the Bluegrass, as newborn foals test their spindly legs and the luscious new grass transforms simple fields into emerald pastures.

At Calumet, the feeling of newness was greater than usual in the spring of 1983, as great perhaps as it had been in the spring of 1932 when Warren Wright launched his thoroughbred empire, in 1941 when his dream of winning the Derby came true, or in 1978 when Alydar brought the glory back. Though hindsight would someday cast shadows on all the days of Lundy's reign, the year 1983 was a time of great hope. It appeared that Lundy meant it when he said he was working toward only one goal: for Calumet to live up to its legend and even to surpass the glories of its past.

By spring, renovations all over the farm were completed or in their last stages. The swimming pool awaited only warm weather, and Gene Markey's log cabin would serve as a cabana for Lundy's sunbathing guests. There were tennis courts, a gazebo, new tanbark paths through the equine cemetery, resurfaced blacktop roads, miles of new fences coated with fresh white paint, new barns, repainted barns, newly graded pastures, new underground water lines, a new surface for the three-quarter-mile dirt track, and four hundred new trees.

Not yet complete were a fully equipped veterinarian clinic and an elaborate equine swimming pool complex including a circular exercise pool, an underwater treadmill, and smaller therapy pools. A big circular barn would be built to house the pools. Lundy planned also to restore the farm's 1939 GMC horse van, which had transported Whirlaway and other champions of the 1940s and 1950s.

"The Legend Lives On" was the headline on one of the pages of the farm's new thirty-page brochure. With stunning photographs of the land and horses, the brochure summarized the history of Calumet—though Mrs. Markey's name and contribution were never mentioned—and ended with the pledge from the Wright heirs and Lundy, "It is our intention to carry on the operation of Calumet based on our heritage while building on a bright to- morrow. We hope this book has made you more familiar with the history of Calumet as we anxiously await the future."

By March 1983, the office renovation was completed. The now two-story

building had its sweeping staircase rising from the center of the lobby and
carpeted in the same shades of blue and red as Calumet's racing silks. On
the walls were oil paintings of Calumet's champion racehorses in heavy
gold-leaf frames. An old, refurbished sulky that was supposedly the one
used to win the Hambletonian race for William Monroe Wright in 1931
hung by chains extended from the high ceiling above the winding stairs.

A large room to the left of the lobby was filled with computer terminals
and lined with hallways of electronically operated files. To the right of the
lobby was the receptionist's desk with its $30,000 computerized switch-
board. Also on that floor were other offices, storage rooms, and a bathroom.
At the back was a hallway that connected the office complex to the stallion
barn.

On the second floor were glass cases filled with trophies and beside them
more paintings. Surrounding a large room with a double-doored entrance at
the top of the stairs were a kitchen, two bathrooms, a small bedroom, an
office, and an attic. In the big room were fine leather chairs and a divan, a
long table for meetings, and bronze sculptures of horses. On the floor was
an expensive Persian rug, and on the walls more oil paintings of Calumet
horses. And there was a special feature. At the center of the high, walnut-
beamed ceiling was an octagonal wooden cupola with eight large windows
and a thin balcony with enough space for a walkway. On one side of the
balcony was a stairway that unfolded from the wall near Lundy's desk below. Climbing up to this balcony, Lundy could see all over the farm, a
feature he relished. He once told employee Michul that standing on this
balcony made him feel as though he truly was the captain of a ship.

Lundy seemed to be checking off items on a lifelong list of wishes. His press
party that year before the Indianapolis 500 was an unprecedented sight at
Calumet: racecars and stock cars parked on the grounds surrounding the
office, massive tents, and hundreds of people. In honor of Foyt and to
publicize Calumet's first sponsorship of an Indy 500 racecar, Lundy, along
with Valvoline Oil Company, a division of Ashland Oil that sponsored Foyt's
car that year, hosted a huge outdoor gala. Local politicians, media celebrities, and Foyt's entire rig of cars were there.

Later a Valvoline executive sent Lundy a letter saying it was the most
successful press party the company had ever seen. Valvoline further publicized Calumet's racecar debut on its radio spots broadcast nationwide on
550 stations. Lundy could hardly contain himself when he saw the Calumet

name splashed across Car No. 1 at the Indianapolis Speedway that May. While Valvoline sponsored Foyt himself, Calumet's driver was George Snider, a Foyt team member who had run the race seventeen times. This was the big time—a world away from speeding cars down county roads in Georgetown, Kentucky.

Standing near the garage shortly before the race, Lundy told one reporter, "This gives us a world of exposure. Not that Calumet's name isn't well-known. But this doesn't hurt us. It's really great advertising, to be seen all over the world on TV." He also said, "We were hoping to win the Derby, then come up here and win the 500."

Calumet's Derby hopeful that year was the horse named Foyt, but the thoroughbred, plagued with physical problems the previous winter and in early spring, couldn't make it to the early May race. By mid-May, Foyt had recovered and was ready to run in a big New York race on May 29, the same day that Calumet raced its first car. Though neither the horse nor the car won, for Lundy, to be surrounded by fast cars and fast horses was dreamlike.

Lundy's image, tainted by his unpopular housecleaning of old-line staffers the year before, was even beginning to change. He was the leader of the fabled stable everyone loved to love, so Calumet's shine and brilliance, for a while, reflected on him. In the days when he was offering his opinions from the barns of his farm in Midway with his shoes caked with mud and his shirttail hanging out, only a tiny group of close friends listened to him. Now he had something he had never experienced before: recognition.

A columnist for *The Blood-Horse* ran a piece about Lundy in 1983 with the headline "The Man in the Limelight." He wrote, "While there has been some criticism of the methods of Lundy in his direction of Calumet, it seems to be based more on envy than fact. Lundy, in my opinion, is doing a great job in rebuilding a grand heritage. . . . To use an overworked expression, he is 'a down-home country boy.'"

With this new spin on Lundy's actions, and especially with the endorsement of a highly respected columnist, the clouds over Lundy disappeared. He was asked to serve on several boards of philanthropic groups, to share his philosophies of breeding, and to spend time with reporters who wanted all the details of the exciting changes at Calumet. He even had a short stint as a hero.

That fall extortion and horse-napping were on everyone's mind. Earlier in the year, Shergar, a racehorse appraised at $13 million and owned by billionaire Aga Khan, son of Aly Khan, disappeared from a stable in Ireland, and by fall was still missing. Then in late September, Calumet Farm and

Spendthrift Farm each received letters with cut-out words demanding $500,000 in $100 bills arranged in random serial number sequence, or the perpetrators would "start shooting horses." All the farms in the area were to contribute to the bundle. The inference was that although Calumet and Spendthrift were targeted, every farm was at risk.

The letters sent ripples of panic through the inner Bluegrass where many farms beefed up security and moved their most valuable horses out of pastures and into stalls. Meanwhile, it was Lundy who got directly involved with the FBI scheme to stop the bad guys.

The letters directed the two farms to respond by placing an ad in the local paper saying simply yes or no to the proposition, though disguising the details of the scheme. The farms were then to await instructions.

Lundy and Leslie Combs II, at Spendthrift, contacted the police, who called in the FBI. A few days later, Lundy placed the following ad in the *Lexington Herald-Leader*: "Yes, we are interested in horse insurance for all horse farms in Fayette Co. Please call J.T. Lundy at 231-8272, between 9 and 5 P.M., reference your letter."

FBI agents watched Calumet's mailbox for more deliveries, since the threats were always unstamped. More agents manned the phones in the Calumet office. For ten days Lundy sat in the office with yet another agent who answered the phone saying he was Lundy. After several conversations the extortionist and the Lundy imposter agreed on a plan.

An FBI agent, posing as Lundy, and toting two canvas bags brimming with $100 bills in the back of his Calumet pickup, arranged to meet a young woman in the alley behind a local shopping center. The woman, barely out of her teens, was an assembly-line worker in a nearby furniture factory, and seconds after she grabbed the first bag, sixteen cops and agents surrounded her. A few days later her alleged accomplice was arrested, too. The frightful incident was over, and Lundy, though all he had done was to volunteer the farm and its premises for the sting operation, was thanked by his neighbors for his role and even received a few notes of thanks from farmers in the region. As usual with stories that churn through the gossip mill, some versions even had Lundy going by himself to the shopping mall because he felt the scheme was aimed at Alydar and he was "spittin' mad."

Also boosting Lundy's status that year was the rising power of Alydar. In 1983, the track performances of Alydar's first crop, some of which had been sold at Keeneland the summer before, were nothing less than spectacular. Two-year-old filly Althea was the first to shine, winning her racing debut by six and a half lengths in June at Hollywood Park. Miss Oceana, another

Alydar filly, won her maiden race at Saratoga in August; two weeks later she won again at Belmont Park in New York. On Labor Day, she won in Chicago at Arlington Park while on the same day her half sister Althea won by fifteen lengths in California. Alydar's progeny earned a total of $1,136,063 in 1983, enough to win him the title of the nation's leading freshman sire.

These were the results of the 1980 breedings that Margaret Glass had matched up and Lundy had criticized in his letters to the Chicago trustees. Though Calumet didn't own Althea, Miss Oceana, or any of the other winning progeny that year, Calumet certainly benefited from their success. When the time came to fill Alydar's book for the 1984 breeding season, breeders from all over the world sent applications asking for a total of more than 350 mares to be mated to Alydar.

The heirs, too, were rolling with the good times, adjusting ever so quickly to a life filled with money—lots of it—for the first time in their lives.

While the redecorating was still in full swing at the main house in Lexington, Bertha began looking into Florida residences, eventually spending $330,000 on a Fort Lauderdale condo, including furnishings. This was also the year that Bertha launched her own business, a women's fashion boutique called Ricco Antonio. The board of directors consisted of Bertha Wright and Lyle Robey. The clothes were the creations of a Filipino designer, Ricardo A. Gorosin, known professionally as Ricco Antonio. Exquisite ensembles, ranging in price from $500 to several thousand dollars, were made from the finest of fabrics and lace, which Bertha imported from Europe. She soon would become immersed in the enterprise, and in the career of the designer, flying with him to Beverly Hills, where he would open a second store, and to other cities to help promote his line.

Though she seemed to be spending a lot of money, Bertha spent relatively little on herself. Her new life was filled with benefit committees, women's groups, and local charities. She sponsored a scholarship program at nearby Transylvania University to keep gifted scholars in the state, and hosted a benefit for the Kentucky Olympic Committee. A firm believer in tithing, she gave $2,000 or more each month to her church. Robey, who handled the donations, was inundated with requests for Calumet's support, his new desk buried in solicitations and invitations. This wasn't surprising considering that during these years Bertha would receive about $5 million a year from the oil and gas assets alone.

The children had each received about $7 million in assets, including their

9.375 percent stake (about $3.5 million) in Calumet Farm. The rest, mostly gas and oil investments and cash, went into Wright Enterprises for Robey to administer and invest. The approximately $700,000 they received annually from the gas and oil properties was a substantial income, and, like their mother, they had little experience handling large amounts of money. But they had their advisers, Lundy and Robey, to help them. Warren III, a conservative spender, had found his plot of land along the Kentucky River. Tommy was still looking at businesses; he'd soon start a local ad firm that did radio spots and he'd invest in a discount cosmetics store.

A September memo from Wright Enterprises to the trustees at Second National indicated that Courtenay was on the verge of closing on an apartment building in Hilton Head for about $225,000. She and her husband were also buying saddlebred horses, a breed indigenous to Kentucky, and sending them to showhorse trainers. Eventually they would own nearly sixty showhorses worth millions of dollars.

Courtenay also would soon be running a chain of restaurants in town called Columbia's—sit-down restaurants with bars and an established clientele. Wright Enterprises, Robey, and a few other partners bought the chain initially and allowed her to run it. Later she bought out the partners for several million dollars, despite the urgings of friends and legal consultants to look elsewhere. The restaurants were decent enough, but the price was too high, they cautioned. Courtenay was familiar with the business and buying this particular chain seemed so convenient. Perhaps when she looked at the price she didn't think about the fact that Robey was compensated at a percentage of all gross receipts that flowed into Wright Enterprises.

Despite the excitement that year, the brighter-than-ever white fences, and the contagious feeling of limitless money, reality had begun to seep through the veneer of Calumet's gleaming image. The farm was beginning to receive bills from the barn builders, the fence painters, the tree surgeons, the architects, and the bankers and lawyers dealing with the Wright family fortune. Second National Bank, which administered the Warren Wright, Jr., Trust, billed the farm $131,256 at the beginning of the year, followed by monthly bills of $15,725; $8,781; $10,324; $8,669; for a total of about $174,758 by June 1983. Among other big bills was one for $404,327 for the use and maintenance of the new Calumet jet.

One of Lundy's dreams was to have an airplane of his own. He loved airplanes, and everybody else he wanted to catch up with, like the Maktoum brothers of Dubai and Robert Sangster in England, had private jets. He told Robey years before that the first thing he wanted to do once he took over Calumet was to get an airplane. Almost immediately, Wright Enterprises purchased a Falcon jet for about $1.6 million.

Calumet's first accounting of the airplane expenses showed that this would be among the biggest costs of operating the new Calumet. One monthly statement revealed that fuel, maintenance, and airport services had cost more than the entire Calumet payroll for the month.

During the Lundy years, Calumet always operated at least one private jet, usually trading the last one for a bigger one. After the Falcon jet, the planes varied in size from a Canadian Air Challenger with a crew of two, to a smallish $1.7 million Hawker Siddeley, then up again to the "Rolls-Royce" of private jets, a Gulfstream G2, and on to a smaller $2.1 million eight-passenger Westwind, 1978 model, with a crew of three. Lundy would even form a company, Southeastern Aircraft Holding Corporation, in Greensboro, North Carolina, to deal with the planes. The company's directors were Lundy and his wife, Cindy Wright Lundy, though Cindy's lawyer would later claim that she was not the person who had signed her name to documents related to Southeastern. The company's president was one of Lundy's attorneys, Gary Matthews. Using Southeastern, Lundy could borrow money to buy a jet and then lease it back to Calumet, charging the farm $30,000 a month. Calumet's payment took care of the money due on the plane, but if the loan was paid off, Southeastern, not Calumet, owned the plane.

The year 1983 also marked the beginning of debt for Calumet. In August, Second National Bank loaned a total of $13.2 million to Calumet on an unsecured basis. The bank, in an unusual move, did not require the farm to supply any collateral in case the debt was never paid. The money was used to buy back, for a total cost of $17.2 million, three thoroughbred stallions and two broodmares that the farm had donated to several universities and hospitals to fulfill the stipulation in Warren Wright, Sr.'s will that 20 percent of the Residuary Trust must be given to charity. It was Robey's idea to donate the horses and then buy them back instead of donating 20 percent of the oil and gas properties and the farm. This way the heirs could continue to own all the assets and the farm, and in buying back the horses, could establish the horses' market value to be used for tax purposes, bank loans, or whatever. In fact, the same horses soon were used as collateral for bank loans. This meant that money from the Warren Wright, Jr., Trust was used indirectly to bring cash from other banks into the Calumet coffers. The problem was that the trust would never be repaid and if the family ever suffered financial problems, there was no collateral to sell to reimburse the trust for this particular loan.

In early September Second National's chairman received a memo from Wright Enterprises revealing a new attitude at the once debt-free stable. "Calumet Farm should easily be able to manage between $10 million and $20 million in debt with $7 million a year in income. As you know, other acquisitions for the farm are in the works, so additional borrowings will be necessary."

But by the start of 1984, Calumet's debt was nearly $27 million—and growing.

7

On the first night of Keeneland's July auction in 1984, prospective bidders crowded into the sales pavilion, leaving no seat or aisle free. Even in the hallway outside the arena spectators vied for space, pressing against the arena's glass walls in hopes of seeing the sales ring, the big digital price board, or the faces of the stars like billionaire Britisher Robert Sangster, the Dubai sheiks, and Nelson Bunker Hunt, the oil tycoon from Texas. These were the high-class gamblers who came to town to roll the dice and bet their millions on the performance of an untested product, a thoroughbred too young to know the smell of a dirt track at dawn, the sound of a cheering crowd, or the sting of a jockey's whip.

Each year the crowds grew as the expectation for thrills was never disappointed. This was the roller coaster of the industry, and the ride each year was wilder than the one year before. Though the top 1982 price of $4.25 million seemed hard to beat, there weren't enough spaces on the big lighted board for the eight digits of 1983's high price, $10.2 million for a son of Northern Dancer.

The Monday-night session in July 1984 would not produce a new record, but it would surpass all past years in the sheer volume of money spent. In that single night nine horses sold for more than a million dollars each: $8.25 million, $6.5 million, $5.4 million, $5.1 million, $3.75 million, $3 million, $2 million, $2 million, and $1.9 million. The average price for the eighty-one horses sold that night was $809,259, compared with a $45,000 average in 1975. For all the days of the sale, thirty-eight horses sold for more than $1 million, compared with four only five years before. The *Wall Street Journal* later reported that by 1984, prices for yearlings at summer sales over the past decade had risen 918 percent to an overall average of $544,681.

Soaring prices encouraged breeders to produce more foals and to offer a larger percentage of their crops to the public, which meant unprecedented numbers of yearlings sold at auction—9,268 in 1984 as compared with 1,717 in 1950. And with headlines advertising the impressive auction results, more and more outsiders were flocking to the Bluegrass each year in hopes of turning a quick profit by buying and selling this hot new commodity.

The contagion had even spread to Wall Street, where investment bankers and stockbrokers had discovered that breeding for dollars was a lucrative game. By 1984, the canyons of Wall Street echoed with the saga of Spectacular Bid, the 1979 winner of the Kentucky Derby and Preakness, who was purchased for $37,000 as a yearling, won $2.8 million at the track, and was syndicated as a stallion for $22 million. The tale of Seattle Slew, a $17,000 yearling in 1975 and a multimillion-dollar stud in 1984 commanding $710,000 for one season's breeding, had made its way to the executive suites of Prudential Securities, Merrill Lynch, and others.

The imprint of Wall Street's own 1980s mania and frenzied deal making was everywhere in horse country. Even Churchill Downs was dancing to the rhythm of the times. On the eve of the 1984 Kentucky Derby, Minneapolis investor Irwin Jacobs and partner Carl Pohlad, owner of the Minnesota Twins, were neck and neck with Leslie Combs II in a race to take over the venerable 110-year-old home of the Derby. Combs, the chairman of Spendthrift Farm, Inc., which owned a 3 percent stake in Churchill Downs, offered shareholders a $100 bond for each of the 383,232 common shares outstanding of Churchill Downs, Inc., or a total of $38.3 million. Jacobs and Pohlad countered with a cash offer of $110 a share, or $42.2 million. Combs warned he might launch a hostile takeover if the board didn't reach a decision before the Derby, but both Combs and Jacobs backed off when several shareholders controlling more than 51 percent of the common stock voted not to sell any of their stock, no matter how high the offer, for the next two years.

Spendthrift Farm's private stock offering during the summer of 1983 drew a roster of thirty-four investors, including Calvin Klein, the designer, and his partner Barry Schwartz; Marvin L. Warner, former U.S. ambassador to Switzerland; Washington timber tycoon George Layman; former U.S. ambassador to New Zealand Kenneth Franzheim II; Verne H. Winchell, founder of Denny's Restaurants; William H. Bricker, president and chairman of Diamond Shamrock Corporation; and Zenya Yoshida, Japan's leading horse breeder. The farm raised $33 million by selling 32 percent of the company, and then, hungry for more, in late 1983 Spendthrift made history by offering to the public 650,000 shares, or a 5 percent stake, for $12 a share. It was the first thoroughbred farm to be traded on Wall Street, and its prospectus featured an impressive illustrated life cycle of the thoroughbred and a glossary of breeding terms for those investors who had never owned a horse or a piece of a horse. The stock value of the farm was $160 million, and soon it would be trading between $8 and $11 a share on the American Stock Exchange.

Brokerage firms and underwriters, once reluctant to buy and sell pieces of a horse, were raising money for thoroughbred and standardbred partnerships and distributing stock in all sorts of equine entities. Prudential Securities did placements for Spendthrift. Merrill Lynch raised $20 million in an equine partnership offering in 1984 and would later, in collaboration with Stephens, the big Arkansas investment bank, create a partnership called Kentucky Heritage "to engage in the business of acquiring, owning, breeding and selling thoroughbred broodmares and their produce, thoroughbred colts and fillies and thoroughbred stallion shares or seasons." Lou Guida, a Merrill Lynch executive, was responsible for $60 million in horse syndications, including a yearling he bought for $100,000 and syndicated for $19.2 million. And small publicly traded companies dealing in some aspect of managing or owning horses were popping up across the investment landscape. Bob Brennan, chairman of First Jersey Securities, created his own firm to cash in on the action: International Thoroughbred Breeders, which was traded on the American Stock Exchange.

There was evidence, too, of the dark side of Wall Street practices, such as high-pressured cold calling, a sales method in which brokers shop for investors by phoning people they've never met. It can be disreputable and even illegal when the brokers sell products of questionable quality at inflated prices. A bloodstock broker from New York might call a retired autoworker in Detroit and try to sell him a share in a stallion or a stallion season. The retiree, whose only connection to a horse was a visit to Hialeah on a Florida vacation ten years before, might reply that he didn't know the first thing about owning a horse or a part of a horse and certainly didn't have a mare to breed to a horse. The odds were good that he didn't even know what a stallion season was. But the broker would explain how the investor didn't have to know about horses. This was a commodity, like a bar of gold, the salesman would say. The investor could buy a season and then turn around and sell it to someone who had a mare to breed to the stallion, and turn a 20 percent profit in the process. That was the pitch, which of course didn't include information about the commission the broker was charging.

There were boiler rooms where salesmen would not only cold call nationwide but also hold investor seminars while strains of "My Old Kentucky Home" played in the background and big banners hung from the walls with such slogans as "You too can be in the winner's circle" and "Be a part of the Kentucky Derby. Own a piece of a horse."

High-pressure salesmen at one company, based outside Miami, sold $9 million worth of thoroughbred horseflesh in eighteen months over the telephone to hundreds of investors from Hawaii to New England. One sales contract promised a 150 percent return on a $10,000 investment in five months. Salesmen referred to the thoroughbred business as "the last bastion of free enterprise." The firm eventually closed shop one day, leaving hundreds of thousands of dollars in unpaid bills and a trail of lawsuits and bilked investors.

Pyramid schemes were not uncommon. In these, a horse agent might buy a horse for $50,000 and then, using a sky-is-the-limit pitch, syndicate it for $500,000, telling unwary investors they'd get their money back and much more when the racehorse proved itself at the track. The investors typically ended up holding the bag—the feed bag, that is—on a lackluster racehorse.

By 1984, anybody could buy a piece of a racehorse, regardless of whether he or she had ever smelled the inside of a barn. "Paper stables"—investment portfolios of stallion shares—were no longer novel. Just like stock in a corporation, a stallion share rose in value according to the performance of the company's product, in this case, the performance of the sire's offspring at the track.

The strange mix of Wall Street and horse country was never more pronounced than in thoroughbred racing's own stock market, the Matchmaker Breeders' Exchange, which began in the summer of 1984. The exchange was a weekly "bid" and "ask" market for the trading of stallion shares and stallion seasons, including "stallion futures," seasons for future years. The *Wall Street Journal* dubbed it "a combination of the Dating Game and the Chicago Board of Trade." Access to the exchange was restricted to members who paid a $400 yearly fee, and every Monday they were entitled to list shares or seasons on the exchange with their asking price by calling a toll-free number before 5:00 p.m. By 10:00 a.m. Tuesday, members received the "ask" list, and potential buyers had until 4:00 P.M. on Wednesday to respond with offers, which had to be at least 80 percent of the "ask." On Tuesday, from 10:00 A.M. to 4:00 P.M. members could offer bids on seasons and shares not listed on the exchange, and the owners of those seasons and shares could accept an offer in the "bid" market between 10:00 A.M. Thursday and 4:00 P.M. Friday. In addition to the weekly trading exchange, that summer Matchmaker began its first members-only auction of stallion seasons and shares.

The exchange gave investors the kind of liquidity they were accustomed to in other markets. The hope was that this would broaden the industry's appeal and bring in more buyers, increasing the demand for the product and pushing up the prices.

Matchmaker's founder, Barry Weisbord, who also headed Matchmaker's New York–based parent, Executive Bloodstock Management Corporation, was an entrepreneur with an instinct for promotion. He had tested the waters the year before when he orchestrated a flashy, black-tie auction at a Lexington hotel to sell stallion seasons. It was a hit and by 1984 a semi-annual event in the Bluegrass. Weisbord also developed what he called a time-saver approach to financing members' equine purchases, Matchmaker Financial Corporation, which provided financing at the prime rate, plus one percentage point and a fee. The loan was based only on the value of the horse. "Our application is one word—the name of a horse," Weisbord once said.

Weisbord was a bold, original thinker who devised creative ways for investors to get into the horse game. His critics and admirers would someday view his work in much the same way as Wall Street looked upon the machinations of junk-bond king Michael Milken. In a few years he would add a loan broker, Equine Capital Corporation, to his expanding empire of equine-service firms, and Calumet's journey would include numerous stops at Long Island–based ECC. One of Weisbord's officers at Executive Bloodstock Management, a man named Marc Rash, would connect Lundy and the farm to bankers and deal makers and help devise ways for Calumet to obtain capital. Weisbord, too, would make deals with Calumet.

Another big part of the boomtime scenario was commercial banking. By the 1980s, bankers were driving their rented BMWs and Mercedes over the winding roads of the Bluegrass, though most of them, averse to getting horse manure on their fine leather shoes, spent little time at the barns. They zeroed in on the main show, the Keeneland summer sales, prowling the corridors of the sales arena and the Keeneland dining room looking for agents and breeders. The locals complained the bankers were far too aggressive.

"They grab you by the arm and hold it up until you've bought the damn horse," Lyle Robey once complained. Behind the bankers' backs, local breeders would chortle over the banking world's naïveté about the horse business, saying things like, "They don't know which end of the horse it eats out of" and "They're idiots with milk on their chins."

But while the cultures clashed, the goals did not. Bankers and breeders needed each other, and as long as prices continued going up and the Bluegrass Bubble expanded, they helped each other line their pockets. But to keep prices up, the industry had to continually bring in new sources of purchasing power. Newcomers were accustomed to leveraging their investments, and prices were so high that even some of the wealthy old-line owners couldn't afford to play the game now without borrowing. At the same time, the banks, facing unprecedented competition in the age of banking deregulation and eager to find new, previously untapped niches to fatten their loan portfolios, convinced one another through sheer competition that the horse industry was safe, clearly more solid than it once appeared to be.

Only ten years before, if a banker outside the Bluegrass or in a state other than those where racing and breeding were a mainstay had even suggested lending money to breeders and securing the loan with the borrower's horses, he would have been ridiculed. But since the mid-1970s, the industry had gained an unprecedented level of credibility. Horsemen were taken seriously, as the hardworking professionals many had always been. The damaging depiction that cast all horse breeders as rich men indulging in an expensive, trivial hobby was fading. This was a business involving all sorts of people with a cash flow that was contributing substantially to state and national economies.

As the industry gained more and more credibility—and brought in more and more revenue—state agencies and equine associations hired consultants to study it. A 1979 study in Nebraska estimated that racing contributed $222 million in revenue to the state economy per year. In 1982 a Joint Legislative Task Force in New York reported that the industry had grown to $2.3 billion in revenue in that state alone. A later study in Ohio showed that breeding and racing accounted for about $450 million of the state's annual output of goods and services; in Texas, the figure was nearly $2 billion.

National studies showed the horse industry, including all breeds and all types of racing, brought in revenue ranging from $12 billion to $20 billion a year, depending on which attendant services were included in the studies. A report in the mid-1980s tried to give perspective to the figures by saying that the industry comprised nearly 20 percent of the gross national product of the agricultural sector of the economy and was equal in value to over 80 percent of the GNP of the textile products sector and 65 percent of the lumber and wood products sector. The report concluded that the horse industry was equal to the combined output of the tobacco and leather products industries.

The combination of such credibility campaigns and the startling auction returns each year made the industry seem a good bet for bankers, though none of this changed the risky nature of the business. The odds that a bank's client would breed a Northern Dancer, a Secretariat, or an Alydar were still about the same as the odds of a teller becoming bank president.

Banks in Kentucky, where horses were the second-largest industry after mining, already had sizable horse portfolios by the 1980s, though separate equine lending divisions were a phenomenon of the boom. One local bank created a logo to go with the trend: a silhouette of a horse's head. Another ran a television ad that showed an elderly black man going to the auctions, picking out a choice horse, buying it for $175,000, and borrowing the money to pay for it.

Banks outside the Bluegrass soon rushed in. Wells Fargo in California made its first equine loans in 1981. European American Bank in New York City was also among the first, and by 1982 had loaned $17 million in horse country. Barnett Banks' Ocala, Florida, office had $22 million in horse loans in 1983, and Sun Trust's Ocala office would have nearly $25 million in equine loans by the mid-1980s. Midlantic National Bank in New Jersey soon had a $100 million portfolio of equine loans, and Crocker Bank and Citibank jumped on the bandwagon. In many of these loans, horses were the collateral, and bankers would lend up to 80 percent of a horse's appraised value, with loan minimums of $1 million. By 1984, banks nationwide had at least $1 billion in outstanding loans to horse breeders.

Lundy's own frantic expansion continued in 1984, but instead of building barns at Calumet he was making deals with financiers and businessmen far from the sweeping savannahs of central Kentucky. This was the year Calumet catapulted out of its staid, stable foundation into the fast lane.

Trips to the Virgin Islands were becoming more frequent now that Cindy Lundy lived on St. Thomas. Her separation from her husband was amicable, and both Lundy and Robey were looking into investments for Wright Enterprises on St. Thomas. Robey seemed particularly intrigued with the idea of building a thoroughbred racetrack in the Red Hook area, the location of the island's main ferry landing. Crews and tourists, waiting for their boats to arrive or spending a day away from the beach, hadn't much to do in Red Hook, Robey reasoned, except to wander through rows of shops. He was interested, too, in buying a chain of Kentucky Fried Chicken franchises on the Caribbean island to diversify the Wrights' investment portfolio. In general he was also looking for ways for Calumet to write off frequent flights to St. Thomas, he said years later.

In March of 1984, Lundy, in partnership with friends John Fernung, Harry Ranier, and A. J. Foyt, purchased Dan Lasater's 1,000-acre Florida farm. Lundy also added Lasater's jet to Calumet's aircraft holdings. As Lundy was building an empire, Lasater was dismantling one. The previous summer, Lasater had begun to disperse his thoroughbred holdings, including more than four hundred horses and his big farm outside Ocala. The reason, perhaps, was that Lasater and Company, his brokerage firm, was expanding after obtaining several big contracts for state bond issues. But around the same time, too, a coalition of local, state, and federal law enforcement agencies, called the Organized Crime Drug Enforcement Task Force, had targeted Lasater in a sweeping investigation that later would result in charges of "conspiracy to distribute cocaine" and a thirty-month jail sentence.

Also that spring, Lundy startled his Bluegrass neighbors with an unusual practice: mating Alydar, a prized thoroughbred sire, with quarter horses. Lundy, who had complained about the mares chosen for Alydar during Mrs. Markey's last years, had cut a deal with a Louisiana politician, state senator J. E. Jumonville, Jr., to mate four quarter horse mares to Alydar. In the view of many thoroughbred breeders, this was tantamount to a marriage between a king and a scullery maid. Quarter horses are strong and agile animals, originally bred as workhorses. They can quickly track down an errant cow or dodge an attacking bull, and they are raced, though only short distances. The racers are adept as sprinters partly because they are heavily weighted up front. This reduces the tendency of a racehorse to lose speed at the beginning of a race by rising up because its strong hindquarter muscles propel it forward. There is nothing wrong with mating quarter horses with thoroughbreds, and it's not especially unusual. Breeders might use quarter horses for the stallion's first year to test his prowess before bringing in thoroughbred mares whose offspring can easily make or break the stallion's career as a stud.

Such matches had been made before, but not with royalty like Alydar, who in 1983 was the industry's champion first-year sire. With sons and daughters selling for an average of $760,000 each—at that time a record for a first crop—thoroughbred breeders were hoping they had mares good enough to be accepted by Calumet for breeding to Alydar. For every quarter horse Alydar was mated to, one owner of a thoroughbred mare was disappointed and the industry was deprived of one more chance to create a superstar. To the thinking of traditional breeders, this practice was truly a waste of Alydar's essence, bordering on sacrilege.

But Senator Jumonville, in his pressed jeans, western shirt, and boots, was thrilled by the prospect of pumping up the quality of the quarter horse breed. By matching his top mares with Alydar, he hoped to produce the fastest sprinter ever. While the amount of money he paid Calumet for this rare privilege was undisclosed at the time, a lawsuit filed years later in Louisiana revealed that he took out a loan for $5 million from a Louisiana bank to launch his Alydar program. Senator Jumonville told a reporter for the Associated Press, "My purpose was to get the quality, and the purpose of Calumet was the money they saw."

But clearly Lundy's most memorable move of 1984 came during the summer when he purchased half a horse for $25 million. The deal came through Harry Ranier's son-in-law, Jesus Colmenares, the former racing secretary at the La Rinconada Race Course in Caracas, Venezuela, who had worked for Caracas entrepreneur and breeder Luigi Miglietti.

Originally from Italy, Miglietti had struck it rich in Venezuela from the success of Aerobuses de Venezuela, an extensive public transportation system he owned. Miglietti was enthralled with racing, whether it was cars, motorcycles, or horses. In Venezuela he owned a 400-acre farm called Haras Monumental, about a three-hour drive from Caracas, and in 1979 he added to his holdings the 125-acre Monumental Farm, near Lexington.

Miglietti seemed to be lucky when it came to horses, but he didn't know the face of lady luck until he came across a particular Northern Dancer colt at the Keeneland sales in July 1982. The colt, a dark bay with three white feet, was a grandson of Secretariat. That year Northern Dancer yearlings were selling for an average price of $857,188, but because this yearling had one crooked leg, Miglietti bought him for $340,000, the cheapest Northern Dancer colt that year. Miglietti named him Secreto.

Two years later, on June 6, 1984, Secreto won England's most prestigious race, the Epsom Derby. And on July 10, Calumet Farm, Inc., announced that it had purchased a half interest in Secreto for an undisclosed amount and that the horse would continue to race until 1985, when it would come to Calumet to begin its career as a stud. The price of Calumet's purchase did not remain undisclosed for long. By the time everyone had gathered at the July sales, it was common knowledge that Calumet had paid $25 million.

Behind the scenes, Lundy, who was acquiring an appetite for deals, had made some interesting arrangements in connection with the purchase. In the sales contract, Lundy agreed to pay $2.5 million thirty days from the date of execution of the agreement, which was July 10; $2.5 million on February 15, 1985, with 10 percent interest; and $2.5 million in the form of a lifetime breeding right to Alydar for Miglietti.

In addition, the farm gave Miglietti a promissory note for $10 million, to be paid in six annual installments of $1,666,666 each plus interest at 10 percent, due on the fifteenth day of November, beginning in 1985. The remaining $7.5 million was to be paid in the form of a demand note, meaning Miglietti could call the loan at any time. Miglietti also received a half interest in the horse Foyt, plus a few broodmares.

To reward those who helped put together the deal, Lundy gave away numerous lifetime breeding rights to Secreto. Each year six people would get a free season to the stallion: Luigi Miglietti's wife; Harry Ranier; Miguel Torrealba, Secreto's trainer; Jesus Colmenares; Janice Heinz, Lundy's assistant; and Lyle Robey. Lundy, who was named the official manager of the stallion, gave himself—not the farm—two free breeding rights per year. In a typical stallion purchase, the trainer might receive a free season annually for his work with the horse, while the stallion manager got two to four rights to breed each year to the stallion. But those rights belonged to the farm, not the manager. The idea is that the seasons are the farm's payment for the cost of managing the stallion.

In this case, Calumet received nothing, yet the money for the purchase and for the expenses of putting the deal together came out of its coffers. And the farm would get less of a return on the purchase each year because eight breeding rights had already been given away. With Secreto's stud fee ranging from $80,000 to $125,000 through the years, the breeding rights Lundy gave away might have been worth as much as $1 million a year to the farm.

The Secreto purchase occurred in July. In August Lundy announced yet another deal: the sale of fifteen lifetime breeding rights to Alydar for about $2.5 million each. The buyers received a right to breed one mare each year and an additional mare every other year, and these rights were good for the entire life of the horse. If viewed as the equivalent of a share in a syndicated horse, which is typically divided into forty shares, Alydar's value could and would now be appraised at $100 million.

But this was not a true syndication. The concept of lifetime breeding rights was a new investment vehicle, a concept Lyle Robey and Lundy created in part to give Calumet a quick bundle of cash to pay down some of its debt. In a syndication, those who purchase a share have the right to breed to the horse each year, just like the holders of lifetime breeding rights, but they also have the right to stipulate such things as how many times the horse will be bred and at what stable the horse will stand. The stipulations are part of the syndicate agreement, and the syndicate manager is bound by the agreement's terms. But holders of lifetime breeding rights had no input into the management of the stallion. Thus Lundy remained in control of Alydar's career while reaping the financial benefits of a partial syndication.

While a certain number of breedings each year were reserved for the holders of the breeding rights, Lundy was free to sell the rest—however many the horse could handle—at his discretion without restraint. Most holders believed this number would never exceed sixty or seventy and were not concerned about relinquishing their control over the stallion's career. Besides, they had the same rights to breed as shareholders did, and they had a tax advantage. At the time, Kentucky sales tax laws exempted sales of "horses or interests of shares in horses, provided the purchase or use is made for breeding purposes only." Lundy, claiming his lifetime breeding rights were tantamount to interests in the horse, did not charge taxes on the $2.5 million purchases.

Although the state didn't collect on the sale, Lundy and company did. On each purchase Lundy collected a 10 percent commission; Robey collected his usual percentage of the gross receipts; and the New Jersey bloodstock agency Associated Thoroughbred Projects, S.I., or ATPSI, whose co-owner Bob Fox put together the bank financing for the deal, made about $1 million.

Midlantic Bank and Trust, of Edison, New Jersey, had been lending to standardbred breeders since 1980. In 1983 it began to tap the rich vein of the thoroughbred market, lending up to 80 percent of a horse's value based on either the purchase price at public auction or a private appraisal or both. Midlantic even included a thoroughbred in its "hungry banker" ad campaign on local television. The concept was that Midlantic's bankers had an insatiable appetite for loans. One ad showed the bank president extolling Midlantic's prowess while feeding a thoroughbred racehorse.

But it wasn't until Fox connected the bank to Calumet that Midlantic's career as an equine lender really took off. In late 1984, after meeting on numerous occasions with Fox, Midlantic agreed to lend Calumet up to $20 million to facilitate the sale of the Alydar lifetime breeding rights. The farm granted the bank a security interest in the promissory notes of the holders of such rights; the buyers were thus obligated to pay back the loans not to Calumet but to Midlantic. Yet although the loans were secured by the notes of the breeding-right purchasers, the guarantors of the loan—those ultimately responsible if the loans weren't paid—were the Wright heirs and the trustee of the Warren Wright, Jr., Trust, Second National Bank.

It seemed like the perfect deal. Midlantic could advertise its association with Calumet, which would help to enlarge its thoroughbred portfolio to nearly $70 million. With the help of master networker and deal maker Fox, the bank now had connections to some of the industry's current high rollers such as Eugene Klein, the former owner of the San Diego Chargers. Fox meanwhile developed a lucrative relationship with Midlantic, earning about $350,000 a year, or one-half of a percentage point of the total portfolio annually, for bringing in the equine business. Lundy could make a killing by selling stallion seasons on a horse that now, thanks to the sale of the breeding rights, had a market value of $100 million. And Alydar had begun a new phase in his career—as the cash machine of Calumet Farm.

Now, as long as the progeny of Secreto and Alydar sold for high prices, stud fees could remain high and everyone with a breeding right would profit. So much depended on the yearling prices, as if they were the steel girders of a skyscraper. If the prices ever collapsed, the breeding-right holders, their insurers, the banks that took the stallions as collateral, and the Wright heirs, all would suffer. But in 1984, it seemed that such a collapse was impossible—certainly it must have seemed that way to the Wrights, Lundy, and Robey.

Secreto arrived at his new home in central Kentucky on October 3, during the same week that Queen Elizabeth II of England visited the Bluegrass. Calumet was on the queen's short list of places to tour, as the owner of Alydar, who was a favorite of the queen's, and now as the 50 percent owner of Secreto, the winner of England's most prestigious race, the Epsom Derby. At Calumet, the queen met Lundy and his friends Ranier and Colmenares, among others. In the upcoming season she sent her mare Contralto to Secreto and mare Christchurch to Alydar.

But despite the privileged life Lundy was leading, he also was learning quickly that managing a huge, famous stable like Calumet could be stressful. Toward the end of the year, he told a local reporter that his job so far was "not as much fun as I thought it would be, and it's not as easy as it looks."

8 By 1985, peculiar things had begun to happen inside the devil's-red gates of Calumet.

At night a Ford Bronco with dark-tinted windows patrolled the grounds, stopping at barns and residences, alternating the order of the stops every other night. The passenger door would slowly open, and the leg of a tall, burly man would appear, his foot and the butt of his shotgun slamming against the pavement at the same time, sending ripples of sound across the dark, otherwise silent land.

The man was one of two high-powered guards hired to protect Alydar and the stallions, and perhaps even Lundy himself. Both were accustomed to jobs like escorting strikebreakers across picket lines during coal strikes in eastern Kentucky. One was in the habit of wearing a big, sweeping overcoat; the other had a business card listing the range of prices for jobs he'd do, like shooting someone in the knee, the eye, or the shoulder. The last item on the list was the cost to help overthrow the government of a small country. Though it seemed like a joke, by most accounts the guard wasn't the type to make up a card just for laughs. He had once served time on an assault conviction.

To make the guards comfortable, Lundy invited them to live in a 2,500-square-foot apartment on top of the foaling barn, which had a cupola with windows on all four sides. Using night-vision glasses, the men routinely surveyed the grounds, watching the comings and goings of the farm at all hours.

Calumet should have hired watchdogs for more than the barns and grounds—perhaps a few with business skills to oversee some of the financial dealings. On March 26, 1985, for example, an executive from Kinderhill Farm, a thoroughbred stable in New York, sent a letter to Lundy saying he had heard the Calumet president was interested in "reviewing a complete package of our top group of yearlings." The letter listed eight yearlings and sales prices based on December 31, 1984, appraisals. On the list was a 1984 colt sired by Green Dancer "out of" the mare Baby Diamonds; the price was $200,000. On March 29, a Calumet check for $300,000 was paid to the order of Kinderhill. The check stub read: "To purchase 1984 Green Dancer–Baby Diamonds colt from Kinderhill Farm." Calumet appeared to have paid $100,000 above the seller's requested price.

It was a puzzling move for the farm's president to allow more money to leave the Calumet account than was necessary, but then Lundy, too, seemed occasionally peculiar these days. The straightforward, down-home Kentucky horse trader was turning into a power-obsessed wheeler-dealer with a mercurial, impatient, and slightly paranoid style. He seemed more like a Mafia boss in a waterfront warehouse than the president of a farm whose office windows overlooked a landscape awash in innocence.

When Lundy was the ruler of his own kingdom and not Mrs. Markey's, he had few, if any, enemies. Though clearly not among the who's who in horse country, he knew enough top breeders and trainers to connect friends with the right people to accomplish whatever they needed. He'd find good bloodstock for Lasater or give Whiteley his best horses to train. He was a generous man. Lundy's mother once told Robey that when Lundy was a toddler he was so generous she'd have to keep track of his toys or he'd give them all away. Shortly after going to Calumet, he paid for a new roof and air-conditioning at a church back home in Scott County.

In 1985, after nearly three years in his new post, there were still signs of the old Lundy and his generosity. "J.T. would rather hide in the barn behind Calumet than say no to anyone," Robey once said. He gave away Calumet stallion seasons to friends and favorite associates, including the gift of a Secreto lifetime breeding right to Robey. He sent Calumet workers to a friend's farm to do work. He allowed another friend to use the farm's vet facilities. Occasionally he'd let friends run horses in their own names just for the fun of seeing their names published in the *Daily Racing Form*. Those who traveled with him were treated to limousines and the best food money could buy. Sometimes he'd take an entourage of friends on the Calumet jet for a day trip, like the time he flew four or five pals to Kennebunkport, Maine, for a lobster lunch, a glimpse at George Bush's house, and back home again. His birthday presents, too, were extraordinary. One person received a weekend at a racecar driving school—a gift costing nearly $1,500. "He picked up the tab for people, everywhere, always," said one insider.

But the generosity of the new Lundy often came at the expense of Calumet. Once when two of his friends owed Calumet $300,000, the debt was redefined in the books as two fees for work done at Calumet, thus wiping out the obligation. For each stallion season Lundy gave away, Calumet lost one season's worth of income, which depending on the stallion and the terms of the breeding right ranged from $30,000 to $300,000. For each break he gave to a friend, whether it was a free breeding right, or Calumet shouldering the burden of expenses for a horse jointly owned by the friend and Calumet, or Calumet forgiving the interest on a promissory note owed to the farm, or the Calumet jet transporting friends, the loss was not Lundy's.

With such generous ways, Lundy's list of friends and business associates kept growing. And his generosity was often reciprocated, resulting in some profitable transactions for him. But despite favors, beneficial deals, and new pals, he seemed more than a little worried about enemies and security. He kept a gun under the divan in the Calumet office and another between the seats of his car, which had dark-tinted glass windows. The windows were tinted, he told a Calumet employee, because he did not want anyone to see who was sitting with him. The same employee walked into Lundy's office one day while he was perusing a catalog of high-security equipment in search of a bullet-proof briefcase. He also began to take different routes to work each morning from Lundy Farm in nearby Midway to Calumet.

Even the topics of Lundy's gab sessions were changing. Though taciturn with the press and not very sociable at big events, Lundy was loquacious with his buddies. He loved the talk of the trade, and at Lundy Farm he'd spend hours chatting about Kentucky-bred horses, their racing potential, their flaws, and the track earnings of their sires. The new Lundy talked deals, deals, and more deals, and when he wasn't, he was spewing out orders to one of his managers or fretting about the way something was or wasn't done.

There were only certain people he trusted now, and increasingly he wanted to keep his business within a small circle of friends and relatives. This was the year he loaned $10,000 of Calumet's money to help his sister launch Equus Unlimited, an insurance brokerage that would handle Calumet's hefty business. In fact, much of Equus's income would come from Calumet and Calumet referrals. A buyer of a Calumet horse would be referred to Equus, and later others connected with Lundy would also refer business to Equus, keeping all the deals close to home. Within the next few years, Lundy would also help his son start a bloodstock agency that would often serve as Calumet's consignor at public auction.

When Lundy was nervous, he'd rub his hands together, back and forth, over and over, as if they were cold. Sometimes, he'd shake his head like Richard Nixon and, between sharp intakes of breath, mutter half sentences about what wasn't being done right at the farm and who was causing the problem. His favorite "fuck it" phrase littered his speech, and it was hard for his staff and advisers to keep him focused on any given topic for more than a few minutes.

If he didn't get his way, he was quick to erupt. Once he wanted to breed one of Calumet's best mares to a stallion at a nearby farm, and because his mare was in heat he wanted the breeding to take place immediately. The stallion's manager, a highly respected owner and breeder, said he was sorry but Lundy would have to wait several days because the farm's breeding shed wasn't open yet. Lundy fumed, then yelled across his office, "Take a letter, take a letter someone! Dear ———, Fuck you. Serious letter to follow. Signed, J. T. Lundy."

Nothing was good enough for him. He wanted better and better airplanes, better and better horses, more and more. When he took charge of the farm, longtime employees were shocked at the extent of the renovations. Though the office needed modernizing, the farm seemed fit enough. Shortly before Margaret Glass left her post, she had even hired workers to clear dead limbs and clusters of old leaves from the thousands of trees on the property. But to Lundy the farm was rundown. It wasn't enough to replace one rotten board in a barn—he'd replace the whole barn. Though Calumet's three-quarter-mile track was one of the finest private racetracks anywhere, he brought in a crew to remove and redo the surface. The new track, which consisted of two or three layers of different types of soil and limestone, hadn't been in place long before he ordered it redone. He apparently spotted a stone on the new surface and worried there might be others that would emerge to harm the horses. The second job didn't suit him either. Grooms and exercise riders couldn't believe their eyes when they saw workmen coming back for yet another resurfacing. He also had a five-eighths-mile turf track built inside the perimeter of the revamped dirt track. An extensive fence repair and replacement in 1982 and 1983 was followed by even more work on the fences. From June of 1984 into the summer of 1985, he was spending more than $12,000 a month on oak planks, locust posts, and the labor to build and rebuild Calumet's trademark white fences.

Lundy appeared to possess the same unrelenting drive that Warren Wright had, but Lundy did not have his style, grace, or intellect. And Wright had not taken money out of the farm in the same way or with the stupefying speed that would someday make Lundy just as legendary.

Lundy was taking himself so seriously that people who had known him for years thought he was becoming a caricature of himself. Not sure how to respond to him, some friends would chuckle and comment among themselves about their old pal's eccentric, sometimes shocking behavior. But on the farm, humor was short-lived. His protean personality, the alternation between Lundy the Generous and Lundy the Furious, was beginning to frustrate farm workers, some of whom quit, they said, because of it. "If you didn't do something right away for him, you were the problem," said one insider.

No one understood why he sometimes seemed intolerant, frustrated, and paranoid. Robey always said someone hurt Lundy "real bad" years back, but he didn't know the details. "He worried that people would somehow take advantage of him," Robey explained. Another old friend said, "He had to get the people before they got him."

Others speculated that he was carried away with his new power and his desire to show horse country that he knew horses as well as any blueblood, even though his daddy hadn't owned land. Those who had known Lundy since childhood said an inferiority complex seemed to permeate his personality and that this was at the heart of all he did. And while the Bluegrass elite mistook his appearance and inarticulate manner for stupidity, those who knew him well recognized that beneath the awkward façade was a streetwise surety driving him to take risks, to make big deals and associate with powerful deal makers—all to show the world the extent of his power.

He believed he knew horses, and now he had the power to tell people what to do based on that knowledge. This might have explained his bossy style with employees, even vets. When a horse was sick Lundy sometimes intervened, watching carefully over the vet's shoulder and then telling the vet how he thought the horse should be treated. The combination of paranoia and interference discouraged one local insurance agent from doing business with Calumet, despite the money that could be made from insuring such pricey horses. The problem, one old acquaintance said, was that "he was smart but not as smart as he thought he was. He was getting just plain arrogant."

Another explanation was stress. The responsibility of managing such a huge farm and such valuable assets as Alydar was perhaps too much for Lundy's nerves. Though he had successfully operated his own 318-acre farm, that was no indication he could manage Calumet, and as Lundy expanded the farm's holdings and mixed the Calumet name into a vat of deal makers from diverse regions of horse country, his responsibilities increased even more.

There was also the possibility that Lundy was running with a fast crowd whose past and present associations could have made him slightly paranoid. Perhaps he knew about the possible underworld connections of one of the businessmen he was dealing with or that two others were convicted felons or that government drug agents were investigating the activities of his friend Dan Lasater.

One of his friends was the New Jersey gambler, racehorse consultant, and notorious fellow Robert Libutti. Though not a familiar face around the farm, Libutti (whose aliases included Robert Presti, Nicholas Spadea, and Ralph B. Libutti) conducted about $5 million worth of business with Calumet, mostly buying seasons and horses for associates and clients during the Lundy years.

Libutti was a loud, flamboyant man who seemed to have a habit he couldn't kick: getting into trouble. This was partly due to his alleged ties to organized crime, including reputed underworld boss John Gotti. His troubles may have begun in the late 1960s when he was barred from racing largely because of such ties. Then in 1971 he filed an income-tax return under the name Ralph Libutti but didn't file a separate return for the $750,000 worth of horse deals he conducted in 1970 using the name Bob Presti. This omission later resulted in an indictment charging tax evasion, to which he pleaded guilty. About the same time, the U.S. House of Representatives' Select Committee on Crime was looking into Libutti's hidden ownership of a well-known racehorse, Jim French, a runner-up at both the Derby and Belmont in 1971. A bank clerk who testified before the committee said Libutti wined and dined him and then asked him if he would do him (Libutti) the favor of temporarily registering some horses in his, the bank clerk's, name. "I was overwhelmed by the glamour of it all," the clerk told the committee. By the mid-1970s, merely associating with Libutti, a short, stout man with a hot temper, seemed to attract swarms of investigators.

Racing's investigative agency, the Thoroughbred Racing Protective Bureau, clearly had it out for Presti or Libutti or whatever he was calling himself. Libutti told *The New York Times* in late 1976 that he felt he was the victim of a "malicious conspiracy" to keep him out of racing, with "constant harassment" of himself, his mother, and other relatives and associates.

"I've never been convicted of any crime. I'm not Lucky Luciano's nephew, like the [Thoroughbred Racing Protective Bureau] told people. I work 14 to 16 hours a day, seven days a week, and I buy and sell $2 million worth of horses a year. I haven't known a bookmaker for 12 years."

The next year he pleaded guilty to "willfully filing a false tax return" in 1971, making him a convicted felon. This would get him into more trouble years later when federal agents found fourteen handguns and a rifle at his New Jersey residence. It's a federal offense for a convicted felon to own a gun, though Libutti would claim these guns belonged to a relative.

By most accounts, it was Bob Fox who connected Lundy and Libutti. They had horses in common and shared an affinity for the word "fuck." Like Lundy, Libutti grew up poor, though in an urban neighborhood in Union City, New Jersey. He, too, had a generous side—for example, giving Lundy's assistant Jan Heinz a champion shar-pei dog worth as much as $100,000. He was known as a heavy tipper. If in a good mood, he might slip $1,000 to the helicopter pilot who had transported him that day, or $100 to a cocktail waitress. Both he and Lundy were superstitious and they both liked to shoot craps, though Libutti was by far the more serious gambler. By the mid-1980s, Libutti was on his way to making a name for himself in the annals of American gambling, as Atlantic City's biggest loser and one of the casinos' most welcome bettors. During the years he was doing business with Calumet, Libutti, who averaged about $12,000 a bet, was also busy wagering nearly $20 million in Atlantic City casinos—and losing about $12 million. To encourage Libutti's habit, the Trump Plaza Hotel and Casino had begun an interesting practice: giving him gifts such as eight Rolls-Royces ranging in price from $155,000 to $250,000, Ferraris, and other luxury cars. Instead of driving the cars, Libutti received money from local dealers for some of them—nearly $1.6 million—and gambled it away at the Trump casino.

Libutti had a penchant for drawing attention to himself, and while he apparently felt like a victim, his own personality and habits seemed to play a role in ensuring an audience for his antics. His tendency during streaks of bad luck to fly into profane rages, during which he allegedly railed against women, blacks, Hispanics, and Jews, was hard to ignore. His arrival at certain casinos was marked by a flurry of activity including the removal of any ethnic personnel at the craps table where Libutti sat—a move that would result in stiff fines for the casinos. But this kind of thing apparently didn't bother Lundy. And Lundy probably didn't know that in 1985 Libutti allegedly began to circumvent banking laws that had prohibited him from borrowing more money from a New Jersey bank. That fall the Urban National Bank had issued all the credit it could extend to Libutti under federal banking regulations. Nonetheless, a bank officer during the next few years would approve $2.25 million in nominee loans, that is, loans to third-party middlemen, though Libutti was the true recipient of the money. The officer also would allegedly allow $1.2 million in overdrafts on Libutti's behalf and issue a $500,000 cashier's check to Libutti though it wasn't approved by the bank's board of directors.

Associating with someone as outrageous as Libutti must have been exciting. The word around the barns behind Belmont and other East Coast tracks was that Libutti was connected to some very powerful people, such as reputed Mafia kingpin John Gotti. Libutti would even be banned from gambling in Atlantic City because of his own proclamations that he was associated with Gotti.

But in addition to the boyish thrill of all this, Lundy might have been slightly intimidated, enough perhaps to be worried occasionally about who might be peering into his car windows or driving behind him on an isolated country road.

For those who watched the activities of the new Calumet president, it was clear Lundy couldn't stand to spend time alone. Some locals dubbed him "the Muhammad Ali of the Bluegrass" because he usually came to events and meetings with an entourage. If he wasn't sitting around his office or on the Calumet jet or at his favorite restaurant with a friend, he was on the phone. An insomniac, he had the habit of calling his cohorts in other time zones throughout the night and early morning to gab. If not on the phone, he was with one or both of his key lieutenants, Janice Heinz and Susan McGee. Because Lundy was secretive about his private life, the local gentry couldn't resist filling the void: rumors circulated about Lundy being involved with one or the other.

Heinz, a strong, big-boned woman in her mid-twenties with strawberry-blond hair and a firm, direct manner, was originally from Pittsburgh, supposedly from a wealthy family. Acquaintances said she spoke of her place on some branch of the H. J. Heinz family tree, had been a debutante in Pittsburgh, and was a niece of Senator John Heinz, now deceased. But when people checked the story, the curator of the Heinz Foundation in Pittsburgh never could find her name on the family tree.

Heinz came to the Bluegrass in 1975. Before teaming up with Lundy, she worked at the Jockey Club for four and a half years writing sales catalogs and later booking stallions at a big Bluegrass stable. Lundy, who had known her since the late 1970s, brought her on board as a consultant for booking mares to the Calumet stallions. Her job was to speak with prospective clients about their mares, advising them on which Calumet stallions best suited their mares. She researched pedigrees of various stallions that Calumet was considering for purchase and was involved in negotiations for acquiring new ones. Lundy also gave her the right to sign his name on the many legal contracts between Calumet and other breeders for the annual matings.

Lundy recognized Heinz's good instincts for quality horseflesh, and as early as the fall of 1982 sent her on a shopping expedition to look for quality mares to bring new blood to the farm. Her official title was executive secretary and pedigree consultant, and, once the renovation was completed, she shared the big main office with Lundy. Though she never received a regular salary from Calumet, her compensation would be more than ample. "I was paid a flat amount whenever I would ask for it," she once said. She also received free lifetime breeding rights to six Calumet stallions and insider prices on breeding to others.

A few months after Lundy hired Heinz he hired McGee. A taciturn woman whose passion for riding seemed to transcend all else, McGee had been friends with Heinz for several years. Before coming to Calumet, McGee, who was a year younger than Heinz, worked at an animal diagnostic laboratory, caring for mares. At Calumet her title was receptionist, though she eventually would take on responsibilities more fitting an office manager.

Though paid a rather meager salary, she, too, would reap extra benefits, including lifetime breeding rights to five Calumet stallions. She and Heinz were treated to trips with Lundy, frequently on the Calumet jet, to cities all over the world, with accommodations in luxurious hotels.

McGee was an ideal employee, tending to her boss's sometimes urgent requests in a calm manner. Despite the elaborate phone system, Lundy was in the habit of yelling his demands from his upstairs office to his downstairs staff: "Susan, there's no pop in my refrigerator. Get some, damn it."

She answered most incoming calls, taking messages and answering questions. Like all receptionists, McGee was, for some callers, their introduction to the corporation, and depending on Lundy's mood and his attitude toward the caller that introduction could be soft and reverent, like the tones of McGee's voice, or brusque and remote.

One of Lundy's business partners complained once that McGee was "unhelpful" because she was so very protective of Lundy. It was impossible to connect with Lundy without first going through McGee, who could be "great as the executive secretary for a wartime general—protective, suspicious, and tough," another friend commented. "There was a lot of red tape. You could not get through those gates unless your visit was preapproved. You couldn't just drop by to see Lundy on the spur of the moment for a Coke or a look at some horses."

If anyone complained about the reception he or she received, Lundy didn't worry. Screening calls and giving preferential treatment to some callers was all consistent with his "for me or agin' me" attitude.

In the spring of 1985, Lundy negotiated another big stallion purchase. This time it was a half interest in Wild Again, a five-year-old racehorse who had won a $3 million purse in the Breeders' Cup Classic at Hollywood Park the previous November. Wild Again's owners were Bill Allen, an insurance executive from Texas and Florida, Terry Beall, also in the insurance business in Riverside, California, and Ron Volkman, a Dallas real estate developer. At the time of the sale, the three men were partners in Black Chip Stables, named after the $100 chip in Las Vegas.

This was the beginning of a long business relationship between Lundy and Allen, who got to know Lundy through a mutual friend, A. J. Foyt. Allen would say years later that he was drawn to Lundy because he admired Lundy's philosophy of breeding "on a volume basis," which meant breeding twice the average number of mares each year to prize stallions to increase the odds of producing a superstar and to make big money. He was also impressed that Lundy had "a lot of connections" in the horse business, which would be helpful in selling the stallion's seasons.

Allen, like many of Lundy's associates, was a successful self-made man with an intriguing past. He was chairman of a public company called Academy Insurance Group and he operated other insurance-related businesses in both San Antonio, Texas, and Miami. But years before his insurance career, in the 1960s, Allen and two other men were convicted of conspiracy and mail fraud in connection with a promotion scheme to lure wealthy patrons into a Maryland country club. The government claimed the trio had per-

suaded prominent businessmen to buy lifetime club memberships for a high
fee, with the assurance that they were an elite group of 150 to 300. On the
contrary, about two-thirds of the 1,850 club members had purchased the
lifetime memberships. The men were also accused of setting up dummy
organizations and diverting membership dues for themselves. Defense lawyers claimed the enterprise was an honest one and that the defendants simply had exercised bad judgment. Allen was sentenced to twelve to thirty-six
months in federal prison. He served three months at Texarkana, with the
balance suspended on probation, and in the early 1970s, President Richard
Nixon pardoned him.

Regardless of past problems, Allen's experience in the horse industry was
charmed. He had done what most horse owners only dream of. In November 1984, he and his partners entered Wild Again, a horse he had purchased
for $35,000 in 1981, in the $3 million Breeders' Cup Classic. This was a
big gamble for a horse who had had knee problems and had won only a
few races, and by entering the race at the last minute the Black Chip partners had to pay a late-entry fee of $360,000. The odds were 30 to 1. Wild
Again won.

Calumet paid $6 million for its half interest in Wild Again—$3 million in
cash and notes, plus Lundy's typical fare of several Alydar seasons, Secreto
seasons, and a share, meaning a season every year during the lifetime of the
horse, in a stallion called Sagace.

Not only did the money for the Wild Again purchase come out of
Calumet Farm, Inc.'s general account, but Calumet-paid staffers would perform all services related to managing the stallion's career, including bookkeeping, advertising, obtaining contracts to breed, and booking of the
mares. But it was Lundy who profited most from the transaction.

The agreement called for Lundy to be Wild Again's syndicate manager
and to receive four breeding rights to the stallion plus the interest accrued
from the stallion's breeding account. The breeding rights, Lundy firmly believed, were his compensation for managing the stallion, and the account
interest was a bookkeeping fee. Yet breeding rights are what farms in the
business of breeding horses typically earn for managing a stallion syndicate;
and it was the farm that was paying the staff to do the bookkeeping. During
the next five years, Lundy would make about $750,000 from the use of the
four breeding rights, plus about $27,000 for his bookkeeping fee. It was
unclear whether the compensation in the form of stallion seasons was ever
reported to the Internal Revenue Service.

Lundy's award of these rights and his compensation in general would one day be a point of controversy. Had he used the corporate assets and his position as Calumet president to make a deal allowing him to manage the breeding career of one of the nation's best racehorses and to reap considerable financial benefits as a result? Or was he justified in taking such benefits as compensation? At the heart of the matter was a key issue during the Lundy years: what the family and the board of directors were told and not told about Lundy's deals and the money he made off the farm.

Board meetings were hardly regular events at Calumet, and records of those meetings, such as agendas or minutes, were even more rare. In the case of Wild Again, the board was informed that Lundy was the stallion manager, but Lundy never told the directors what his compensation would be. He certainly never explained that his gain in this deal would be the farm's loss. And Robey, who prepared the Wild Again agreement, would later be unable to recall a specific meeting during which he, Robey, had explained the arrangement to the heirs or its implications for the farm. Warren Wright III recalled being informed about the Wild Again purchase, but he wasn't aware of the four breeding rights or the bookkeeping fee.

By 1985, secrets had become a way of life at Calumet, from the big iron gates and the guardhouse at the farm's entrance to the paper shredder in the office and the habit of neglecting to outline to board members the financial implications of major purchases before the deals were done. There were myriad little details the heirs were not aware of, matters that appeared unimportant in the early years but later would seem suspicious, even sinister, like those breeding rights Lundy gave away in the Secreto deal. This was Calumet's biggest-ever purchase of a stallion, yet the board didn't vote on the details, nor did anyone bother to explain to the heirs the significance of the giveaway breedings. There was never a vote or discussion about Lundy's compensation of 10 percent from the sale of Calumet horses, a commission he had also taken on the Alydar lifetime breeding rights. Nor was the board privy to the additional payments he took, such as free breeding rights in several Calumet stallions. In the beginning, Lundy refused a salary, but no one grasped the advantages in not having a fixed salary, the utter freedom in taking what one felt one deserved or wanted. This was a double-edged sword, with generosity gleaming on one side and greed glaring on the other. Robey said in later years that the board of directors "had just a vague idea" about Lundy's compensation.

Then there was Lundy's penchant for creating companies, such as Maricopa Ranch, Renwar, and C.C. Air in Kentucky, as well as Southeastern Aircraft in North Carolina, and Vaca Cut in Florida. Lawyer Gary Matthews, who incorporated several of Lundy's creations, was sometimes listed as director.

Vaca Cut, for example, cropped up in the town of Marathon, in the middle of the Florida Keys, during the summer of 1985. Its initial officers were Lundy, Robey, and Janice Heinz, but in later years Robey would drop out and the company would merge with another entity, Henry Jay Contracting Company, a Matthews-incorporated Kentucky entity. After the merger the company was called Vaca Bloodstock, which sounded like an agency for buying and selling horses though no one in the horse business had ever heard of it. The Florida Keys seemed an unlikely place for such a business, and it was unclear what Vaca did. It might have been just a name Lundy gave to a company he established to own property in Marathon. There were five lots registered in Vaca's name at a place called Hawaiian Village, and in 1985 Lundy hired a contractor to build an extensive estate for Vaca's officers, including a main house made of stucco with a red barrel-tile roof, four master suites and master baths, a big pool overlooking the Gulf of Mexico, a Jacuzzi, and sauna as well as a guesthouse with two bedrooms, two baths, a living room, and kitchen. There would also be a boat dock to accommodate a captain-equipped boat. Calumet staffers began to notice Lundy's frequent trips to what they referred to as "Marathon House." Some believed he went fishing; others thought perhaps his mother spent time there and he was visiting her; still others claimed his friends were taking "wheelbarrows of cash" from Calumet to Marathon for reasons they didn't quite understand. In Marathon, his visits were noted by the locals as being quite frequent, especially for a horse farmer from Kentucky. But then, the house and estate were so lovely it would be hard for anyone to stay away for long.

The family trusted Lundy and Robey and rarely questioned the farm's operations. No one ever asked to see financial records. Warren Wright III would later testify at a trial that he visited the Calumet offices every two or three months "to say 'hi' to J.T., maybe to get a [Calumet] coat or hat."

The heirs clearly didn't know about Lundy's method of beating the odds in the breeding game. It wasn't just luck that the mares he bred to Wild Again, using his own four seasons, always produced foals. Lundy had devised a shuffle system of stallion management, which was tantamount to placing a bet after rolling the dice. It worked like this: When a horse is syndicated, the syndicate owners hold a certain number of breeding rights each year. Breedings beyond that number can be sold to anyone and are placed in what is sometimes referred to as the extended book. The syndicate owners split the proceeds from the extended book. The syndicate agreement for Wild Again called for a lottery system of choosing which mares at Calumet would be bred to Wild Again when a season holder in the extended book didn't send his own mare and opted to let Calumet choose a mare for the breeding. But nothing was left to chance. The designation of which mares were assigned to which seasons was often made after the mare proved to be in foal or barren or slipped (a miscarriage).

With Lundy's system, barren and slipped mares bred to Wild Again were routinely reassigned to the extended book. This postbreeding allocation process ensured that no unsuccessful mares were assigned to Lundy's four breeding rights. Hence he typically had four foals each year from Wild Again, which he could sell as weanlings or yearlings, or place in training. They belonged to Lundy, the syndicate manager. Meanwhile, the syndicate owners, including Calumet, lost income from their extended book by having perhaps more than the average number of barren or slipped mares. The problem was that 50 percent of the losses resulting from this system were shifted to Calumet as a 50 percent owner in Wild Again.

Warren Wright III acknowledged that the directors were informed when the corporation was planning to borrow money. Family members, he said, "signed a lot of notes" and "borrowed a lot of money." But he also said he didn't really understand what was going on at the farm. He and his siblings routinely, without review, signed legal documents presented to them by "their representatives." Sometimes they'd go to Wright Enterprises to sign them; other times, a messenger would bring the documents to their homes. While they were aware of agreeing to deals ranging from bank loans to stallion purchases, none knew or understood the financial arrangements behind the deals. No one explained to them exactly what the impact of their signatures might be—not on the farm, on the family fortune, or on their futures in general. There wasn't even a summary of Calumet's finances at the annual shareholder meeting held before the Calumet Christmas celebration each year. The Wright family would gather in the living room in the early evening, and Lundy would offer his state-of-the-company report for the previous year in five or ten minutes.

"J.T. would tell us about what horses had raced, which ones had done well," according to Warren III. "If he had done any purchasing during the year, he would tell us during some of those meetings, possibly what races he was going to be entering for the next year and which horses he felt would be good for the upcoming Derby."

Lundy and Robey took the attitude that if the heirs wanted to see a contract or review a loan document, all they had to do was ask. Robey held a few meetings in his office, he said, to report the overall debt to the family, and he circulated memos outlining how much money they had borrowed or guaranteed in the various loans. Unfortunately, the heirs didn't know what to ask, and they clearly did not understand their responsibilities for their own wealth as members of the Calumet board. They simply did as they were told, signed the papers they were asked to sign, and took what they wanted for themselves.

A lawyer asked Warren in a legal case years later if Robey requested that he sign "certain resolutions from time to time."

"Yes," he answered.

"Would they represent that it was appropriate that you sign them?" asked the lawyer.

"Yes."

"And would you accept that representation and sign what you were requested to sign?" asked the lawyer.

"Yes."

Tommy Wright, also in a deposition, said Robey "would advise us whether it was good or bad or—and it never—we never got to this—to the point where there was discussion as far as contracts or anything like that. He would just say, 'This looks good. Do it.' "

Cindy Lundy said that from time to time she had received copies of financial statements.

"Did you read them?" a lawyer queried in a deposition years later.

"Sometimes."

"Did you on any occasion find errors or inaccuracies in the statements?"

"I probably didn't because I wouldn't know enough about it to be able to know that it was wrong."

Courtenay Wright Lancaster said her brother-in-law had threatened her into agreeing with the way he was running the farm. She alleged he intimidated her and other family members "into believing that only he could manage Calumet Farm, Inc., that they should sign any document presented to them by him without question or there would be bad family and business consequences."

Lundy made it clear, she said, "on several occasions" that he didn't want her involved in the farm's operations.

Lundy and Robey longed for complete control, the kind of freedom few businessmen ever experience, the kind of independence that Warren Wright,

Sr., and his son had sought to prevent with provisions in their wills, and the kind of power Warren Sr. knew could stop the flow of a fortune to future generations. The target was the bank that managed the Warren Wright, Jr., Trust. And the best way to control the bank was to buy it.

As early as 1983, Lundy and Robey began exploring the acquisition of Second National Bank and Trust Company, the one-hundred-year-old Lexington bank responsible for the trust that controlled 62.5 percent of Calumet Farm's stock. Second National was a family-owned bank, run for many years by the locally prominent Graves and Clark families and staffed by many people who had worked their entire lives at the bank. It was a farmers' bank with a strong, conservative image, a steady 9 or 10 percent share in the Lexington banking market, and an aura of the Old South where employees and their fathers and grandfathers had worked side by side with generations of Clarks and Graveses. It was the kind of bank that inspired confidence, and clearly Warren Wright, Jr., and his advisers felt it was solid and reputable enough to protect the Wright treasures.

Robey enlisted a local financial consultant who had worked at the bank and was familiar enough with its operations to prepare a study. The purpose was to determine why it would be smart for Lundy and the Wrights to take over.

"If the bank were to be 100% owned by the Wright family," the report read, "problems involved with Calumet Farm being interfered with by the bank would be minimal. After all, if anything went wrong, the only people who would really suffer, with the exception of the Federal Deposit Insurance Corporation, would be the stockholders. . . . In addition, in 1982, the bank charged $200,000 for services as trustee of the Wright trust, and it appears that those fees in 1983 will run between $200,000 and $400,000. In the event the Wright family took over the bank, the fees could still be charged and would be tax deductible to the family but it would be more on the order of taking money out of one pocket and putting it into another. . . . There is a very real danger that the bank will be sold to someone whose involvement in Calumet Farm and the Wright family business could be much more extensive than it is currently. Ownership of the bank is entree to Calumet Farm. . . . Second National Bank is worth more to the Wright family than it is to an outside acquirer."

But by the fall of 1985, bank representatives were talking to an outsider, First Kentucky National Corporation of Louisville. First Kentucky was interested in buying both Second National Bank and Bank of Commerce and Trust Company, also in Lexington, and then merging the two. What Second

National was planning appeared beyond the scope of Robey and Lundy. Robey believed he had a commitment for rights of first refusal if the bank's controlling shareholders decided to sell or merge their interests, but the bank didn't seem to agree that such an understanding existed. One day Robey and Lundy would open the morning paper and read news of the merger. Soon after, Robey would move his Wright Enterprises office out of the bank's building to a new location.

Another way to cut the ties that bound the Wrights to the bank was simply to eliminate the Warren Wright, Jr., Trust. In the fall of 1985, Bertha Wright and her children notified the bank that the trusts created under the will of Warren Wright, Jr., were terminated, effective immediately. "The basis for termination," the letter read, "is that all of the beneficiaries have entered into agreements which accomplish the purposes of the trust. The last will and testament of Warren Wright, Jr., does not prohibit the termination and the beneficiaries have elected to so terminate."

The letter asked the bank to deliver the trust assets to Bertha Wright and her children. At this time there were still millions of dollars in the trust, whose purpose, according to the wishes of Warren Jr., was to ensure that his widow would always have an income.

The bank struck back. On September 26, it filed a complaint in Fayette County Circuit Court against the Wright heirs asserting that the trust was not terminated and could not be terminated as long as Bertha Wright was still alive. The bank's attorneys asked the court to rule on the continued validity of the will of Warren Wright, Jr.

Then, as if stoking a fire with a stick of dynamite, the family filed a motion complaining that the trustee had charged "excessive and unreasonable fees" to manage the trust. The bank had been paid $200,000 for its services as trustee the previous year, according to the claim, and in return for the fees, the heirs asserted, the trustees had done nothing but mismanage the trust assets, failing to act in the best interest of the family.

At the 1985 summer auctions bidders were still riding the fast track. At the Matchmaker auction of seasons and shares in January, a breeding right to Danzig for the 1987 season had sold for $250,000 and one to Northern Dancer for the upcoming 1985 season went for $1 million. At Keeneland's July sales, the top price set another record, $13.1 million for Seattle Slew's half brother, later named Seattle Dancer. And new investors were still entering the game, like corporate takeover artist Carl Icahn, who was part of a syndicate that bought a horse for $7 million.

But by 1985, there was a new element in the Bluegrass, floating across the land like some toxic cloud: skepticism.

A few party poopers had preached caution throughout the boom years. While everyone else was toasting windfalls, they'd mutter caveats about the dangers of fast money, hungry bankers, and overproduction. They were the ones who had read the fine print in the Spendthrift prospectus that revealed how Spendthrift's banks had forbidden it to pay dividends and how, at the time of the stock offering, Spendthrift's earnings were declining.

The horse industry was not without wise souls. A Florida breeder wrote a letter to Barnett Bank early in 1984 warning about the pitfalls of a plan to finance purchases of horses at auction. Calling it a "very poor and dangerous plan," he explained: "Imagine if an unscrupulous person wanted to borrow $300,000, but only wanted to utilize a small portion for the acquisition of a broodmare. He could easily buy a $50,000 mare prior to the sale, then bid the mare up to $300,000 without so much as raising a few eyebrows.

"Worse yet," the letter continued, "someone in the capacity as an agent could persuade an innocent buyer to acquire financing and buy his consigned mare. By manipulating the price, the agent could cause the unsuspecting buyer to purchase a mare far beyond her value. In effect, the bank would be unwittingly aiding a nefarious individual and accepting collateral of bogus value. All the time, the borrower would be innocent of any wrongdoing."

Another breeder, in the midst of the most spectacular night in Keeneland's history, July 24, 1984, told reporter Andrew Beyer of the *Washington Post*, "When this is over, most of the sellers are going to feel fortunate to have gotten out with their lives." Beyer was prescient to include the quotation in his review of that glittery eve, but his source would not allow attribution. Beyer referred to the voice of doom as "one expert"; no one would want to be connected with such outlandish pessimism.

But by the end of 1985 the skeptics were gaining an audience. Clouds were gathering, and anyone who bothered to look up from his calculator or checkbook could see the storm ahead.

9 At Calumet, 1986 was a year like any other during the Lundy era, with money flowing in and out at a fearless pace. The farm appeared as prosperous as ever, its image as pristine as its bright white fences, its reputation glowing in the eyes of bankers and deal makers, despite the gathering gloom.

In July, the industry's barometer swung wildly into a new zone. The average price for yearlings in the sales ring at Keeneland sank 24 percent below the 1985 average. The tempest some horsemen predicted as early as 1984 had come, and it was brutal.

At dinner parties, in hotel lobbies, and by the barns at Keeneland, there was still talk of hope. No one could believe the boom was over. The July sale was indicative of only the fact that the fierce competition between Sangster and the Arab sheiks had ended. Everyone knew they had achieved a truce and might even be working together on certain deals. Without their competitive thrust and speculative energy, prices were bound to slip. The dip, breeders assured themselves, would be short-lived.

But in the fall, at Keeneland's September sales, the story was much the same: prices plunged 13 percent below the previous year's average. Before the year was out, it would be even worse. At a Matchmaker auction in December, a season to Spectacular Bid, a horse that had been syndicated for $22 million, sold for a mere $27,500.

In any industry this would be a devastating drop, but in the business of thoroughbred breeding, where the lead time between investing in the product and selling it is two years at the very least, the plunge was doubly bad. A yearling that sold in the summer of 1986 was a foal of 1985 and had been conceived in 1984. This meant that the owners of the yearlings in the 1986 auction had paid stud fees at the peak of the boom. Breeders during the 1980s expected a yearling to sell for about 2.5 times the stud fee. It was not uncommon in 1984 for a breeder who had paid $125,000 for the mating that produced his 1986 yearling to sell the horse for only $50,000. On top of the stud fee, the breeder had spent at least $40,000 to raise the horse. The cost of bringing the 2,377 horses to the fall sales that year was an estimated $86 million—about $58 million for stud fees and $28 million to raise them. But the horses sold for a total of only $64 million.

Breeders at every level of the game took a bath. The atmosphere at all the sales was filled with trepidation that could turn to panic at any minute. If prices continued to fall, so would stud fees, causing the value of the horses to diminish still further. It was only a matter of time before the banks would realize that the value of their equine collateral was falling with a force as compelling as gravity. And everyone knew that when the banks called their loans, the bloodletting in this highly leveraged industry would begin.

While some horsemen bemoaned the wretched luck of 1986, others knew the crash was long in the making. And though an uncanny number of unfortunate events converged in one horrific year, the tragedy of 1986 had little to do with chance. One economic fact superseded all other reasons for the debacle—overproduction.

It was a simple lesson in supply and demand. In 1986 there were 51,293 foals registered at the American Jockey Club, up from 26,810 in 1973 and 35,613 in 1980. One reason the Bluegrass had achieved its stature as the thoroughbred capital of the world was that it had avoided overproduction during other speculative eras. But in the 1980s few breeders could resist the temptation of making big money fast. The way to do so was to meet the seemingly endless demand for their products. Short-term thinking, a 1980s trademark and a by-product of greed, was anathema to the patient, careful art of horse breeding, which is based on a long-term investment of money and hope.

As the thoroughbred market moved toward saturation, changes in the U.S. tax laws began chasing away thousands of investors, further decreasing the demand for horses. It was tough love in horse country, as horsemen were forced to face the errors of their 1980s ways while the government zapped them with a new tax structure.

When it comes to taxes, horsemen will always feel misunderstood. The problem stems partly from the government's habit of lumping all farms together for tax purposes. Every farmer shares the potential for cash-flow problems during the period between planting and harvest. There is always the possibility that at the end of the growing season parts of the crop won't be fit enough to sell. The risks are similar for crop farmers and horse farmers, but the financial planning is completely different. A farmer who takes his crop of corn or wheat to market each year has little in common with a horse breeder who must wait two to four years to make money, depending on whether the horse is sold or raced.

Horse farmers, who must continue to pour money into their crops for feed, medical care, and training before they see one cent of profit, are more like real estate developers than wheat farmers. While equine investments had become more like stocks and bonds in the 1980s, the government continued to treat them like so much alfalfa.

The government's intent in changing the tax structure was to lower taxes as an incentive to spend, and to eliminate as many tax shelters as possible. In the agriculture industry, the goal was to get rid of investors who seemed more intent on reaping profits from the tax code than on harvesting crops. The reforms delayed deductions for expenses in raising plants or livestock until the assets were productive or sold. This effectively stymied the flow of cash for horse farmers, who depended on tax benefits each year to bridge the gap between investment and earnings.

For an industry in which losses are a way of life, the reduction of the income tax rates from 50 percent to 28 percent was disastrous. While the lower rate meant taxpayers could keep more money, it also meant that the maximum tax savings from a loss was 28 percent, rather than 50 percent. With the new tax act, the horse industry effectively lost the best partner it ever had: the government.

Just as bad for the breeders was the end of the capital gains exclusion. In the old days, a horseman could exclude 60 percent of the profit on the sale of a horse and pay taxes on only 40 percent. Now there was no exclusion at all.

In attacking tax shelters, the government aimed at limited partnerships in all businesses, including real estate and gas and oil. In the horse industry limited partnerships had become almost as common as horseshoes. The racing partnerships typically bought yearlings, with profits depending on winning races. Breeding partnerships, considered much safer investments, usually involved the purchase of shares in mares or stallions, and profits came from the sale of the foals that resulted from the breeding. Brokers liked to use oil and gas analogies, saying that the racing deals were like wildcat drilling whereas breeding partnerships were more like developmental operations.

Before tax reform, losses from these partnerships, which were classified as passive investments, could be used to offset taxes on active income, such as salaries. Now, investors had to be actively managing a horse in order to write off the losses of owning that horse, or a piece of the horse, against other income. Investors who simply bought a horse, like any other commodity, at arm's length in a partnership could write off the losses only against income from other passive investments, though most investors wouldn't have enough passive income to take advantage of the losses.

Horsemen felt the government didn't realize how dependent the horse business had become on outside capital, how much the $16 billion industry had expanded in recent years, how many jobs its boom had created, and how much its exports had contributed to the balance of trade. Furthermore, the horse industry took a double hit. Other industries such as real estate that had poured new money into the Bluegrass for the past fifteen years were also dramatically affected by the government's crackdown on tax shelters.

The impact of the reforms on equine investors was not unlike the reaction of a stable of horses to the smell of burning straw. Even before the new laws took effect, accountants and consultants were steering their clients away from the horse industry. Because of tax reform and the weakened energy markets, the sound of crisp new money and the sight of Texas tycoons and their fat wallets were conspicuously absent at the 1986 sales.

Also gone was the dramatic dueling between the Maktoums and Sangster. Their apparent bidding truce put a lid on prices at the 1986 sales, meanwhile moving the auction results off the front page and onto the back pages of the sports section. As this free advertising was taken away from the industry, its ability to reach new markets diminished.

Even Spendthrift Farm, the horse industry's great experiment on Wall Street, was falling apart. Spendthrift had been the top seller at Keeneland's yearling sales eighteen times, and its flashy owner Leslie Combs II was as much a part of the landscape as Calumet's white fences. But that year, Spendthrift posted a loss of $9.4 million on revenue of $33.4 million. By November, its stock, which had sold at $12 a share in 1983, was fetching a mere $2 on the American Stock Exchange; it had nearly collapsed under the weight of a debt load of about $57 million. Once a glittery inducement to come to horse country, Spendthrift was now a red flag waving bankers and investors away and sending a message of restraint to breeders.

Spendthrift was only a few miles away, but no one at Calumet saw the red flag. In 1986, there was no evidence of restraint.

Alydar's stud fee had reached the high range of $250,000 to $350,000, depending on whether the contract included a guarantee of a live foal, and his breeding schedule was booked solid for the following spring, with at least seventy mares. The farm's managers were so confident about the stable's financial viability that they even loaned $8.1 million to the Wright Enterprises partners, up from a $6 million loan to them in 1985.

In the summer Calumet purchased a half interest in yet another stallion, Mogambo, a three-year-old racehorse whose sire, Mr. Prospector, had produced two outstanding runners, Fappiano and Conquistador Cielo. Mogambo was running in the Derby that year, and Lundy sealed the deal a day or two before the race. The seller was Lundy's Connecticut friend Peter Brant, and the price, undisclosed at the time, was about $10 million. "He's one of the best looking horses I've ever seen in my life," Lundy said, waxing enthusiastic to the press. "He reminds me of Alydar."

The agreement called for Lundy to manage the stallion and gave him— not the farm—four free breeding rights each year. He paid for the horse with a $6.5 million note and his favorite form of currency: seasons in Alydar. Considering the $350,000 rate at the time, Lundy had to give away ten seasons to come up with a value of $3.5 million. The note was to be paid in five installments of $1.3 million plus quarterly payments of interest.

In a truly unspectacular run, Mogambo came in tenth at the Derby that year. But by then Lundy was on to the next deal—one that neither Warren Wright nor Mrs. Markey would have ever considered. He and Robey mortgaged the farm for a $20 million loan from Mutual Benefit Life Insurance Company of Newark, New Jersey.

Mutual Benefit, which had begun lending to horse farms in the early 1980s, now had a loan portfolio of nearly $50 million to thoroughbred operations in Kentucky alone, including an earlier loan to Shadowlawn Farm, the home of Lundy's friend Harry Ranier. A lawyer for Mutual Benefit would say years later, "Calumet had the reputation as a money machine. Calumet was the absolute king. You could just look at it and know, this is a safe loan."

The deal was struck shortly before the Keeneland sales, and the loan, secured by a first mortgage on the farm, was guaranteed by the Wright family. Years later, Courtenay Wright Lancaster would say that Lundy pressured her into signing the $20 million note and that he or one of his minions "misrepresented the nature of the document" she was signing.

By the close of Calumet's fiscal year on September 30, debts were piling up. In addition to the $20 million owed to Mutual Benefit, the stable owed more than $13 million to Second National Bank, which was now CommerceNational Bank, about $25 million to Citizen's Fidelity, a considerable amount to Brant for the Mogambo purchase, and for the Secreto deal several million was owed to the heirs of Luigi Miglietti, who had died from a massive heart attack in January.

• • •

Lundy's buddy Lasater was indicted in October that year with eight others on cocaine-related charges following a three-year government probe. In December he was sentenced to two and a half years in prison. (Governor Bill Clinton, in a controversial move years later, pardoned Lasater.) Meanwhile other relationships in Lundy's inner circle were picking up speed. Bill Allen, the Wild Again partner, would be doing deals with Lundy periodically for the next four years or so. Gary Matthews, the tax attorney whose license plates on his Corvette one year read "Go For Mo," seemed to be spending more and more time at Calumet and would soon be appointed Calumet's chief financial officer. From the East Coast came New Jersey bloodstock agent Bob Fox, who with his partner Alan Krutchkoff stayed many days and nights at the Calumet guesthouse. And there was New York businessman Robert Perez.

Perez, a stout, bespectacled construction contractor from Queens, bought and sold horses from and to Calumet for several years during Lundy's regime. He bred his own mares to Calumet's stallions, including Alydar, and had an eighty-acre farm, Lucy Grace Farm, near Otisville, New York. He seemed genuinely passionate about horses and racing, which might have been one reason for his bond—by all accounts a strong one—with Lundy. But Lundy was likely intrigued more by Perez's rags-to-riches story and his power.

Perez came to America in 1960 from Argentina, where he grew up a block from the racetrack. In the states, he got a job as a construction worker in Queens, but several years later, in the autumn of 1966, was arrested for allegedly heading a ring of Argentinean nationals who were swindling insurance companies. The next year he pleaded guilty to defrauding two insurance companies and was sentenced to two and a half to five years at Sing Sing prison in New York. Perez, who stalwartly believed he was wronged, wrote letters to judges and to his attorney, claiming he had been guaranteed probation in exchange for pleading guilty. Still, he served time from July 25, 1967, to November 22, 1968.

Shortly after his release, he started Perez Utilities, which did construction work for utility companies. In the late 1970s he bought an old New York company called Sicilian Asphalt Paving Company, and by 1986 he operated Perez Interborough Asphalt Company, one of the largest minority-owned firms in New York, employing hundreds of workers and snatching up millions of dollars in city contracts.

Perez would have another brush with the law, though a minor one: an arrest for allegedly attacking and chasing a city inspector who went to Perez's Brooklyn office to deliver a summons. The summons resulted from a complaint by an elderly woman who couldn't get out of her apartment because Perez's workers, on one of his street projects, had blocked the door. Perez later told a reporter he thought the inspector was wearing some sort of wire or bugging device for the government. (The case was eventually dismissed.)

Perez's career as an owner and breeder of thoroughbred horses was trouble free. One of his accomplishments was the mating of his mare Lady Abla to a son of Northern Dancer, producing a filly named Cupecoy's Joy, one of the best ever bred in New York State. For a while, Perez co-owned her with Robert deFilippis, the owner of a Queens-based construction equipment company and at one point a business partner of alleged Genovese crime family associate William Masselli. But that association didn't deter Perez and didn't stop Cupecoy's Joy from a spectacular racing season in 1982 that included winning a prestigious New York race called the Acorn. "After the Acorn," *The New York Times* reported, "nobody is about to underestimate Perez and his filly again."

Lundy connected with Perez through New Jersey agent Fox, who had also brought Lundy together with another East Coast pal, Bob Libutti. By 1986, Fox, whose thickset build resembled Lundy's, was so much a part of Calumet that people talked about the farm's business possibly being operated out of Fox's Teaneck, New Jersey, offices.

Fox raced, bought, sold, syndicated, and appraised horses; he arranged financing for horses with major lending institutions; and he was a writer and video producer. But of all his enterprises, his work with Calumet was the most profitable and probably the most fun. Fox made a small fortune during these years just by repeating one simple sentence, "I can get you in at Calumet; J.T. will listen to me." In later years Fox's résumé, listing breeders he had done business with, read like a directory of Calumet deals in the 1980s. A clever, quick-witted man, Fox loved to talk and tell stories. He was a networker by nature, connecting breeders and trainers nationwide to Calumet. He also did many of the appraisals of Calumet horses.

It was Fox who negotiated numerous sales of lifetime breeding rights to Alydar, and Fox who arranged for the $20 million in financing at Midlantic, the New Jersey bank. His agency, Associated Thoroughbred Projects, S.I., made $50,000 per sale from Calumet plus money from the buyers. On eight sales the agency made about $640,000, and Midlantic paid Fox another $500,000.

Fox and his partner, Alan Krutchkoff, had clearly found a profitable niche at Calumet. Their agency would make about $5 million from commissions for arranging the Calumet deals, and they would travel all over the world with Lundy, often on the Calumet jet and the Calumet expense account. These were some of the perks for bringing business to Lundy, Fox would say years later.

Fox had known Lundy since the mid-1970s but didn't begin to do business with him until 1984, the year he was producing, directing, and writing promotional videos for the Thoroughbred Racing Association. Ted Bassett, president of Keeneland, suggested that Fox talk to Lundy, who might be interested in videos to promote Calumet. Out of that came *Queens of Calumet*, a video about Calumet's five finest mares. The same year he put together a promotional video about Senator Jumonville's deal to breed Alydar to the quarter horses.

Fox had other ventures in the 1980s such as creating a video-cassette subscription sports magazine, and he also helped start Thoroughbred Broadcasters, with the assistance of Lundy and Calumet. This company televised several big races, including the Arkansas Derby in 1985, and later produced *Racing Across America*, a cable program.

Fox could be charming and endlessly funny, though some of the Bluegrass elite found his aggressive, fast-talking style offensive and claimed Lundy had "let the fox into the chicken yard" the day he opened the Calumet gates to the New Jersey deal maker. Still, to be with Fox was like being in the high school in-crowd. He was a born raconteur with the animated style of a stand-up comic. He could make a fast-food cashier feel important by asking questions about his or her work, telling stories, or sending compliments to the kitchen. Lundy took to him like a magnet. He seemed to revel in Fox's ideas and the way Fox connected him to an array of investors. And Fox had an outrageous, lewd side to him, like Robey and others in Lundy's circle.

When Lundy and Fox sat in the main office at Calumet, howls of laughter sometimes could be heard all through the building. Lundy would be laughing at Fox's latest joke or some outrageous gossipy tidbit about another breeder or some funky name Lasater might have given a horse. One such name was Somfas, which according to Fox meant "Sit On My Face And Spin." Once at a restaurant, Lundy was laughing so hard over one of Fox's jokes he had to leave the table.

The joke, in Fox's words, went like this: "Two guys are pissing next to each other in a public restroom. One's a big tall Texan, and the other is about three and a half feet tall with a big pecker. The Texan looks over and sees this big pecker on the little guy, and the little guy says [in an Irish brogue], 'I see that you're lookin'; you're lookin' at my big dick, and I know you'd like one too. Well I'm a leprechaun, and I can be granting you three wishes. First you'd be wanting a big dick; then you'd be wanting the women for the big dick; and then the money to get the women. Well, now, if I was to be granting you these three wishes, which I can do, I'd be likin' just one wish of me own first. I'd like to take this big dick of mine and ram it up your ass.' The Texan agrees that he wants the wishes and if this is what he has to do to get them, he'll do it. So he bends over, and they go at it. And afterward, the little guy says, 'So tell me, laddie, how old are you?' The Texan says he's thirty-five years old. 'You mean to tell me that you're thirty-five years old and you still believe in leprechauns?' "

That joke so tickled Lundy that he named a 1986 colt So Tell Me Laddie, and in future negotiations for sales of seasons, if there was a long silence during a meeting or some sort of stalemate, Fox would suddenly say to the buyer, "So tell me, laddie, how much would you be willing to pay if we throw in [this or that season]." At that point Lundy would burst out laughing.

Until the late 1980s, it seemed that anywhere Lundy went so did Fox, who referred to his friend and associate as "Chief." It was easy to trace their globe-trotting steps by looking at the ads Fox and his partner Krutchkoff produced for ATPSI. At least half the photos were taken during trips with Lundy.

The full-page ads ran in the *Thoroughbred Record*, a trade publication owned then by Peter Brant, and no one in the Bluegrass had seen anything like them. The ads typically featured a photo of Fox alone or with friends or with Krutchkoff in a foreign country or at a famous U.S. landmark. Beneath the photo was a poem, short essay, or adage. More than anything, the ads symbolized the horse industry's wild ride during the 1980s—and Calumet's in particular.

In the September 1986 ad, Fox stood in a terry-cloth bathrobe on the balcony of the Mandarin Hotel in Hong Kong. In October 1986, he knelt in snow on a Colorado mountain ridge. "We worked hard to reach the top," the ad read. Under the picture was ATPSI's list of accomplishments, including the fact that his agency "arranged over $65 million of thoroughbred financing and sold over $60 million in thoroughbred stock in 1985."

In the November 1986 ad, Fox, in clothes covered with racecar emblems and team patches, was standing at Daytona with racecar drivers Richard Petty and A. J. Foyt. The message: "In 1986, we booked hundreds of mares to our special group of stallions. It's now time to think of the 1987 breeding season. We can make some wonderful things happen with live foal seasons, foal sharing arrangements, season swapping and other very creative deals. We specialize in Affirmed, Alydar, Fast Gold, Highland Blade, Judge Smells, Mogambo, Raise A Cup, Sagace, Secreto, Secret Prince and Wild Again. If you want to breed a fast horse, deal with people who really know high speed."

10

The end of a bull market is like the last move in a game of musical chairs. When the music stops, some player inevitably ends up with nothing. The trick to sustaining an image of bullishness is to enhance the value of what you have, to pretend as long as possible that the music never stops and the chairs are never taken away. After 1986, this was the challenge in the horse industry, and Calumet had the tricks.

By 1987, the Bluegrass was saturated with economic worries: how to keep stud fees from plummeting; how to prevent banks from calling loans; how to continue bringing in cash from investors, from banks, from fellow breeders. But Lundy was able to accomplish the impossible. Over the next two years Calumet would borrow millions of dollars from several big banks, expand its list of clients, and create new partnerships. While banks, high-rolling investors, and limited partnerships seemed part of an era that ended with the fall of the gavel at Keeneland in July 1986, the boom times lived on at Calumet.

What Calumet management was able to pull off during the next several years was partly a tribute to the power of the Calumet name. Bankers, insurers, and investors associated it with words like "reputable" and "stable," "rich" and "superior." There was something glamorous about having Calumet listed in a loan portfolio. The farm's Camelot-like aura made it seem invulnerable to the vagaries of economic cycles, and there was the mystique of Alydar, whose stud fees were still in the range of $250,000 to

$350,000. For Calumet to have money problems seemed about as likely as the lights going out at the Smithsonian because of unpaid electric bills.

But behind the postcard-perfect façade was a repertoire of schemes and shams using the Calumet name in ways that would have horrified Warren Wright—ways that propped up the prices of Calumet horses and seasons and kept the farm's financial statements looking good.

Equine lenders required documentation such as appraisals and year-end financial statements to assure them that a farm had a healthy income from sources such as stud fees and yearling sales. They often consulted auction records to assess the market values of horses, which in turn would give an indication of how much an owner could charge for a stud fee and, hence, the potential earning power of the horse and the owners. As long as a stallion's progeny were selling well at auctions or privately, its owners could maintain high stud fees. Using transactions that were possibly fraudulent, Calumet made certain that these records were as spectacular as its very name.

The smoke-and-mirrors deals would include hyping prices of the offspring of Calumet horses at auctions with the help of bidders that were either friends of Calumet or entities owned by the friends. This tactic enabled Calumet to maintain high values for its equine collateral as well as profitable stud fees. Hyping auction prices was a handy, short-term way to get cash out of banks, establishing a market value for horses used to secure loans. There would also be instances of sham private sales of horses, allowing the farm to include the impressive prices on its financial statements; favors done for a bank executive who was later convicted of money laundering; and, among other questionable practices, the use of a company legally unrelated to Calumet to borrow money used by Calumet and secured with Calumet-owned collateral.

The schemes allowed Calumet to maintain a nearly constant flow of cash. And from 1987 on, the need for cash was endless. In the last three months of the year, for example, the farm was borrowing $200,000 or $300,000 every few days from Citizen's Fidelity, eventually adding up to about $8 million for the quarter. Though cash flow is always a challenge for horse breeders, Calumet's cash needs were so intense that even participants in some of the sham deals were baffled. Said one such individual years later, "I didn't question it as I didn't want to know anything that didn't concern my immediate deals. I just didn't want to know, but I have never seen such an appetite for cash."

To be sure, by 1987, the Calumet way of life included excessive prices for equine purchases, globe-trotting, sweetheart deals, and debt payments. But offsetting that were high prices for Calumet-bred horses, high stud fees—especially Alydar's—and the bank loans. Calumet was like a pool that could never fill no matter how much water was poured into it. It didn't take an expert to surmise there might be a leak.

Lundy would later claim that the effort to bring back Calumet's glory years, as he'd promised the family he would do, was more expensive than anyone anticipated. Still, it was clear he was paying himself handsomely to keep this promise. His sales commissions and his free breeding rights could be viewed as a blatant conflict of interest amounting to nothing less than self-dealing. Former Kentucky lieutenant governor Steve Beshear would someday claim in court that "any time a choice came of whether to benefit J. T. Lundy or Calumet Farm, J. T. Lundy won out." Regarding the breeding rights he took for himself, Lundy said, in court, "I didn't think about Calumet being entitled or not. I think I'm entitled."

Lundy appeared to buy into the belief that you're smart as long as you're aggressive and playing the game. And as long as you're doing deals and making money, you're in the game. It was an attitude indigenous to the 1980s, when deal making became the essence of running a business. At Calumet, business was no longer a simple matter of buying or selling a horse; business now meant structuring a deal that might involve cash, a loan, a swap, notes, seasons, stallion futures, lifetime breeding rights, any combination of goods and services and favors. And the more deals Lundy made, the more successful he felt, much like a trader on the floor of one of the stock exchanges. Even as the equine industry faced tough times, Lundy's attitude, his friends said, was that he had always worked a deal in the past, he'll work a deal again. But soon he would have too many balls in the air.

With the wisdom of hindsight, some Calumet insiders would say that 1987 was a turning point. If the farm had stopped borrowing money and cut expenses then, its prosperous image might have matched its condition. Instead, Lundy, like an addicted gambler who just couldn't leave the table, made deals that took the farm deeper into the red. The problem was that the schemes, typically devised to bring in quick cash, were shortsighted moves. Hyping prices, for example, at auctions or even at private sales was a formula for disaster. Clearly, as long as the progeny of Alydar, Secreto, Wild Again, and other Calumet horses sold at good prices, those who had breeding rights, like Lundy, could make big money each year and the stallions could be appraised at high values. But, in the long run, the more inflated the prices, the further the values would fall as the equine market continued its dive. And if the value of the horses used as security for bank loans was hyped, then both borrowers and lenders would be in a precarious position if there was ever a need to sell the collateral to pay back the loans.

Lundy, it seemed, had an unstoppable urge to take risks, always moving closer to a dangerous edge. As the son of a tenant farmer, he had lived most of his life on the fringes outside the blueblood world of Fayette County waiting for his moment to enter. Now he had arrived, to a secure, enviable spot, sitting on top of a pot of gold. He had all the money, power, and prestige a person could want. In early 1987, he was even able to get a power of attorney giving him legal access to his wife's fortune. He could now if he so desired borrow money and use her considerable assets as collateral. A financial statement in early 1987 valued the net worth of the five Wright heirs—Bertha and her children—at $251 million. The following year assets of the Lundys, husband and wife, would be assessed at $55.4 million.

But all the power and money he had wasn't enough. He wanted more of both. It appeared that in 1987 Lundy had made a choice, though likely an unconscious one, to take his world, including Alydar and Calumet Farm, to the edge of destruction.

Each summer there are three major U.S. sales of yearlings, two in Lexington in July and one at Saratoga Springs in August. The first sale is presented by Fasig-Tipton Kentucky, a subsidiary of Keeneland's arch rival Fasig-Tipton Company, a New York–based auction company that started in 1898. In 1987 the average price at this sale plummeted 28 percent below the year before.

The second auction is Keeneland's "select" sale, which offers the finest yearlings Keeneland will sell that year and some of the best bloodstock in the world. This was the one that in the early 1980s had evolved into a multinational, standing-room-only orgy of deal makers, bankers, and fat wallets. By 1987, potential bidders and spectators had no problem finding seats. There was already talk about the good ol' days, as everyone stared at the big board and recalled that moment in 1983 when there weren't enough spaces to register the highest bid. It seemed so easy then, like money rolling out of a slot machine in response to every quarter spent. Now it was rare for a seller to get a price as high as $400,000 or $500,000.

In 1987, the average price for the "select" yearlings was down 9 percent from 1986 and off more than 50 percent from the average on the Monday night in 1984 when euphoria filled the Keeneland sales pavilion. Two nights later, at the second part of the sale, there was a glimmer of hope with the average price rising 2 percent over 1986.

Then, in Saratoga Springs, at the third big sale, optimism, like a familiar, pleasing scent, wafted through the sales arena as 194 yearlings sold for a total of $46.9 million. The average price rose 29 percent over the year before, and suddenly recovery seemed more than just a matter of hope. With this sale, all the dips in Lexington began to seem like a bad dream. But unfortunately for the rest of the industry, this wasn't an auction that could be used as an economic indicator. Because of Calumet, the percentage of increase was a bit illusory.

In February, a group of investors headed by Peter Brant had agreed to buy 62.5 percent of the outstanding stock in Fasig-Tipton. The group, which included J. T. Lundy, paid $16.5 million for their stake in the New York–based company. Fasig-Tipton, host to the yearling sales every August in Saratoga Springs, owned more than 40 percent of Fasig-Tipton Kentucky. It also owned horse sales organizations in California, Florida, Louisiana, and Maryland; a thoroughbred training center in Maryland; a horse appraisal service in New Jersey; an insurance group with branch offices in New York and Florida; a lending organization, Thoroughbred Equity Company, known as TECO, in New York; a public relations firm in Lexington; a bloodstock agency in New York; and 50 percent of Stallion Access, a stallion futures exchange much like Matchmaker Breeders' Exchange.

The rivalry between Fasig-Tipton and Keeneland for the highest quality in horses, buyers, and sellers was as much a part of the horse business as the Derby parties in May. And Fasig-Tipton's new owners wanted to turn up the heat on Keeneland.

One strategy was to focus more attention and resources on the Fasig-Tipton Saratoga auction than on the Kentucky sales. This meant persuading sellers who planned to sell in Lexington in July to wait and bring the best of their crop to Saratoga in August. Thus the horses at the Fasig-Tipton Kentucky sale were not as high quality as usual, and they sold for less, bringing the average of that sale lower than expected and having the effect of focusing even more attention on the Saratoga sale. But what really put a spotlight on the Saratoga sales ring that year was Calumet.

For one of the few times ever, Calumet planned to sell some of its legendary bloodlines at public auction. The star-studded group included four Alydar daughters, three Alydar sons, one Secreto filly, and two sons of Triple Crown winner Seattle Slew. One of the sons of Seattle Slew was a son of

Alydar's mother, Sweet Tooth, making him a half brother to Alydar and all the more valuable.

But something peculiar happened on the first night of the sale. All but two of the successful bidders who signed the tickets for the Calumet horses were friends and associates of Calumet and Lundy, and the horse vans that waited near the barns at Keeneland to transport the yearlings to their new homes took all but two of the Calumet yearlings back to their old Kentucky home: Calumet. Calumet had never intended to sell the horses—just to create the appearance of a sale in order to give the horses an official market value.

Thanks to the generous bids for the Calumet horses, including $2 million for Alydar's half brother and $1.5 million for the other Seattle Slew colt, the average price that opening night was more than 70 percent above the average on the first night in 1986. Though the world might have been impressed with such results, insiders knew there wasn't all that much to celebrate. Without the Calumet sales averaged in, there was an increase, but one of barely 11 percent. Instead of the sweet scent of success, astute horsemen smelled the sour whiff of scandal.

Four of the Calumet sales tickets were signed by Axmar Stables, a company based in West Palm Beach, Florida. The stable was a division of a family partnership called Axmar Investment Company, consisting of Robert P. and Betty G. Marcus, along with Betty's mother, Mrs. Akston—hence the name Axmar. Betty Marcus might be remembered best in the business world as the individual who inspired the Q-tip. When she was only six months old her father invented the cotton swab and started a small business which her husband developed into a much larger enterprise before selling it in the 1960s.

Sometime during the late 1970s, the Marcuses decided they wanted to get into the horse business and so created Axmar Stables. It was not a farm; it had no training facilities, no stables, no breeding facilities. It was a company established for the purpose of buying thoroughbreds and racing them to increase their value enough so their progeny would bring a lot of money at the annual sales.

Because the Marcuses knew little about the horse business, they called a friend at Fasig-Tipton for advice. He referred them to a bright young accountant with an expertise in equine accounting practices, Marc Rash.

The Marcuses retained Rash, in the beginning, to explain to them and to their own accountants the nature of equine accounting. When Rash went to work at Executive Bloodstock Management, the parent company of Matchmaker Breeders' Exchange, the Marcuses began using that group for various services, including advice on the buying and selling of thoroughbreds.

The Marcuses knew Rash was friends with the president of Calumet—a connection that increased their confidence in his ability to advise them on purchases of fine horses. It was only logical that he told them about Calumet's plan to offer horses to the public for the first time and that he would suggest they might want to purchase some of the horses and even enter into a partnership with Calumet.

Before the sale Mrs. Marcus was given a number for each of the Calumet horses, a number beyond which she need not bid in order to buy the horse. "I had advisers. They told me we have looked at the horses, they are worth x amount, don't bid more than that, and I didn't," Mrs. Marcus said later in a deposition.

The number was Calumet's reserve price, that is, the lowest bid the stable would accept in order to sell the horse. Not all horses have reserves, and the auction house doesn't always know the reserve. But if there is a reserve of which the auction house is aware and bids don't reach it, the horse is officially unsold. The audience of bidders often doesn't know that the horse didn't sell because the auctioneer and his spotters behave the same way in either case. The spotters are told through the auctioneer's signals that the reserve hasn't been attained. Then a fake bidder will chime in and win the bid; the spotter will take the sales ticket to the bidder or to the auction house office, all the while going through the motions of an official sale. Only later will auction records show that the horse didn't sell. If the final bid reaches or goes beyond the reserve, the horse is considered sold and the permanent records of the auction house will show who signed the ticket as the buyer and the amount of the successful bid.

Reserves are an acceptable practice at horse auctions—as at most public auctions—to give sellers the right to refuse a sale if the price doesn't give them the desired return on their investments. The reserve is effectively the asking price. The difference between the auctions and other retail sales is that buyers at auctions don't know the asking price.

Sellers and their agents at thoroughbred auctions are permitted also to bid on their own horses. The auction houses disclose such practices prominently at the front of their sales catalogs, under the section "Conditions of This Sale," noting, for instance, that according to the laws of Kentucky, "the right to bid in this sale is reserved for all sellers, including their disclosed and undisclosed agents." Though buyers prefer to bid against other buyers, the industry, with this type of disclosure, seems to take the point of view that the buyer is effectively warned that some sales might be bogus and that, if so, there is nothing illegal or fraudulent about these practices. What happens after the sale and how the auction records of sale prices are used are not the concern of the auction house, and, in an unregulated industry, the deals surrounding the auctions are private matters between buyer and seller.

Still, the system is fraught with the potential for fraud when these practices are applied to artificially inflating the prices of horses in prearranged deals. The horse auctions of the 1980s provided not only an opportunity to buy the best of the breed but also a perfect front for all kinds of deals. The auctions could, for example, be used as conduits for funneling cash from one corporate entity or individual to another. A seller might run a horse through the ring for a certain price, then after the sale make a secret sale for less money and kick back a portion of the difference, splitting it between himself and the buyer. Sometimes mock buyers, typically friends of the seller, would bid up prices to give the horses an established market value—printed in the auction house records—that could then be used in financial statements for a multitude of purposes, such as borrowing money from banks. The sales results could also be used to promote a stallion's career by showing how much his progeny were worth. And the higher the price of a stallion's offspring, the more the owners could charge in stud fees. Bankers during the 1980s often used the auction records as a way to assess the value of horses pledged as collateral for loans. It was at this intersection of horse trading and banking that questionable, potentially fraudulent transactions would occur.

At Saratoga that summer, there was no problem in reaching the reserves set on certain Calumet horses because friends of Calumet in the audience would serve as shills, bidding up the price to the amount Mrs. Marcus was told. Mrs. Marcus didn't need to fret about the prices she was paying because—trusting her advisers, Marc Rash and Barry Weisbord—she believed the horses were worth what she bid and that buying Calumet horses was a unique opportunity to improve Axmar. Besides, she had a partner in the deal—Calumet—and she was told that if the yearlings did not prove to be profitable, Calumet would compensate her for any loss through breeding rights to Calumet stallions.

At the sale, Mrs. Marcus bought an Alydar colt, later named Joymaker, for $600,000; Alydar's half brother and a Seattle Slew son, later named Calumar, for $2 million; another Alydar colt, Full Blooded Boy, for $475,000; and an Alydar filly, Lady Hoolihan, for $300,000. Six other Calumet horses were sold that night. The sales tickets for four of them were signed by friends of Lundy's or Rash's, for $1.6 million, $285,000, $1.5 million, and $310,000. But the signers of these tickets hadn't really bought the horses. It would look highly suspicious for Axmar to buy all the horses, so friends pitched in to give the appearance of buying the horses that were then, after the auction, given back to Calumet to be added to the new Calumet-Axmar partnership along with the horses Mrs. Marcus had purchased.

Calumet wanted the partnership to have a value of $10 million. Its contribution would be the four sale horses plus one more horse—a package it would say had a value of $5 million. Calumet would also pay all board, feeding, and breeding expenses for the partnership horses. To pay Axmar's 50 percent stake in the partnership, Mrs. Marcus borrowed $3.3 million on Axmar's line of credit at Citizen's Fidelity Bank and wrote a $1.625 million promissory note to Calumet for the rest. The money she borrowed from Citizen's Fidelity was immediately returned to the same bank to pay down Calumet's huge Citizen's Fidelity debt. The partnership would commence without any operating capital.

Mrs. Marcus said later, in a deposition, that she was told this was a "no-risk situation" for her and "that we would go into a partnership in which Calumet, who needed cash at the moment, they were having a cash problem, would be able to get cash from us in return for the purchase of—we would get horses. They would get cash. It was a finite deal. At the end of a certain period they could regain the horses and we would get our cash. . . . They had two purposes, they needed cash and they wanted somehow to retain the bloodstock." With Calumet supplying the horses and paying the expenses, it looked like a good deal for Axmar. There was also the Calumet name, which Mrs. Marcus later said was part of what she counted in the value of the partnership: "That's a value just like the name Mercedes has a value vis-à-vis a Ford."

But Calumet-Axmar was a better deal for Calumet than for Axmar. Calumet received the cash it needed in the form of an interest-free loan from Citizen's Fidelity via the Marcuses, who would be responsible for the interest. And without spending a cent, Calumet was a 50 percent owner in a $10 million partnership—a stake it could use as collateral to borrow more money.

Calumet paid Bob Fox's ATPSI $100,000 as consignor for the Calumet horses at the sale. The Marcuses paid Rash, as their adviser, and, though the Marcuses later claimed they didn't know it at the time, Calumet also paid Rash at least $100,000.

As for the Calumet horses that Axmar bought that August, four years later the values looked like this: Full Blooded Boy, which Axmar bought for $475,000, would sell for $6,500; Joymaker, a $600,000 Axmar buy, for $20,000; Calumar, bought for $2 million, would sell for $105,000; and Lady Hoolihan, a $300,000 purchase, for $200,000. A package of horses valued at $3.375 million according to the sales records at Saratoga—a package that would soon become part of the collateral for a big loan—would be sold at a sale four years later for a total of $331,500, a drop of about 90 percent.

In the upper echelons of Calumet management, Rash seemed to be the new favorite. A tall thirty-nine-year-old man from Philadelphia, Rash could always devise a way to get what Lundy wanted: millions of dollars in cash and connections with banks. He was even squeezing out Lundy's longtime adviser Robey.

Robey had laid the legal groundwork for Calumet's new order through the incorporation of the farm, the creation of Wright Enterprises, and the composition of the board of directors and executive committee. He took credit, too, for the Secreto deal, and he negotiated for Calumet, along with Fox, on the Midlantic deal.

But by 1987, Robey was spending less and less time with his high school buddy. He kept his distance from the Axmar deal, which was orchestrated almost entirely by Rash, as well as other partnerships Lundy would soon create. Although he was still collecting his percentage of gross receipts coming into Wright Enterprises and the farm, he was no longer absorbed in scouting for deals and deal makers for Calumet.

Robey could ill afford associations with any potentially dicey deals. In August, Kentucky governor Wallace Wilkerson appointed him to the coveted post of chairman of the Kentucky State Racing Commission, and as the man in charge of regulating thoroughbred racing in Kentucky, Robey had to, according to legislative edict, "maintain the appearance as well as the fact of complete honesty and integrity" in the industry. Kentucky's governors typically gave this job to people who had helped arrange contributions from the state's wealthy horse breeders. Calumet, for example, had contributed a healthy amount to the governor's election campaign. It was also a post tainted by past chairmen who had resigned amid cries of regulation by special interest, allegations of kickbacks, hidden ownership of tracks, and conflicts of interest.

But it wasn't only Robey's new duties and a desire to dodge conflicting and coinciding interests that diminished his involvement at Calumet. The stable's needs, defined mainly by an unrelenting desire for cash, seemed beyond Robey's reach. His regional network of influential people wasn't big enough for Calumet anymore. While Robey had once seemed like the cleverest man in town, Lundy had new idols now, those with connections outside the Bluegrass.

To be sure, Fox was still on the scene and still traveling with Lundy. In 1987, the ATPSI ads would picture Fox at the Vatican, on the Great Wall of China, in front of a castle in northern France—"Can we interest you in a castle?"—in Greece, and in Egypt.

But back home, Lundy would sit in the Calumet office talking to his new buddy, Rash. On the phone or in person they'd chat about deals, while lawyer Matthews sat waiting in a chair at the foot of the sweeping staircase in the lobby. Suddenly Lundy would come to the top of the stairs, lean over the wood railing, and say to Matthews, "C'mon up here and bring that legal pad of yours with you."

A bright fast-talker, Rash fit the profile of someone Lundy would listen to and learn from. Nobody knew equine accounting better than Rash, who was part of the package of expertise that came with doing business at Equine Capital Corporation, a loan broker affiliated with Matchmaker Breeders' Exchange. Barry Weisbord, the whiz kid entrepreneur who devised Matchmaker, was a shareholder and officer of ECC along with Rash and others.

ECC's president was Michael Lischin, a lawyer who had worked briefly on Wall Street and at an Albany law firm whose clients were mostly banks. In the 1970s, a man Lischin had met on Wall Street told him that Fasig-Tipton was starting the Thoroughbred Equity Company, or TECO, which used horses as collateral for loans as a way to augment its auction sales. If a bidder couldn't afford a horse, the new company would loan money based on the value of the horse the money was used to buy. Lischin took a job at TECO, whose shareholders were largely Wall Street brokers and investors, and soon became its president. But in 1987, when Carl Icahn, Peter Brant, and the new group, including Lundy, took over Fasig-Tipton, Lischin left to start two new equine lending companies, ECC and Matchmaker Financial Corporation. Calumet would do deals with both, though mostly with ECC.

The timing was perfect for loan brokers like ECC. No longer were bankers holding up the arms of bidders at Keeneland and Fasig-Tipton, hoping for pricey purchases so they could swoop in, loan money, and fatten portfolios. ECC's plan was to be the liaison between breeders and reluctant bankers, to find banks willing to lend to an industry with an unstable market. An all-purpose firm, ECC would find the banks, do the appraisals on the collateral, file all necessary documents, and review insurance policies. Its clients were often horse breeders who were having problems paying their debts. ECC was willing to go where banks feared to tread, sometimes loaning to breeders teetering dangerously close to bankruptcy.

ECC would arrive, like a traveling medicine wagon in the nineteenth century, at the gate of the troubled farm and offer to work with the farm to prevent bankruptcy. It helped that ECC had a strong relationship and a very big credit line with Citizen's Fidelity Bank and Trust in Louisville. ECC borrowed the money from Citizen's and reloaned it to breeders. From the breeder, ECC obtained a promissory note, collateral in the form of horses, and a handsome fee.

Lundy saw the broker's ability to persuade banks to lend to breeders as a valuable resource, as was ECC's bulging credit line with Citizen's Fidelity, where Calumet was wearing out its welcome. For the next several years, ECC, Rash, and Rash's own companies, MMR Equine and Gray Cliff, would all play a large role in Calumet's quest for deals and money. It was ECC's Lischin who would connect the farm to a big-time New York bank. Rash would arrange sales of Calumet horses and seasons, such as a four-horse sale for $1.2 million to Robert Perez in New York. And Lundy would give Rash considerable power within the Calumet kingdom. Once after Rash sold $450,000 worth of seasons for Calumet, he wrote a memo to Matthews that offered a glimpse of that power. Rash informed Matthews that a Texas breeder would be sending Matthews a check for $450,000 worth of Alydar seasons. The check, which Matthews would receive on Monday morning, would be made payable to Calumet Farm, Inc. Rash wrote, "I need $50,000 of this money to help with interest payments regarding Calumet horses and also to help J.T. with some interest payments. Please have Calumet Farm issue MMR Equine Services, Inc. a check for $50,000 representing a purchase of a 1/9 interest in Secreto/Lady Abla colt. I can then use this money in MMR Equine Services, Inc. to make the interest payments. Thanks for your help in this matter."

July, August, and September were prime times for Lundy's deal making. Because of the yearling sales in July and August, this was traditionally a time when horse traders quickened their pace, but for Calumet, there was the additional factor of a fiscal year that ended on September 30. By then, tax-related deals had to be locked in, and because several large bank loans had originated during those months, interest payments came due about that time, too. Each year the frenzy seemed to escalate, and 1987 was no different.

The day before the Saratoga sales, Lundy sealed yet another stallion deal. He purchased a half interest in Capote, a sleek, black racehorse who was a son of Triple Crown winner Seattle Slew and who had earned $714,470 in his racing career. Calumet paid $6.4 million for its 50 percent stake, and Lundy agreed that if Capote won the Eclipse Award that year, Calumet would pay $1.6 million more, or a total of $8 million. Lundy paid for the deal mostly with his favorite currency: Calumet stallion seasons. Lundy received four annual free breedings to the horse, and gave six additional free seasons to Capote each year to Bob Fox and his ATPSI partner, Alan Krutchkoff; trainers Wayne and Jeff Lukas; and two horse agents, Phil and Norman Owens.

The week after sales at Saratoga, Riggs National Bank, the largest bank in the District of Columbia, loaned $20 million and extended a $3 million credit line to a new partnership called Calumet-Gussin No. 1. Most of the money went to Calumet.

Calumet's partners in this deal were Renwar Corporation, a subsidiary of Calumet, and two Maryland businessmen, Fred Gussin and his father, Paul. The Gussins began investing in thoroughbreds around 1984 after selling Gussini's, their shoe store chain. They hooked up with Calumet through Bob Fox.

The partnership's connection to Riggs came from the Gussins, who had banked at Riggs for their shoe enterprise. Riggs's chairman, Joe Allbritton, who already had personal investments in the horse business and loved the races, decided Riggs should become the banker of choice for the thoroughbred business, especially in Kentucky. The Gussins, meanwhile, knew through Fox that Calumet was hungry for cash.

With the $23 million Riggs loan, on August 20, 1987, Calumet-Gussin bought from Calumet Farm, Inc., the assets pledged to the bank as collateral for the loan, including top-pedigree broodmares May Day Eighty, My Juliet, Lady Abla, Davona Dale, Before Dawn, Sugar and Spice, 'N Everything Nice, and Baby Diamonds. The deal also included a 25 percent stake in the Calumet stallion Criminal Type, three Calumet racehorses, several weanlings and yearlings, and $1.5 million worth of seasons each year to the Calumet stallions. The partnership was supposed to pay the bank $4 million a year in cash on the note, which was payable in about five years. To make payments, the partnership would sell the offspring of the broodmares, certain horses in the package, and some of its annual allotment of stallion seasons. Both Calumet and the Gussins guaranteed the loan, but any shortfalls or deficiencies, the agreement said, were the responsibility of Calumet. Though a different set of transactions, the deal was similar to the Calumet-Axmar partnership in that Calumet formed a partnership and received millions of dollars as a result.

The cash flowed out of Riggs and to Calumet via the partnership's purchase. Before it was deposited in the general account, however, Calumet records show that Lundy collected a $150,000 fee on the transaction. For its usual role as facilitator and matchmaker, Bob Fox's ATPSI made about $500,000.

Around Labor Day that year, Lundy, under Robey's legal guidance, acquired more power than ever over the fate of Calumet. This maneuver began on August 5 when a state judge put an end to Lundy and Robey's hope of legally wresting control of Calumet from the corporation's majority shareholder, CommerceNational Bank, by terminating the Warren Wright, Jr., Trust. After a two-year deliberation, the judge said the intent of Warren Jr.'s will was to provide Bertha Wright net income only—and never the principal—from the trust for the rest of her life. The remainder would be left to whomever she stipulated as beneficiaries in her will. Warren Jr.'s will, the judge wrote in his opinion, implied that the trust, with its spendthrift clause, could not be terminated.

Though disappointed, Robey saw a way to parlay the loss into a victory and perhaps in the process to regain some of his power in the Calumet hierarchy. Robey knew that the judge's decision didn't prevent the Wright heirs from proceeding with their 1985 counterclaim, in which they accused the bank of mismanaging the trust and charging exorbitant fees. So Robey informed the bank that the family would drop the suit if the bank agreed not to interfere with the management of Calumet Farm. The family, at Robey's behest, signed papers to dismiss the claim. Then Jacob Graves III, the bank's representative on the Calumet board and Lundy and Robey's only colleague on the board's executive committee, stepped aside to be replaced by another banker, who would be perhaps less assertive with Lundy than Graves had been. Years later Bertha would say, "I remember being told by someone that Second National [CommerceNational in 1987] had agreed to leave J.T. alone and let him run Calumet Farm and that another banker would replace Jacob Graves III on the Board of Directors of Calumet Farm, Inc., which did happen." Timothy Cone, a Lexington lawyer who worked for the Wrights at this time, added, "I understood that J.T. was going to have a freer hand in running the farm. This was intended to attempt to resolve previous bad feelings which J. T. Lundy had toward Mr. Graves."

By the end of the fiscal year, with the help of the $3.3 million from Citizen's Fidelity via the Axmar partnership and the millions from Riggs via the Calumet-Gussin partnership, the farm was able to whittle down its $25 million Citizen's Fidelity debt to $12 million and to send $2 million to a bank in the Netherlands Antilles for a payment on the Secreto note.

But more was owed on Secreto and the other stallion purchases, millions more to Midlantic, Mutual Benefit, CommerceNational, and now to Riggs. Millions were also due in premiums on the equine insurance for the stallions and the pricey broodmares. Then in 1987 the state of Kentucky joined ranks with those seeking money from Calumet, claiming the stable owed $916,230 in back taxes on sales of Alydar lifetime breeding rights from October 1982 through February 1985.

Perhaps it was this debt load that compelled Lundy to allow Calumet to borrow millions more from Citizen's Fidelity. On October 1, the first day of the new fiscal year, Calumet borrowed another $2.96 million from the Louisville bank to pay down its mortgage. Four days later, an additional $350,000 was wired to Calumet's general account from Citizen's. A week or so later it was $489,000 and $15,000. On October 20, the farm borrowed $400,000 from Citizen's. In November, the loans went like this: on the sixth, $250,000; the tenth, $500,000; the eighteenth, $2.33 million. On December 3, the farm borrowed $500,000, and on December 14, $400,000. By the spring of 1988, the total of Calumet's debt to Citizen's Fidelity would be up again, to a whopping $25.48 million.

11 As Calumet's debt increased, so did Alydar's workload. By the late 1980s, most thoroughbred stallions were servicing fifty or sixty mares during the 135-day breeding season from mid-February to early July. The average cover rate, that is, the average number of breedings it takes for a stallion to impregnate the mare, was in the range of 1.6 to 2.5. In

1988 Alydar, whose rate was about 1.8, covered ninety-seven mares, which meant he made nearly two hundred trips to the breeding shed, an above-average workload.

His breeding season that year began on February 12 with a mating to a Calumet mare named Best Decision. On the fifteenth he resumed with two mares, Honor Guard and Too Bald. He mounted one mare on the sixteenth, two on the seventeenth, and one on the eighteenth. Then after a day off, he worked every day for two weeks, most of the time servicing two or three mares a day. In March and April he was bred dozens of times, covering three mares a day. The season was full until the end of June; in July he worked only a few days.

Most stallions will cover an average of one mare a day. Twice a week they'll cover two a day, and every few weeks they'll get a day off. Alydar had the 9:00 A.M./ noon/ 3:00 P.M. schedule on many days, plus sometimes an appointment at 7:00 P.M. Alydar also mounted several mares during the autumn months, the Southern Hemisphere's breeding season. His last breeding of 1988 was on November 6.

Whether or not breeding a stallion so many times was abusive was a much-discussed topic among those who knew of Alydar's schedule. Some believed such excess couldn't be good for the horse, though it wasn't necessarily abusive. The problem was the horse might lose interest and just burn out right in the middle of the season. When former Calumet farm manager Melvin Cinnamon was asked about the practice during a magazine interview, he said his preference was to limit the stallion's books to thirty-five to forty-five mares. "Their semen is a lot stronger and they cover the mares better," Cinnamon said.

Other horsemen viewed Cinnamon and his ilk as simply old-fashioned. Stallions liked their jobs, and it couldn't hurt them to breed a few more times every year. From Lundy's point of view, the more times a stallion was bred, the better the odds of producing a superstar. To breed often was "like shooting a shotgun instead of a BB gun," Lundy once said. And the more times a stallion was bred, the more money came into the stable.

While the rest of the equine market was suffering from decreasing demand, recent victories of Alydar's progeny helped to steady the market for Alydar seasons. With Lundy and his friend Fox marketing the stallion's breeding prowess, Alydar's semen was as sought after as gold or oil. His stud fee, in the context of the industry-wide slump, defied the laws of gravity. At the Matchmaker public auction of seasons in January that year, a right to breed to Alydar for one season sold for about $240,000. Two months before, at Matchmaker's November Selected Sale of stallion shares and seasons, a lifetime breeding right to Alydar had sold for $1.5 million.

One of Lundy's first acts as Calumet president had been to double Alydar's stud fee for a mating with a guaranteed live foal to $80,000. In 1983, he raised it again, to around $125,000. In 1984, the fees ranged from $175,000 to $225,000, depending on whether the contract included the live foal guarantee and whether the farm was charging insider prices for long-time clients and friends. In 1985, the fee was as high as $450,000, though the average price was $350,000. In 1986, it slipped to a range of $215,000 to $380,000; then to an average of $310,000 in 1987, and to about $250,000 in 1988.

By 1988, Alydar was a superstar stud. With sons and daughters earning millions of dollars at the track, he was the industry's second-leading sire. His reputation soared in 1987 when his son Alysheba won both the Kentucky Derby and the Preakness, the first two races of the Triple Crown. In 1988 at age four, Alysheba won the Horse of the Year award in the category of Champion Older Horse, and soon he would be the world's leading money winner with nearly $7 million. At the same awards ceremony in late winter of 1988, another Alydar son, Easy Goer, was the Champion Two-Year-Old Colt. In 1986, Turkoman, a son of Alydar, had won the Champion Older Horse award. Among the champion fillies Alydar had sired were Miss Oceana, Clabber Girl, Althea (Champion Two-Year-Old Filly in 1983), and Alydaress (Champion Three-Year-Old Filly in Ireland). These were tremendous accomplishments, especially considering the range of competition in the 1980s compared with earlier decades. When Bull Lea was the sire of champions, the number of thoroughbred foals registered at the Jockey Club each year was in the range of 5,000 or 6,000—5,696 in 1938 when Whirlaway was born, for example. The year Alysheba was born, there were 49,244 registered foals.

The feats of Alydar's progeny also drew some attention to Lundy's philosophy of high-volume breeding and to Heinz's ability to put together a good stallion book each year. Unfortunately for Calumet, the stable owned very few of Alydar's big money winners.

And despite the stallion's popularity and the apparent advantages of Lundy's the-more-the-better theory of breeding, to push so many Alydar seasons and offspring onto the market was a shortsighted strategy that would soon prove self-destructive. Regardless of whether it was ethically wrong to work Alydar so hard, Lundy's methods were economically devastating, eventually causing a market glut. And with an oversupply of Alydar fillies and colts, his stud fee could fall despite the performances of his progeny.

By 1988, the excessive breeding of Alydar was beginning to falter even as a short-term strategy for bringing in cash. His workload at the 1988 rate indicated he was bringing bushels of cash to Calumet, as much as $20 million or $25 million a year. These were the numbers often repeated in the press and in casual conversations during the public sales or over dinner at the Thoroughbred Club in Lexington. And indeed there had been years like that. But by 1988 Alydar's earnings were dwindling, despite his stepped-up schedule.

This was another reason that Alydar had to work so hard in 1988 and every year from then on. Because Alydar seasons had become a form of currency for Calumet, more and more seasons already were committed at the beginning of each breeding season, thus diminishing the number of income-producing seasons available. Numerous investors owned lifetime breeding rights to Alydar, and there were the seasons committed in stallion purchases, such as the ten pledged in the Mogambo deal. Seasons were used to pay interest on loans, wages, and even bills for horse feed. The vet Dr. Alex Harthill received an Alydar season as a bill payment. The only way to keep the cash flowing was to increase the number of seasons sold each year, which meant more work for Alydar, an eventual market glut, a fall in the price Calumet could charge for Alydar's stud fee, and an inevitable decrease in the value of Alydar himself. And because there was ultimately a limit to the stallion's capacity, the farm would soon begin to leverage seasons into future years. Then, if stud fees decreased, as they inevitably would, satisfying consumers of stallion futures would require the farm to somehow compensate for the loss of value, either by paying money or promising additional matings with Alydar or another Calumet stallion.

Someday it would be clear that Calumet was overpledging seasons to breeders and bankers who had no idea that the arena of Aldyar investors had become so vast. Calumet's management of Alydar was beginning to resemble the movie *The Producers,* in which dozens and dozens of investors buy the same 50 percent stake in a theatrical production.

William Monroe Wright (1851–1931)

Warren Wright, Sr. (1875–1950)

(right to left) Elizabeth Arden, Prince Aly Khan, and Lucille Markey at a party in the Calumet log cabin

ABOVE: Gene Markey, c. 1950

LEFT: Leslie Combs II, 1947

A Markey Christmas greeting: *(left to right)* Gene Markey, Lucille Markey holding Timmy Tammy, and Charles Rankin

Margaret B. Glass and Whirlaway, 1943

Main residence at Calumet

Aerial view of a portion of Calumet

Calumet Farm office

Alydar and his trainer, John Veitch, 1978

LEFT: Bertha Cochran Wright, 1991

RIGHT: Warren Wright, Jr., 1954

J. T. Lundy (*above left*) at the 1984 yearling sales, with John Fernung, one of Lundy's partners in purchasing a 1,000-acre Florida farm from Arkansas businessman Dan Lasater

RIGHT: Lyle Robey

BELOW: At the Keeneland yearling sales, July 1985, a half-brother of Triple Crown winner Seattle Slew sells for $13.1 million.

Alydar's stall door

Alydar's grave

Henryk de Kwiatkowski, the "count of Calumet,"
standing in a Calumet barn, May 1992

12

In 1988 Calumet continued to dance its way into the American banking community and past the scrutiny of the Wright heirs. As if lulled into a romantic state by a tune conjuring up sentimental images of past glories, everyone—the bankers, the trustees, the family—agreed to most everything the farm's representatives wanted. No one was willing to say no to Calumet or to question why the farm couldn't get enough money, why it needed even more than the nearly $100 million it had already received from Mutual Benefit, Citizen's Fidelity, CommerceNational, Midlantic, and from Riggs, via the Calumet-Gussin partnership.

Early in the year, Rash told the Marcuses that Calumet needed cash yet again and wanted to use the horses in the Calumet-Axmar partnership to obtain a loan from IBJ Schroder Bank and Trust Company of New York. Schroder was the U.S. commercial banking subsidiary of the Industrial Bank of Japan, the world's fifth-largest bank. Since 1982 it had loaned about $25 million to horse breeders and owners.

Rash and ECC president Michael Lischin first linked the Wright heirs and Calumet to Schroder. Lischin had brought business to Schroder through his job as head of TECO, the financing arm of Fasig-Tipton. Now he and Rash were colleagues at ECC, which was brokering loans for Calumet. Schroder knew all about Calumet and its owners. By 1988, it had extended a $3.2 million credit line to the Wright heirs as well as a $1 million short-term loan to Calumet for insurance premiums. In their research before granting the loans, Schroder officers had flown to Lexington to meet with Lundy, who once greeted them wearing a Hawaiian shirt. Sitting in his office drinking soda pop, Lundy would point to the portraits on his wall and talk about the stable of champions and its bright future. He'd regale them with Alydar's breeding prowess, and with stories about the stallion's feisty personality, like the time Alydar bit him in the chest. "That damn horse was trying to spite me for something," he told the bankers.

The Schroder officers asked around the horse business and the banking community about Calumet's reputation. "Everything was excellent," one officer later said. "It was one of the premier farms in the country and pretty much what you had heard about the farm at that time, a lot of great winners, and so forth." A 1987 interoffice memo at Schroder showed the value of the farm as follows: "On a cost basis, Calumet has a net worth of $33.9 million. However, when restated at current market value, the net worth of the farm increases to $226 million after allowing for the effect of income taxes." And as additional assurance, the memo noted that "the family does not withdraw funds from the farm."

Now Rash was talking with Schroder about a $3 million loan to Calumet, using the horses in the Calumet-Axmar package as part of the security. Mrs. Marcus, as 50 percent owner, agreed to this "in reliance on representations of Marc Rash that Schroder would make a separate loan to Axmar for $2 million on the same terms as the loan to Calumet, secured by the same collateral, the horses of the partnership." She would use the proceeds to pay off Axmar's $1.625 million note to Calumet.

It seemed an appealing offer to the Marcuses, who could use the proceeds to pay their debt to Calumet without having to use their own cash. But later there would be much disagreement over what had happened in relation to that loan, especially about what Rash had promised the Marcuses in exchange for the right to use the partnership horses as collateral. In the end, Calumet got its $3 million loan, but Axmar never received its money. Using a partnership consisting of horses with inflated values, Calumet had managed to get more than $6.5 million in cash from two banks—Citizen's Fidelity via Mrs. Marcus, and now Schroder.

At the Fasig-Tipton sales in Saratoga Springs that summer, the average price for yearlings fell 16.6 percent to $201,419. The gross sales total, $36.05 million, was 23 percent below 1987 and the lowest since 1982. Based on the theory that what makes a good horse sale is the quality of the horses, the promotion, and the credibility, this was an abysmal event. Buyers complained that the quality of the yearlings was not as high as usual, and worst of all, in a business where perception is everything, Fasig-Tipton had a credibility problem.

As prospective buyers toured the barns behind the sales pavilion during the days before the sales, examining horses and scribbling notes in the margins of their sales catalogs, many skipped the stalls housing Calumet horses. Some breeders had noticed the year before that several horses Calumet appeared to sell had left the auction in Calumet vans and were now the property of a Calumet partnership. The Calumet way of selling horses at auction seemed to be: sell them and keep them. By 1988, word was out that the legendary stable had rigged certain 1987 sales of its yearlings, and distrust hovered in the air like smog.

What happened at the Fasig-Tipton Kentucky sale in Lexington that July didn't help blot out the past. The sale brought a 13 percent increase in average price over the previous year, compared with a 28 percent decrease the year before, and the leading consignor in gross sales receipts was R.S.L. Sales Agency, co-owned by Lundy's son, Robert. Successful bidders of R.S.L.'s offerings included some new companies on the scene—such as Zoonis Management, a Bob Fox entity.

A month later in Saratoga, the Calumet-Gussin partnership was the leading seller in terms of gross receipts. With Calumet Farm acting as its agent, the partnership sold eight yearlings for $3.9 million. But prices were well below those of the year before, and to wipe away any suspicions, John Finney, the chairman and chief executive officer of the auction house, was compelled to tell the press, after the sale, that the Calumet horses "were clearly on the market here. . . . They went to perfectly customary, creditable buyers, and the prices clearly reflect the market reality."

Meanwhile, in another part of the country Calumet was cooking up some new deals. Four days after the Saratoga sales, the *Houston Business Journal* ran a half-page display announcing Calumet's latest coup in the banking community. Headed by "Calumet Farm" and the Indian chief logo in devil's-red and blue, the announcement read:

$20,000,000 Revolving Credit Facility
$15,000,000 Term Loan
Financing arranged by
FIRST CITY, TEXAS
First City Bancorporation of Texas
First City National Bank of Houston

Despite the state of the thoroughbred industry and Calumet's bulging portfolio of debt, First City trumpeted the addition of the legendary farm to its list of new loans. The final agreement called for a $50 million revolving line of credit as well as the $15 million loan. First City and Calumet were a perfect match. Calumet's cash needs meshed well with First City's equally pressing need to drum up new business.

First City, the fourth-largest bank in Texas, was about to enter a new era when Calumet signed on. In 1987 the bank had failed, one of many Texas banks brought down by the heavy burden of bad loans resulting from plummeting oil and real estate prices in the mid-1980s. But First City didn't close its doors. The Federal Deposit Insurance Corporation allowed the bank to continue operating while seeking investors to buy and reorganize it. The government would loan investors money to cover estimated losses, so investors, as if bidding on a contract, submitted their proposals. The winner was Robert Abboud, a Chicago banker, and his investment banking partner, Donaldson, Lufkin and Jenrette Securities Corporation.

Abboud, a hard-charging banker with an abrasive style, had a reputation as an ultraconservative lender but with a history of diving into territory where others feared to venture. In the 1970s, Abboud, armed with his Harvard M.B.A. and more than a decade of banking experience, orchestrated a stunning turnaround for the deeply troubled First Chicago Corporation. But during the 1980s, he was fired twice: first as chairman of First Chicago, and then as president of Occidental Petroleum Corporation. In his 1987 book *Money in the Bank,* Abboud defended his philosophy of conservative lending practices and blamed his dismissal from First Chicago on the board's inability to resist the quick profits of risky loans.

Abboud began his crusade to bring First City out of the ashes in 1987. To help him, he brought along another Chicagoan and banker named Frank Cihak to be First City's vice chairman. Cihak also became one of J. T. Lundy's pals.

Like his Kentucky friend, Cihak, once described in the *Wall Street Journal* as looking like a Chicago Bears lineman, had a beefy physique, and, like Lundy, he loved to talk for hours on the phone. Cihak was a former amateur boxer who grew up in an orphanage on Chicago's South Side, the toughest part of town. A cigar smoker who seemed to suck in the entire room with one inhalation, Cihak exuded the toughness of a backroom deal maker.

Until the mid-1970s Cihak had worked at First Chicago as a commodities lender, and then became involved in the financing and management of some small midwestern banks. In 1984, Cihak's focus shifted to Tennessee, which was suffering from the impact of more than a dozen bank failures. Cihak and a few other investors created a new holding company that financed the merger of the failing Butcher Bank of Commerce, of Morristown, Tennessee, and Southern Industrial Banking Corporation. He then became the CEO of the new Bank of Commerce.

Cihak got into the horse industry, by most accounts, during the 1970s when Bunker Hunt, the Texas oil magnate and horse breeder, hired him as a financial consultant to help restructure Hunt's debt and consolidate dozens of loans. Hunt was supposedly indebted to Cihak for this help and so teamed up with another businessman to back Cihak in an Illinois bank. Hunt also connected Cihak with a group of Illinois horse breeders who served as Cihak's conduit to many more horse traders, including Lundy, in the late 1980s. But before that he hooked up with an eager, resourceful entrepreneur named Lloyd Swift. It was through Swift that Cihak learned about the horse industry, 1980s-style.

Swift, then a six-foot peroxide blond, was a horse farmer from Missouri whose smooth, fast-talking style was more suited to Wall Street than the Midwest. Swift had bright ideas about horse partnerships and a surefire plan for making money.

His scheme called for buying mares at cheap prices and syndicating them at inflated values, sometimes selling ten units each for the price he had paid for the entire horse. He bought one mare for $42,000 and syndicated her for $300,000; another, purchased for $30,000, was syndicated for $550,000. He held informational seminars, replete with a slick video of his own horse farm, to inform prospective investors about the potential windfall in owning a piece of a horse. He acquired some clients while playing golf at a big resort hotel in Scottsdale, Arizona. With the energy of a religious zealot and the charisma of a practiced salesman, he found wealthy people who practically begged him to take their money to buy them an ounce of horseflesh and turn it into gold.

It was a no-lose proposition for his clients, who were typically wealthy retirees. They believed they could recoup their investments plus a profit after the racehorse had proven itself at the track. Because Swift arranged for them to borrow money from a bank, they didn't have to put up their own cash, and returns on the investment would pay off the note. Even if the horse broke down or wasn't a winner, the investors, who were mostly in high tax brackets, could benefit from big tax write-offs.

Swift would take care of breeding, racing, and selling the horses, while his investors could sit back and wait for the money to roll in. As it turned out, though, Swift allegedly didn't spend all that much time developing the horses; he was too busy selling the syndications and rounding up clients. If investors did earn money, it was from the proceeds of more syndications— for example, syndications of the progeny of their horses—not necessarily from the performance of any horse. As with a classic Ponzi scheme, the profit came out of the scheme, not the value of the actual commodity.

For Swift's plan to work, he needed a bank willing to finance his investors. The Bank of Commerce, under the leadership of Cihak, became that facilitator, and by January 1986 it had financed horse syndications involving at least fifty-four investors in eighty-eight separate transactions, amounting to $3.6 million, disbursed directly to Swift. Only one loan for the purpose of investing in Swift's syndications was ever refused. Cihak later denied he ever got a cut of the syndication proceeds.

Late that year, the FDIC examined these eighty or so transactions and learned that the money was loaned to one person, Swift, as opposed to individual borrowers—a questionable move though the FDIC apparently never brought charges. Investors, however, did.

In the fall of 1987, shortly before Cihak took a new, highly visible job at the big Texas bank, a group of investors in Arizona filed a suit against Swift and others, including the Bank of East Tennessee, the new name of the bank Cihak once headed. The investors, who by now had defaulted on their notes, claimed they were defrauded of hundreds of thousands of dollars in deals that violated securities laws and the federal racketeering law. The case was subsequently moved to Tennessee, where Cihak's name turned up frequently in documentary evidence during the fact-finding process called discovery, but by then the statute of limitations in the state of Tennessee prohibited plaintiffs from adding Cihak to the list of defendants.

Defendants claimed the investors were sore losers smarting from the recent market crash that had left them with assets with a depleted value. Outraged, the investors argued the horses' values were so inflated to begin with that the slump in the equine market was immaterial.

At the heart of the case was the question of whether the bank knew it was being used and whether it participated in the alleged swindle, so the plaintiffs' attorneys worked hard to demonstrate a strong link between Swift and Cihak. In the process, they uncovered many documents, including Swift's personal journal in which he wrote that Cihak advised him to "sell, sell, sell" more horse syndications despite the fact that Cihak was "really worried about [the] FDIC."

Certain exhibits offered a chilling glimpse into other horse dealings of the era. Of particular interest was a letter exposing how a classic swindle in the horse industry works. The letter was allegedly written by Swift and addressed to Cihak, and referred to transactions involving Alydar seasons as an example. Though undated, it was clearly written before Cihak's appointment to First City.

The letter says clients "foreign to the horse business" can be drawn into a scheme in which they pay inflated prices for thoroughbred horses while certain "silent partners" skim money off the deal. Horse appraisers, the letter says, are bribed so they anoint the horses with greater value than they are worth. The partners, including a horse farmer, an insurance agent, and a thoroughbred horse agent, might also overcharge investors for equine insurance.

The four major "ingredients" to the swindle, according to the letter, were a "bloodstock agent with access to major stallion shares; owner with quality mares and working knowledge of Kentucky and farms; insurance agent with horse representations with major equine company; and access to wealthy clients foreign to horse business who need tax benefits."

The letter also details formulas for milking investors: "1) major shares in stallions are always offered on terms but can be bought considerably lower for cash. . . . Sometimes deal is structured where farm selling share will not directly sell at lower price but will give agent buyer an extra breeding season in another stallion that agent can sell season for cash and split with silent partners. Non-traceable in share transaction.

"2) share in Alydar can be sold in $1.6 million to $2,000,000 range retail with bona fide appraisal from certified agents. Appraisers are given small breeding season by agent as incentive to certify high appraisal. Alydar share can actually be purchased for $1,200,000. Either $400,000 or [unreadable, possibly $800,000] depending on retail price is profit split by silent partners."

The letter explained the ways in which the silent partners make money. Among them: "Seasons are sold in stallion by bloodstock agent each year. Group pays commission and this fee is split as profit for silent partner group, usually at end of breeding season. Usually at least one breeding bonus from owning share is kept by silent partner group and another at time share is eventually sold. Can mean as much as $500,000 extra for silent group. . . . Agent also usually charges purchase[r] of each year's season a finders fee commission in addition to seller paying commission. This also goes into silent partner pool."

The letter, which was authenticated at the trial, introduced into evidence, and blown up on a big board for the jury to see, concluded that this process was a "very well guarded business," "common practice" in the horse industry, and "non-traceable because of the way it is transacted unless it is contested in court thru discovery."

In court testimony, Swift admitted he had written the letter to Cihak to warn him about an investment Cihak had made in a certain thoroughbred, though the name of the horse was never revealed. Swift also testified, however, that he never sent the letter, and Cihak denied ever receiving such a letter.

When Cihak arrived at First City, the controversy over what he and Swift had supposedly done at the Bank of Commerce hadn't yet erupted. Though the fourteen Arizona plaintiffs had filed their suit, it would not begin to have reverberations until the case was later moved to Tennessee. Eventually the FBI would initiate a probe into horse partnerships, paying particular attention to the situation in Tennessee.

Abboud quickly appointed the enterprising Cihak to First City's second-highest post. Almost as fast, Cihak allegedly became involved in fraudulent practices, such as paying Swift thousands of dollars in consulting fees out of First City's coffers and taking some for himself. In one instance, First City paid Swift $61,500, which was deposited in Swift's account at Worth Bank, one of several Illinois banks partly owned by Cihak. Nine days later, $40,000 was transferred from Swift's Worth account to Cihak's account at Citibank in New York. Another time, Swift received a $40,000 consulting fee, of which $30,000 made its way back to Cihak. In yet another transaction, out of a $90,000 consulting fee paid to Swift, Cihak allegedly received $45,000. Among other things, he would someday be accused of illegally falsifying financial information related to loans to Swift.

The president of Calumet Farm met Cihak through the same Illinois horse breeders who had introduced Cihak to Swift. These were Cihak's partners in a lifetime breeding right to Alydar, though no one outside Calumet knew about Cihak's stake in Alydar because the breeding right was listed under the name Triple C Thorostock.

Lundy and Cihak seemed to hit it off instantly. For Lundy, Cihak fit into the Calumet scheme of things as well as a saddle fits the contour of a horse's back. Lundy admired Cihak's ability to rise above his hardscrabble past with a toughness that propelled him into powerful positions. They shared a lewd and raucous humor and even had some deal makers in common, such as ECC. During this time, for example, as much as $1 million flowed from Calumet to First City through ECC, supposedly for some sort of tax deal for Cihak.

Perhaps most of all, Lundy and his advisers appreciated Cihak's style of lending. As Robey once said, "Cihak had this ability to borrow big sums without committees and stuff. That had a sort of appeal about it."

One of Cihak's first big loans was to Calumet Farm. The loan emanated from the energy department of the bank—perhaps because Robey, Lundy, and Wright Enterprises had contacts in the Texas oil business from previous investments—and totaled almost $32 million. For the next three years, Calumet was now obligated to pay First City $750,000 every fiscal quarter, with the final payment due November 1, 1991. The collateral included Alydar and seven other stallions plus a number of broodmares. The Wright heirs signed a document guaranteeing the loan.

With the new cash infusion, Calumet paid off its debt to Citizen's Fidelity (which now totaled $25.48 million), sent $6 million more to the Miglietti estate to whittle down the Secreto debt, and used $40,000 to get rid of a Wild Again note to one of the former partners of Black Chip Stables.

First City banked on Calumet's reputation and its appearance as a reliable financial performer. The farm's financial statements and appraisals showed Calumet had stallions whose manes seemed to be sprinkled with diamonds. For Calumet to connect to First City, a big Texas bank with $14 billion in assets and with a friend of Lundy's in the number two post, was a fantasy come to life. Over the course of the next year, Calumet would borrow several million more from First City, bringing the total Calumet debt load to a monumental $44 million by the end of fiscal year 1989.

Lundy put the finishing touches on Calumet's fiscal year with a highly questionable transaction that made the farm look even more solid to the financial community while giving his Miami friend Bill Allen some nice tax breaks. In late September Lundy sold four broodmares for $3 million to Allen: twenty-two-year-old Spring Sunshine, twenty-one-year-old Moonbeam, twenty-three-year-old Royal Entrance, and thirteen-year-old Lucinda Lea. Allen agreed to pay $500,000 for each of the older mares—a generous price considering that one of the mares had not produced a foal since 1985 and another had been barren since 1986—and $1.5 million for Lucinda Lea.

After they had agreed on terms and prices, they met with attorney Matthews to wrap legal paper around the arrangement. Matthews, a neat, compact man with a nervous, fidgeting manner, was Calumet's "cleanup man." Lundy made the deals and Matthews gathered loose ends, applying the finishing touches. Since late 1987, Matthews had been gaining ground in the Calumet power structure, as a tax expert and a liaison with Calumet's commercial lenders. Taxes were clearly his specialty. After graduating from the University of Akron Law School and practicing law for four years at a Pittsburgh law firm, he was a tax manager for a big accounting firm, Alexander Grant and Company. From 1982 on, Matthews, while at Stoll, Keenon, and Park, did some work for Calumet, often referred from Robey, who had worked at the same firm. Then, after Robey became chairman of the state racing commission, Matthews's Calumet workload increased. One of his first major deals was the 1987 Calumet-Gussin partnership. From then on, he usually negotiated the loan covenants and terms of Calumet's numerous loans from commercial banks. By 1988, Matthews was so involved with Calumet that he resigned from the Lexington law firm to take a new post as Calumet's chief financial officer. Matthews literally filled a void. Lundy was frequently out of town, and lenders couldn't always find him when they wanted to. Even when he was in town Lundy was sometimes inaccessible. "It was really difficult to get him to communicate with the bankers," said one insider. "He didn't like to do it and would even physically hide when they'd come to the farm. [Gary] fronted for him." An accessible CFO inspired a lot more confidence than an absentee president.

On the day of the meeting with Allen, Matthews, in his typical efficient style, pulled his legal pad out of his briefcase, placed his pen flush against the side of the pad, adjusted his thick-lensed spectacles to a firm spot on the bridge of his nose, and began asking the usual questions. "What exactly is it that you want to do this time?"

As a tax expert, Matthews knew a few tricks, legitimate schemes regarding the horse industry, mostly involving ways to accelerate depreciation, the times of the year to make big purchases, and when a big sale might help. But Lundy had a habit of putting his own spin on things, to the frustration of both Matthews and Robey. Matthews wrote Lundy memo after memo about the mounting debt service, the unpaid insurance premiums, Calumet's dwindling resources, and the dangers of short-term "Band-Aid" remedies. Lundy would wait until shortly before an interest payment was due to begin to figure out a way to get the money; then, if necessary, he'd resort to selling future seasons in Calumet's stallions, sometimes two years in advance, to come up with the money. The shoot-from-the-hip management style supposedly made both Robey and Matthews nervous.

Allen told Matthews he wanted to make the deal with Calumet "for tax reasons." But he wasn't sure he'd need all four broodmares to get the tax benefits he sought, so he wanted the legal right to terminate one or more of the sales in the future. Matthews prepared a "Limited Put Option," allowing Allen, after a certain amount of time, to "put" any of the mares back to Calumet for the same price he had paid. If Allen exercised the option, Calumet would refund to him any interest he had paid on the promissory notes he signed for the purchases of the horses.

Allen also was concerned about the advanced age of the mares and the possibility that one might die before he "put" the horse back to Calumet and was able to cancel his debt. So Lundy wrote Allen a letter saying that if any of the horses died, Calumet automatically would cancel Allen's promissory note for that particular horse.

It seemed like a normal sale, with lawyers drafting official papers such as bills of sale and with the buyer and seller signing them. But the mares never left their stalls at Calumet; papers at the Jockey Club Ownership Registry were never transferred to Allen's name; and Calumet never got its $3 million.

The purpose of a horse sale is usually for one person to get money and another to get horses, but this transaction had other aims. For one, Allen wanted to record the $3 million purchase on his tax records, which he did. Allen denied later that the sole purpose of the sale was for his tax benefits; he did have another goal, he claimed, in making the deal, and that was to own those horses. Still, he never took possession of the horses nor did he pay for them.

Calumet, meanwhile, included the $3 million from the sales of the four horses as income on its own tax returns and financial statements used to extend its loans with First City. The bills of sale also allowed Calumet to show that, despite the news that prices were falling elsewhere, its horses were selling at prices such as $500,000 and $1.5 million, even at such advanced ages as twenty-two and twenty-three.

These sales figures established market values that could be shown not only to banks but also to insurance companies. On January 16, 1989, Calumet increased the mortality insurance from $100,000 to $1 million on Lucinda Lea, the only one of the four mares covered by insurance.

At about the same time as the Allen deal, Lundy, following Bob Fox's suggestion, sent some Calumet horses to a Florida trainer named Louis Gurino. It wasn't unusual for Calumet to send racehorses away. By 1988, the farm had nearly fifty horses in training at tracks and stables all over the world. Calumet would find a trainer with a good reputation, like D. Wayne Lukas who resided in California, and send certain horses to that trainer's facility. Gurino was at Lou-Roe Farms in the Ocala region of north Florida.

It was unusual, however, for Calumet horses, including progeny of the top-notch racehorse Wild Again, to be sent to an unknown trainer such as

Louis Gurino. His name wasn't listed in the 1988 edition of *American Racing Manual,* which tracks the careers of horse trainers, showing how their horses have placed in races each year. For a novice trainer to test his prowess and build his skills using horses from a renowned stable like Calumet was, to say the least, different. Fox figured that Gurino was in fact a good trainer but needed to work with high-class horses to prove himself professionally. It was Lundy's generosity in wanting to help a young, hardworking trainer, Fox said, that led him to do business with Lou-Roe.

But in the upcoming years, the name Lou-Roe would look suspicious in the Calumet files. As it turns out, Anthony Gurino, who was Lou-Roe's founder and Louis Gurino's father, was an associate of reputed Mafia kingpin John Gotti. And law enforcement officials would someday call Lou-Roe "part of Gotti's empire."

Gurino created Lou-Roe Farms, a paper stable without any land, in 1977 to buy, sell, and race thoroughbred horses. At the same time, he owned and operated the Arc Plumbing and Heating Corporation in the New York City borough of Queens. Arc listed among its employees a $25,000-a-year plumbing salesman named John Gotti. For years Arc had been suspected of being a front for the Gambino crime family, a vehicle for laundering dirty money.

During the spring of 1985, Gurino bought more than one hundred acres of land near Ocala, Florida, under the name Lou-Roe Properties. He called that land Lou-Roe Farms. A few months later the U.S. attorney in Brooklyn charged Gurino with obstruction of justice in a narcotics case, and the next year Arc, which held contracts from the New York City Housing Authority, the New York City Parks and Recreation Department, the New York Department of Sanitation, and the New York City School Construction Authority, was banned from city contracts for three years because Gurino had failed to disclose his 1985 indictment. Two months later, in July 1986, Gurino created a new company called Hi-Tech Mechanical, allegedly to replace Arc, but without any visible connection to him. Fronting for Gurino, Hi-Tech then entered into plumbing contracts with the New York City Housing Authority. Gurino allegedly used various other companies to secretly channel about $1 million from Hi-Tech in New York to Lou-Roe in Florida. Gurino claimed he was persecuted by government agents because he had once employed Gotti and he and Gotti were childhood buddies.

The government would someday label Hi-Tech "an alter-ego of Arc" and claim that Gurino used tainted money to develop Lou-Roe's elaborate estate of Spanish-style stucco barns topped by red-tile roofs, a fifteen-room mansion with marble floors, and huge towering palm trees, with a black iron electric gate protecting it all. Money transferred through companies, mostly in Queens, came to Lou-Roe in various amounts, from $25,000 to $100,000 and often in small $5,000 checks.

Calumet boarded several horses at Lou-Roe from 1988 on. So did Lundy, and so did Robey. A few of the horses were even jointly owned by Calumet and Lou-Roe, such as a horse named Sixth Sign and one named Miglietti. The latter was a Secreto colt that Louis Gurino had purchased for $150,000 through the agency owned by Lundy's son, Robert, at the 1988 Fasig-Tipton sale in Lexington. The first check from Calumet to Lou-Roe, only $943, was for a board bill for a Wild Again colt, paid in November 1988. In January 1989, Calumet would pay $2,720 to Lou-Roe; in February, $5,303; in March, $3,068—and so on until the spring of 1990. The reasons written in account books varied from board bills to training expenses and upkeep of the animals.

Few people knew about the link between Lou-Roe and Calumet, a tie that could have been exactly what it appeared to be—a relationship between two horse farms. On the other hand, Lou-Roe's alleged association with Gotti in combination with Calumet's thirst for cash and high-stakes transactions inspired speculation that the relationship might be more complicated than that.

In late fall, Eunice Kennedy Shriver, chairman of Special Olympics International, joined several others at Calumet for a news conference. The occasion was what Shriver called "the largest single contribution ever made to the [Special Olympics] program." Calumet planned to donate four Alydar seasons, a value of nearly $1 million, to help Kentucky Special Olympics in its drive to enroll more learning disabled children and adults. Three-time Olympic gold medal winner Mary T. Meagher of Louisville attended. So did Matt Biondi of California, who won five gold medals at the 1988 Summer Olympics in Seoul, South Korea, and former U.S. track star Lee Evans, who won two gold medals in 1968. Alydar, too, made a special appearance. The executive director of Kentucky Special Olympics said he hoped others would be inspired by the Calumet donation. What he didn't know was that Calumet would soon owe his group $875,000.

Meanwhile Fox's 1988 ads showed Fox in Australia holding a koala bear, Fox standing on the equator in Equador with one foot in each hemisphere, and Fox at Easter Island. The last ad seemed more like a message from its author's subconscious than an ad for a horse broker. It read:

> Things are sometimes done and nothing is ever said. You may not know why it was done or, for that matter, what or how it was done. Maybe we don't need to know everything.

In mid-December Fox's ATPSI appraised the nine stallions in the Calumet stallion group at a total value of $201 million. Except for Alydar, whom Calumet owned in toto, the farm's stake in the stallions was typically 50 percent, so the farm's value in the stallion group was $136.7 million, according to the ATPSI appraisal. Secreto was valued at $75 million, Alydar at $66 million, Mogambo at $13.8 million, Highland Blade at $8.9 million, Wild Again at $16.5 million, Capote at $15 million, Foyt at $2.9 million, Tim Tam Aly at $2.3 million, and Judge Smells at $1 million.

Fox's system for establishing the value of a horse was predicated on the earnings potential of the stallion for one year, that is, the stud fee multiplied by sixty (for an average of sixty mares bred each year to the stallion), projected for five years, which is what he considered the minimum useful life of the horse. While he knew his appraisals were used by banks to evaluate the value of the assets of a borrower, Fox believed the assets were only part of the banker's picture. It was the bank's responsibility to examine the expenses of the borrower against its assets. Fox's only job was to appraise the horses using a system he firmly believed was logical and fair.

This appraisal, dated December 16, 1988, and intended for First City, read:

> It is impossible to think that anyone, with the exception of the Calumet Ownership Management and Staff, knows the Calumet stallions better than we do at ATPSI.
>
> We have been and all still are instrumental in much of the business of booking and dealmaking with the Calumet Farm stallions.
>
> In addition, I have inspected all the stallions at Calumet Farm and have found them to be above average, excellent examples of correctly built, strong Thoroughbreds.
>
> As such, I can certainly state that Calumet Farm Management is, by

far, the most progressive, ingenious and intelligent in the entire horse industry, period!

Stallions succeed at Calumet Farm. When we appraise, we do so knowing that Calumet Farm makes stallions and Calumet Farm makes big money in the industry.

Very simply put, I can state, first hand, "at Calumet Farm, they make it happen."

By the close of 1988, the list of lenders fueling Lundy's frenzy was longer than ever—Midlantic, Mutual Benefit, CommerceNational, IBJ Schroder, First City, and Riggs.

But the very last deal of the year defied all tradition at Calumet and would have shocked Lundy's predecessors more than all that had occurred since Mrs. Markey's death. On December 24 the farm announced that it was considering developing a thirty-five-acre tract of land, if the city would allow the required zoning change. The plan was to build a hotel, office park, and conference center and call it Calumet Business Park.

An equally alarming event closed 1988: Spendthrift Farm filed for bankruptcy. The great experiment of mixing the cultures of Wall Street and horse country had failed. Spendthrift's stock had plunged; its shareholders were alleging fraud. Its debts of nearly $57 million far exceeded its assets of $7.67 million. Secured creditors, owed $7.9 million, included NCNB, a Charlotte, North Carolina, bank; Manufacturers Hanover Trust Company of New York; and Central Bank and Trust Company of Lexington. The largest unsecured creditors, Shearson Lehman Hutton, Merrill Lynch, and Cede and Company, were owed a total of nearly $26 million. A slump in the horse industry, a deluge of litigation, and management problems appeared to be the culprits, though industry insiders spoke too of the deleterious impact of hyped prices.

Leslie Combs II, who had founded the farm in 1936, was devastated. His innovative strategies had paved the way for a business boom whose spirit and participants were now self-destructing. Reached at his home in Bal Harbour, Florida, the night after the bankruptcy petition was filed, Combs, eighty-seven years old and retired from the farm's management, said he blamed the farm's woes on "people running Spendthrift who overdid everything." Later, Combs told a friend, "I saw this coming, but I couldn't stop it. . . . . [It's like] when a horse you've loved is about to die."

13 In early August 1989, streaks of lightning filled the night sky above Calumet, illuminating the red-trimmed cupolas and tall trees and lighting the way for dozens of people as they rushed from their cars up the front steps of Calumet's main residence, trying to shield their sequined dresses and perfectly pressed tuxedos from the pouring rain. These were among Bertha Wright's two hundred or so guests at a gala to raise money for the American Cancer Society.

Bertha had hosted other big events—one year she allowed the Friends of the Library to use her house for a fund-raiser that featured the then–vice president's wife, Barbara Bush—but this "Evening under the Stars" orchestrated by the cancer organization on August 5 was probably the biggest of all. For their $100 donations guests were promised dinner, valet parking, live music by the Lexington Philharmonic, dancing, and a chance to tour the landmark farm, which had been closed to the general public throughout the Lundy years.

Whether she was donating thousands of dollars to her church or hosting a dinner, Bertha liked being a philanthropist. Years before, when she and Warren Jr. had lived away from the farm, she had thought now and again about what she'd do if someday she lived in the big house at Calumet. She had visions of summer afternoons spent staring out windows at rolling pastures dotted with grazing thoroughbreds. She had ideas for decorating, such as tearing out the wall-to-wall carpet and restoring the wood floors. She thought about entertaining friends in the huge formal dining room. But a favorite fantasy was to be known as a Bluegrass benefactor, hosting galas.

After days of preparation for the big outdoor event, late in the afternoon of the fifth it began to rain. The guests were invited for 7:00 P.M., and every half hour until the moment the valets were dispatched to the wide circular drive in front of the pillared house, the rain intensified. By seven o'clock, there was thunder and lightning, and throngs of people filed into the house, past the portrait of Lucille Markey holding Warren Jr. on her lap and past the long divan with a needlepoint cover Mrs. Markey had made while she was married to Warren Sr. The guests filled every corner of the mansion that Warren Wright had built for Lucille and Warren Jr. over fifty years ago.

Many hostesses would have been flustered when rain forced a well-planned out-of-doors event suddenly indoors. Bertha was not. The rain meant more people would come into her house; more people would ogle the gilt-framed portraits of horses, the fine Venetian glass, and the huge photomural of an aerial view of Whirlaway crossing the finish line in 1941. Bertha was proud of where she lived, proud of what Calumet meant to the Bluegrass and to racing. She was the first lady of the showplace of the region.

Bertha was perhaps all the more grateful that night to be the highbrow philanthropist because other dreams had fallen apart. In early July her fashion boutique Ricco Antonio, which Robey had incorporated in December 1983, was legally dissolved, filed away in the state's corporate records with the status "inactive in bad standing." At the same time she was locking horns with Ricco, aka Ricardo A. Gorosin, in a messy court battle in California.

Ricco and Bertha had once jetted around the nation together to market the name and the designs, which were eventually sold at such ritzy stores as Saks Fifth Avenue. One or two Miss Kentuckys had worn the Ricco Antonio evening gowns at Miss America pageants. And best of all perhaps, Bertha had a young escort to parties and an excellent dance partner. But the partners parted ways in 1987, largely over money and over her suspicions that he might have been taking advantage of her. In September 1987 Gorosin sued Bertha and Ricco Antonio, Inc., in Los Angeles Superior Court on claims including fraud, slander, wrongful discharge, breaches of oral and written contracts, emotional distress, and—strikingly—palimony. He wanted in excess of $30 million in damages.

Gorosin alleged he and Bertha had begun to live together in January 1985. She promised to provide financial support for him for the rest of his life, he claimed, and said they were equal partners in Ricco Antonio. In what he described as an "oral express" agreement, he promised in return to act as her "companion, social host, and confidante." After they split up sometime in June 1987, he claimed that she refused to transfer his share of the stock and earnings of the company to him and to provide him with adequate financial support "consistent with the style and manner established for him during the time" they had lived together. She slandered him, he claimed, in July 1987 by telling people he had stolen money and fabric from the business.

Bertha retaliated. She demanded that he pay back cash advances from the company, and she wanted thousands of dollars in monthly rent on a Los Angeles apartment that she or the company had paid; funds for materials, equipment, and inventory she said he took from the company; and thou-

sands more for medical and dental bills, entertainment, and travel expenses
unrelated to the business of Ricco Antonio, Inc. Bertha claimed, too, that he
had defaulted on a note for a loan from Citizen's Fidelity, for $25,665.60,
and left her with the payments and the obligation. She had never lived with
him, she said, though on occasion he had stayed at Calumet in a guest room
at the main house.

It wasn't losing the money that bothered her. Bertha, much like her son-
in-law Lundy, had the notion perhaps that the money would never run out.
What troubled her was fighting with her former partner, the embarrassment
she felt for failing to sustain a thriving business, and the painful realization
that perhaps she was totally inept at managing money.

Money to her mind was not about numbers and budgets but about security and nights like that of August 5. Warren Jr. had understood this about
his wife, which is why he had left his money in trust to her, giving her an
income for life and providing for their children as well. Despite the troubles
she and Warren Jr. might have had through the years and her resentment
toward Mrs. Markey, she was grateful to them for what she had now. A
shiver raced up Bertha's spine every time she thought of how her grandchildren and their children, and on and on, would be running up and down the
wide front staircase, sliding down the walnut banister, long after she had
passed away. On the night of the gala, Bertha proudly shook the hands of
many guests and listened to the compliments of the Cancer Society representatives about the magnificence of her home and her generosity.

Meanwhile, her son-in-law and some of his advisers were struggling with
a cash crisis—yet another cash crisis. The farm hadn't made its quarterly
payment of $2.2 million to First City (due on August 1), and it was unclear
where that money would come from. If Bertha that night had known the
extent of Calumet's problems, how close the farm was to the brink of destruction, she would have cherished her gala all the more.

Companies in trouble typically cut expenses and restructure the ways they
do business. Not Calumet. In 1989 Lundy and company continued the
frantic spending and yet borrowed more and more just to pay the bills. Early
in the year the farm took out millions on its huge First City credit line, thus
upping its quarterly interest payments. In the next five months the farm
would borrow over $12 million: on February 3, the farm drew out $2.575
million; on February 21, $75,000; on March 2, $45,000; March 8, $7.175
million; March 16, $150,000; March 23, $160,000; March 30, $250,000;

April 7, $250,000; April 14, $250,000; April 20, $200,000; April 27, $200,000; May 18, $500,000; June 14, $25,000; June 22, $135,000; and on June 29, $200,000.

The year had begun with a ruling against Calumet in its big tax squabble with the state, which claimed the farm owed nearly $1 million in back taxes on sales of Alydar lifetime breeding rights. The defeat didn't seem to worry Robey, who appealed the case, taking the battle to a higher court. Nor was Lundy cowed. Lundy was busy with other details of running the farm, such as traveling.

Oddly enough, despite the farm's problems paying such essential bills as insurance premiums, travel expenses seemed to be escalating. In February, for example, in addition to the $30,000 monthly cost of leasing the Calumet jet from Lundy's company, there were $27,831.42 in plane-related expenses, up from $8,000 in January.

Racehorse owners typically travel a lot, visiting their horses in training and watching their horses race, but these trips appeared to be to destinations without tracks or horses in training and not just one trip but several. On the first of February the plane flew from Lexington to Baltimore to Teterboro, New Jersey, a small airport used for private jets in the Newark area, and back to Lexington. The flights for the rest of the month looked like this:

Feb. 2: Lexington to Ocala, Florida, and back to Lexington
Feb. 6: Lexington to Teterboro and back to Lexington
Feb. 10: Lexington to Atlanta to Ocala and back to Lexington
Feb. 11: Lexington to St. Thomas
Feb. 12: St. Thomas to West Palm Beach to Lexington
Feb. 13: Lexington to Houston and back to Lexington
Feb. 16: Lexington to Ocala to Miami to Fort Lauderdale
Feb. 19: Fort Lauderdale to Ocala to Lexington
Feb. 20: Lexington to Denver
Feb. 21: Denver to Miami
Feb. 22: Miami to Lexington
Feb. 26: Lexington to St. Thomas
Feb. 26: St. Thomas to West Palm Beach to Lexington

This frantic globe-trotting continued into March, with a trip on the first and second to Louisville and Chicago, back to Louisville, and then home, only to return to the runway on March 3 for a $7,000 trip to West Palm

Beach, then to Houston, then to Las Vegas, and back to Lexington. It's unclear what was so pressing about rushing to these particular destinations at this time.

While Lundy took to the skies, Robey stayed in Kentucky. As the racing commissioner, he gave keynote speeches at political fund-raisers and at dinners honoring the elite of the racing world. He received honors and awards from various political and industry associations, and was even 1989 Man of the Year for the Horsemen's Benevolent and Protective Association. But life wasn't as rosy as it seemed for Robey.

Robey, who harbored the secret desire of someday running Calumet if Lundy ever stepped down, had felt his control dwindling over the past two years—especially regarding farm finances. A large percentage of the Calumet transactions still crossed Robey's desk, and the family depended on his judgment for investing their inherited wealth, as they had for years now. But Lundy no longer consulted with Robey about everything he was doing, nor did he seek advice from his longtime counselor. Robey had become a distant voice on the phone. "There were things J.T. kept from me, that I didn't know about until they were already done," he said years later.

When Robey offered advice, Lundy didn't always listen, according to Robey. Whether he felt threatened by those who seemed to have Lundy's ear or he didn't like the way they did business is unclear, but he expressed his concern on several occasions. He didn't want Lundy to allow Fox, for example, as much power as he had, and he tried to steer Lundy away from Marc Rash. The farm didn't need the expense of middlemen like them.

Deals requiring the signature of family members, deals pushing the debt ever higher, were frequently faits accomplis by the time Robey knew about them. There were times now when Robey couldn't even reach Lundy. If Lundy was in town, Robey might be told that he was at the dentist or on an errand and that the call would be returned later. After many such excuses, Robey confided to his sister, "J.T. must have the worst set of teeth in the state of Kentucky."

And Robey wasn't the person First City called if there was a question or a problem with the loan. CFO Matthews now handled most of Calumet's communications with the banks, and was edging in on Robey's legal territory as well. Robey's friends talked about how Matthews was making $20,000 or more a month, compared with Robey's $125,000 annual salary. At IBJ Schroder, in New York, Calumet's link was Rash. It was Lundy's friend Gussin who made the connection with Riggs Bank in Washington, D.C. Robey had little, if any, involvement in the Axmar partnership or the Calumet-Gussin partnership. None of this sat well with the former Green Beret captain.

Robey could have resigned but didn't. In later years he attributed his willingness to stay to his loyalty to Lundy, though this seemed a rather simple explanation for such a complicated situation. And Robey's habit of drinking revealed an inner conflict that his clever, good-ol'-boy conversation did not. While his friends joked about raucous times with Robey and his outrageous sense of humor laced with bawdy language, those who cared about him worried. And they had reason. Robey, like Calumet, was on a collision course with disaster—the events of April 1 being a perfect example.

At about midnight on March 31, Robey was driving along a Lexington road when his Porsche veered off the pavement and flipped over. Within seconds the police came to Robey's rescue, though he likely would have been pleased if they hadn't. One of the officers smelled alcohol every time Robey opened his mouth and asked Calumet's general counsel to count backward from fifty-nine to thirty-five. Robey became confused at fifty-seven. The red-faced forty-eight-year-old wasn't able to stand straight for a heel-to-toe walking test and refused to take a Breathalyzer test. Early on the morning of April 1, he was arrested and charged with driving under the influence of alcohol.

Later the same day, Lundy, with the help of lawyer Matthews and partner Allen, was busily putting together a new deal. Allen was selling Calumet five mares and a 50 percent interest in eight two-year-olds. Calumet paid $2,567,375 for the package—$1.8 million in notes and part of the rest in assigned receivables from breedings the farm had sold to hotel magnate Woodrow Marriott. Allen was given the right to receive the income from those breedings—one to Secreto and one to Alydar—plus three future Alydar seasons for 1990, 1991, and 1992. Calumet and Allen then contributed their half interests in the two-year-olds to yet another new partnership, called Cal-Allen.

If every investor could profit as much as Allen did in this 1989 transaction, no one would invest in anything but thoroughbred horses. Allen bought the mares from various sellers for a total of about $149,450; a few he bought the day before selling them to Calumet. Calumet paid $1,062,375 for the five horses.

For its half interest in eight two-year-olds, which Allen had purchased for a total of approximately $126,000, Calumet paid $1,505,000. With

Calumet's purchase, however, the Cal-Allen partnership was able to establish the value of its assets at about $3 million, which meant a huge tax-beneficial loss for the partners when later they sold three of the eight horses for a total of $46,500. Calumet's share was half, or about $23,250. Of the other five, one was sent to "the killers" or "dog food people," as one court record put it. Two others were given to riding schools and two to friends.

Later Calumet would lose even more money on the deal. The farm paid $280,000 for Joey's Dream and eventually sold her in 1991 for $35,000. Millie Do was bought for $216,187.50 and Calumet sold her in 1991, in foal, for $60,000. The farm tried to sell Wise Madame, bought for $200,000, in 1990 at Keeneland, but the last bid for the horse, $11,500, was below what Calumet was willing to accept and so the farm took her back. Soon thereafter, she died. Birth of a Nation, bought for $216,187.50, also died at Calumet, uninsured. Turf Club Honey, on the other hand, was sold. Calumet paid $150,000 for the horse in 1989 and sold her in 1990 for $1,200, a loss of approximately 99 percent on the farm's investment.

The April transactions allowed many things to happen. For one, certain of the yearling purchases and later sales provided both partners in Cal-Allen with big losses for tax purposes. Consider that Calumet purchased a 50 percent stake in the two-year-old Native Tango for $225,000 in April 1989 and the Cal-Allen partnership sold the horse in October 1989 for a net of $31,500. In six months the farm suffered a loss of 93 percent on its investment of a 50 percent interest in the horse. Another advantage in the April deal was that the purchases of the five mares allowed the farm to claim that the value of its assets was more than it really was.

On May 1, Lucinda Lea died. She was one of the four mares Allen had supposedly purchased from Calumet during the fall of 1988. When mortality insurance for the fourteen-year-old horse had soared from $100,000 to $1 million in January, Allen canceled his purchase of the horse and Lundy canceled the note. Thus it was Calumet that collected the $1 million insurance on the dead horse.

As if trying to assure the family, banks, and maybe even himself that things weren't all that bad, in midsummer Lundy commissioned a financial portrait, though it would seem more like a self-portrait. The accounting firm Deloitte Haskins and Sells (later Deloitte and Touche) was to compile a report of his and his wife's financial worth, though the accountants' cover letter carefully stated that the record was not an audit for tax purposes but merely a "representation of the individuals whose financial statement is presented." Later in the report, the accountants wrote, "values are based upon estimates made by Mr. and Mrs. Lundy unless otherwise noted."

It was a cheery picture that would have impressed or reassured any bank. Personal assets were listed at $66 million and liabilities at $10.6 million, leaving a net worth of $55.4 million.

Cindy's 9.375 percent stake in Calumet was set at $15.7 million, which established the farm's value at nearly $170 million. Southeastern Aircraft, Lundy's holding company in North Carolina, was worth almost $5 million. Lundy's 7 percent stake in another company called C.C. Air was $2.1 million, and among his other corporate holdings was an entity called Farm, Inc. —valued at $8.9 million—that held his Fasig-Tipton stock. The value of the Warren Wright, Jr., Trust was $17.4 million. And then there was the real estate: a condominium in Key West valued at $418,000, a house in the Virgin Islands appraised at $2.5 million, and a $500,000 condominium in Vail, Colorado.

In the liabilities column, the Lundys owed about $900,000 to the Schroder bank, $1.8 million to Wright Enterprises, $225,000 to Bertha Wright, $200,000 to Citizen's Fidelity, and a total of $831,000 to Matchmaker Financial Corporation. On mortgages they owed $6.3 million to Citizen's Fidelity and $332,000 to Dime Real Estate in Key West for the Florida condo.

Even considering that the Lundys were guarantors on $80 million worth of notes issued by the various entities in which they had ownership interests, the statement's message was clearly positive. Calumet, which had had a value of $21 million in 1982 when Mrs. Markey died, suddenly had a value of about $170 million based on the value of Cindy's 9.375 percent stake.

Years later, the statement seemed questionable. Had Lundy begun to believe such figures? Was he no longer able to see through the veil of illusions? Or was he trying to buy time against a clock that was running out?

In August, a few days after Bertha Wright's gala, Alydar was inducted into racing's Hall of Fame. Just as meaningful perhaps to the farm, Matthews and Lundy arranged a short-term loan of $2.2 million from Bank One in Lexington which the farm received on about August 15. It was used to make Calumet's big payment that month to First City. But the relief was short-lived.

About a week before the end of Calumet's fiscal year, Matthews sent a six-page memo to Lundy revealing the shockingly fragile financial state of a farm supposedly worth $170 million.

The memo had a tone of urgency about it, which may have been inspired in part by the recent bankruptcy of Ranier Properties, a company that included Harry Ranier's Shadowlawn Farm. In the past, whatever Harry Ranier touched had turned to gold, but the equine economy seemed to destroy the alchemy of his touch. Did Matthews sense that Calumet could be next?

Matthews was painfully blunt, as if he were slowly walking his client toward the guillotine and wanted to explain step by step why the end was near. He began with the status of the farm's shaky relationships with lenders. Matthews wrote that he had asked Mutual Benefit for a deferral of $2.5 million from Calumet's due date on October 1, 1989, to January 1, 1990. He was also thinking of a roll-up of the mortgage with the First City loan, he said, which would effectively refinance the mortgage and eliminate the issue of current payments. By then Calumet's debt to First City had increased from $32 million to more than $44 million.

The farm still owed Peter Brant an annual principal payment of $1.3 million plus one quarter's interest on the Mogambo note. On October 1 the farm, Matthews wrote, might owe $545,000 to Manganaro Stables, a Massachusetts stable owned by John Manganaro, who was in the construction business in Boston. Matthews explained to Lundy that in December 1988, Marc Rash "did a race horse deal for the farm" with Manganaro that gave Manganaro the option to get out if the racehorses didn't live up to expectations. There were two option dates, October 1, 1989, and another in early 1990. Manganaro notified Rash that he wanted to exercise his option and terminate the deal on October 1. "Rash has talked to Manganaro and has told him that for his particular tax position it would be beneficial if he waited until 1990 to exercise the option." If Manganaro didn't wait, Matthews warned, the farm would have to come up with the $545,000 within the next week or so.

Then as if pointing to which part of the guillotine's blade was the sharpest, he discussed the increasingly touchy subject of insurance premiums. In June, Matthews had written a memo to Lundy saying the farm had to come up with the money for the insurance premiums on Alydar or the insurance would have to be canceled. Now, three months later, the situation wasn't much better. One problem was that the farm had had several pricey mares die over the past year; as a result, insurance premiums would go up. Matthews warned that with the premiums due and other miscellaneous operating expenses, the farm would need at least $1.5 million over the next ninety days.

"Obviously, with the deaths this year to the insured horses, it will be hard to get favorable terms in February when the policy is renewed," he wrote. "You may recall that the London underwriters were not too happy with the 1988 losses. I was able to convince them that it was an unusual year and the farm had been timely on its payments. If the farm continues to be delinquent on the premium payments, it will be difficult to negotiate with the underwriters in January and February. In addition, failure to pay breeds the risk of cancellation, which would cause a default under the loan agreement."

Logical, methodical Matthews, with his thick glasses and nervous manner, suggested getting money to plug the dam by collecting the many debts owed to Calumet, especially those owed by some of Lundy's friends. Though "a review of the account receivables" did not give Matthews "any great confidence in their collectability," he encouraged Lundy to pressure these friends to pay.

He brought up the subject of First City executive Cihak, who at the time of the memo was apparently sending $50,000 on a note owed to Calumet. Cihak, though the vice chairman of the bank from which Calumet borrowed heavily, apparently had borrowed money from Calumet, perhaps a lot of money.

"This [the $50,000] is not a lot considering the amount he owes the farm," wrote Matthews. "However [Cihak] has skillfully put himself into a position with Calumet which makes him a critical party in its transactions to reduce its debt. This position will enable him to defer payment as long as there is a chance that he can put together a deal. If the farm pushes him for a payment, he could conveniently drag his feet." Matthews was polite enough not to mention that such back scratching is a clear conflict of interest that any banker knows is looked upon as highly unethical, at the very least.

Advising Lundy on how he might escape the fall of the guillotine blade, Matthews, who would soon resign as Calumet's chief financial officer, ended the memo as follows: "The farm needs to put a deal together which would raise $6 million to $7 million. The farm has not done a deal of this type since Axmar and that deal is unwinding. Maybe the farm could work with Rash or maybe you have some ideas but something needs to be done soon."

In December, Calumet borrowed another $2 million or so from IBJ Schroder, adding to its extant $3.3 million loan that had not been paid down. What allowed Calumet to expand its Schroder debt was the dissolution of the Calumet-Axmar partnership. With Betty Marcus out of the picture, Calumet could present its 100 percent interest in the partnership horses, persuading Schroder that the loan was a solid investment.

The rounds between Marcus's lawyers and Calumet's had begun in the spring of 1989. Finally, in early December an agreement was struck. Axmar would give up its interest in the partnership horses. In exchange, the partnership, now solely Calumet, would give Axmar $1.7 million in the form of 1990 stallion seasons, cancellation of the $1.625 million note, and a note to Axmar for the remaining $1.675 million. The breeding rights included three Alydar seasons, four Secreto seasons, five Wild Again seasons, five Capote seasons, and five Mogambo seasons. If Axmar didn't use the seasons in 1990, Calumet was supposed to sell them to another breeder and forward the proceeds, up to $1.675 million, to Axmar.

In the end, Marcus lost her interest in the horses, owed Citizen's Fidelity at least $3 million for the loan to enter the partnership, and was owed $1.675 million by Calumet. Also, Marcus separated herself and Axmar from her longtime agent and consultant Rash.

Seven months later, Marcus sued Rash, Executive Bloodstock Management, and Barry Weisbord, accusing them of a pattern of fraudulent and illegal misconduct that violated the federal racketeering laws. The complaint cited examples of horses being sold for more than they were worth, Axmar paying the price, and its agents taking "secret commissions, amounting to the difference between what the agent paid for the horse and what Axmar paid the agent to buy the horse."

Meanwhile, as a result of the Axmar partnership, Calumet had indirectly been able to borrow about $8 million from two banks: $3.3 million from Citizen's Fidelity via Marcus at the beginning of the partnership and over $5 million from Schroder using the partnership assets as collateral. On the debt side, it had leveraged $1.7 million worth of stallion seasons to Marcus, owed a $1.6 million note to Marcus and $5 million plus interest to Schroder, and had pledged ten more horses to a bank (Schroder) for collateral.

By now, Calumet's finest broodmares were collateral for the Riggs loan; a dozen or so more horses secured the loans through Equine Capital and Gray Cliff; still others were pledged to Bank One; interests in Alydar secured the Midlantic loan; and a long list of Calumet horses, including Alydar, were pledged to First City. It seemed that everything at Calumet except the portrait of William Monroe Wright had been leveraged.

14 In 1990 Calumet's troubles were as deeply hidden from the outside world as the caves beneath its Kentucky pastures. By spring, the stable's image was better than it had been since the days of Alydar's run for the Derby roses in 1978. An almost giddy Lundy stood in the winner's circle at Pimlico Racetrack in May holding a big silver trophy for winning the prestigious Pimlico Special. The winner was Criminal Type, a son of Alydar, half-owned by Calumet and trained by D. Wayne Lukas, one of racing's hottest trainers. This was the first $1 million race at the Maryland track, but more important to Calumet, the Pimlico was a race that Calumet champions such as Whirlaway, Citation, and Twilight Tear had dominated in days past.

In New York, only minutes before Criminal Type crossed the finish line, another Alydar offspring, 'Tis Juliet, won the Shuvee Handicap, a big race at Belmont Park. The almost simultaneous victories seemed to signal the beginning of Calumet's return to glory, but the real victor that day was Lundy.

At Pimlico, as Lundy accepted Criminal Type's trophy, a crowd formed around him. Until now, he had been inconspicuous, milling about the grandstand and the barn area, rubbing his hands together, and looking occasionally at the television monitors to catch bits and pieces of the races. He was wearing his usual informal attire, sport shirt, gray pants, navy blazer—an outfit he would wear to several more races that summer, just for good luck.

Someone in the crowd asked him how long it had been since the farm had won such an important race. Lundy didn't have to pause. He answered quickly that it had been 1978 when Alydar won the Blue Grass Stakes and came in second in all three Triple Crown races. And as if suddenly in that moment he realized that this was the comeback he had been promising to produce, he smiled and said, "It has been mostly a matter of bad luck. That's the way racing is. If you are unlucky you have a bad year. Now Calumet has got a good racing stable again, with a lot of nice horses coming out."

With Lundy's 1980s-style emphasis on breeding to sell rather than breeding to race, the farm was not a major winner at the track in the 1980s. Relative to the millions of dollars spent on horses, on the renovation of the physical plant, and on a stepped-up training program, the farm's track earnings and its horses' performances had been disappointing. Until 1990, the farm's top earnings in the past twenty years had been $1.2 million in 1979 under the guidance of trainer John Veitch and the management of Margaret Glass and Melvin Cinnamon. In Lundy's first year, 1982, earnings were $561,264; in 1983, $645,685; 1984, $303,453; 1985, $703,529; and in 1986, $811,202. In 1987, the farm was finally over the $1 million mark again with earnings of $1,040,060, and in 1988, $1,018,144. In 1989, earnings dipped to $837,880.

In the 1980s, no one believed there could be a return to the glory days when Calumet horses brought home trophies for simultaneous victories and first and second place race after race and the stable was the nation's leading breeder for eleven consecutive years. But in 1990, beginning with the Pimlico Special and the Shuvee Handicap, the devil's-red and blue silks appeared in the winner's circle again and again, and mostly for victories of the sons and daughters of Alydar. That year the farm would earn $3.9 million at the track.

By midsummer, new trophies were filling the glass cases at the Calumet office, and the press was buzzing with the stable's tales of success. Articles appeared with headlines such as "Return of the Devil's Red," "A Different Breed: Calumet's Lundy Is a Racing Maverick," and "Lundy Brings That Old Gleam Back to Calumet."

Lundy's image was rapidly changing. What were once viewed as his flaws were not only forgivable but even laudable. The lavish spending seemed like a solid business strategy now that the farm was producing winners. Lundy's unconventional breeding techniques and the style of secrecy beyond the big red gates were no longer suspicious. Rather, these were the trademarks of an individual.

Lundy's peculiarities, through the microscope of success, were beginning to look like the eccentricities typical of trailblazers and risk takers. While his social skills and taciturn behavior were once the subject of criticism, he was now referred to as an efficient, succinct talker who didn't waste time on lavish verbal descriptions and didn't dwell on his own accomplishments. His simplicity was interpreted as modesty and humility. One writer dubbed his unconventional attire at the track and his habit of avoiding the Calumet box and the clubhouse as "vintage Lundy." In a *New York Times* story that summer, trainer Lukas said it best: Lundy's successes were "wearing down his critics."

Lundy appeared to be donning the mantle of an unsung folk hero; at the very least he was the off-center iconoclast of the horse business. His image had transformed from the rebel without a cause to the rebel with a definite goal, which he was now achieving.

In interviews at tracks and at home, Lundy was asked things a celebrity is asked. What was his favorite horse of all time? Mrs. Edith W. Bancroft's 1967 Horse of the Year Damascus. What was his favorite Calumet horse of all time? General Duke. What was his favorite Calumet horse now? Criminal Type.

His opinions about everything from management techniques and breeding philosophies to taxes and simulcasting suddenly counted. On taxes, he told one reporter, "When they [the federal government] took away many of the advantages, that caused the slump in the horse business. I'd like to see those advantages reinstated so we can get investors in there to bring in new money."

In an interview for an article in *The Blood-Horse* that summer, Lundy stressed the importance of current farm practices as setting the stage for the farm's future. He talked of the commitment of the Wright heirs to continuing the operation for many years to come. Calumet's horses were "on a roll," he said. Calumet's reputation could now stand on its own again without the crutch of its past glories. The article ended, "Why live in the past, when tomorrow looks so bright?"

Meanwhile, along the farm's inner roads, far from the public eye, Calumet's trademark white fences were beginning to show wear. The paint on random planks was cracking, and tiny white chips were falling onto lush meadows below. Even the fields offered hints of hard times with the appearance of an occasional patch of dandelions—an unprecedented event at a farm whose groundskeepers were renowned as the best. But not even the best could function without money, and by the summer of 1990 funds for the grounds had severely diminished.

In fact the need for cash was formidable. Proceeds from transactions such as recent horse sales rarely made it into the Calumet general account anymore. The farm was now asking buyers to wire the funds directly to the banks it owed money. In the eight years since Mrs. Markey had died, leaving the farm debt free, Calumet had accumulated more debt than any other horse farm in the history of the Bluegrass. Whatever had happened to the millions and millions of dollars flowing into the farm from banks and deals over the past few years, now there was barely enough to make the payroll. And there was nowhere to run—no bank to add to the list of Calumet

244 WILD RIDE

creditors and few, if any, horses that had not already been pledged at least once as collateral.

Selling seasons and horses was not a simple solution because by now the market for seasons of Calumet horses was diminishing. Whereas the rest of the market had suffered such a blow in 1986, Calumet had been able to stave off a recession until late 1989. Things had become so bad in the rest of the equine economy that it was difficult for Calumet to continue to prop up its prices, and it could not hype them in the way that it had done on occasion at auctions because such tactics had so shaken the farm's credibility. It seemed that despite the successes at the track, the Calumet bubble was deflating.

Still, in the first half of 1990, Calumet informed several breeders and agents that it was planning some private sales, even publishing a 205-page private "Catalog of Calumet's Racing and Breeding Stock." With the catalog tucked under their arms, prospective buyers toured the barns and surveyed the horseflesh, and by the end of February the farm had sold nearly $5 million worth of horses. But that was not enough. So the farm tried to sell as many stallion futures as it could. This required delicate maneuvering because so many of the horses were already pledged as collateral with banks, and selling interests in the horses' future earnings could jeopardize the value of the banks' potential property. It was like collecting the rent several years in advance on apartments in a building that had secured a loan. If the loan went into default and the bank took over the building, the building would be worth much less without rent coming in for the next two or three years. But in 1990 Calumet had few alternatives.

By summer the farm was furiously selling seasons to Alydar, sometimes for two and three years in advance. Lundy had been preselling Alydar breedings for the past few years but never at such a pace as in 1990, when packages of seasons might include three seasons, one for 1991, 1992, and 1993. To encourage people to buy so far in advance, the farm offered incentives, such as deferring the stud-fee payment until after the foal was sold. There were also three-season foal shares, in which the farm would share the foal with the mare's owner for two years and then give the foal to the buyer for the third year. Alydar, as a Lexington attorney would say months later, had become "Lundy's ATM machine."

In 1990 Alydar's stud fee was in the range of $165,000, down from $190,000 in 1989 and $250,000 in 1988. Despite the dip, this was far more than any other Calumet stallions were bringing in. Wild Again's fee peaked at $50,000 in 1988 and 1989 and by 1990 was down to $35,000 to $40,000. Capote never brought more than $35,000. And Talinum, a Calumet stallion purchased in 1988, brought $15,000. Even Secreto, the $50 million horse once appraised by Fox for $75 million, brought in $140,000 tops in the late 1980s and would soon slip to the $75,000 range.

The demand for Alydar was still high, though by now there were thousands of Alydar progeny throughout the world. In 1989, Easy Goer, an Alydar son, placed second at the Derby and the Preakness and won the prestigious Belmont Stakes. Criminal Type would win seven major races and place second in two others in 1990, enhancing Alydar's reputation all the more. Alydar had sired forty-six stakes winners from just eight crops of foals.

His workload continued to increase. After a full schedule in 1988 of mating to 97 mares, he serviced 104 mares in 1989, including seven Australian mares during the autumn months. His first trip to the breeding shed that year was on February 11 and his last on December 6. In 1990, he would mate with 107 mares, meaning at least 200 trips to the breeding shed, with his last breeding for the year to an Australian mare named Stravaganza on November 1.

But Alydar's earnings seemed to evaporate as quickly as morning dew on Calumet fields. Whatever cash the farm received from Alydar breedings soon vanished. The excessive spending continued, despite the farm's obvious problems. In August, for example, travel expenses were approximately $35,000 while the payroll that month was $19,924.51. By 1990, Alydar's busy schedule wasn't bringing in all that much cash because so many seasons each year had been presold or pledged in connection with one of Calumet's deals. As the economy worsened, the number of foal-sharing agreements—deals where the owner of the mare wasn't paying a stud fee—increased. Instead, the owner of the stallion received one-half of the proceeds from the sale of the foal that resulted from the breeding. A certain number of seasons were reserved for Calumet's own mares, too. With twenty or so foal-sharing agreements; one or two breedings for each of the approximately twenty holders of lifetime breeding rights; perhaps fifteen breedings reserved for Calumet mares; fifteen to twenty breedings prepledged in relation to various deals and several more used to pay bills related to the stable's operations, it's possible that as few as fifteen seasons would generate cash during 1990. That meant Alydar would earn no less than $3 million in cash for 1991, and whatever he earned, at least $2 million was already earmarked for insurance premiums.

Beginning as early as 1989, Calumet was lucky to sell twenty seasons to Alydar that weren't already committed through some sort of prior arrangement. Sales records for the seasons sold in 1989 showed only three breedings bringing in cash, for a total of $650,000. Two of those breeders paid their bills but one didn't, which meant that the cash yield was only $450,000. The figures bolster the notion that Calumet's chief earner wasn't bringing all that much cash into the farm's coffers. The ATM machine was nearly empty.

Besides the quest for cash, the biggest challenge for Lundy and his advisors was to prevent the banks from calling the loans. This required maintaining the stud fees at a decent level to impress the banks with the value of their collateral: presenting solid financial statements and appraisals; and keeping up with the insurance premiums due on the collateral.

One default could bring down the house of cards. The Wrights, whose names appeared as principal guarantors on most, if not all, Calumet loans, would suddenly wake up to the significance of all those papers they'd been signing, and they might panic enough to seek help outside the Calumet board. This would be tantamount to throwing a lighted match into a hayloft.

To keep the peace at Calumet's biggest creditor, First City, Calumet managers knew they needed to keep their connection, Frank Cihak, happy. In the context of Calumet's urgent need to keep First City on its good side and considering its continuing cash crunch, what Lundy and Matthews did in early 1990 was almost understandable. Out of context, it was bizarre.

On February 7, 1990, Lundy signed an agreement to purchase two oil paintings and a 10 percent stake in a resort on the island of Majorca off the coast of Spain from a family in Madrid. The paintings were *L'Araignée de Mer* by Pablo Picasso, 1940, signed and dated, and *Femme et Oiseau dans la Nuit*, a 1968 work by Joan Miró, also signed. Appraisers had set the market value for the assets at approximately $12.5 million, and Lundy's purchase price was $5.2 million, which he borrowed from First City.

Lundy was not an art collector, nor had he ever shown the slightest interest in Picasso or Miró. In a deposition later he would say, "I don't know anything about art and don't care anything about it." But he did have an interest in doing favors for his buddy Cihak.

What Cihak wanted Lundy to do that February involved minimal effort for Lundy, and if everything went according to plan, Lundy could get $650,000 in return. It all seemed so simple.

Cihak, through one of the First City chairman's Middle Eastern friends, had heard about a wealthy family in Spain that could be a good client for First City. The Coca family owned millions of dollars in fine artworks and resort properties, but it also owed a lot of money to a Spanish bank. First City came to the rescue in 1989 and guaranteed a loan of 14.1 billion pesetas (then about $120 million) from Citibank Spain to the Coca family to pay off their other bank debt. The arrangement earned First City millions of dollars in fees. The Cocas were to pay back the Citibank loan through sales of their assets.

But by early 1990 the assets weren't selling. Knowing that a default would be disastrous for First City, its shareholders, and its executive officers, Cihak was worried about the Cocas' ability to make the Citibank payments. The immediate concern was an upcoming $11 million interest payment. So Cihak allegedly concocted a plan that, with Lundy's help, funneled $5.2 million from First City to the Cocas via the president of Calumet Farm.

First City's Dallas bank loaned the $5.2 million to Lundy, who then bought the two treasured Coca family paintings and shares in the Coca company called Golf de Poniente. The loan was made to Mr. and Mrs. John T. Lundy, whose net worth was listed, in loan documents, at about $55 million. The loan proceeds—$3.2 million for the paintings and $2 million for the stock—were transferred, at Lundy's direction, to an account of the Cocas at Citibank, and they used the money to satisfy a portion of the interest obligation due Citibank.

The family, according to the agreement, had the right to repurchase the paintings and stock by August 6, 1990. If they did, Lundy would get $650,000 above his purchase price—$400,000 for the paintings and $250,000 for the stock—in five months with no effort whatsoever. And if they didn't repurchase the assets, Lundy could sell the assets valued higher than his purchase price to pay off his First City loan and make a profit in the process.

The loan did nothing for Calumet and its debt problems. Though the intent might have been to create more leverage for the farm's corner-office deals with First City, the deal made Calumet's president and one of its attorneys, who both signed legal papers related to the transaction, accomplices in a highly questionable scheme—one that some banking officials and lawyers would claim a few years later had defrauded the shareholders of the bank and, though perhaps unintentionally, might have violated federal banking laws. The deal would be part of the allegations of mismanagement and self-dealing in a $1.18 billion lender liability case—one of the largest such cases in history.

By the fall, Calumet was selling horses again. With silver trophies and cups continuing to arrive at the main office and a sizable crop of new foals and yearlings frolicking in the pastures, it was a propitious time for agents and breeders to tour the farm and peruse the animals. But as the boxes were unpacked and the trophies carefully placed in the glass cases outside Lundy's office, the pressure inside his office seemed to intensify with each hour. The Calumet calendar was filling with dates for payments due. The pressure was even worse than the year before when Matthews had written his state-of-the-finances memo.

Axmar tried persistently to collect the proceeds from the sales of the 1990 seasons Calumet had agreed to give the Marcuses when their partnership fell apart. The group had written to Calumet in January instructing the farm to sell the seasons it was owed and send the proceeds. There were three $250,000 Alydar seasons; four $100,000 Secreto seasons; five $50,000 Wild Again seasons; five $30,000 Capote seasons; and five $30,000 Mogambo seasons. Calumet was obligated to reimburse Axmar for the seasons within thirty days of Axmar requesting that the farm sell the seasons. At the end of February, Axmar called and wrote, but Calumet still didn't send the money. To make matters worse, the farm was obligated to pay Axmar the first installment on its $1.675 million note in December. And for Lundy there was the added stress of the ugly battle between his two friends, Marc Rash, who had helped Lundy and Calumet on numerous occasions, and Betty Marcus, whom Lundy wanted to appease.

The IBJ Schroder bankers in New York were also frustrated. The last time a payment had been made on the Wright heirs' loan was December 1989, and the farm, which also had a Schroder loan, had failed to meet a pay-down requirement in October 1990. Neither did it send the bank its year-end financial statements, which the bank had requested on several occasions.

Around the same time, in early October, Calumet defaulted on its Mutual Benefit loan. The farm hadn't made a payment for a year and a half on its $20 million loan from Mutual Benefit, which was paid down to only about $18 million. The collateral was a first mortgage on Calumet's land.

The state of Kentucky, too, was getting into the act, with a tax lien against Calumet, claiming that the farm owed $3.7 million in back sales taxes due mostly on sales of breeding rights from 1982 through 1989.

Besides the Calumet debt, Lundy had debts of his own. By December 1, he was supposed to pay to Citizen's Fidelity $4.8 million, the amount still owed of the $6.65 million he and his wife had borrowed in February 1988, using as collateral his own 318-acre farm and the St. Thomas house he and Cindy had bought in 1984. Also due in December was a $1.6 million loan from Citizen's Fidelity that Lundy and the Wright heirs had guaranteed on December 1, 1987.

As creditors closed in, there were more quick-hit deals. Lundy called Matthews at the beginning of October to tell him he was selling some horses to his friend in Queens, Robert Perez. On October 8, Matthews received a memo from Executive Bloodstock Management Corporation prepared by Marc Rash, outlining the details of the sale of four horses to Perez for $1.2 million. On October 10, Calumet sold an Alydar filly born only a few months earlier for $750,000; the buyers were Irish breeders tied to Robert Sangster. A few weeks later Calumet sold five more thoroughbred weanlings to the same group, this time for $2 million.

The sales brought in cash, but the horses were encumbered by liens— some held by the Calumet-Gussin partnership, some by Riggs, some by Lundy's friends such as Frank Cihak, some by Equine Capital Corporation, and so on. Matthews cleaned up the deals by obtaining lien releases, but in the end, Calumet didn't receive much money from the sales. For example, Matthews instructed the agent for the Irish breeders to wire-transfer $1.05 million to Riggs and $600,000 to Citizen's Fidelity for the ECC account.

Also in October, Criminal Type, the symbol of Calumet's renaissance, was injured and couldn't run, as planned and hoped, in one of the biggest races of the year, the Breeders' Cup Classic.

At about the same time, Lundy was finding it difficult to sell his fine art. The Cocas did not exercise their option to buy back the paintings and the stock by August 6, 1990, and now Lundy was stuck with another First City debt and with the difficult job of selling the assets. The logical step was to place the paintings in a public auction, but here, too, he was stymied. Though Christie's and Sotheby's were both interested in the paintings for their fall sale, the Cocas were still in physical possession of the works and refused to allow them to be sold.

Still, the worst news of all that fall came out of Texas. The Calumet jet traveled to Houston twice in October, on the sixteenth and on the twenty-first. The flights cost almost $11,000, but that was nothing when so much more was at stake. Calumet, in coping with its enormous First City debt, had fallen into a classic debtor's trap. To make its quarterly payments on the First City term loan, Calumet had begun to draw on its credit line from First City. For some time now the farm had hoped for some sort of restructuring of the debt, perhaps to ease the monthly payments or extend the due date beyond November 1991, the date established in the July 1988 loan agreement. But on October 16 the bank announced a $102 million loss for the quarter—largely owing to defaults on loans vice chairman Cihak had initiated, including the Coca family loan. That same day Cihak, Lundy's strong link to the bank, resigned.

Now First City was scrutinizing the loans Cihak had made, including the ones to Calumet. First City's board was more than a little worried about the possibility of another bad loan. And Calumet, after all, was one of First City's biggest borrowers, with the same status as Saddam Hussein who earlier in the year had borrowed about $50 million from the Texas bank.

On October 25, the bank restructured Calumet's debts in the form of a second mortgage for $44.75 million, using as collateral the farm and more bloodstock, adding to the package of horses, including Alydar, pledged in the past. At least 75 percent of the Calumet horses were now pledged to First City. Since July 1988, Calumet had amended its security agreement at least three times, adding more and more horses to the collateral list as its debt increased. The October 1990 transaction was in the form of two notes, one for $42.25 million, which was the consolidation of the debt, and the other for $2.5 million, to allow Calumet to clean up some of its delinquent premiums on the insurance for its many horses, now First City's security. The farm applied the $2.5 million toward the Alydar premiums. At the same time, the bank issued a letter of credit for $1.5 million to Calumet for interest payments due Riggs National Bank.

The restructuring was designed to use the proceeds from the upcoming January sales at Keeneland to repay a large portion of the Riggs loan. The second mortgage was guaranteed by the Wright heirs. The first interest payment was due November 28, 1990, and the new due date for the principal was February 28, 1991. The due date on the original loan had been November 1991. For Calumet, the pressure was intensifying. And First City now just about owned Calumet Farm.

15 In November 1990, Calumet's financial condition was still a well-kept secret. Banks were hesitant to face Calumet's reality after literally stampeding to the big red gates in the 1980s in hopes of adding the prestigious farm to their loan portfolios. In 1990 the name still sparkled for them; there was no reason to suspect that behind the pastoral serenity was a state of panic.

While the need for so many loans and so much cash during previous years was mysterious enough to be suspicious and what happened to all that money was never clear, the reason for the panic was. Without the ability to sell more seasons and more horses or to take out more loans, Calumet would not be able to service its debt. How could it possibly prevent an avalanche of defaults? Worst of all, it looked as if a big cash deal, preferably with Japanese investors and bankers, might not come to the rescue soon enough to save the farm.

Nearly two years before, in his quest to turn dross to gold, Lundy had looked to the Far East for an alchemist with the resources to save Calumet. Nobody else, and certainly no American buyers, could come near the prices the Japanese were paying. Racing and breeding thoroughbreds was big business in Japan. In 1990, the Japanese wagered about $23 billion at the track, compared with $12.5 billion in the United States. And they seemed as serious as the Arabs had been about bringing home some of the world's best bloodstock. In 1989, Zenya Yoshida, the foremost Japanese breeder, paid $2.8 million for Northern Dancer's last yearling to be sold at public auction. At Keeneland in 1990, breeder Tomonori Tsurumaki spent $4.9 million for two colts. In 1990, Japanese breeders had imported more than two hundred mares, compared with four in 1985, and half of the imports were in foal. The island of Hokkaido, which some regard as the Bluegrass of Japan, soon would be home to 1989 Kentucky Derby winner Sunday Silence, champion filly Tiffany Lass, and another top American filly, Open Mind. It wasn't a return to the boom, but exporting to the Japanese was keeping the wolves from many a breeder's barn door. Lundy had tried twice and was now in the midst of a third attempt to make a deal.

The first idea, which was Bob Fox's, in the fall of 1988, was for certain American breeders, including Lundy, to lease some of their best stallions and mares to the Japanese, shipping them to Hokkaido for a number of years, where a network of brokers connected with Sanwa Bank would find buyers for each year's progeny. What the Japanese didn't buy would be shipped back to the United States in time for the Keeneland yearling sales in July. Calumet would send Alydar and possibly Secreto as well as some mares. The U.S. breeders could make between $150 million and $300 million during a time when business was bad in America, and they might also have a cut of the racing purses, which were far bigger in Japan than in the United States. (The biggest races in Japan were restricted to Japanese-bred horses only.) The downside was that the sons and daughters of some of America's best bloodlines would reside in Japan.

It's unclear exactly what went wrong with the deal but Sanwa backed out, and so a few months later Matthews was called to the farm for a meeting with Lundy and others to discuss Japan. Lundy was also trying to finesse a deal in Hong Kong, but Japan was the obsession of the day, or rather the obsession of the year. In 1989, everything seemed on hold at Calumet in anticipation of a Japan-Calumet pact, the big deal that would bring in the cash no longer coming from U.S. banks. Matthews encouraged Lundy to do smaller deals and to continue selling horses because prices were slipping each year. But Lundy placed his bets on the Japanese. They had what he wanted—cash; and he had what they wanted—horses with superb pedigrees.

After the meeting, Matthews was dispatched to figure out the pros and cons of a deal involving the sale of a package of horses and breeding rights to the Japanese. He quickly surmised that the sale wouldn't supply the fast money Calumet needed. There would be promissory notes and partial payment through the sale of the horses' progeny. The returns were just too slow in coming. So in autumn 1989 Matthews began talking with Nomura, Babcock and Brown, a partnership between Japan's Nomura Securities and Babcock and Brown, an investment house in San Francisco, about the potential for an equine partnership with Calumet. NBB would put in cash, and Calumet would contribute horses and seasons, much like other partnerships Calumet had formed in recent years. Matthews flew to Japan, touring Hokkaido and meeting with NBB representatives in Tokyo, and though he felt they had a sincere interest in the partnership proposal—for Calumet, a $50 million deal—he sensed they were not going to jump into anything at this time. Still, Lundy wanted to push, so in the spring of 1990 Calumet sent a letter of intent to Nomura.

Nomura replied that it was putting the proposal on the back burner until fall 1990. In a meeting with Matthews and others during April, Lundy said that if the Nomura deal or a similar transaction was not consummated by fall 1990, it would be impossible to operate the farm without the sale of a substantial portion of the horses, mainly to service the First City debt. Matthews cautioned that selling horses, which eroded the asset value of the farm, was not a favorable long-term method for debt reduction. He stressed the need to raise "significant cash" to reduce principal as opposed to asset liquidation to meet interest payments.

By fall many of those horses had been sold or pledged as collateral for Calumet's recently restructured loan from First City. At the same time, nothing was happening with Nomura. Then, in late October, more bad news: one of Calumet's equine insurers had pulled the plug.

For a long time, during the same period that Calumet was trying to impress the Japanese, the farm had been struggling to pay its insurance premiums. Paying the premiums was crucial for two reasons. If one insurer lost confidence in Calumet's ability to pay and canceled a policy, other insurers might do the same. And without insurance for the pricey collateral securing Calumet's loans, panic would spread to the banks.

Lundy's sister, insurance agent Kathy Jones, would later say that Calumet was missing its due dates on premiums as early as the beginning of 1988. "It began to get harder at that time, and then it just got progressively worse as time went on. . . . They did make payments early on. It was just they were slow, and then it became harder to get money. And then it became impossible to get money."

As of February 1990, Calumet held policies for Alydar alone worth $20.5 million. All of this coverage was assigned to First City except for $2.5 million to Midlantic Bank, meaning that if anything happened to Alydar, most of the claim money would go to the banks. The horse was insured for a total of $36.5 million, with the holders of lifetime breeding rights who were insured accounting for the difference. Policies totaling $17.5 million of the coverage were set to expire on December 26, 1990: $12.5 million covered by Lloyd's and $5 million by Golden Eagle Insurance.

Golden Eagle was a reputable equine insurer owned by a longtime horseman who knew the horse business and its players better perhaps than most insurers. In fall 1990, the San Diego–based firm informed Calumet that it wanted to lower its Alydar coverage, possibly to $2 million, after the current policy expired in December. It was increasingly clear that overbreeding Alydar had produced a glut of Alydar offspring in the marketplace, which according to the laws of supply and demand would bring down the price of his yearlings and lower the amount Calumet could charge for stud fees. To astute industry observers, it was even clearer that Alydar's value in recent times had been artificially inflated. But Calumet and its insurer couldn't agree on the issue of Alydar's value, so in late October Golden Eagle notified Calumet's broker that it would not renew the Alydar coverage.

PART IV

FRENZY

1 Alton Stone knew he had done his best on the night of November 13. He knew that anything could have happened the minute he left the stallion barn and that while he was driving down the road to finish his rounds, he wouldn't know about it, wouldn't hear a sound, wouldn't see anything except the two streaks of light reaching out from the front of his Bronco into darkness and space. Only a twenty-four-hour guard in the stallion barn could have prevented Alydar's pain. He knew that, and everybody assured him that they knew it, too. But he still blamed himself for what happened, and he couldn't tell the story of finding Alydar, withers covered in sweat and eyes popping out with fear, without his own eyes filling with tears. It was the image of Alydar's leg, dangling listlessly, that most haunted him. "It looked like the only thing holding the leg on was a piece of skin," he'd say later. And the sound of Alydar's faint nickering, a soft cry of surrender compared with his usual king-of-the-realm snort and whinny, would come back to Stone at moments when he'd gaze into Alydar's empty stall and wonder what had happened that night.

If only someone had been there to calm the horse after he kicked the door or somehow caught his foot between the stall door and the wall or was frightened by something or someone coming toward him. Just someone to give him a carrot, thought Stone. That might have saved his life.

Alydar had a habit of getting mad; over what, nobody really knew, but he would do so and break into a sweat. And it was well-known in the barns that a carrot would calm him. Stone always thought Alydar was a horse who wanted people to adore him, to hover around him. He loved the attention, and just one carrot somehow reminded him that he was the great Alydar. But if he didn't get the carrot, Stone knew, he'd start pawing at the wall or the stall door. And if he still didn't get attention, he might start to kick. Then he'd get impatient, and soon impatience would turn to anger. Sometimes he'd try to bite whatever was in front of him, even people, though he never meant any harm. He was just a big, powerful animal who wanted attention.

On the night of Alydar's accident, after the vets, Lundy, and the insurance adjuster had arrived, Stone fetched coffee and helped where he could—between rounds, of course—as a way to distract himself from his own pain and worry. But the thoughts kept coming into his head, like hailstones on the tin roof of a barn. He knew in his heart the whole thing might not be as simple as carrots.

He had noticed the bracket from the stall door lying in the hallway and wondered, if Alydar had kicked the door so hard as to cause the iron bracket deeply embedded in cement to burst from its mooring, why didn't the wood on the door give in before the bracket sheared off? And why, Stone asked himself, wasn't there a bigger dent in the door where Alydar had been kicking? He seemed to remember that Tim Tam Aly, an Alydar son, had kicked his door so hard he splintered it. That horse kicked in the whole bottom half of the door, Stone recalled, but the bracket was still in place. The wood on the lower half of Alydar's stall door was rough, pockmarked, and filled with little nicks and partial hoofprints, but not indented to the degree that Stone thought the power of a horse could cause. In fact, that first night he didn't remember marks on the door. The idea had crossed his mind that the door was loosened before Alydar started to kick it. Was it possible that someone who knew Alydar's excitability just bent down and somehow sheared that bracket off, knowing that the weight of a loosened door might eventually harm the horse's leg? And that the same person, though not touching the horse, agitated him somehow so he'd kick the door? This might mean that Alydar kicked the door only a few times before its weight had swung back with a force strong enough to cause the break.

Or perhaps he got his leg stuck between the loosened door and the stall wall, then panicked, as horses tend to do, causing the bone to fracture as he pulled his leg out. Everybody knows that for a horse a broken leg usually results in death, so it was possible that someone set the trap for the break instead of directly causing it. At the very least, Stone believed, if the horse in fact kicked the door, as the farm officially stated, then the horse might have kicked in response to something—something more than the need for attention and the desire to be pacified with a carrot. There was also the possibility that the bracket was sheared off as a tactic to divert attention from the real cause of the horse's demise.

During the thirty-six hours of Alydar's struggle, Stone wished for nothing more than the triumph of Alydar's will to live, that fighting spirit that was so legendary, a spirit that had kept him pushing for the number one spot in the three races of the 1978 Triple Crown. But this time, as in 1978—the two biggest battles of his life—Alydar's willpower came up short.

Stone wasn't among those Lundy asked to attend Alydar's burial, but the thirty-two-year-old groom went on his own. He drove his Bronco to a bend in the road about two hundred yards from the Calumet cemetery, and as he leaned against a fence post with the breeze blowing his long, thin blond hair, he watched as Alydar's body was lowered into the ground. When the grooms began shoveling dirt onto the horse's dark chestnut coat, everyone except Lundy and Fox walked to their trucks and cars. Nobody noticed Stone, or if they did they didn't acknowledge him.

At the graveside, Fox reminded Lundy of a 4:00 A.M. phone conversation he and Lundy had had several years before concerning the death of a stallion named Norcliff. Once a champion racehorse, Norcliff had died in Kentucky shortly after a road trip from Florida. "Better him than us," Lundy had said to Fox that night on the phone.

On this day, Fox, his hands stuffed in the side pockets of his black leather jacket, said, "Remember Norcliff, Chief? Better him than us, remember? Is that the case here?"

Lundy, looking down into the slowly filling hole before him, said, "I'm not sure."

2 Alydar's mourners far exceeded the small gathering at the Calumet cemetery. In the days following the burial, hundreds of news stories in France, Australia, Venezuela, Ireland, Germany, Japan, and the United States eulogized the horse, poring over every detail of Alydar's suspenseful moments at the track and his profitable years in the breeding shed.

Fans spilled out of the backstretch and the balcony boxes of every racetrack in the world. At Santa Anita, the horse's former exerciser Charlie Rose, whose license plates bore Alydar's name, told reporters Alydar was the most intelligent horse he'd ever ridden. "I feel like you'd feel if a close friend had died," said Rose, who took Alydar on morning gallops during the horse's early days with trainer John Veitch.

Veitch told reporters, "I was on the phone at an airport when I heard the news. I just started to cry, in the middle of the conversation."

Alydar fans commented on the horse's self-assured personality, his high intelligence, and his determination. One Chicago sportswriter, discussing the legendary 1978 duel between Alydar and Affirmed, wrote that Affirmed's move in 1986 from Spendthrift Farm to a stall next to Alydar's at Calumet was akin to Muhammad Ali and Joe Frazier sharing an apartment on New York's Park Avenue.

The impact of the horse's death on Calumet was not really an issue during the fall of 1990. It was inconceivable that the stable, on a winning streak all year, could be ruined by the death of one horse. At almost the same moment when Alydar was lowered into the ground, one of his many sons, Strike the Gold, won his first race by eight and a half lengths at Aqueduct Racetrack in New York. To the media, this was a sign that the stable could rebound quickly from the death of its superstar. Unnoted was the fact that Calumet, to stay afloat, had sold Strike the Gold in a package with five fillies and one colt two months before Alydar's death.

The big question for the press and the big story was what Alydar's demise meant to American racing in general. Commentators talked of the death as a devastating blow in a tragic year that had begun with the death of Secretariat. The 1973 Triple Crown winner was humanely destroyed in October 1989 after developing an incurable hoof inflammation. A few months later two prolific stallions, The Minstrel and Fappiano, were euthanized on the same day because of illness and injury. And at one of the sport's biggest televised races, a favorite filly, Go for Wand, stumbled one hundred yards before the finish line, shattering her ankle and crashing onto the turf with such ferocity that she was "put down" moments later before thousands of spectators. Then on November 15, the very day Alydar died, another great sire, Northern Dancer, suffered an attack of colic. Because he was twenty-nine years old, surgery was out of the question. He was put to sleep the next morning.

The sport was losing its superstars, and Alydar's death triggered the fear that such a loss, in combination with foreigners snatching up some of the finest bloodlines at the auctions year after year, might cause a shift in the industry's power—and money—away from central Kentucky and America to Japan or Europe.

Through all the speculation and commentary, there was never a question about Calumet's ability to handle the loss or even much discussion about how Alydar was injured that night. Alydar, a feisty, headstrong horse, had simply kicked his stall door a little too hard. In the fall of 1990, the public accepted this explanation without question, and Calumet's image remained stellar. Soon the white fences and red-trimmed cupolas would be the back-drop for a Ford Motor Company commercial touting the excellence of cer-tain American institutions like Ford and Calumet.

Letters, cards, and flowers continued to come in as fans expressed their sympathy. Some preferred to remain anonymous, like the person who threw four red roses on Alydar's grave about a week after the burial. A day or so after a granite headstone was erected at the grave, fresh roses ap-peared again. Through every season, for nearly eighteen months, there would be fresh roses on Alydar's grave, adding to the mysteries enveloping Calumet.

3 Tom Dixon never claimed his investigation would bear any resemblance to a police probe. He didn't request depositions or poke around the barns or the courthouse in an effort to piece together every detail of what had happened in the hours leading up to Alydar's injury. He was an insurance adjuster, not an investigator. His job was to take state-

ments, relay information to Lloyd's of London, and get the claim settled to everyone's satisfaction as soon as possible. There was never a doubt in Dixon's mind that in the case of Alydar he did the best he or anyone could do.

Dixon, a Lexington native, was the preferred adjuster in the region for Lloyd's, which handled more than 50 percent of the worldwide equine insurance market. After quitting a job at the post office and enrolling in a correspondence course in insurance adjusting, Dixon during the early 1960s took a part-time job as an adjuster at United Underwriters, a firm partly owned by Warren Wright, Jr., that handled a broad range of insurance. Soon he secured a better post with Kentucky's state insurance department, working his way up to chief enforcement officer. In the late 1970s, Dixon astutely recognized that the horse boom would soon deliver big business to equine insurers. With prices going sky high for shares and seasons, buyers needed insurance, and as more buyers borrowed money for equine investments, banks would demand insurance on their equine collateral. Knowing there was only one equine adjuster in town, Dixon launched his own firm, Dixon Adjusters. In 1979, his first year, he had 290 claims; by 1985, he had 1,500. And by 1990, he worked with twenty or more agencies, including Lloyd's, an exchange of insurance syndicates similar to the stock exchange in which individuals and businesses invest.

Dixon knew that the Alydar claim, the largest equine insurance claim in history, could take months to close. While most of the $36.5 million coverage was Lloyd's, $5 million was covered by Golden Eagle, a San Diego firm, and there was also the insurance of several holders of the lifetime breeding rights. In such a high-profile case no agent wanted to be caught dragging his feet. This was a time to show just how efficient the insurance business could be, especially for Lloyd's, which in recent years had been criticized for delays in paying claims on equine policies.

"Every agent was wanting to be the first one to pay on it. Everyone wanted to show how good they were at honoring claims," Dixon said later.

Dixon saw no reason to start his investigation the night after Alydar was hurt, or the next day, or the day Alydar was put down. Everyone he needed to talk to was busy, and he didn't want to interfere. But once he began, several days after Alydar's burial, he was lightning fast. He talked with the vet Dr. Lynda Rhodes, with Alton Stone, and with office assistant Susan McGee; he got reports from vets Baker and Bramlage. He didn't take Lundy's statement because, he said later, he was with Lundy throughout the ordeal.

"We arrived at about the same time, so it seemed to me no reason to do that."

On November 19, six days after Alydar's injury, Dixon met with Stone at the Calumet office. McGee was there, too. Dixon asked Stone for his address and birthdate and explained that the interview was being taped.

DIXON: Now, we are going to talk about the events of November 13th, 1990, and if you could, it's my understanding that you were filling in for the night man, that ordinarily you are the day man.

STONE: Yes, sir.

DIXON: Could you just kinda describe your routine for me beginning about oh 9 or 9:30 and just kinda bring me up to when you found the horse.

STONE: Okay, I was patrolling the whole area at the time and I come up here [to the stallion barn] just like 9:30, check the horses, did all of the other routines I normally go through. I come back like at 10:05 and double check myself just for the safety.

DIXON: Is that kinda an ordinary routine or did you have some reason to come back?

STONE: I just came back on my own just to check. Then I found Alydar standing there sweating.

DIXON: Could you describe the door for me?

STONE: I didn't look at the door at all.

DIXON: His door was closed?

STONE: Yes, he was standing there facing me, wringing wet of sweat. So I immediately got on the radio and hollered for Sandy to come to the stallion barn.

DIXON: Sandy, is Sandy who?

STONE: Sandy Hatfield.

DIXON: She's what, your broodmare manager?

MCGEE: She's actually Alton's supervisor through the day.

DIXON: Okay, I'm sorry, go ahead. I just want to identify these people. So your first call was to Sandy.

STONE: Yes and at the same time I was walking to the phone to call Lynda Rhodes, our veterinarian.

MCGEE: Both of them live on the farm.

DIXON: That was going to be my next question. So you came in the office here to use it or do you have a phone . . .

STONE: We have a phone in the back [of the stallion barn].

MCGEE: It's in the barn.

DIXON: When you saw him standing there, did you try to open the door or did you just immediately go to call Sandy and Lynda?

STONE: I just immediately went to call, done nothing.

DIXON: Can you remember what you said when you called Sandy?

STONE: Oh, shit.

(Laughter)

DIXON: I assume she and Lynda came on up here [meaning the stallion barn]?

STONE: Yes, they were right here. I walked in and caught him and when I first saw him I didn't even notice the leg. I just seen the sweat and I thought maybe it was colic or something. So I went on and caught him and that's when I discovered the leg like that.

DIXON: Did you all have any difficulty opening the door?

STONE: No, sir.

DIXON: When did you notice that he had apparently, had kicked the door?

STONE: Just shortly after we hooked onto him, I mean, it was just obvious all out of place, cause I was coming out with the vet and I kinda looked down and seen a piece of the roller laying out on the floor and I said something's wrong.

DIXON: When you saw him in the stall was he standing free or did he have that leg in between the door and the wall?

STONE: He was standing facing me, at the stall door.

DIXON: So it would just be guessing if he ever had his leg in between the door, the stall door and the wall. I mean, did anybody actually ever see it in there?

STONE: No, sir.

DIXON: I'm just trying to figure out how, if he might have got it in there in the excitement trying to get it out, snapped it. But you never did see it?

STONE: Never did see it, no.

DIXON: And this would have been 10:15 or 10:20.

STONE: 10:20.

MCGEE: There were scrapes on the wall, right by that door, where you came in.

DIXON: I arrived just about, shortly after that. You mentioned about the horse acting colicky, you gave me the time, you told me about the routine . . .

MCGEE: The horse was never colicky, the horse was sweating and he didn't know what it was. He just knew something was wrong.

DIXON: I'm putting words in Alton's mouth, when he saw the horse standing there sweating he thought possibly he was colicky.

MCGEE: Yes, he didn't know what was wrong. The horse was just standing there, making no movement at this time.

DIXON: Okay, I stand corrected. And you told me who you called first. Did you stay with the horse waiting on Lynda and Sandy?

STONE: Yes.

DIXON: And I assume they are here within . . .

MCGEE: Seconds.

STONE: A couple of minutes.

DIXON: I notice, I think the next morning, I think it was the left eye that was closed. Do you have any idea how that might have happened? I know he went down that night after they put the cast on him and I'm wondering if he hit his eye when he went down [the first night] with the cast.

STONE: I didn't really notice.

DIXON: That's about all I had. Is there anything I haven't asked you that you think is important?

STONE: No, sir.

DIXON: I don't know of anything you could add to it. Susan, is there anything . . .

MCGEE: There's nothing, you arrived shortly after I did. We were here about 10:30. We were here as quickly . . . (inaudible)

DIXON: That's it then, you don't have anything else to add?

STONE: No, sir.

DIXON: Okay, we appreciate your cooperation. Thank you.

Dixon knew that soon theories about why Alydar died would spread like a virus through the Bluegrass community, but he was the one taking statements and he had been there to see the valiant efforts to save the horse. Dixon was as certain about what he had seen that night as a horse with blinders is sure of the track directly in front of it. He knew Alydar had broken his femur two days after the surgery on his fractured cannon bone, on the same leg as the first break, and that the stallion was euthanized moments later. That's how the horse had died. A postmortem, sometimes required after a horse's death, wasn't necessary. It wasn't as if the horse had died and the owners called Dixon two days later to report it. Dixon had been on the scene, doing his job, witnessing every moment leading to the horse's death. And though he conceded that no one really knew what had happened in the minutes before Alton Stone discovered the horse, he was fairly confident that Alydar had injured the first bone while kicking the stall door.

That was it. There wasn't a lot to pull together, Dixon would say later. "They had already figured out before I got there that he had kicked the door. They didn't get together and have a story ready. It seemed to be the general consensus."

It was true that Dixon had never seen a bracket and roller sheared off the floor of a stall, but while it seemed strange at first, he believed that the farm's official story explained away any doubt. A horse is a powerful animal, and Alydar simply kicked that door hard enough to shear the bracket right off. The time to have probed for more concerning the bracket might have been in the first hours after the injured horse was discovered. But Dixon, being sympathetic to the concerns of all present that night, refrained from asking. "We're looking at the leading sire in the world standing there with a fractured leg. I can't be running around asking a bunch of dumb-ass questions when we're worried about this stallion," he said later.

Alydar was a spoiled horse, Dixon said on more than one occasion, and was known to kick his door. "People would comment on the noise from J.T.'s office, which was connected to the stallion barn. 'Oh, that's Alydar kicking on his door. He does it all the time,' J.T. would tell them," according to Dixon. "There was some talk that Alydar had got his leg hung between the sliding door and the main wall. Well, there wasn't room in there for his leg to get in there, and there would have been a whole lot more tearing of tissue. There would have been a whole lot more blood. He just happened to kick that door too hard in the wrong way, once too often. . . . There've been a lot of cases I wish there had been a video camera in the stall. This is one of them."

As Dixon continued to take statements, it never crossed his mind that what happened to Alydar could have been intentional. If there had been any "hanky-panky," Dixon reasoned, someone would have contacted him, perhaps anonymously and perhaps for a price, asking him for money in exchange for the truth. "Any police investigator will tell you, you break cases like this with informants," he said.

The Calumet press release that Lundy issued in the midst of the maelstrom immediately established the kicking-the-door theory as the cause of Alydar's injury. The problem was that there were farm workers who didn't recall this habit of Alydar's. He was known for pawing at the stall door and the wall, both of which were filled with the nicks and rough spots that such pawing, over time, might cause. But he wasn't known as a persistently violent kicker, and it seemed only logical that regular kicking, over time, would cause large indentations on the door.

Stone's initial reaction to the horse's sweaty appearance was that Alydar was colicky. Colic is when a horse's delicate intestinal tract blocks, causing a painful buildup of gases. In severe cases the intestines literally implode and spread toxins through the horse's body. The pain of colic is intense enough to make a horse feel crazed, go wild, or kick. Horses sometimes try to relieve the pain by rolling in fields or on the floors of their stalls. Was it possible that Alydar, in the frenzy of seeking such relief, had jammed his foot in the space between the stall door and the wall? Those who were there that night commented that the sweat had subsided after the splint was placed on Alydar's leg and there were no later signs of the colic. The possibility of Alydar having had an attack of colic that provoked him to move in such a way as to hurt his leg was never really considered. "There were no secondary signs of colic," said Dixon later. Still, Stone mentioned colic on the night of the accident, and again during his interview with Dixon. And it was possible that the tranquilizers and painkillers that Alydar received had diminished such secondary symptoms of the condition. However, none of these possibilities was enough of an incentive for anyone to demand an autopsy.

Dr. Bramlage, one of the nation's foremost experts in equine surgery, had seen a lot of broken cannon bones in his time, but he'd never seen a bracket and roller sheared off the base of a stall door. It wasn't uncommon to see a roller wiggle loose over time, but to see it just break off was a new experience. If the stallion had kicked the door every day for a long time, it was possible that the roller had been loose enough to be ready to break. Still, it seemed unlikely that no one, in the course of sliding the door open and closed several times a day, had noticed a roller loosened in such a way.

Bramlage never believed for a second that Alydar was hit by a bat or a crowbar or any outside force. If so, the bone would have shattered. Instead, Alydar had what is called a butterfly break, a low-energy fracture caused by a bending pressure rather than a direct hit. "The fracture looked like the leg had been bent to the side," he would say later. It was the kind of break that might occur as a result of getting a leg caught in a door or a hole.

Bramlage also wasn't convinced either that the break was the direct result of kicking the door, though it was possible, he said. What the vet believed was that Alydar caught his leg for a split second in the small gap between the stall door and the wall. This space is at the point where the door overlaps with the stall wall, after sliding across the entrance to the stall and attaching to the wall with a brass latch. The horse might have kicked the wall or perhaps the door once or twice and during the last kick, hooked his foot in this gap. When he tried to pull it out, he ran into trouble because a horse's hoof is bigger than the rest of his foot, fanning out at the bottom. Getting the hoof caught in the gap in the midst of a kick was possible because the hoof might have angled in sideways. But when he tried to pull it out, the shape of the hoof would prohibit its release—and cause the horse to become hysterical with fear. In the struggle to free his hoof, Bramlage theorized, Alydar might have slipped, causing the cannon bone of the trapped leg to break. The fractured leg was then limp, making it easier for the horse to pull the hoof out of the gap.

Whatever caused the injury, Bramlage had been pleased with the results of the surgery, believing Alydar, despite the odds against him, had a decent chance for recovery. This made the outcome all the more disappointing. In a report addressed "To whom it may concern" dated November 20, 1990, Bramlage offered his version of the last moments of Alydar's life:

> The sling was removed at 8:15 A.M. For 10 minutes, he seemed comfortable and reasonable on his limbs. His head was up and his ears were pricked. He seemed much happier about his environment. I left the hospital at that time . . . but as I understand it, as he began walking across the stall, he stumbled on his left fore as he was moving forward, and the cast, still foreign to him on his right hind leg, caused him to fall towards the cast side, with the cast going under his body and his body sliding down the wall, fracturing his femur. His temperament, both resenting the maintenance of the sling, as well as wanting to move across the stall unrestricted, certainly contributed to his problem. We fully expected to lose the horse due to the severity of the injury, but I did not expect to lose him for this reason.

There was little else anyone spoke about at the Keeneland sales that November. An early rumor, the day after Alydar's injury, had Alydar out of his stall and kicking at Secreto's stall. A farmhand told the story of how a negligent worker had forgotten to fasten the latch on Alydar's stall before

Stone came on board for the night shift. After years of spending most of their days in stalls, horses know every detail of their surroundings, how everything works, and especially how to get out when the opportunity presents itself. Alydar had spent some time that night slowly nuzzling the heavy door open, so the story went. Once in the cement corridor outside his stall, his first sight was Secreto, whose stall was directly across from Alydar's. In recent years the two horses hadn't gotten along. Secreto taunted Alydar, who responded by kicking the outside wall of Secreto's stall, which was made of concrete. A scared farmhand found the horse, led him back into the stall, and then sheared off the bracket to make it look as if Alydar had kicked his own stall door.

In bars and restaurants that story would be told with all sorts of twists and variations during the next several months. One version had Alydar and Secreto in a war of the stallions, like mythological beasts, outside the stallion barn. In all versions Lundy was not told of the mishap because the workers feared the consequences.

Such talk was nonsense, according to Dixon, who believed the rumor had been sparked by the fact that one of the vets had to tranquilize Secreto the night of Alydar's accident. A groom might have witnessed the injection and concluded that Secreto was somehow connected to whatever happened to Alydar. The truth was that Secreto "was all riled up," Dixon said, probably because of what had happened in Alydar's stall, which was directly across the corridor from his.

There was talk, too, about the possibility of someone hitting Alydar with a crowbar or baseball bat. Dixon said there was no way for that to have happened because, as Bramlage said, the leg wasn't shattered and there was very little blood on the straw. Besides, Alydar was an aggressive horse who wouldn't allow anyone close enough to his hindquarters to hit his rear legs.

A former Calumet employee talked among friends about the mysterious circumstances in the last seconds before Alydar's femur bone cracked. While everyone wondered what in the world had caused the horse to stir in those minutes after the sling had been removed, that employee believed the horse was pulled by his halter too quickly. That sparked another round of rumors about the circumstances after Bramlage and Lundy left the barn and the possibility of sloppiness or intentional harm in pulling the horse perhaps toward his water bucket. Dr. Baker, who was there, said nothing of the sort had happened.

Some wondered why Dixon had been called to the scene instead of Calumet's normal adjuster, Terry McVey. Dixon and Lundy didn't always get along, though Dixon downplayed the conflict. "He wanted things done yesterday," according to Dixon, "but we didn't really have words." But McVey's firm Equine Adjusters had handled the accounts of Calumet's insurance broker Kathy Jones and her agency Equus Unlimited since the spring of 1987, and McVey's firm had a good reputation and several big clients. He had been one of the adjusters, for example, when Secretariat died in 1989.

Jones, who was Lundy's sister, called Dixon the night of Alydar's injury only after first trying to reach McVey at his home. At that moment McVey was in his car, and when his pager went off, he was only ten minutes away from a phone. It was about 10:30 P.M. when he got the frantic messages and called back only to find both Jones's home line and the Calumet phones tied up. About forty-five minutes later he finally got through to Dr. Rhodes, who told him Alydar had been seriously injured and Dixon was at the scene for Lloyd's.

McVey, a stocky, six-foot-tall man with short black hair and a black mustache, arrived at his office the next morning to find a message from Golden Eagle, the California underwriter that only a few weeks before had informed Calumet's broker it would not renew its Alydar policy. Golden Eagle wanted McVey to serve as adjuster in the Alydar case.

McVey wasn't bothered about Dixon representing Lloyd's but he was confounded when he visited Alydar's stall to examine the scene of the accident. It was about 2:00 P.M. on November 14, only seven hours after Alydar had been moved to the clinic, yet already the stall showed no hint of the struggle that had just transpired. The red floors and red-and-white walls were scrubbed so clean they even appeared to have been repainted, and the floor was covered with fresh straw. A new bracket was bolted to the floor.

To have swept away the traces of Alydar's struggle was the height of efficiency for a farm in the midst of such turmoil. McVey appreciated this, but the fact that no evidence remained bothered him. He needed details, such as blood-stained straw or marks on a wall. Besides that, with a fresh pair of eyes, he might be the one to notice something the rest, in their panic to save the horse, might have missed. Now he had to depend on people who knew what had happened only after the horse was injured, after the horse had paced his stall swinging his broken leg in hysterical attempts to fling it back into place, after Stone had discovered the stallion's trembling body in the steam-filled stall. But McVey never expressed his dismay and only went about his business, asking questions, gathering facts.

McVey was told that the horse had kicked at the door until the bracket had broken off, and then the door came back and hit his leg. He knew that Alydar was aggressive, territorial, and difficult, but he hadn't heard that the horse had a habit of kicking the door. And he had trouble rationalizing how much force it would have taken to push the door out far enough so that it could swing back with enough power to break the horse's leg. If the door was heavy enough to break the leg, how could the horse have had the strength to kick it out?

Dr. Lynda Rhodes was not one to talk much about the details of Alydar's last days. She was particularly reticent about the cause of injury, saying only that the physical evidence was there, on the barn floor. "I don't know what happened. I don't know, and I don't think anyone will ever know," she would say months later. She described Lundy's actions as those of a man stunned by the event and very upset. "There were times he would be in the stall, and he would break down in tears. It wasn't a for-show thing on his part."

Robey would say that however Alydar had broken that first bone, Lundy didn't know a thing about it. He wasn't there, and he didn't know everything that happened in connection with Calumet, even if he thought he did. Robey sincerely believed that Lundy was involved in so many complicated deals by 1990 that he couldn't keep everything and everybody straight.

The mortality claim—the largest in the history of equine insurance—was settled in thirty days, with almost all of the $20.5 million going to First City. Holders of breeding rights had their own coverage, ranging from $250,000 to more than $1 million, bringing the total Alydar coverage to $36.5 million.

Dixon was proud of the way things progressed in the Alydar case, saying later, "We just about set a world record." The speed of payment on the claims was even more phenomenal considering that Calumet still owed at least $1.2 million on its premiums to Lloyd's.

Everyone agreed that it was extraordinary for a farm's number one stallion, a horse that would be named the industry's number one sire for 1990, to be injured in a freakish incident. But from Dixon's point of view—and everyone else's—there was no motive for wrongdoing and so no reason to even suspect it. Alydar, everyone believed, was worth much more to Calumet alive than dead. What madness would provoke anyone to kill the goose laying the golden eggs?

Besides, few people during the fall of 1990 had the slightest hint of how bad things had gotten at Calumet. Very few knew that Alydar, despite his stepped-up work schedule, was no longer the cash cow of Calumet and that the golden eggs had turned into promissory notes. The stable was in the midst of a comeback; its power and the power of those who ran it seemed greater than ever. Its image was like a bright light shining in the faces of all who came near, blinding them in the process.

But considering Calumet's fragile financial condition, its long list of debts, and its struggle to pay insurance premiums and operational costs, there was every reason in the world to suspect something evil—something that happened in those moments before the first bone broke, something that none of the caretakers, the vets, and all the good people who tried to save the stallion's life could have known about. The motive could easily have been to pay down the First City debt, the most onerous of all Calumet's obligations, a loan that held most of the farm's horses as security. The farm couldn't sell those horses unless it turned over the proceeds to First City, and any potential buyer of the farm would find the liens and the debt prohibitive. If the farm defaulted on the loan, a loan whose principal was due in only a few months, it could lose the assets. The insurance claim, in combination with the horse sale planned for January, would greatly diminish the $44.75 million debt, making the farm's financial state less onerous to outside investors, such as the Japanese. This would also allow the farm to release some of its assets from the grasp of First City. And while it seemed the farm would be less attractive without Alydar, Calumet did have a new rising star, Criminal Type, who was a top contender for the 1990 Horse of the Year award. Despite appearances, Alydar was worth more dead than alive.

During the weeks following Alydar's death, few people were suspicious, and those who harbored doubts kept quiet. The ones who were powerless, such as farm workers, were afraid to question publicly the farm's official story. Employees of insurance companies feared they would be alone in their suspicions and knew if they were wrong, if they questioned the crown jewel of the industry at a time when sympathy was the appropriate response, they could jeopardize their positions. Those with power within the industry or the insurance community feared that a scandal might hurt a business already suffering from plummeting sales prices and dwindling investments. Because of Alydar's high profile, an investigation would attract a good deal of attention, raising doubts among the general public about the industry's ethics. The horse's fame, Dixon and others believed, was one reason not to suspect any wrongdoing. Why would anyone want to get rid of a horse whose death would draw so much attention? Yet it was the prospect of this attention, which intensified the penalties for being wrong, that might have kept those suspicious few quiet.

Doubts, suspicions, and investigations reflected poorly on the industry, and even if there was an assassin and he was found, the horse was still dead. The damage was done, and now there seemed to be no place for heroes. Besides, who would have believed that a farm dedicated for decades to the production of animals and superior athletes could be so desperate that it now could survive only by destroying what it had produced?

4 While Lundy lost his ATM machine when Alydar died, the impact was more like the collapse of a bank. If there was anything that might have caused Lundy's ulcer, it was the aftermath of Alydar's death.

For days and weeks after the tragedy, the din of ringing phones and beeping faxes filled the Calumet office. At first there were messages of sympathy and requests from the media for comment. Then came the demanding voices of bankers and investors; creditors panicked about collecting on their Alydar seasons and worried about how even the seemingly invincible Calumet could withstand such a loss. Everyone wanted to be paid immediately.

If they had come in person to the farm to collect, the line would have extended from Lundy's door down the winding staircase of the Calumet office, through the office parking lot, across a mile or so of fields, and all the way to Alydar's grave. Besides the seasons held by Calumet, by certain deal makers, and by the owners of the insured lifetime breeding rights, at least sixty more 1991 seasons were pledged to Riggs National Bank, Betty Marcus, Marc Rash, Midlantic Bank, Black Chip Stables, Peter Brant (who got his seasons from the Mogambo purchase), several bloodstock agents and appraisers, the new owners of Strike the Gold, Manganaro Stables, feed companies, blacksmiths, vets, and a long list of people who had come to Lundy's rescue when he needed money and had swapped cash for an Alydar season. Nearly eighty seasons were already pledged for 1992, and perhaps as many as fifty for 1993. The prices ranged anywhere from $300,000 for a three-year package to $150,000 for one season. Records of who was owed a season were incomplete because Lundy had bartered some seasons in oral agreements with no formal contracts. And, as usual, he had given some away. A Calumet insider would later say that the farm typically gave away at least twenty breeding rights to its stallions each year.

It was clear that Alydar's death had solved a short-term problem by reducing the monstrous debt owed Calumet's largest creditor, First City. And because so many Alydar seasons were presold and prepledged, the farm did not suffer the debilitating loss of Alydar's supposed $20 million annual income. But there was nonetheless a devastating result: a tidal wave of demands for restitution. Without money and without a bank willing to lend the millions of dollars Calumet owed Alydar season holders, Lundy and his advisers did the only thing they could do: barter the seasons of other stallions in the Calumet stable.

Stallions that may have been bred only 50 or 60 times in 1990 would be bred many more times in 1991. Wild Again was bred to 102 mares for the 1991 season, compared with 82 the year before. Mogambo, bred to 20 mares in 1990, covered 58 in 1991; Capote went from 45 in 1990 to 60 in 1991; Criminal Type serviced 82 mares during his first season at stud. The farm also leveraged the seasons of its stallions, as it had done with Alydar seasons, into 1992 and 1993.

The flaw in the plan was that an Alydar season was worth far more than a Criminal Type season, then selling in the range of $50,000, and more than Wild Again at $35,000 or $40,000. In one case, an Alydar season was traded for eleven Wild Again seasons; another time, the farm swapped one Alydar for three Wild Again seasons and five to Criminal Type.

Considering the joint ownership of some of the stallions, the replacement process was complicated. Calumet and Black Chip Stables were co-owners of Wild Again. Lundy was stallion manager; Calumet did the bookkeeping. Calumet sold all the seasons each year, and the two owners divvied up the proceeds. Calumet would typically sell half the seasons for itself and half for Black Chip. If Calumet oversold its half, it would pay back Black Chip out of its "bank" of future seasons.

After Alydar's death, Calumet sold far more than its half of the Wild Again seasons, which were going for $35,000 that year: the farm ended up owing Black Chip approximately $1.2 million. But with all the 1991 seasons sold and almost 50 percent of 1992's sold, Calumet's "bank" of Wild Again seasons went bust. Though selling Wild Again seasons might stave off a creditor or two, the farm created a new debt—the $1.2 million owed to Black Chip.

Banks, though for the most part unaware of the replacement frenzy, would someday be upset by this process. For one, First City, which would soon hold Calumet's 50 percent stake in Criminal Type as collateral, was unaware that many breeders had been given chunks of that interest in the form of stallion futures, way into 1993. It was like buying a house and finding out later that the property was a time-share and that three months out of the year someone else had the right to live there.

Promissory notes flew back and forth. Calumet would issue a note to the Alydar holder and secure it with seasons to other stallions. If Calumet could put off the due date long enough, it could use the seasons for replacements in 1991 and then either pay back the note or give up the collateralized seasons for the next year.

Manganaro Stables, a Lexington-based partnership whose partners lived in Massachusetts, had two 1991 seasons to Alydar as of March 28, 1990. After Alydar died, Calumet agreed, in November, to pay Manganaro $300,000. In early January 1991, the farm issued Manganaro a promissory note for $300,000 and secured the note with twelve seasons to Criminal Type and twelve seasons to Wild Again. In the note Calumet claimed the collateral was free and clear of all liens. The twelve seasons, in each case, were divided into four for 1991, four for 1992, and four for 1993. With both Criminal Type and Wild Again jointly owned, this was a messy arrangement. But nothing was simple now.

Further complicating matters, Lundy, in the habit of doing favors for certain friends, not only reimbursed some who were owed but also helped others who were not, such as certain holders of lifetime breeding rights. The rights were supposedly good only as long as the horse was alive, and besides, most holders had insurance in case the horse died or became unfit for breeding purposes. Still, on November 21, Lundy sent a letter to Fred Gussin explaining that he would receive ten 1991 Wild Again seasons in place of his Alydar breeding right, which Gussin had recently purchased from Peter Brant for $1.1 million. "I think that you will be able to sell these seasons for enough money to recover," Lundy wrote.

While the individuals with Alydar seasons stormed the Calumet gates in the days after the horse's death, the bankers were initially less agitated. To most, Calumet was still a farm with a great reputation, a glorious past, and a spectacular year at the track. By now it was clear that the farm would make almost $4 million in purses for 1990. Alydar's death, though a tragedy, didn't seem to be impeding the farm's progress; there were plenty of other big-name stallions in its stud barn.

The farm's lending officer at IBJ Schroder, Deborah White, heard about Alydar's death on the evening news. Though confident in the farm's ability to withstand the blow, she still called Lundy the next morning. Just to be cautious, White arranged a trip to Lexington with her boss to discuss the status of things. Lundy took the two New York bankers to lunch at a local mall. Over orange pekoe tea and fried salmon, Lundy assured them that Calumet could honor its $3.3 million debt. His plan was to bring in some extra cash at the January sales at Keeneland by selling a broad range of Calumet bloodstock. He'd then make the Schroder payments.

At First City, within hours of Alydar's death, a bank representative called the farm. On November 15, Terry D'Souza, a First City vice president who took over the Calumet loan after the departure of Frank Cihak, was in a routine midafternoon meeting at the bank's offices in Houston. An executive vice president was called out of the room and returned minutes later with a furrowed brow. Afterward, he pulled aside D'Souza and told him Alydar was dead. While the farm could now pay down the $44 million–plus debt to the Houston bank, $20 million was still owed, and one of the first concerns was whether the insurance was paid up on the collateral for that debt. Besides Alydar, First City's collateral included most of Calumet's bloodstock as well as the value of the land over and above what the farm owed to Mutual Benefit. But First City knew the farm hadn't been paying its premiums since February or March. A bank with uninsured collateral is a nervous bank, especially with collateral as fragile as horses.

D'Souza, who for weeks had been studying the troubled portfolios of First City, worried that without Alydar the farm might be shaky. In his new job, D'Souza, a diligent man with a rapid-fire style, was anxious to get beyond the somber circumstances that forced Cihak to leave. First City was a bank looking for heroes, and D'Souza would qualify if he kept certain portfolios, such as Calumet, stable. On November 19, First City loaned the farm $2.58 million to make an interest payment back to First City. The collateral for this loan was Calumet's 50 percent stake in its new superstar, Criminal Type.

Lundy tried to ease First City's jitters with the same assurance he had given Schroder. In January he would sell some of Calumet's best bloodstock, nearly one-third of its horses, at public auction.

5 On January 3, 1991, Lundy could have celebrated more than his fiftieth birthday. In the past year he had brought Calumet back to the top of the business. The farm closed out the year with fifty-four wins, fifty-five second places, thirty-nine thirds, and $3,827,961 in earnings, and the odds were good that Criminal Type would be named Horse of the Year at the prestigious Eclipse Awards in February.

But for Lundy, Calumet's cash crunch ruined the festive spirit. A week or so after his birthday, Lundy made a deal with Texas breeder Craig B. Singer to loan Calumet some cash. On January 14, the farm issued a promissory note for $689,487 to Singer, using collateral consisting of twenty 1991 seasons to Criminal Type, ten 1991 seasons to Wild Again, and ten 1991 seasons to Secreto—all supposedly lien-free. The note was due in just two months.

So desperate was the farm for cash that Calumet was willing to pay huge interest rates. In a few cases, Calumet borrowed money from an individual in exchange for stallion seasons; the farm would then turn around and buy back the seasons at an inflated price so that the lender was getting 40 percent or so interest on its loan as a service fee for helping Calumet get the cash infusion.

At the same time, Lundy was planning the big sale of Calumet horses at Keeneland and fussing with First City over some of the details. The main point of contention was that Lundy wanted to put the horses into the sale without setting a reserve, or minimum bid for each horse, while First City demanded a reserve. Lundy wanted the horses sold no matter what, and he figured the horses weren't worth as much as First City thought they were. Panicky about the potential for another bad loan, First City wanted the full value of its collateral. Reserves, the bank reasoned, would protect them. First City's vision of value was based on the farm's quarterly reports to the bank, which might include any number of business records, including appraisals of the equine assets, year-end financial statements, or tax returns with records of sales proceeds.

Where once Calumet might have inflated those values in order to increase its borrowing capacity, Lundy and company now needed First City to be frighteningly realistic. "Apparently you do not understand what I am trying to do on Tuesday," Lundy wrote. "I am trying to sell horses to reduce Calumet Farm's debt. . . . The prices I had previously given you reflected a price if the horses were sold at a more opportune time. An auction is something I cannot control."

At the same time, the agents who conducted the last appraisal of the horses First City used as collateral wrote to the bank with an equally foreboding message: "Our records indicate we have not done an appraisal for the First City National Bank of Houston since March 15, 1990." The letter then listed fifteen reasons why the value of horses appraised in March 1990 might be much less in January 1991. Among them: "weakening demand; Mid-East crisis and uncertainty; time of year; general weather conditions; general economic conditions."

The bank won a modified victory, but the reserves were set at about 10 percent of what First City apparently believed the collateral was worth. Horses that bankers thought were worth $250,000 were placed in the auction with a $30,000 reserve bid.

The January Keeneland sale began on the fifteenth, with three full hours devoted to the dispersal of Calumet horses. In the barns behind the sales pavilion where consignors show the horses to prospective buyers and prepare them for the sales ring, there were two topics of conversation: the Persian Gulf War and Calumet. The horse industry had a particular interest in the Gulf. For a decade, Arab buyers had been spending millions at the Keeneland and Fasig-Tipton auctions. Arabs—mainly the Maktoums who were members of the royal family of the United Arab Emirates—typically accounted for 40 percent of total sales. At the Saratoga Springs sale in August 1990, held one week after Iraqi troops marched into Kuwait, there was barely an Arab presence.

Now, in the barns, owners and consignors waiting to lead their horses into the sales ring fretted about the prospect of another Arab no-show. As a distraction, they chatted about Calumet. A big dispersal sale like Calumet's, with nearly one hundred horses of all ages, was a sure sign of trouble. Among the horses were twenty-nine yearlings, thirty-four two-year-olds, and thirty-two broodmares, some in foal to Alydar, Seattle Slew, and Wild Again.

Lundy was accustomed to sidestepping skepticism. The reduction, he said, was devised to free up space, though he also wanted to streamline expenses. "You just breed so many horses and there's nowhere to put them," he told a Lexington reporter. "It's just horses and horses and horses." The farm was not financially strapped, he assured the reporter.

The sale, with an average price of $75,212, was a disaster. The Arabs' conspicuous absence was sorely felt. Agents for Japanese horseman Zenya

Yoshida paid the top price—$525,000 for Calumet's four-year-old filly A Wild Ride—but seventeen of the twenty-nine Calumet yearlings that walked into the ring that day failed to reach their reserve bids. Nor did sixteen Calumet broodmares. One horse, appraised for $750,000 the previous spring, sold for $32,000. Of the ninety-five horses Calumet put on the block, the farm was able to sell only sixty-two for a total of $4,867,500—hardly enough to satisfy the bankers in Houston. This was a stunning outcome considering the sales figures and appraisal values in Calumet's recent past. One 1986 appraisal, for example, written for a Citizen's Fidelity loan of $20 million, valued seventy-two horses at $40 million. At the 1987 Saratoga sale, five Calumet horses had brought a higher total than the sixty-two in 1991.

For First City, the sale was like a match igniting an ever-shortening fuse. Prior to the sale, First City officials had learned that Calumet hadn't made a payment on its Mutual Benefit loan for eighteen months before its October default. In addition, First City hadn't received Calumet's year-end statements, as it requested numerous times, and phone calls to Calumet were not being returned. In late December, First City, seeking more attention, had contacted the guarantors of the loans, the Wright heirs; the family's surprise over the current state of affairs troubled the bankers. Then came the fuss over reserves, the sluggish sale, and the fact that the bank learned that in addition to the usual commission taken by the auction house, 5 percent was taken off the sale proceeds as a commission for the consignor, Lundy's son. First City was also beginning to realize that because of the replacement chaos after Alydar's death, its expensive piece of collateral, Criminal Type, was now laden with liens in the form of pledged seasons—some committed as far into the future as 1993.

First City demanded a plan. D'Souza and Lundy, accompanied by Robey, who was now beginning to panic, too, would soon meet to discuss the formulation of a new course to appease the bank.

6 On the second weekend in February, racing's elite gathered at the Fairmont Hotel in San Francisco for the Eclipse Awards. This year they would highlight the official return of the Calumet glory, but no one suspected the ceremonies also would expose the strained relations behind the glory.

On Saturday afternoon, the industry's leading breeders and owners filed into a spacious room with high ceilings dripping with crystal chandeliers for the nationally televised announcement of the winners. After the awards for Jockey of the Year, Trainer of the Year, and a dozen or so other categories were disclosed, the announcer took a deep breath before revealing the biggest honor, the award for 1990 Horse of the Year.

"We have a felon in our midst," he began. "Criminal Type is the winner."

Lundy, dressed in a navy jacket and a red tie, walked sheepishly to the podium to accept the trophy. His quiet, seemingly humble demeanor gave him a dignity that his appearance did not. This was a moment of great achievement for Lundy, who regardless of his unconventional ways wanted to be accepted and recognized in his industry. On this day in February he would get that respect, despite his hardscrabble past, the way he dressed, and the manner in which he sometimes conducted business.

"I don't know what to say," he began, as he clutched the award with both hands. "On behalf of the people at Calumet, and all the employees . . . thanks to Wayne [Lukas], the turf writers and everyone—this is something. . . . I just don't know what to think."

At the black-tie dinner that evening, award winners gave their speeches and officially received their trophies, but this year the occasion seemed as much a celebration of Calumet's apparent comeback as a tribute to the year's accomplishments in racing. Calumet received the Breeder of the Year award, and before Lundy accepted it, there was a short video about the farm. With scintillating pictures of the Calumet landscape and old stills of Warren Wright, Sr., in his homburg hat and rimless spectacles watching the 1941 Derby through binoculars, the narrator intoned:

> The name Calumet Farm instinctively brings memories, memories of Whirlaway and Citation, eight Kentucky Derbies, and a general dominance of a sport. Happily, however, Calumet Farm also stands

proud today, based on its current record. Under direction of J. T. Lundy, president of the historic Kentucky farm, Calumet's breeding operation in 1990 was represented by no fewer than eleven stakes winners. . . . When you think of Calumet, you are justified in remembering yesterday, but what the farm is achieving today is also the stuff of history.

Comedian Tim Conway was the evening's master of ceremonies. He directed James T. Bassett III to present the Breeder of the Year award to Calumet, and in his presentation speech Bassett, too, referred to the sense everyone had of a comeback. "The fabulous silks of Calumet Farm have now risen to the forefront of American racing, with twenty-one stakes winners, fourteen grade I winners, $3.8 million in winnings."

Lundy, with a calm gait that belied the stress his job had recently wrought, moved to the stage and said simply, "I would like to thank everyone on behalf of the people at Calumet for this honor."

Soon, another video was shown, another glimpse of Warren Wright, Sr., in his box at Churchill Downs with his binoculars, and more panoramas of the farm, and a voice-over:

In recent years, Calumet Farm has often been able to wake up the echoes of past glories. . . . it has been up to Calumet president J. T. Lundy to guide the farm through new chapters of the glory days. In 1990, Calumet's Criminal Type, a homebred son of Alydar, added his name to the honor roll of champions old and new. . . . And so once more racing has a champion from Calumet Farm to salute.

Lundy came to the stage yet again, this time to accept a bronze trophy for Criminal Type as Best Older Male Horse. While on stage, he was once again awarded the gold trophy for the Horse of the Year award. Lundy, who after sweeping up the biggest prizes of the year was beginning to relax a little on stage, said with a chuckle, "This gold looks better than the bronze." With a smile he went on to say, "But I want to give credit to Wayne [Lukas] because he's responsible for this happening, because he did a great job with [Criminal Type]. Thank you all."

Clutching a big trophy in each hand and holding them against his waist for balance, Lundy moved to the back of the stage as the tall, urbane Lukas came forward and began his own acceptance speech. He talked of what a privilege it was to win such an award, considering the number of good horses in competition that year. Then, as he was saying, "And I just want to thank the Calumet family for giving me—" he was cut off by a loud throaty cry from the audience.

"I think the Wrights had something to do with that, and there are two here today. . . . By damn, we're gonna be recognized," the voice shouted.

Necks strained and eyes scanned the audience, trying to find the source of the voice. Lukas remained composed, and looking out into the maze of black ties and diamonds saw Bertha Wright coming toward him.

Smiling he said, "They're recognized."

Barely missing a beat, he drew a breath and continued his speech. But as he opened his mouth to speak, so did Bertha: "I'm Warren Wright, Jr.'s wife. By dern you're going to recognize the Wrights."

Lukas graciously nodded and said, "Thank you . . . Mrs. Wright, ladies and gentlemen . . . now I'd like to add just one more thought here."

Bertha was now in front of the podium. Lukas smiled and said, "Here we go."

In her black satin ensemble with red sequined trim, and perhaps tipsy from a few too many glasses of champagne, Bertha had nonetheless accomplished what appeared to be her goal: to sweep away the dust on the Wright family name. Looking up at Tim Conway, she said, with a wide grin, "I love you as a comedian, you're great."

Conway, easing tensions, leaned over the podium: "You didn't have time to talk, with everybody up here screwing around collecting awards."

As she turned to face a confused audience and take a deep breath in preparation for the journey back to her seat, Bertha caught a glimpse of Lundy. She frowned for a split second, stamped her right foot, clapped her hands once, and said, "Warren Wright, Sr., did it." Then she stomped away, back into the blur of breeders and owners who again turned their attention to Wayne Lukas.

Bertha returned to her table, pulling up a chair next to her son Tommy Wright and his wife. This was a big night for Bertha. Knowing that Calumet was to win the top awards, she had flown to San Francisco that morning with a brand-new dress and with thoughts of her husband and his father and how she would honor them both. She had expected to be called up to the podium with her son-in-law Lundy.

Don S. Sturgill, a Lexington lawyer who had known Bertha for many years and sat at her table that evening, later said, "Sixty years of the Wright family and no acknowledgment that night. . . . It's hard to get just one of those awards, rare to get both ever for one farm, and unprecedented to get both on the same night. . . .

"I'd say that was the straw that broke the proverbial back. Calumet meant a great deal to her, and to be ignored in its moment of glory was just too much. . . . Lundy was so wrapped up in trying to thank Wayne Lukas that he forgot her. It was a big mistake for him. It was one of those moments, you know, that can change the landscape."

Until that night, Bertha had never believed anyone who criticized her son-in-law. For some time her daughter Courtenay had been telling her that things at the farm just weren't the way they ought to be; friends had warned Courtenay that Lundy might be taking advantage of her family. But Bertha did not want to strain family relations any more than they already had been strained through the years. Most of all, for the sake of her grandchildren, she was determined to avoid another scandal. This was a family affair, not to reach the world outside the white fences. She had lived through the rift with Mrs. Markey, the exile from the farm, her husband's prison term, the dissolution of her fashion business, and the palimony suit that followed. She had even survived a bout with cancer in the early 1980s. Now, at seventy-one, she simply wanted the privilege of drifting into old age peacefully and with her family intact.

Lundy was the father of her grandchildren, and she would continue to defend him as long as she could. But that one moment, that seemingly small incident at the Eclipse Awards dinner, jolted Bertha into reality. The next morning on the plane going back to Lexington, she asked Sturgill to work for her, mainly to find out exactly what was going on in the management at Calumet.

7 Toward the end of February, during commercials on *60 Minutes, PrimeTime Live,* and basketball games, Americans were treated to a bucolic scene of a yearling trotting across a field. This was followed by racing scenes and an enumeration of Calumet's champions. "When excellence becomes a tradition, there's no end to the greatness," the narrator said,

"and it doesn't happen only in horse racing." Suddenly Ford's stable of cars replaced the horses, and the narrator extolled the excellence of the car company. Later, a Ford spokesman told the local paper, "We at Ford Motor Company like to be associated with winners like those at Calumet." And Lyle Robey added, "We're very pleased with it, believe me. You don't get that kind of nationwide publicity very often for nothing."

But while Calumet seemed as accessible to most Americans as switching on their televisions, the farm's bankers and investors were finding Calumet more and more elusive.

Some complained bitterly that no one answered the phone and that Lundy was impossible to reach. The deadlines involving First City, IBJ Schroder, Bank One, and countless individuals were coming fast. The vise was tighter than ever before. To placate creditors and to scan the financial landscape for deals, Lundy was on the road or in the air almost daily. He made frequent trips to New York, where Calumet had retained an attorney to help devise a plan for managing its debt, and to Chicago, where the farm hired a financial consultant.

With Betty Marcus's note due to Citizen's Fidelity at the end of March, Axmar was tightening the screws. Calumet still owed the $1.625 million note and the $1.7 million in seasons. Axmar had been trying for months to get some word from Calumet, but the bright white fences seemed to be turning into brick walls.

Axmar's Washington, D.C., attorney Austin Mittler had met with Lundy on December 17 and stressed that Axmar couldn't make its own loan obligations to Citizen's Fidelity until Calumet began making at least a few payments. On January 4, Mittler spoke with Matthews and urged him to make a partial payment. Ten days later, he sent Matthews a letter asking for a reasonable portion of the amount due and a schedule for future payments. In his response Matthews said he had "impressed upon [Lundy] the need to formulate a plan."

In the midst of the Axmar mess, Texas rancher Craig Singer alleged Calumet still owed at least $300,000 on his $689,487 note from January. If Calumet didn't pay, Lundy would have to hand over the ten Secreto seasons, ten Wild Again seasons, and twenty seasons to Criminal Type that Lundy had pledged to him as collateral.

Two big notes to Matchmaker Financial Corporation and one to Equine Capital Corporation were due on March 1. Gray Cliff, a shell company once owned by Rash and now a subsidiary of Calumet, owed Matchmaker nearly

$1.45 million and ECC about $181,000. And Calumet owed $1.12 million to Matchmaker. Matchmaker and ECC had taken out the money from Citizen's Fidelity for these loans, as they so often did.

During the same month, Calumet lost about $693,000 from its general account at the First National Bank of Georgetown. In a highly unusual situation, a bank employee allegedly misread a statement and wire-transferred $770,301.58 to Peter Brant's White Birch Farms rather than the $77,301.58 Calumet claimed it instructed the bank to wire.

The $300,000 note of Manganaro Stables concerning the two Alydar seasons matured during this period. When Manganaro demanded its rights as a secured creditor, it found trouble. The equine collateral was full of liens—by Riggs, by the state of Kentucky, by First City, by Craig Singer.

The Calumet board, accustomed to meeting infrequently, now convened every week. There were also new faces present, such as Bertha's lawyer Don Sturgill. High on the list of priorities was the task of devising a plan for First City. Lundy had never experienced such pressure. In mid-March he even wrote a letter of resignation but never sent it. Instead, according to Robey, Lundy folded the letter several times and stuffed it into his hip pocket as he went about his business.

What might have been most frustrating to Lundy was his inability to complete a deal with the Japanese. By the time the Nomura deal had fallen through the previous fall, Lundy had another deal in the works. The new plan called for representatives of Mitsui and Company, an industrial conglomerate and Japan's second-largest trading house, to find Japanese investors to buy 75 percent of Calumet. The Wright family would continue to own the remaining quarter interest. Coolmore Stud, the Ireland-based farm owned largely by British magnate Robert Sangster, would manage the farm for the Japanese. Early in 1991, an attorney representing Riggs and Fred Gussin, Calumet's partner in the Calumet-Gussin partnership, visited Japan, Ireland, and Kentucky, sometimes on the Calumet jet, in an effort to fit the pieces together. Riggs and Gussin apparently were motivated by the $9.2 million that Calumet, because of its liability in the Calumet-Gussin partnership, owed Riggs. If the deal worked, Riggs would get its money. But by March, though Calumet's accounting firm had compiled a prospectus showing the farm's value at $160 million, the deal wasn't going anywhere.

On March 27, Lundy traveled to New York to meet with Asher Fensterheim, Calumet's new attorney, and Mittler about Axmar. For Lundy, who hated confrontations, the hours-long meeting wasn't much fun. Mittler claimed Lundy had communicated with Betty Marcus throughout 1990 without ever telling her there would be problems with Calumet's ability to meet the terms of the redemption agreement. This he called "unconscionable," and he told Lundy that he believed Calumet had sold at least some of the 1990 seasons to the stallions designated as Axmar's and that the cash had been diverted. Lundy didn't deny it. At the end of the meeting, Mittler said Axmar was considering a lawsuit against Calumet, a course it would surely pursue unless Calumet sent cash payments immediately.

On the same day in Houston, First City's chairman and Cihak's old boss, Bob Abboud, stepped down from his post. The event sparked rumors that the Federal Bureau of Investigation might be looking into some of the bank's dealings that involved Cihak. Abboud's resignation might mean more intense examination of First City's troubled portfolios, such as Calumet.

In Lexington that day, a few hours before the weekly Calumet board meeting, another gathering that would have yet more impact on Calumet's future was taking place at a Chinese restaurant on the west side of the city. At the end of the luncheon rush, three cars drove one by one into the small parking lot in front of the August Moon. The first was a red Volvo station wagon driven by horse trainer John T. Ward, Jr. A minute or so later a black BMW pulled in. Its driver was Paula Cline, a small, muscular woman with thick shoulder-length brown hair. About ten minutes later, a white Blazer arrived with Lundy's sister-in-law Courtenay Wright Lancaster at the wheel.

Cline entered the restaurant and immediately spotted Ward sitting in a booth in a far corner of the nearly empty dining room. Cline, who regularly exercised racehorses at Ward's stable, also managed his horse sales at Keeneland. Two months before, at the January Keeneland sales, Ward and Cline had had a conversation that led to the August Moon encounter. That day, in the tack room of one of the barns, Cline had asked Ward what he thought might be happening at Calumet. Cline knew Courtenay Wright Lancaster from church and had picked up on her friend's anxiety about the farm. What concerned Cline was that Lancaster seemed reluctant, almost afraid, to press Lundy for details about the farm's operations—details that every Wright heir had a right to know. She seemed intimidated by the man entrusted to manage a large portion of her inherited wealth. And part of her intimidation, Cline knew, was that she had limited knowledge of how the horse business worked.

Ward had been watching the Calumet state of affairs for some time. He knew little about what happened inside its gates, but he read every detail about sales and purchases of horses, about seasons, about the auctions. A third-generation horse trainer, Ward, like most Kentucky-bred horsemen, was in love with the Calumet legend.

In the barn as they fought off the January chill that day and listened to sales results on the speakers outside, Cline and Ward talked at length about Calumet. Cline expressed her concern for Lancaster and her suspicion that Lancaster's brother-in-law could be deceiving the Wright heirs. Ward seemed intrigued, and as Cline left the sales that day, she felt she had found the perfect person to help Lancaster figure out what was really happening at Calumet.

Now, at the August Moon, Lancaster joined Ward and Cline. She smiled timidly as Cline introduced her to Ward. She began with a few questions about who Ward knew in the horse business and then eased the conversation cautiously toward Calumet. Though Ward's honesty was Lancaster's biggest concern, she was impressed with his knowledge of the industry and his outsider's perspective on her farm. By the end of the luncheon, Lancaster decided Ward was someone she could trust.

8

Lundy spent part of April Fool's Day completing a deal to borrow $193,629 from Citizen's Fidelity for himself, pledging shares of horses and breeding rights as collateral. On April 2, he sent a fax to Betty Marcus offering shares in two Alydar foals, for a value of over $400,000, as a way to pay down the debt of more than $3 million owed to Axmar Stables. "Dear Betty, I have some new Alydar to add to your list. These new ones will help bring up total values for you. . . . This is the only cash we have. We are trying to get more for you and I'll call you tonight. J.T."

The next day was the board meeting of Calumet Farm, Inc., in the dining room of the main residence. Shortly before 2:00 P.M., family members, lawyers, and bankers filed into the long, cavernous room with the bay window that Gene Markey had added in the 1950s. As Stephen Foster and General Lafayette stared down from portraits, the board members took their seats: Lundy; Bertha; her children, except for Lundy's wife who was in France, and their spouses; Robey; Matthews; Sturgill; the president of CommerceNational Bank and the bank's trustee of the Warren Wright, Jr., Trust. Briefcases clicked opened. One or two individuals, in tones soft enough to be whispers, exchanged greetings. A few reached into breast pockets and purses for pens.

The purpose of the meeting was for Lundy to deliver a plan that would put Calumet on a firm schedule to pay its debts. Ever since Calumet's January sale had fizzled, the banks, in particular First City, were demanding payment schedules be met. So far there had only been delays.

Throughout March, Lundy had insisted that the banks wait until summer when he could sell the yearlings he had failed to sell in January. And the broodmares, he said, would sell for a handsome price by autumn when Keeneland held its annual breeding stock sale. Then of course there was the possibility of the Japanese saving the day. He had told the Calumet board on several occasions that negotiations in Tokyo, ongoing for several months now, were progressing, and with the horse market the way it was, both Lundy and Robey believed it'd be smarter to try to sell Calumet as one big package, a unit of horses and land, retaining some rights for the family. The horses could bring higher prices, they thought, if sold with the land and the facilities. The farm with the horses was simply more attractive than just a plot of land.

Lundy needed time; in the end, he assured them, everyone would be glad they had waited. Besides, if the Japanese balked, then possibly after the heat was off the Middle East, the Saudis would be interested in some sort of deal. There was also the suggestion of a public offering, though Spendthrift's collapse in combination with the sluggish equine market lessened the likelihood of Calumet going public.

The family and the banks were sick of promises. By now, no one had the patience to give Lundy the time he wanted. The meeting would be short and the atmosphere about as cool as a drafty barn.

The spokesman for the bank pressed Lundy for a plan one last time. Lundy wasn't defensive, but, feeling that everyone had made up their minds before the meeting not to listen anymore, he seemed agitated enough to punch the next person who spoke. His response was simple.

"You step outside and we'll talk about it," he told the banker. The banker declined.

Bertha, desperately seeking some solution, offered to sell her finest china if that would help.

Lundy then said, "The bank doesn't control me." Staring down at the table, he continued, "But if the family wants me to leave, what I'm saying is, I will."

Lundy, looking at Robey, placed a resignation letter, dated March 15, 1991, on the table. Then he stood up from the table, looked around the room one last time, and left, never to return.

The room was silent except for the sound of Lundy's footsteps moving across the wooden floor of the front hall to the door. Though the moment was dramatic, it wasn't a shock to anyone present and Lundy wasn't exactly walking off a cliff when he closed the front door. He had, after all, just taken out a loan from Citizen's Fidelity for more than $193,000. He had his farm in Midway, Kentucky, and property in Florida. In a few weeks, he would borrow $500,000 from the First National Bank of the Florida Keys, mortgaging the property in Marathon that belonged to his company Vaca Bloodstock. Lundy was not suffering nor was he without a plan for his own well-being.

Robey was the first to speak. "You don't understand the implications of what you've just done. Discharging him at this time will create irreparable harm to Calumet." Robey recognized that Lundy was balancing more balls in the air than anyone at that table knew, more than even he was aware of. While Lundy had lost track of money and seemed sometimes confused by the interdependence of deals and deal makers, it was clear to Robey that without the juggler the balls would fall on Calumet, perhaps crushing the farm when they landed. In recent months the situation had become more than frustrating to Robey. He wanted to find a solution to the problems and to propose the plan everyone was demanding but he didn't have all the information he needed to do so.

In January shortly after the horse sale, Robey's sister had found him sitting in his Wright Enterprises office staring at the walls in a deep depression. She asked him if there was anything she could do to help.

"This place . . . they don't listen to me," he told her, still in a daze. "I feel like we've made so many mistakes."

"You can advise and counsel," she said. "But you can't make anyone do it, do what you want."

"Yeah," he responded, clearly not listening.

Now, as if Robey's credibility had plummeted the moment Lundy shut the door, no one responded to his comment. Seconds later, from somewhere inside the house, John T. Ward, Jr., appeared. The banker announced to the board that the family had decided Ward should take over. His title would be chief operating officer, though a few weeks later he'd be appointed the official president. Ward said a few words about going over to the office and talking to the staff; then one of the bankers asked everyone to leave.

But the transition wasn't over. Down the hill from the main house and across a few pastures, Lundy's assistants Heinz and McGee, as well as two or three office staffers, had gathered at 3:00 P.M. in the lobby of the Calumet office, as instructed by one of the bank officers. They were joined by four men including bank president Roger Dalton, Heinz would later swear in an affidavit.

Dalton, Heinz recalled, announced that Calumet was getting a new president. He said a lot had happened to Calumet since Alydar had died, and as if reminding them of why the bankers had the right to be there, he said the bank, as trustees for the Warren Wright, Jr., Trust, was the majority shareholder of Calumet Farm, Inc. And now the bank was going to try to run the corporation. The office would be closed, he said, for the rest of the day, and he instructed the staff to write their names, addresses, phone numbers, and job titles on a legal pad, and then to go home. Someone would get back to them within ten hours and let them know if they could keep their jobs.

Then one man accompanied each employee to her desk. Dalton went with McGee. Another officer escorted Heinz. He searched her purse and another larger bag before permitting Heinz to leave. That afternoon, with the staff gone, the office was "swept" for bugs and the locks were changed.

At the main house, Bertha told a reporter for the Associated Press that "J.T. has done what he set out to do and has brought Calumet back to a position of prominence. He now wants to do some of the things that he neglected in his personal life in the last decade while running Calumet."

Lundy's reason for leaving was much simpler. "It was just time to quit," he told the reporter.

9

Almost every day of his life, John T. Ward, Jr., had passed by the white fences of Calumet Farm. His boyhood home, a white frame house on a one-hundred-acre farm down the road from Keeneland, was just a mile or so away. As a boy, he had seen Calumet on his way to and from school, and in the barns at Keeneland he had listened to his father and other trainers talk about the latest feats of the unbeatable Calumet. Now he had his own John T. Ward Stables, and every trip to town and back meant a drive past Calumet.

On the morning of April 4, as he drove to Calumet from an early workout at his stable, Ward thought about his father, who could break a yearling better than just about anybody John Jr. had ever watched. His uncle, Sherrill Ward, was a Hall of Fame trainer, and his grandfather, John Sherrill Ward, was a trainer, too. His great grandfather had shoveled coal at the local coalyard to earn the keep for one racehorse. Passing the familiar half mile of white fences preceding the Calumet entrance, Ward thought about his father's life, how some hopes had been dashed by luck or by timing, and how he, John Jr., could now make up for what his father might have wanted but never had. It was a nostalgia-filled ride until he reached the Calumet gates; then his thoughts turned to Lundy.

As Ward waited for the guard to open the gates, he thought of how the farm was no longer a factory designed to produce racehorses who after their racing careers would retire on the farm to produce another generation of racehorses, as Warren Wright had intended it to be. Under Lundy, despite recent successes at the track and many horses in training, it had seemed more like a factory of horseflesh to buy and sell as a commodity. He thought, too, about the farm's debt and wondered how many months it would take to turn things around and get the farm back on course.

Ward moved his old red Volvo through the entrance and as he watched his bumper clear the closing gates, he decided the gates should be open from now on. When he was growing up, there had been no gates. It was Lundy who resurrected the gates, which Warren Wright had discarded in the 1930s, and it was Lundy, so secretive and private, who had kept them closed for nearly nine years. To open them now and keep them open would signal a bright new start. It would be a symbol of an open-minded and hopeful regime.

After parking his car, Ward walked toward the office with slow deliberate steps as if he were savoring every breath of the air around him. These were special, untainted moments. He could bask in the glory of his new post without the burden of his new responsibilities. His charge was not only to manage the showplace of the Bluegrass but to bring it out of a deep hole. He knew from talks with the family and the lawyers that the farm owed at least $20 million to Mutual Benefit and more than that to First City, but Ward believed that was a workable situation, considering the potential earning power of the stable. For a while everything seemed possible.

Ward, a trim, six-foot-tall man in his mid-forties, stood for a moment in the office lobby, looking up the sweeping staircase. He had thick blond hair and blue eyes that seemed all too often focused on the ground, as he typically walked slightly slumped over. This was more a product of shyness and fatigue than of a moody, somber disposition. In a flash, with the help of a friend's prodding, he could burst forth with an impish grin and a witty remark that seemed to reverse time and give his blond eyebrows and fair complexion a youthful blush.

Ward had never ventured into the Calumet office. He wandered from room to room. There was the big computer complex to the left of the lobby and shelves of electronically operated files behind metal gates. To the right was a big reception area, another office, and a bathroom. Up the stairs, he saw the sulky that had belonged to William Monroe Wright and glass cases filled with the many new trophies. Then his eyes fell on the paper shredder in the hallway and the big duplicating machines nearby. Through the double doors to the big office, he saw portraits of recent Calumet stallions and a 1940s bronze sculpture of Citation with a peculiar-looking copper ashtray strapped to its back. And there were telephones everywhere: telephones in bathrooms, telephones in offices, even a telephone in the tiny kitchen only a few steps from Lundy's desk phone.

There was nothing unusual about paper shredders, copiers, or telephones in a farm office, but somehow their presence clashed dramatically with Ward's image of Calumet. Horses were his passion, and horses, in his estimation, were what Calumet was all about. Calumet's office could have been on the top floor of the World Trade Center. Its atmosphere seemed so far away from the farm. The feeling of contrasting worlds Ward felt that morning was his first sense of how far Calumet had drifted from its foundation in the Bluegrass.

Standing in the upstairs hall, he suddenly walked to the nearest window, in the door of the second-story entrance, and looked out onto the vast acres of farmland, as if needing to remember why he wanted this job at all. The miles of white fences gave Ward a rush of serenity. It was something he would do often in the next several months.

That first day Ward chose what he called his transition team, people whose judgments he trusted. One was Ron Sladon, a local thoroughbred breeder with more than twenty years' experience as a lawyer in Florida, where he had prosecuted criminal cases as city attorney for Fort Lauderdale and West Hollywood and had done civil litigation in private practice. The other was David Switzer, an equine insurance agent who was also a lawyer.

Sladon's official title was secretary-treasurer and Switzer's, director of sales. Sladon dubbed the group "the three musketeers."

Ward's main motive for bringing the two on board was that he wanted to work with and occasionally lean on "friends who had the same code of ethics." He also called on an old college friend, Steve Beshear, a former Kentucky lieutenant governor and local lawyer, as a legal consultant.

Ward's salary at Calumet was $10,000 a month and Sladon's about $40,000 a year. None of the three ended their regular work. Ward insisted on this since he wanted to be able to take risks for the good of the farm, if necessary, and not put his own business at risk in the process. At first they divided their time between their enterprises, but soon Calumet took over their lives.

The first order of business was to assure the staff, in the offices and out at the barns, that all operations would continue. Ward had asked Heinz and McGee to leave, but the rest of the office staff could keep their jobs. It was the middle of breeding season, and Heinz and McGee had been handling the bookings; without the two women, the first few weeks would be mayhem.

Next there was the seemingly endless task of combing through all the books to figure out how much was spent for everything from hay to airplane maintenance and where expenses could be cut. This was not easy. The financial records for the fiscal year that ended September 30, 1990—the year-end results that First City, Schroder, and others had been clamoring for—had never been completed. Ward learned that very few, if any, bills had been paid—for oats, for straw, for anything—since the beginning of the year. Also disturbing was the fact that though the farm was in the middle of the breeding season, there was no cash flow.

The telephone rang almost every second from April 4 onward. One of the first calls was from Axmar; the Marcuses were fed up. Dozens of other calls came from breeders and businessmen who wanted to know when Calumet planned to give them their seasons or pay them their money. If there was no record of something Calumet owed, the caller often said the deal was an oral agreement with Lundy. At that point Ward would deploy Calumet accountant Todd Wright to investigate the problem, and Wright—no relation to Warren Wright—would scan files somehow connected to the horse or the deal in search of a letter or a memo that might prove Calumet indeed owed the individual a season or cash.

The only bills that had been paid in 1991, it appeared, were those for the water, telephone, and electricity. Calls came from almost every big track in America complaining about unpaid Calumet bills—and not just thoroughbred racetracks. The farm received a bill for $450,000 to sponsor a national racecar team, and when the bill went unpaid, the farm got another, from A. J. Foyt's office, for $50,000 to pay for removing the Calumet emblem from the team's overalls.

Certain Japanese investors were calling, too, though not with complaints. They hoped to visit before the Derby to discuss the possible purchase of a farm they believed was solvent and enormously profitable. They had seen a prospectus that valued the farm at $160 million.

The magnitude of the problems would hit Ward and company only in the few seconds between phone calls. Within a few weeks, they realized there was only $400 left in the Calumet general account at the Georgetown bank. During Lundy's regime that account, Ward estimated, had seen about $350 million come and go. They also had a new estimate of the debt: $56 million.

Soon Ward managed to cut Calumet's operating budget from about $1.3 million a month to $300,000. To do this, horses were reappraised at much lower values, which caused the equine insurance premiums to drop substantially. And insiders no longer got "in-house" commissions for selling the seasons to the Calumet stallions each year. First City, in the interest of keeping the farm functional, agreed to provide the $300,000 for several months.

One of the biggest challenges for the new regime was to keep the Calumet image intact while repairing its shaky foundation. The image got a big boost, though short-lived, when, on the first Saturday in May, a home-bred Calumet horse, Strike the Gold, won the Kentucky Derby. Though Lundy, in a quest for cash, had sold the horse the previous fall and the Wright heirs were reportedly furious when they found out, the rest of the world saw the victory as further proof of the Calumet magic. On the same day as the Derby victory, a son of Secreto won a big race in England. Bertha Wright bolstered an upbeat image when she told the press how pleased she was for the sake of Calumet's "new generation, my children. . . . I'm pleased and we hope to continue."

But for Ward and his crew, as more and more Calumet creditors expressed frustration and threatened to sue, the magic was slipping away. On April 25, what Ward dreaded finally occurred. Bank One, of Lexington, sued Calumet. The bank, after extending deadlines and refinancing Calumet's debt to it at least once, finally reached a point of no return. The farm, the bank claimed, owed it $221,662 plus loan fees due March 15 on a $450,000 short-term note renewed November 1, 1990, by Lundy.

By the first week of May, the Persian rug on the floor of the second-floor office was covered with sixty or more files and yellow legal pads. On the long conference table lay diagrams showing money in and money out for particular years, for particular bank transactions, and for particular stallions. There were charts made in an effort to figure out which investors had a right to which seasons and shares and which banks had liens on which horses. And there were lists of Calumet horses and their locations on tracks and at farms all over the world.

Ward never figured out how Calumet horses ended up in Tasmania, an island off the south coast of Australia, but with the help of lawyer Sturgill he finally fit together the pieces of Calumet's Australian outpost. There was no land and no farm, as he first had hoped. Instead, Calumet Australia, as it was called, was a Wright family partnership that owned stallions and boarded them at the ranch of an Australian breeder. And it was not a boon to Calumet's disappearing bottom line, as Ward had hoped upon discovering the offshore enclave; it was just one more complication. It would cost at least $7,000 to ship each of the animals to the United States, an expense neither Calumet nor the partnership, which also had huge debts, could afford. Selling the horses in Australia wouldn't take care of much more than the partnership's debt, so the thrill of discovering Calumet Australia was short-lived. Soon it was simply one more file in a growing pile of entities that troubled and stymied Calumet's new regime. Ward, Sladon, and Switzer worked many nights until 11:00 P.M. struggling to solve the mysteries that were quickly becoming Calumet's legacy.

From the start, trust had been an issue, for Ward and for the Wright family. The more Ward and others understood about the farm's finances, the more important trust became. There were rumors that the Calumet offices had been bugged, which is why at the beginning of Ward's regime the building was swept for them, from lamp shades and curtain rods to desk drawers and file cabinets. But after several weeks it became apparent that the farm was getting calls about transactions that Ward and Sladon had discussed in the second-floor office only the day before. Uncanny coincidences began to pile up. To check for bugging again seemed melodramatic, and it was unlikely that someone had sneaked into the office and wired it. Finally, they discovered that one of Lundy's former staffers who had survived the transition was reporting to Lundy on the activities of the new regime. Ward asked her to leave.

While Ward found ways to cut expenses, Sladon read through reams of

files looking for money owed Calumet, either because of favors granted to
certain investors or uncollected bills. He called every track in the country
hoping to find some money on deposit in a Calumet account. There was
none. One day accountant Wright recalled that somewhere in the offices
there was a vault where Lundy was known to keep thousands of dollars in
petty cash.

"Well, let's find it," said Sladon, with the zeal of a twelve-year-old looking
for buried treasure. He nearly slid down the railing of the office staircase
after Wright said the vault might be somewhere in the computer room. It
was a steel vault, about three feet high, Wright remembered, and it was kept
in a closet.

With the pent-up frustration of the past few weeks fueling a burst of
energy, Sladon threw open the closet door. Before him were old Styrofoam
cups emblazoned with the Calumet Farm emblem, boxes of computer paper, and some bright red Calumet jackets, but no vault. Sladon then slid
open a steel cage that separated the main room from shelves of documents.
There, on the floor, buried in bank files, was the vault, its door slightly ajar.
In it were nine one-hundred-dollar bills, some empty envelopes that bore
the Calumet insignia, and a note from a former secretary saying she owed
petty cash in the amount of $3,500.

Sladon's other explorations were more successful. He found records of a
$3,000 mobile phone billed to Calumet and located in lawyer Matthews's
car. He wrote a note demanding its return, and shortly thereafter Matthews
brought in the phone.

But Sladon's biggest discovery came in relation to the Ford Motor Company ad. He had recently received a call from an air-conditioning manufac-
turer that, like Ford, wanted to film ads at Calumet, using the farm as a
backdrop. Sladon took the call. The first question was about the farm's fee
schedule. The filming involved background shots with models, so Sladon
asked for $1,000 a day plus insurance coverage. No problem, the caller said.
As Sladon chastised himself for not asking for more, he began thinking: If
that was so easy, how much did the farm make from the Ford commercial?

The Ford contract, which Sladon excavated from a mound of documents,
stipulated that Calumet was to receive a brand-new Thunderbird in exchange for the use of the property. Sladon surveyed the cars on the farm but
found no new Ford. After talking to some of the farmhands, he learned that
Lundy had been driving a Ford in recent months, a brand-new Ford. He
then called local Ford dealers and found Lundy had recently traded a new
Thunderbird for a four-door Crown Victoria, valued at around $20,000.

Sladon called Lundy, and the next day the car appeared in the parking lot outside Matthews's office. Sladon dispatched a Calumet staffer to fetch it, and within twenty-four hours it was sold. Sladon used the money to make the weekly payroll.

Sladon's greatest contribution may have been his work with the public. He could be calm and even witty in the face of mounting pressure from creditors, lawyers, or the press. He had a penchant for storytelling, which was a refreshing diversion for his colleagues and for Calumet's many anxious callers. His patience had the effect of a cool balm applied to a rash.

While an utter nuisance to most people, the unending stream of calls seemed almost an adventure to Sladon. Everyone wanted something from the new Calumet regime. One day Bob Fox called to ask if he might be able to work out a deal for his friend Robert Perez to buy Calumet's box at Saratoga Springs. Sladon, not knowing Calumet's future, said no; besides, he was sure Calumet didn't even own it. There was a call from the nephew of Kentucky governor Wallace Wilkerson who planned to come to Calumet to retrieve a horse he was boarding there. With a little research Sladon learned that the nephew had a $3,000 unpaid board bill. Before he could jump in his car, Sladon called him back and said, "The horse doesn't leave until the board bill is paid. No payment, no horse."

Meanwhile, the weekly board meetings seemed to get longer and longer as the family and Ward, the bankers, and the lawyers searched for ways to maintain the farm. After one such meeting, Bertha told a *New York Times* reporter, "I'd like the world to know we're standing together. It's an uphill course, but we're working on it. We're trying to see if we can work as a family together."

But for Ward, it was increasingly difficult to present a positive view and to say that the ills of the enterprise could be remedied. Each day "the three Musketeers" uncovered new facets of the Calumet condition, and each day Calumet's future looked grimmer.

Instances when former Calumet deal makers came to the farm to talk about money they believed they were owed could be particularly frustrating because so often there were no records to back up the claims. Prior to one such meeting, Sladon had concluded that the farm owed nothing to one particular gentleman; on the contrary, Sladon believed the man owed the farm about $200,000. The businessman and his lawyer stood in front of the big wooden desk where Sladon sat, while Ward watched from a nearby chair. After a pause, the lawyer suggested that this matter might be resolved very easily through a simple bookkeeping entry. The room was silent, and all eyes shifted to Ward, who so far had said nothing. Training horses is a profession of observation and patience. It was Ward's style to watch and wait. Without saying a word, he shook his head no. What he believed he was hearing was that a little fine-tuning of the books would allow a friend of Lundy's to receive $200,000, though the Calumet records, as they now read, didn't reflect such an obligation.

After the meeting, a wave of doubt swept over both Ward and Sladon about why they were doing this job and what the consequences might be. How could they clean up the Calumet mess when it was becoming increasingly clear to them that the records might be incomplete? New deals seemed to surface almost daily. Without complete paper trails they had no idea who and what they were really dealing with. As the magnitude of the debt and the layers of convoluted deals increased, so did the new regime's fear of what they might have gotten themselves into.

There were troubling details that no one could understand. Sladon was bothered in particular by an exchange of checks in the fall of 1990 between First City and Calumet. In early September, a $500,000 check was sent to First City; the same day a second check, for $1.5 million, also went to First City. On September 14, Calumet got a letter from First City saying it had received the checks and voided them. A few days later Calumet received a check for $500,000 from Lundy's friend at First City.

Even more perplexing was a check to First City that drew $1 million out of the Calumet general account that was returned uncashed to Calumet in an envelope with no explanation. Filed with the check, Sladon found a letter that was sent from First City to Calumet several months earlier in the fall of 1990 requesting a $1 million payment for "services." During the months between the check's being sent to First City and the check's return, the million dollars was never debited in the Calumet accounting records. There were also large checks in relation to certain Calumet stallion purchases that had been deposited in an offshore bank in the Netherlands Antilles.

Letters reflecting transactions in which stallion seasons were apparently used to move money back and forth from person to person or bank account to bank account were scattered through the files. Money was paid for the seasons, but the seasons apparently didn't change hands. Letters also revealed instances where Calumet had paid the interest on somebody else's or another entity's loans. It was clear that any number of these transactions might be illegal.

Calumet's accountant mulled over the meaning of certain letters and memos. Even transactions that seemed so simple on the surface were wildly complex, like Calumet's 1988 purchase of the stallion Talinum.

Calumet bought Talinum, a son of Alydar, from Ontario breeder John Sikura, who had purchased the horse, among others, from Texas oilman Nelson Bunker Hunt. With its superior pedigree and earnings of $740,000 in racing purses, the horse had a good chance at being a leading sire.

Sikura, a big player in the international horse market for many years, was a dark, handsome man with the fast-talking, streetwise style of a hood. In Canadian racing circles he was known as a wealthy man, but the source of his money was unknown. He came to Toronto at age sixteen from Czecho-slovakia nearly penniless. Some seemed to remember that years back he sold cars for a living; others recalled he had worked as a dishwasher at a Toronto hotel. It was rumored that he or his father had made a killing in the U.S. stock market in the 1960s; or perhaps it was real estate where they struck gold. Now Sikura was a guy who made a lot of money in the horse business, had bred some fine racehorses, and was connected with some of the wealth-iest breeders in the world. His connections included some people who also had links to Calumet and Lundy. Bunker Hunt, for example, had worked with Cihak, Lundy's pal at First City, and with Sikura. And Sikura, who commuted regularly between Toronto and Lexington, bought his Bluegrass farm from a Venezuelan businessman who was at one time closely associated with Luigi Miglietti, the man who sold Secreto to Calumet.

By the time Sikura began discussions with Lundy over Talinum, he al-ready had some offers for the stallion, the highest coming from the Japanese. But these were cash offers, and Sikura didn't want the attendant tax liabili-ties. Calumet's representatives, too, offered cash, about $800,000, plus two Alydar seasons and two seasons to Wild Again, for a total of $1.425 million for a half interest in Talinum. But Calumet, with the expertise of its lawyers, was also willing to work with Sikura in structuring a deal that would allow Calumet to purchase the horse for this amount through deferred payments, thus precluding any tax liabilities for Sikura, and eliminating the need for Calumet to pay up front for the horse.

Sikura asked his auditors to come up with a figure that would net him $1.425 million in six years—Calumet's suggested purchase price—plus 11 percent a year in interest. Effectively, Sikura was loaning Calumet the money to buy his horse. The 11 percent interest was what Sikura could have gotten if Calumet had paid him the $1.425 million in cash and he had invested it for the six years. The total came out to be $3.6 million. Under the terms of the sale agreement dated December 15, 1988, Calumet purchased all of Talinum for $3.6 million from Northern Equine Thoroughbred Productions in Ontario. This was the document that Calumet used to back up its financial statements and the official record of the ownership of Talinum. Yet verbally it was understood between Sikura and Lundy that Calumet was really buying only a 50 percent interest in the horse for $1.425 million. Sikura's half was taken care of in an addendum to the sales agreement, called "A Limited Price Call Option Agreement," that allowed another of Sikura's companies, 724334 Ontario, Ltd., to buy back one-half of Talinum for one dollar after Calumet finished making its payments.

The most intriguing aspect of the deal, however, was Lundy's roster of associates who were given free lifetime breeding rights to the horse. Lundy, as stallion manager, got his usual four breeding rights, typically given to the farm. Fox and his partner Krutchkoff each got a breeding right, as did attorney Matthews, Lundy's colleagues Heinz and McGee, and the trainer D. Wayne Lukas.

Ordinarily Calumet in a deal like this would lose the income from the giveaway breeding rights each year, but this transaction was even worse for the farm's general account and more confusing to the new regime than other stallion purchases. Though in essence the deal set up a partnership and Calumet owned only 50 percent of the property, Calumet was responsible for all the costs of maintaining the property—feed bills, bookkeeping, breeding costs, and so on. Sikura was guaranteed six seasons from 1989 to 1994 and Calumet six. Proceeds from the rest of the seasons—above the twenty-one committed—would go to Sikura every year until the horse was paid for. This was only one of many deals Ward had to decipher.

Ward had an image of how he thought things had worked. He envisioned a big wheel. The hub was Calumet, and the spokes extending out represented the banks and the partnership deals bringing money in and taking money out of Calumet. Then there was the rim where the partners made deals with one another, back and forth, over and over, trading horses and seasons and shares and cash. At the rim, there were common threads and patterns in the loans the partners got to facilitate the deals. The problem with the wheel image was that Ward couldn't take it to the next level, if there was such a thing. That is, he couldn't determine whether it was just a lone wheel rolling along for the ride or a wheel that was part of and supporting a much larger vehicle filled with deals and deal makers. The patterns and the potential for a larger scheme—perhaps money laundering, perhaps bank fraud alone—began to worry Sladon and Ward after their first two months on the job.

One day in late spring, Sladon and Ward left the premises, jumped into Sladon's pickup truck, and drove to a secluded corner of the Calumet property to talk. The stress and intrigue of daily revelations about the Calumet way of doing business had made them paranoid, or perhaps wisely cautious. For about an hour, as they watched the sun setting over the red-trimmed cupola of a nearby barn, they discussed the pros and cons of staying on. Both admitted it was ego that kept them going and that the hope and desire for the farm's survival was partly selfish. If the farm survived, their toil and sacrifice would be rewarded by the opportunity to remain in charge of the legendary stable. Then there was altruism. If they didn't go to the trouble to save Calumet and to understand why it was in such dire straits, who would? They decided to stay but also to hire a law firm outside Lexington to help them, one that had no ties to the horse industry.

When they returned to the office, one problem seemed to be clearing up, but the fax machine delivered yet another. A group of Japanese businessmen from Mitsui were planning to come to Calumet to tour the farm and talk about the Calumet prospectus, which they hoped could be updated by the time of their arrival.

Shortly after Ward took over, a lawyer representing Japanese investors had asked him to update a prospectus compiled in 1990 in time for a late April trip to the Bluegrass. They wanted to meet with the new Calumet management before the Derby to discuss the document, which had valued the farm at $160 million. At this point the Japanese were unaware of the extent of Calumet's troubles, though they must have suspected something or they would not have asked for an updated prospectus.

The Japanese deal was a dilemma for Ward and the new regime. While they were scraping together enough money to keep the bins filled with oats, the Japanese had visions of a farm worth five times its market value, if the horses were included. The abrupt change in management had shaken the confidence of the Japanese, as Robey and others had feared, and Ward's crew was well aware that these potential buyers were disappointed with their communications so far with the new management. Sladon said the Japanese viewed the post-Lundy administration as the "Dr. Death" group. Ward had a cards-on-the-table style that wasn't as much fun as believing the farm was worth more than it was. And Ward, convinced the prospectus was completely off base in its appraisals, couldn't possibly redo it in time for a pre-Derby visit.

Now, after the Derby, the Japanese still wanted to check out the farm, though this time a lone representative from Mitsui would arrive in just a few days.

When the day came, Sladon and Ward rolled out the red carpet as well as they could. They gave the Mitsui man a grand tour of the farm and drove him to Louisville for an afternoon at the races. In the car about halfway to the Churchill Downs track, Sladon and Ward told the representative about Calumet's onerous debt. He admitted he had been concerned because of rumors and that was why he had pressed for more numbers. Ward urged him not to drop the idea of buying the farm and explained why such a purchase was a once-in-a-lifetime opportunity, even with the burden of so much debt. As they parked the car, the man from Mitsui said he would be in contact with Ward. Nothing more was said as they all enjoyed their day at the races.

For the rest of May and into June, the fax machines were screaming with memos from all over the world, demanding this and threatening that. Ward's walks to the windows to catch a glimpse of the serenity outside were becoming more frequent. And so were the lawsuits.

About the time Bank One sued, Peter Brant, Lundy's former partner in Fasig-Tipton, filed a suit against the farm for nearly $3.4 million due on its 1986 purchase of the stallion Mogambo. Calumet's former partner Axmar Stables sued the farm and Lundy for more than $3.3 million. On May 10, Manganaro Stables sued the farm for $300,000. Ten days later, Equus Unlimited, Lundy's sister's insurance business, sued Calumet for failing to pay it $1.2 million in premiums and fees. John Sikura's Northern Equine Thoroughbred Productions sued claiming the farm had defaulted on the terms of the 1988 agreement to buy Talinum—he wanted the stallion back.

Midlantic National Bank claimed more than $2 million was owed on its loan, which the bank alleged should have been paid with the Alydar insurance funds but wasn't. Equine Capital Corporation and Matchmaker Financial Corporation sued Calumet and Gray Cliff, saying they had defaulted on two loans that were extensions of three other loans, and that, as of June 1, Calumet owed them nearly $3 million. Both Matchmaker and ECC requested the sale of several horses that were pledged as collateral, including one of Calumet's prized stallions, Capote. But the biggest of all suits so far, the tenth to date, was Riggs National Bank's, claiming nearly $10 million due on a 1987 note.

On July 10, Ward informed all Calumet employees that they were to report to the main office at the end of the day to pick up their paychecks.

He then went to the bank and got about $20,000 in cashier's checks, to be distributed to the staff. Ward wanted to be certain that the employees were paid while there was still money, while it didn't require the approval of a judge, and wouldn't be contested by a creditor's lawyer. He didn't tell them what was about to happen. But everyone knew.

On July 11, the most shocking news to hit the horse industry since the death of Alydar ran on newswires nationwide. Calumet Farm had filed for chapter 11 of the federal bankruptcy code.

Just about every newspaper in the country carried the story of Calumet's fall from glory. Even the New York syndicated gossip columnist "Suzy" wrote a lengthy piece with the headline "Down on the Farm—Glory Takes a Powder."

"Calumet Farm, once the pride of Kentucky racing, mysteriously crumbled," she wrote. "It seems Calumet owes a staggering $118,050,732 to banks all over the country from Houston to Lexington, and the well has run dry." She called Calumet the "showplace of the South, with its magnificent rolling pastures surrounded by pristine white fences and impeccable barns and appointments all trimmed in red. Sic transit gloria equus mundi—or something like that." Its collapse, she wrote, "has scared the riding britches off some of those Blue Grass 'hardboots.' "

The initial filing listed debts of $118.05 million, of which $85.47 million was secured debt and $32.58 million unsecured. By August the liabilities would be $127 million, with assets of $87 million including the farm, the bloodstock, artwork, furniture, equipment, and vehicles. On the same day the Calumet-Gussin partnership declared bankruptcy, listing liabilities of nearly $17 million.

Calumet's secured creditors included:

First City	$32.4 million
Mutual Benefit	$21.9 million
Riggs	$9.6 million
IBJ Schroder	$5.2 million
Midlantic	$2.6 million
ECC	$1.8 million
Matchmaker	$1.2 million
MMR Equine Services	$943,694.44
First National Bank	$513,194.44
Warren Wright, Jr., Trust	$502,625.00

Bank One, Lexington	$229,288.79
CommerceNational Bank	$150,583.33
Others = Craig B. Singer; Manganaro Stables	

Among unsecured creditors:

Warren Wright, Jr., Trust	$23.3 million
Peter Brant and White Birch Farms	$4.0 million
Gray Cliff	$1.2 million
Calumet Farm Aircraft	$1.1 million
J. T. Lundy	$448,246.00
Lyle Robey	$189,373.00
Kentucky Special Olympics	$875,000.00

While the family and Ward had begun the process of rebuilding with the notion that the farm was no more than $60 million in debt, the final registry of claims, filed in February 1992, would total $167.23 million.

Not only was the Calumet general account, which had seen hundreds of millions of dollars come and go during Lundy's regime, down to a mere $400, the supposedly secure Warren Wright, Jr., Trust, which had amounted to nearly $50 million in 1982, was now worth barely $6 million. Wright Enterprises, the family partnership, had zero value despite the nearly $18 million it had received from Calumet's own account over the past several years and all the assets and cash that had flowed into it.

While the four Wright grandchildren had each received about $7 million in assets, including their shares in Calumet, in 1982, they were now liable for nearly $80 million in loans they had guaranteed by signing the many documents presented to them over the past nine years. Whatever assets remained were now at risk because most of the loans were in default. The great American fortune amassed by Warren Wright lay in ruins.

10

On a late October morning, 126 thoroughbred horses, their coats glistening in the sunlight, were led single file across Calumet's rolling fields. Through openings in the white fences and along winding back roads, the funeral-like procession slowly walked a three-and-a-half-mile path to the barns behind Keeneland.

No fanfare, no advance billing, no headline announced this event, but to those who led the horses that day, to Ward and to Sladon, and to everyone involved with Calumet, the convoy marked the unofficial end of the dynasty Warren Wright had created sixty years before. In three days, at a special Calumet dispersal sale held in the auction ring at Keeneland, the Calumet horses would be sold to breeders all over the world and the bloodlines of Calumet would be dispersed to Japan, England, Germany, Ireland, Venezuela, and Mexico. While someone might someday use the Calumet name and even occupy its land, this sale would put an end to Calumet's thoroughbred breeding based on lineage that began with Warren Wright's stallions Bull Lea and Blenheim II and his early broodmares, Nellie Flag and Dustwhirl.

The Bluegrass had never witnessed a procession such as this. Grooms who held the halters of broodmares they had brushed and fed for many years knew this was their last task at Calumet. After the sale, their jobs and the animals they cared for would be gone. Only a few, including Alton Stone, would be asked to stay another month to tend to the six or seven Calumet stallions whose destinies were still tied up in court battles. There was little talk, only the sound of hooves and shoes crunching the fallen leaves and an occasional whinny. Walking single file made socializing difficult, and most everyone was lost in thought, recalling this and that about the horses and worrying about the future.

Though the spectacle would go down in history as the symbolic end of Calumet, its purpose was not drama, but rather economic. The cost of transporting the horses in vans from Calumet to Keeneland was $40 per horse. The farm couldn't afford it. Ward had tried to sell the farm and the horses as a package, but there were no takers. Mitsui had disappeared over the horizon. And so Ward was selling the horses, eight at Keeneland in July and then one hundred at Keeneland's September sale. Still believing a buyer might appear, he waited until almost the final possible second to let go of the rest, so long that there wasn't enough cash for the horse vans.

Ward stood teary-eyed as the procession moved past him. Without these horses, Calumet was simply a plot of land and a lot of memories. There were also the lives of the dozens of Calumet workers to worry about. While Lundy had successfully purged the office of Mrs. Markey's loyalists, he had allowed numerous farm workers to stay, as he knew their experience was invaluable. Some of these workers knew no other life than Calumet. Some were born on the farm and marked the turning points in their own lives with the births, deaths, and victories of the Calumet horses. Others bore their children on the farm. Ward had these people in mind as he tried for months to find cash, to keep the farm operating, and to find a buyer for it. One of the reasons for declaring bankruptcy was to gain time to find a buyer.

But so far there had been no formal bids. Interested, enthusiastic investors would call, schedule a tour and meetings, and then back out. Immediately after the bankruptcy filing, the farm had been deluged with inquiries. In response, Ward sent out informational packets with appraisals of the farm, a list of all its horses, and a ten-minute video about Calumet. Inquiries came from Lundy's old friend Dan Lasater; Giancarlo Parreti, the former CEO of MGM Communications Corporation who asked questions through Eugenio Colombo; real estate agents in New York, Kentucky, California, Indiana, and New Jersey; lawyers from several states; a financier from Zurich; and some Japanese companies.

Lewis Burrell, the father of rap singer M.C. Hammer, had visited the farm in May but later said it was too expensive and there were "just so many things surrounding it, like lawsuits." An agent from Bakersfield, California, made an offer in late summer for $68.5 million over the phone but didn't reveal his client and never called back. There were always one or two "mystery buyers," it seemed, keeping the farm dangling by a thread of hope, and Ward asked the bankruptcy court to approve loans from creditors, mainly First City, to keep the farm operating as long as possible.

By August there were four interested parties, but Ward never disclosed their names. In October the local paper ran stories about two mystery buyers, but soon it was clear that the cost of keeping the 120 or so horses was more real than the hope of selling the package.

On November 3, the day of the horse sale, a stiff wind whipped across the Calumet grounds, whisking leaves from trees and blowing branches against the windows of empty stalls. The sun, which only three days before had caused red and yellow leaves to glisten across the hills as the horses marched to Keeneland, was dimmer now. For the first time that season temperatures dropped below thirty degrees.

At the barns where grooms rubbed their hands to keep warm, prospective buyers, wrapped in furs and scarves, examined horses up to the last minute before the sale began at 2:00 P.M. The talk, as the grooms walked the horses in circles before the many shoppers, focused on Calumet.

Leaning against a wooden rail at barn 9, a bloodstock agent from the Seattle area lamented: "It's a shame what's happening. Calumet is history. I think, though, they'll sell well today because of the image. It'll kind of be a status thing to own a Calumet horse."

At one of the barns a visitor talked with a Calumet groom as he prepared a mare for the walk to the ring. "This is my last day. But it's not just me feeling the loss. The industry feels it, too. It's like the farm lost Alydar, and now the industry's losin' Calumet."

Pointing to a stall behind him, another groom, James Gilliam, said, "That one there, it's a great-granddaughter of Bull Lea. Her mother and her brothers and her sisters all lived at Calumet."

Near barn 10, three Calumet grooms talked of the farm's collapse. "It tears my heart out to see this," John Simpson said, as he turned on the closed-circuit TV screen mounted at the end of the barn. "It makes me want to cry. It's sad because Calumet is a legend. These last few days. It's like getting ready for a funeral."

Ed Simpson, his brother, talked about the horse he'd been grooming, 'Tis Juliet. "It must be hard for anyone to sell a horse that fine," he said.

At about 1:55 P.M., a man in a bright red Calumet jacket with a cellular phone attached to his hip and a large red notebook in his hand called out, "The first four have to go in five minutes!"

Ninety mares and thirty weanlings would be led one by one to the ring. No reserves had been set; it was a closeout sale. The first in line were Macau, Jiggy Dancer, Tru's Cheer, and Hot Aly. One at a time they were brought out of their stalls and held still by one groom while another wiped them with a yellow cloth, a third brushed their tails, and a fourth shined their hooves.

The arena was packed. Bidders and curious onlookers talked of Calumet's state. Those who traveled the auction circuit noticed that some of the Calumet horses supposedly sold at other public sales in 1987 and 1988 were on the block again, as if they had never been sold at all. They talked among themselves about how things had gone wrong, using words like "mismanagement" and "bad deals," "wake" and "funeral." There was even the type of reunion that funerals sometimes inspire. John Veitch, who had trained such Calumet champions as Alydar and Davona Dale, came from New York for the event. Trying to be as inconspicuous as possible, he stood at the back and watched, with a feeling of anger mixed with sadness, as horses he had known for years came on the block. Citation's trainer, Jimmy Jones, now eighty-five years old, came from his home in Parnell, Missouri. "My father [Ben Jones] and I worked hard for twenty-five years to keep this place in the black. I thought this place was as staunch as the Capitol building in Washington."

The last horse scheduled to go on the block was Before Dawn, a twelve-year-old broodmare whose grandfathers were Tim Tam and Raise A Native and whose ancestry went back to Blenheim II. At half past five, the last of the sunlight filtering through the trees cast shadows on the floor of Before Dawn's stall. Three grooms brushed and shined her deep brown coat, her long tail cut straight across at the bottom, and her short-cropped mane. As if in protest over losing her home and her stallmates of many years, Before Dawn kicked and bucked and snorted all the way into the ring and even after she arrived. Two minutes later, the digital sign flashed the sales price: 6-4-0-0-0-0.

When the sale was over, the horses were loaded on vans bound for their new homes, and the grooms who had cared for them headed home. The sale had grossed $10.2 million, a pittance compared to the Calumet debt and even less compared to the priceless tradition that had just been destroyed.

As a group of the now-former Calumet grooms walked toward the parking lot at Keeneland, one, Ed Simpson, had a large red comb sticking out of his back pocket. It was the comb he had used to groom 'Tis Juliet, an Alydar daughter and, in Simpson's estimation, one of the finest horses Calumet had ever bred. The comb was something to remember her by.

The day after the sale, the staff was cut from eighty-eight to twenty, and all stalls, except those in the stallion barns, were empty for the first time since they were built. That morning Ward walked at a weary pace to the barns to begin putting away saddles, bridles, and blankets. As he shut the stall doors, he glanced occasionally at the gold plates bearing the names of the horses and their ancestors. But Calumet without the horses was like a person without a soul. It was as if the cold, remote ambience he had found in the office on his first day had spread now to the entire farm. When the horses were gone, so was the dream. What Ward had believed was possible when he drove through the gates that first day or when he sat down proudly at that first board meeting could not be done. He would not be the head of the nation's premier stable, nor would he be able to work with the progeny of Calumet's superior bloodlines. Instead, in the months to come, he and Sladon would have to meet with creditors, give depositions in relation to the many lawsuits, and sort through the Calumet records to answer the questions of investors, lawyers, and reporters. Besides the family, the investors, the banks, and the Calumet staff, Ward, too, was a victim of the collapse.

Back at the office that morning Sladon chatted with visitors who had come for the sale. The procession and the sale were like "turning out the lights at the Smithsonian," he told one reporter on the phone. Sladon tried to describe his morning of gathering gear with Ward in the barns. He took a deep breath, inhaling the essence of his cigarette, and slowly began his tale, "I was putting away the saddles and bridles, and oh, it's so sad. . . . I'm sorry. . . . Call me back in an hour or so." Sladon was choking back sobs.

11 In wintertime, at dusk, thousands of birds flock to the two trees in front of the Fayette County courthouse. The sound is deafening. Children waiting at the bus stop point to them and scream, making the scene all the more unsettling. Mothers pull the hoods over their children's heads and warn about a "sprinkle" that is on its way. Old men open their umbrellas, occasionally peeking beyond the edge at the phenomenon before them. As the birds swoop back and forth from tree to tree, some land on the front of the courthouse, others rustle the branches of a pine tree that by early December is decorated with Christmas lights.

The man behind the soda fountain at the pharmacy across the street says it happens only in winter. They migrate from the farms, he says, because it's warmer in town. "They'd get their heads blown off out in those fields in winter. There must be 6,000 or more of them starlin's just in those trees. It's a blizzard of birds you see; that's what, a storm comin' down on the courthouse."

By mid-November 1991, the birds had begun their journey from the farmlands to the courthouse. So, too, had Calumet. The business of Calumet

Farm was conducted almost entirely in a courtroom now, as an unending barrage of creditors sought money and horseflesh, while family members sought answers and culprits. Although the bankruptcy legally prevented any new lawsuits from being filed against the farm itself, there was still a constant stream of Calumet-related litigation against the Wright heirs, against Robey, against Lundy, between and among the Calumet deal makers.

Like a powerful twister, the case seemed to be pulling into its center every lawyer in the region who had experience in equine disputes or an understanding of the horse industry. Each bank had its hometown lawyer in Houston, New York, Washington, D.C., New Jersey, or Florida, as well as its Lexington counsel. By winter, orders and motions in the bankruptcy and copies of new suits were sometimes duplicated for as many as eighty lawyers. By January 1992, nearly 150 attorneys were involved in the many cases the bankruptcy had provoked. Whatever was left of the Wright fortune would now go to lawyers.

Because of the complexity of the deals during the Lundy era, the bankruptcy was mercilessly convoluted. It was an unusual bankruptcy to begin with because most of the assets were live animals. So while there were disputes about who owned which animals or which percentage of the animals or which seasons, these assets had to be fed and cared for, bred and birthed. Selling them was difficult because of the number of liens on each horse. Everyone with a claim had to agree before the horse was sold; sometimes this process took months. As Ron Sladon said, "In court these days you just say good morning and eight guys stand up and object."

The stallions remaining at Calumet had been bred to an average of seventy mares a year at prices ranging from $20,000 to $500,000. That meant at least 600 deals each year and nearly 4,000 transactions from 1984 on. "There was a deal a day ranging figuratively from a used car to a Rolls-Royce to a huge estate," said one insider. The collapse provoked an avalanche of claims regarding those transactions, and the bankruptcy judge learned quickly that there was not always documentation for every deal.

After the November 1991 sale, the next imperative was to sell the stallions to bring in operating cash and money for creditors. With Wild Again considered the leading sire that year, this was perhaps the finest collection of stallions at a single stable anywhere. Ward wanted to schedule an auction, dubbed the "stallion spectacular," for December 9.

At a hearing in mid-November, Ward told the judge the farm had only enough money to operate until December 11. Calumet, which owned at least 50 percent of the nine stallions in question, had asked for an emergency order to sell them. The plan was to sell each horse, take Calumet's half, and let the claimants divvy up the other 50 percent. In theory selling 100 percent of the horse would bring a higher price for the creditors than selling Calumet's own half interest alone.

But the minute Ward stood up in court to plead his case, more than a dozen attorneys jumped to their feet to object to the sale. Most of the stallions, or Calumet's interests in them, had been mortgaged, sometimes to more than one lender. There were also a slew of people with breeding rights to the stallions. Largely because of the replacement frenzy after Alydar's death, no one really knew how many people had claims to the horses. Lundy may have given six Wild Again seasons to one breeder in a replacement package, and that breeder might have peddled three of the six to another breeder. Suddenly the lawyer for the breeder with the three peddled seasons would come out of nowhere with a claim. Sorting these out and deciding which interest, Calumet's or the other owner's, the claims would be taken from was a painstaking process.

At the end of the stallion hearing, bankruptcy judge Joe Lee rejected the plan for the sale, saying it was impossible to sell the stallions without considering the breeding rights, liens, and various other claims held on them.

The disputes over the stallions would continue for years, and complications, such as the validity of the breeding rights the farm allegedly had given away each year, would arise continually. First City, the Texas bank, felt the holders of those rights had no claim to them because Calumet didn't have the right to give away seasons for horses it had pledged as collateral to secure First City loans. The bank wanted to count those rights as its own and collect money on them. There would be trials to settle some claims. There were even disputes about where the stallions should be sent for the interim, because Calumet no longer had the staff or the funds to take care of its horses.

Judge Lee, a tall, slightly stooped man with bushy gray brows, had seen many bankruptcies in his thirty years on the bench, and in recent years farm bankruptcies involving pigs, beef cattle, or horses had abounded in his central Kentucky courtroom. But none could compare in complexity and intrigue to the Calumet case. Each hearing seemed to reveal a new set of circumstances bringing to light, piece by intricate piece, the astonishing variety of deals Lundy and his cohorts had fashioned. Judge Lee seemed fascinated by an operation that took to extremes all the habits of the thoroughbred industry during the 1980s—from excessive breeding to excessive borrowing.

One day lawyers competing for rights to Capote agreed that Calumet could sell its 50 percent interest in the stallion. Judge Lee immediately turned the courtroom into an auction house. He was not about to let the moment pass; by the next hearing the disputes over Calumet's share could erupt all over again. Attorneys whipped out their cellular phones, calling clients and horsemen worldwide to inform them of the auction, and soon the courtroom was buzzing with potential buyers. Only the horse was missing from the ambience. By 8:00 P.M. the half interest had sold for $4 million, considered a good price.

While one category of the litigation dealt with horses, the farm, and its creditors, another focused on the former board of directors of Calumet Farm, Inc., the heirs, and the issue of blame.

Robey was among the first to pick a fight. Since the day Lundy resigned, Robey had been aggravated with the Wright family. He believed he of all people should have taken over the farm after Lundy's departure. As a member of the executive committee, Robey could pick up where Lundy had left off. A change within the current regime would have been much less disruptive to creditors and clients than an entirely new administration, he reasoned. Robey knew, too, that some of the farm's creditors were Lundy's buddies who would have far more patience with Lundy's or Robey's efforts to pay them back than with a newcomer's. But no one listened to Robey anymore.

The ruddy-faced ex–Green Beret was also furious because he felt the family had gotten exactly what they wanted out of him and out of Lundy and now that the money was gone, they were pointing fingers at the very people who had helped them. No one talked about how much money the family took out of its own coffers, Robey bitterly complained. "They thought it [the farm] was Fort Knox," he said. At one point the farm gave Wright Enterprises nearly $16 million, some of which went to the Wright heirs, he said. During the past several years, the farm had given Courtenay Wright Lancaster and her husband $560,000. Of this, $45,000 was given in 1990 when "the fort" was nearly empty. Lundy allowed the farm to forward $96,000 to Bertha over the years, and in the early fall of 1990, he gave $55,000 from the Calumet account to Tommy Wright.

Robey had resigned from his post at Calumet on April 23. A month later the family fired him from Wright Enterprises, the family partnership. Robey responded in June with a lawsuit in Fayette Circuit Court against the family and the partnership, charging he had been dismissed without cause and demanding his job back. The family, he said, owed him nearly $200,000, and they had breached his contract, which he claimed was good until 1993. He did, however, exempt J. T. and Cindy Lundy from his attack.

In August the rest of the Wrights accused Robey of failing to protect their interests and to keep them adequately informed about financial developments. They contested the charge of breaching the contract, and their friends railed against Robey, saying that he'd seen every transaction at the farm and Wright Enterprises. He could have stopped the madness, but he was too busy making money. And so what if the family had taken money—it was theirs. And if the reserves were running low, then Robey, as an adviser, had the responsibility to tell them.

Lundy's and Robey's way of keeping the family out of their way was to give them exactly what they wanted, whether it was cash or a ride on the Calumet plane or a trip on the Concorde. How could anyone complain or be tempted to probe into the inner workings of the farm if every wish was fulfilled and there seemed to be no problems? Despite the documents they had signed, they didn't sense any urgency about Calumet's condition. They also didn't understand their positions and duties as corporate directors.

But the squabble between the family and Robey was minuscule compared to the battle between the Wright heirs and CommerceNational Bank, the trustee for the Warren Wright, Jr., Trust and largest shareholder in Calumet Farm, Inc.

The bank's job as trustee—for which it was paid about $12,000 a month—was to manage and control the assets and to pay the income derived from the trust to Bertha Wright until her death. Whatever remained in the trust after that would be divided among the Wrights' children, grandchildren, and great-grandchildren. There was now barely $6 million in the trust, and dozens of creditors were questioning their lawyers about whether it was possible legally to pry open and get at the principal in this type of legal stronghold, called a spendthrift trust. If so, the last of Warren Wright's legacy would disappear in a heartbeat.

The issue at the heart of this mudslinging dispute couldn't be more basic: who was responsible for the financial ruin of farm and fortune? Money had flowed out of the trust into the Calumet account—some to purchase horses and some to Wright Enterprises—but none had returned to the trust. Was it the bank's fault for allowing such a drain? Robey and Lundy's, for initiating it? The family's, for failing to stop it?

The heirs made the first move, filing a lawsuit accusing the bank of "gross negligence" in its role as trustee. Decisions made and documents signed during the first moments of Calumet Farm, Inc., were suddenly key pieces in the puzzle Calumet had become. The bank, the family claimed, should never have allowed Lundy the right to borrow up to $10 million in the name of Calumet Farm, Inc., without prior approval of Calumet's board of directors. Calumet at that time was valued at about $21 million, so the entire equity of the corporation could be encumbered in just two $10 million loans. That, of course, happened more than twice. Worse than that, the bank also loaned $13.2 million to the farm out of the trust on an unsecured basis. Moreover, in July 1988, when Calumet took out its first huge loan from First City, the Wright heirs signed an agreement that subordinated the trust's loans to the loans of First City; at the same time they agreed to indemnify and "hold harmless" CommerceNational from any damages that might result from this so-called subordination agreement. This meant that the trust had lost assets it could claim if the farm did not reimburse the trust—which is exactly what happened. Now the trust was an unsecured creditor, which meant it would be reimbursed only after other creditors, such as First City, got their millions. The trust, in other words, would likely never be replenished. How could the bank permit this to happen?

There was also the matter of Calumet's executive committee, which consisted of Robey, Lundy, and one bank representative. How could the bank, as the majority shareholder of the company, allow itself to be in a minority position on a body that effectively controlled Calumet? The family even accused the bank of not attending all meetings of the executive committee and of not investigating thoroughly enough the proposals and deals discussed at such meetings. The family accused the bank of "unlawfully and imprudently causing or permitting the encumbrance of all or substantially all of the assets of Calumet Farm, Inc., over an eight-year period without sufficient assurance that the debts secured thereby could be repaid within the stated maturities out of earnings." The heirs demanded that the bank reimburse them for their lost fortune.

The bank denied all charges and in its counterclaim reminded the family that in 1982 Bertha had signed the "hold-harmless agreement"—the document that effectively released the bank from any responsibility for what happened to the trust. The stated purpose of the document was "to indemnify and hold the trustee harmless against any and all loss, damage, claims, suits and attorneys' fees in defending claims, suits or demands which in any manner arise out of or result from the retention of Calumet Farm or any interest therein and the operation thereof as an asset of the trust." This was perhaps the messiest part of the dispute. From the bank's point of view, the family had no grounds for complaint because of this two-page agreement. To complain about the bank's performance as trustee was tantamount to crying about a runaway horse after leaving the stall door open. One lawyer, slightly more cynical, said, "It's like someone complaining about being an orphan after he's killed his parents."

The family fumed over this and claimed the document was "unfair, unconscionable," for it granted immunity and impunity to a paid corporate trustee for future breaches of fiduciary duty. They said no one explained to them the consequences of the agreement before they signed it, and a contract of this sort simply wasn't enforceable without complete disclosure of all rights—at the very least the knowledge of what they were giving up and of what the document permitted Lundy to do.

Each side looked at the other in total amazement. How could a bank stand on the sidelines while the assets so carefully guarded by Warren Wright, Sr., and his son slipped away? Was it legally possible for a bank to waive its responsibility as a trustee and still be paid for the service? And why wasn't the farm's first big mortgage, from Mutual Benefit, a red flag for the trustees, a signal that something wasn't right? On the other hand, how could a family guarantee one loan after another, signing this paper and that paper for nearly eight years, without understanding what they were doing to their fortune? If the case ever went to trial, lawyers claimed, it would be the largest fiduciary trust case ever.

The feud would last for years. In early 1992, the bank asked Judge Lee's permission to sue Bertha Wright, Lundy, and Robey, claiming they had misappropriated funds and owed Calumet, a company in which the bank was the majority shareholder, more than $25 million—the $18 million taken out of Calumet's account without approval of the Calumet board and sent to Wright Enterprises, plus at least $7 million in interest. But the judge denied the request. The bank had a conflict of interest because the Wrights had sued the bank and it was the creditors' job to go after the Wrights and other Calumet board members. The judge, however, did say that if the creditors did not pursue the directors, the bank could try again. Unwilling to give up, the bank, a year or so later, sued Bertha, claiming that she and the other partners in Wright Enterprises had misappropriated, converted, and embezzled nearly $27 million between October 1984 and April 1990. It was a nasty fight.

Meanwhile, the twists and turns of litigation would throw the family and the bank, though still spitting fire at each other, on the same side of yet another dispute: the creditors of Calumet attacking the board of directors, which consisted of the family and the bank, for breaching their fiduciary duties. While the heirs appeared to be the victims of a pillage, they were also, as members of the Calumet board, accused of perpetrating the pillage. The creditors in one lawsuit claimed that the heirs—minus Cindy, who was not on the board—"failed to carry out their fiduciary obligations as directors for the corporation by allowing J. T. Lundy and Lyle G. Robey to make all decisions regarding the operation of the corporation and to deal with the corporate assets without any measure of control from the board of directors." It was a perplexing position for the heirs.

The family blamed the bank. The bank blamed the family. The creditors blamed the board of directors, meaning Robey, Lundy, the bank, and the family. Robey blamed tax reforms, greedy bankers, a family that spent too much money, and, on rare occasions, Lundy for his choice of deals and friends in the late 1980s. Robey claimed the heirs wouldn't listen to him; the heirs said Robey didn't advise. Oil was another culprit, according to Robey, who had invested family funds in all sorts of Texas oil ventures, most of which failed. There seemed to be more finger-pointing and side-taking in Fayette County than at any time since the Civil War.

Calumet creditors soon claimed, in a lawsuit, that Robey had committed malpractice by failing to advise the Calumet board of Lundy's actions and the financial consequences of many of his deals. They accused Lundy of taking breeding rights and other forms of compensation out of the farm's coffers without authorization from the board. Lundy, the creditors alleged, had also caused Calumet to make payments to various entities in which Lundy had a financial interest. Because of him, they claimed, Calumet purchased horses for excessive prices, horses that later sold for less than 5 percent of the purchase price. This was hardly just a market drop due to a downward swing in the market. Because of Lundy and Robey, they claimed, the farm had borrowed money beyond its ability to pay, resulting in the complete destruction of the net worth of the farm. At the same time, both men had allowed Calumet to loan millions of dollars—without the board's approval—to Wright Enterprises, which now had no assets and no conceivable ability to reimburse Calumet.

Regardless of who was shouting at whom and what was said in a lawsuit, a deposition, or a court hearing, Bertha Wright never publicly blamed her son-in-law for the troubles that now filled her days. In various interviews with reporters around the nation she described Lundy as a quiet man whom the family had trusted. "He does things his way: 'I'm the leader. You follow.' And we did follow," she told Joe Durso of *The New York Times* a few days after the bankruptcy. When Durso asked whether Lundy's methods "split the family," she said, "Well, it happened. He resigned. Nobody will ever know what happened."

She did, however, tell at least one writer that she placed the blame on the fact that Lucille Markey left all her money to charity and none to her son's children. Bertha felt that some of the money Mrs. Markey had given to cancer research should have been left to the children as a capital base for running the farm.

But more than anyone, Bertha seemed to blame herself. She was the only one willing to take some responsibility. In an interview with a local reporter on July 11, 1991, a few hours after the Calumet bankruptcy papers were filed, Bertha wept as she said, "I feel like I let the Wrights down. . . . I'm the last of the four. You know, the mother and father and Warren and me— and I feel badly that I can't do any better than take advice from those who would advise me."

12 Christmas in the white-pillared mansion with the devil's-red shutters and the tall front door draped in greens was Bertha Wright's favorite holiday. She loved the sounds of great-grandchildren, grandchildren, and her own children gathered in one place for the day; the sight of dolls and stuffed animals crammed onto the satin window seat at the landing halfway up the wide stairway, the occasional toy truck lunging across a hallway; and the tree, nearly as tall as the fourteen-foot ceilings. This was perhaps the best part of living on the farm.

But 1991 was different. It was the last Christmas for the Wright family at Calumet. Numerous pieces of furniture, paintings, and bric-a-brac were already missing, for Bertha was slowly moving her possessions into storage, in preparation for the big move after the holidays.

A week after New Year's, a moving van motored up the long drive to the columned house, around the circle driveway, past Gene Markey's log cabin, and past the two stone steps that Lucille Markey, when she was still Lucille Wright, had used to ease her climb onto the back of a horse. It stopped near the front door and remained there for hours as movers emptied the Wright residence.

Out came the oil portraits of Calumet champions, the nineteenth-century paintings of horses and riders, the Venetian glasses, goblets, and plates painted with dainty medieval scenes, the ten-and-a-half-foot-long dining room table, the needlepoint rugs, the late-eighteenth-century camelback sofa, a portrait of Henry Clay, a color photo of Bull Lea taken in 1938, the portrait of William Monroe Wright sitting in a Victorian chair, and the portrait of Lucille Wright holding her toddler son Warren Jr. which had hung in Calumet's main residence since 1937 when the house was built. Some items would be stored until an auction could be arranged. Others Bertha would take with her to her new abode, a rental townhouse in Lexington.

The lawsuits were still rushing in, whittling away at family members' self-esteem and dignity. Citizen's Fidelity had just sued the family for defaulting on a $1.6 million loan to Wright Enterprises in December 1990. None of the $75,000 quarterly payments had ever been made. Bertha's own debt tally was increasing. Calumet bankruptcy files now showed she owed the farm several hundred thousand dollars, including back rent on the main house, which she had leased from the farm.

In a television interview a month or so after her move, Bertha showed the strain and sadness of the ordeal. Calumet's collapse, the storm of litigation, and the plight of the family were big news in the Bluegrass. The showplace of the region was now the setting of the biggest bankruptcy in horse-industry history. The local citizenry had grown up with the legends of Calumet. This was their symbol of perfection, and someone had made a mess of it. How could the family allow it to slip away? Were they negligent, ignorant, irresponsible? Or were they the victims of bad, perhaps deceitful, advisers? The public wanted answers.

Sue Wylie, the sprightly, blond host of the show, understood her audience and their fascination with the unanswered questions. The interview lasted about twenty minutes. Bertha, in her simple royal blue silk dress accented with a light-blue scarf, slowly and carefully answered every question, occasionally looking behind her to get the nodding approval of an adviser backstage.

Wylie began with some background information: "It was less than a decade ago that Bertha Wright inherited 62.5 percent of Calumet and moved into the great white house, her share of the farm established then at $13 million. Her four children also shared in the will, each getting 9 percent of the farm, with a total value placed then at $21 million without a penny owed to anyone. But everything changed . . ."

Q (WYLIE): Do you feel like a victim?

A (BERTHA): Yes, I do. When you don't know what's going on, you feel like a victim. . . . I want to correct one thing, though. It wasn't Lucille Markey who made this farm. It was her husband. She did not hurt it, but he made it.

(After talking about the devastating effects of tax reform on the horse industry—a turning point for Calumet, Bertha told the audience—Wylie probed deeper:)

Q: Everyone in and outside the thoroughbred industry knows bad times have fallen on the industry, but Calumet's troubles are so much more dramatic than anyone else's. Did you lay out a master plan with your son-in-law?

A: I didn't lay out any sort of plan. I was just supposed to live there, and everyone said everything would be all right.

Q: Who's everyone?

A: Everybody around us.

Q: Financial advisers and J. T. Lundy and everyone just kept saying this is the way to do it?

A: Uh-huh.

Q: Did you realize that the farm was going into debt?

A: No, not right away.

Q: No one told you?

A: No, not till much later . . .

Q: You really thought it was a short-term, sort of tide-us-over kind of loan.

A: Yes.

Q: Did you want to take a more active role in the farm?

A: I didn't think I was capable of it.

Q: Why not?

A: Because I hadn't been trained to do anything like that.

Q: You didn't consider yourself a businesswoman?

A: Absolutely not. I was told when I lost the money on Ricco Antonio [the dress shop] that I shouldn't conduct any kind of business. My

Nashville lawyer told me, don't get into another business. He said it's like putting a paper bag along the side of the road with cash in it and somebody comes along and says it's mine, nobody else owns it.

Q: Didn't that bother you?

A: No, I took his advice.

Q: So you were just going along living on the farm, enjoying the horses and the industry and the social life and so forth. Did you feel in any way you were living beyond your means?

A: No.

Q: No one said we have to trim costs?

A: At one time we were told oil and gas was going down in 1986 and 1987 and that we should be slowing down on our budgets.

Q: Well, you did by many other people's standards—[have] a lavish lifestyle. Calumet got involved in racecars—

A (*interrupts*): I did not live lavishly. . . . I just lived on a nice farm. I mean . . .

Q: You're a simple person who doesn't need a lot . . .

A: Yes, that's right. We did enjoy flying. We understood the plane was supposed to be for business. And I'd use it to take clothes to Ricco Antonio shows and to go to the racetracks.

Q: Did you have homes in other places?

A: I had a condo in Lauderdale for about four or five years and didn't think I was staying there long enough to warrant it, so I sold it three years ago.

Q: And you had utter faith in the people advising you?

A: Yes, I always have.

Q: Have you learned a lesson?

A: Yes, I have.

Q: Are you embarrassed?

A: I certainly am. Wouldn't you be?

Q: Embarrassed still?

A: I am.

Q: Do you feel guilty?

A: No, not really. Don't feel guilty 'cause I don't know. . . . Nobody knows . . .

(After talking about rumors of as much as $350 million missing from Calumet, Wylie asked:)

Q: Do you think there's a missing fortune?

A: I hope they find it if there is.

Q: Do you feel there is?

A: I have no idea.

Q: Do you feel that you have been ripped off in any way?

A (*while looking backstage*): I don't know—that's not what I should be saying at this time.

Q: What has this done to your family?

A: It's hurt them . . . oh . . .

Q: What about the family unit?

A: We're still together, but they all hurt in different ways. . . . They never expected to be caught up in something like this, and we've had to go to meetings once or twice a week since the last part of February [1991] trying to find a solution to all this, and every time we had a meeting we'd find a way to make it somehow and then the next week we'd go and they'd say, "Can't do that."

(Here Wylie gives the audience some basic facts of Calumet's recent past.)

Q: Some of your family relationships have been lost besides the fortune and farm?

(*Bertha nods.*)

Q: Do your children feel cheated out of their legacy?

A: Yes.

Q: You're sad, aren't you?

A: Wouldn't you be? I certainly am sad. I'm smiling, but I'm sad. It's bad to be sitting here in front of people and talking about your problems. Nobody likes to do that.

Q: But people feel sorry for you, you understand. The public considered Calumet a treasure, their treasure, too.

(More questions followed then:)

Q: What do you think Mr. Wright would say if he knew what was going on?

A: Like the old term, he'd turn over in his grave.

Q: And Mrs. Markey?

A: She was already concerned before she died.

Q: Why was she, and how do you know?

A: She talked to me. . . . She had a difference of opinion. She knew what route we were going, and she was concerned. . . . She knew we were going to try to run the farm, and I guess she wanted me to have somebody other than family to run it.

Q: Did she advise you to hire someone?

A: No, she didn't advise me.

Q: And she didn't give you any names of people she thought could run the farm better than your son-in-law, J. T. Lundy?

(No answer.)

Q: What have you learned from all this?

A: Life is very real and not like living in a fairy-tale dream house. . . .

13 By 1992, J. T. Lundy was nowhere in sight, and his disappearance had spawned a new sport in the Bluegrass: J.T. sighting.

A local trainer said he saw Lundy having dinner at an elegant restaurant in Louisville with former Kentucky governor Wallace Wilkerson. The next day, a bloodstock agent spotted him lunching at one of his favorite hangouts in Lexington, the luncheonette at Kroger's Supermarket. In the training barns at Churchill Downs, Dr. Alex Harthill, the veterinarian, told a trainer he had just seen Lundy in Prestonsburg, the eastern Kentucky coal town that was home to Lundy's friend Harry Ranier. There were sightings in parking lots, at stoplights, on turnpike exit ramps. Someone who had recently visited Spendthrift Farm claimed he caught a glimpse of Lundy pulling back a curtain and peeking out from an upstairs window of the white-columned main house. Someone else saw him at Pimlico Racetrack in Maryland, and another claimed to see him boarding an airplane in Miami. A friend of Margaret Glass's told her about a friend who had spoken with a mail carrier who said he had handled a package with an address for Lundy in Argentina. Still others said they knew "for a fact" that he was spending most of his time in Australia, where they were certain he owned a plot of land in someone else's name. There were rumors about Lundy living on an island off the coast of Honduras, buying into a coal partnership in eastern Kentucky, dressed in black with his hair slicked back at a restaurant in London, taking it easy in Key West, standing in front of a bank in the Cayman Islands, and hiding out in secret underground quarters on his own farm in Midway.

In a region rich with folklore where storytelling is about as natural as talking, "J.T. sighting" was almost as much fun as going to the races. One reason for the intrigue was simply a matter of arithmetic. For most people, the numbers in the Calumet debacle just didn't add up. So much money flowed into the farm during the Lundy years that no one could understand how it was possible that nothing was left. This image of a gap between money in and money out, in conjunction with the fact that Lundy was bringing into his own coffers millions of dollars in commissions and breeding rights, led to the suspicion that Lundy had stacks of money hidden away—money of his own and money that might be legally construed as Calumet's.

Part of the new sport was speculating about just how much money he had and where he had stashed it. Bankers, journalists, horsemen, and lawyers, during spare moments at their desks, in court hearings, or at lunch, scribbled numbers in margins of notebooks, on napkins, and on backs of envelopes to estimate how much money might be missing. The question that plagued anyone who knew about Calumet was how it was possible for the legendary farm to go so far into debt. Spendthrift had died a similar death, but its debt was not quite $57 million. Calumet's was a monumental $167 million.

To be sure, expenses were high. Ward had estimated that operating the farm under Lundy cost at least $12 million a year, far more than the $2 million to $2.5 million annual expenses during the Markey years. Added to this were the multimillion-dollar stallion purchases, the initial renovations, the commissions, the hefty insurance premiums, legal fees, and deals that perhaps were not accounted for on paper in the Calumet records.

But despite the expenses, many bills and interest payments were clearly unpaid, hence the millions of dollars in creditors' claims against the farm. Moreover, the farm had not spent as much cash as it appeared to, often using seasons to pay for goods and services. Even some of the pricey stallion purchases that everyone referred to as part of Calumet's monstrous costs were bought with notes and seasons and little cash. So if there was so much money coming into the farm and yet bills went unpaid and purchases often involved no cash, where was the money?

Some of the millions pouring into Calumet spilled right back out again to Wright Enterprises. Several million dollars went to Wright heirs; Robey had invested several more in oil and gas companies that appeared to be real losers. But Wright Enterprises had a cash balance of zero and debts of $30 million. Where was this money?

Using rough estimates of income and expenses, some people placed the sum of missing cash at a stunning $300 million. Others with a more realistic eye placed it in a range from $25 million to $100 million. Ron Sladon estimated at one point that nearly $100 million was unaccounted for. "Proceeds from all sources when J.T. was there generated nearly $350 million, including bank loans and revenue. Then the farm ended up $150 million in the hole, so there is about $200 million unaccounted for. Against that you have $12 million a year for running the farm or less than $100 million plus stallion purchases, though a lot were paid for by Alydar shares. So, it's somewhere around $90 million or $100 million unaccounted for."

Where these millions had gone was the titillating part of everyone's speculation. Courtenay Wright Lancaster told a friend she was certain Lundy had money stashed away in either the Cayman Islands, Australia, or a Swiss bank account, but she didn't know anyone who could afford to look for it. One individual who had known Lundy for many years claimed that in the late 1970s and early 1980s several people he knew had established accounts in the Caymans and Lundy was among them. He remembered this distinctly, he said, because at the time it seemed unusual. But, he added, he had no tangible proof to offer and he didn't know whether this had continued after Lundy became Calumet president because he and Lundy had drifted apart.

A few former employees recalled Lundy's frequent trips to the house in Marathon. Here, one dramatic theory went, someone from Calumet would bring suitcases full of cash and hand it over to someone else on a boat nearby or on a plane landing on Marathon's airstrip, bound for a bank somewhere in the Caribbean. Marathon was only an hour from the Bahamas and another forty-five minutes from the Cayman Islands—both places where money can be hidden easily. Those people who knew about Robey's house on an island off the coast of Belize also concocted theories about planes stopping there on their way to South America.

These were the people who loved to say things like, "You know the book *The Firm*? Change the 'i' to 'a' and well that's the story here: *The Farm*." To some, what had happened at Calumet appeared to be the kind of "bust-out" the Mob might orchestrate: First you use an organization to get money out of banks; then you drain the business of cash; and in the end, you leave both the banks and the business high and dry as well as dozens of creditors. With the money gone, no one has the financial ability to search for lost millions.

But nothing so dramatic was ever proven. Some Lundy insiders said they knew nothing about a house in Marathon. Others said it was better not to ask questions about Marathon or Vaca, the company that apparently owned the house. As for Robey's island retreat, it was a dome-shaped pink house on a small plot of land that he told friends he used occasionally for vacations devoted to fishing.

In the barns behind the tracks, at Saratoga Springs, at Belmont, at Churchill Downs, and at Keeneland, there was always someone who said he or she knew the real story but it was too dangerous to tell. What had happened was all too shortsighted, too stupid, too greedy, too cash intense, and too heartless for someone who cared about the farm to have orchestrated. Behind the scenes there must have been a mastermind, an evil force, someone who was making Lundy do the things he did. The endless stream of money from banks, the excessive travel to places such as Hong Kong, Australia, the Caribbean, and many other locales, the alleged Mob contacts, as well as certain business practices, pointed to culprits much more sinister than a cyclical business slump, a saturated marketplace, or a deal-addicted Lundy.

Ward and Sladon had heard the rumblings about money laundering or some Mafia-related scam. They joked among themselves about car bombs and things like cement blocks and bottoms of rivers. This was why, Ward said later, with a chuckle, he and Sladon had sent someone else on the Calumet staff to pick up that Ford of Lundy's, the one that Lundy or someone had left in the parking lot next to Gary Matthews's office.

No one in the Calumet offices apparently noticed a blurb in a *USA Today* column "Across the USA" in late August of 1991 that read: "Robert Libutti, 59, who lost $12 million to casinos over 6 years, was banned from state casinos. Cited: Libutti made racist comments to workers; has ties to reputed mob boss John Gotti."

If they had, they might have felt justified in worrying about what was behind the Calumet debacle, though still there would be no proof. Libutti, who did millions of dollars' worth of business at Calumet during the Lundy years, repeatedly claimed that the government was out to get him and that his Gotti ties were bogus. In 1992 he was indicted for bank fraud, income tax evasion, possession of firearms by a convicted felon, and conspiracy to commit bank fraud. A former president of a New Jersey bank was indicted with him, in part for his role in funneling millions of dollars out of his bank to Libutti via loans to third parties, from fall 1985 to spring 1987.

Ward and company did notice, however, in early 1992 that Lou-Roe Farms was busted on charges of fraud and money laundering. Lou-Roe's founder, Anthony Gurino, was indicted on twenty-one counts alleging that dummy companies were used illegally to divert funds from a New York City company acting as his front to Lou-Roe. His son, Louis, and his wife, Barbara, were also charged. What was particularly unnerving to the Kentucky crowd was the government's underlying intention in bringing the charges. "The Gurinos are documented as associates of Gotti and his crime family. This is part of Gotti's empire . . . the purpose of the indictments is to take a chunk out of it," said Lieutenant Frank Alioto of the Marion County Sheriff's Department in Florida.

Calumet's "three musketeers" talked about the link between Gurino and Gotti and about Lundy's prior connection to Lou-Roe. It was meaningful that Lundy had done business with an alleged division of Gotti's empire, but exactly what it meant, no one knew.

Lundy's own evasiveness did more to fuel rumors than anything else. His flight seemed an admittance of guilt, though anyone who knew him understood it was part of his personality to duck and hide. His friends knew how he hated confrontation and how he had hidden on the farm, even in the office, to avoid meeting with bankers or deal makers with confrontation on their minds. But now, with lawsuits and creditors, the stakes were higher.

It was one thing to avoid the public or certain kin, but he was also avoiding servers of court summonses, creditors and their lawyers, and journalists. He was sought for depositions in ongoing cases and for money in the judgments against him in the few closed cases. Trails of the searches were scattered through the Calumet-related court files, where big manila envelopes, used to send documents by certified mail, were covered with crossed-out addresses and scribbled messages saying Lundy was not there to sign for them. In the files there were reports from "warning order attorneys," lawyers appointed in a case for a specific purpose such as finding a defendant and making certain he has received certain court papers. Once a secretary at Lundy Farm in Midway, Kentucky, signed for two packages and then sent them back with a letter saying she had signed for them in error. She advised the sender to contact one of Lundy's attorneys. One package was hand-delivered to the offices of Lundy's Lexington attorney, who said he was not authorized to accept or open Lundy's mail. Next the sender tried an address in Florida. Finally, weeks later, the return-receipt card was mailed back, from an address in Venice, Florida.

Local columnist Don Edwards put Lundy into a story involving a ficti-
tious character, "the pseudonymous social arbiter" Buffy Bleugrazz. In the
story, Buffy is speaking with her rural cousin, Barbara Jean. Buffy says:

> "On a morning in early spring, the mist is rising from a horse pas-
> ture. Suddenly an apparition appears in the mist. It floats above a
> green hill, then descends slowly to the ground. Hundreds of people,
> their empty hands outstretched, are waiting for it. Many have been
> waiting ages for its return."
> "Good grief," says Barbara Jean, "who is it? Can you see the face? Is
> it some great spiritual leader?"
> "Actually, no, darling. I think it might be J. T. Lundy."

Around the same time, some reporters having lunch after a Calumet-
related court hearing swapped stories about their own efforts to find the
elusive Lundy. All agreed that Lundy had achieved celebrity status and had
been spotted and talked about almost as often in Kentucky as Elvis was in
Tennessee.

Lundy's main attorney, Montjoy Trimble, didn't understand what all the
fuss was about. A tall, bespectacled man with a penchant for one-liners,
Trimble was a Scott County boy, like Robey and Lundy, and had known
them both for many years. Even more than Robey, Trimble was a great
defender of Lundy, not only because Lundy was his client, he would say,
but because he believed Lundy was a scapegoat. People were taking out
their frustrations not just for what had happened at Calumet but also for the
depression of the entire industry. It was so easy to point a finger at Lundy,
Trimble would say. He believed, too, that jealousy might be a motive for the
condemnation.

"He [Lundy] might not have been the best businessman, but what he did
for the farm . . . well last February you know he got an Eclipse Award and
the Horse of the Year award. A lot of people would give their left nut just to
win one of those awards. . . . But for J.T.'s leaving, that farm would still be
afloat. He was working things out, looking for the angel to buy half the farm
and get it on financial footing.

"You want to know what happened? Exactly what happened? The truth? I
can tell you that, pure and simple. I can tell you that as we sit here today.
Calumet is a symbol of what happened in the industry because of the
1980s." During a court hearing in the fall of 1991, Trimble, standing tall and

facing the court, said he firmly believed the bankrupt corporation Calumet was simply "trying to poison the public eye against J. T. Lundy."

From the sometimes dramatic mix of rumors and facts surrounding Lundy, several theories had emerged. Lundy's "against me or for me" view of the world was becoming his legacy. A common supposition, usually referred to as the "mastermind" theory, was that Lundy, with Robey's help, had conspired from the start to drain the farm and the trust. "They wanted to deplete as much capital as was possible," according to one oldtime Lexington breeder who admitted he based his idea strictly on his knowledge of the personalities involved. "The plan was to milk everyone dry, the family and the banks, to put them into a posture of loss, so that by the end no one would have enough money to fight back."

Even those who were more informed about the case advanced this theory, basing their belief largely on the evidence of the legal foundation Robey had created for the new Calumet in 1982. There was something suspicious about the way the executive committee gave Robey and Lundy so much power. There were things like the "hold-harmless" agreement and the right to borrow as much as $10 million without board approval—things that made it look like they had a grand scheme rather than a simple desire to manage the family's assets because the family was incapable of doing so. Now that the family was knee-deep in creditors and attorneys' fees and unable to fight back, the way the corporation was set up pointed to something potentially sinister. Because of the legal structure of Calumet Farm, Inc., the family had a dilemma: every time they blamed Lundy or Robey for doing something, they, as members of the Calumet board of directors, were also blaming themselves. They had the responsibility to oversee financial matters as much as their fellow directors Lundy and Robey.

The intriguing question was: Who might be the mastermind? Was Lundy the man behind the scenes? Robey did say on several occasions that "[Lundy] did everything. He was in charge of all aspects of Calumet Farm, Inc." Or was it true, as many others said, that Lundy was intellectually incapable of devising such a scheme and therefore must have been under the influence of either Robey or someone outside the Bluegrass such as his New Jersey associates at ATPSI, the casino gambler Libutti, someone connected with the Florida farm indicted for money laundering, or someone tied to the Houston bank, such as Frank Cihak?

Those who had seen Matthews's name on so many official documents and knew that he was often the farm's representative while Lundy traveled the world speculated that Calumet was really run out of Matthews's office. This irked Matthews, who claimed he was only doing his job and had done his best to keep the farm alive. To be blamed for orchestrating its demise was "beyond belief."

There were those, too, who, like Trimble, had compassion for Lundy in his exile from the once-premier stable. Lundy had simply done what the Wright family asked him to do: bring back the glory years of the 1940s and 1950s. To accomplish that in the boom-boom times of the 1980s cost more money than anyone realized. Others unabashedly said that what Lundy did, whether it was pumping up prices of bloodstock at auction or borrowing millions from banks that were eager to be part of the gold rush in horse country or perhaps skimming a little off the top of a deal, wasn't necessarily unusual in the horse business during the wild and woolly 1980s. According to them, Lundy was taking the heat for the practices of an industry and an era, for things other people had done with impunity.

Lundy's defenders liked to stress that the Wright heirs spent a big chunk of the fortune on themselves. They bought their businesses and properties. Bertha used the Calumet jet for her fashion boutique. In 1989, she, her son Tommy, and his wife flew to London on the Concorde and returned on the luxury liner *Queen Elizabeth II*. Tickets started at $4,000. Cindy had her house in the Caribbean and more recently a condo near Vail.

Robey was a Lundy defender, despite his intense frustrations in trying to rein in Lundy's zeal for making deals. This, he said, was a matter of loyalty more than anything else. There was also the possibility that he knew if Lundy went down so would he. Robey blamed Calumet's demise on the industry's downturn, and he blamed that on tax reform and on banking practices of the 1980s. Bankers "were hustling at Keeneland like whores on 42nd Street," he said. "The banks made a false assumption; they assumed horses were like stocks. . . . J.T. did what he was asked to do, what he was mandated to do by the family, to make Calumet number one again."

Robey was only critical of Lundy for the company he kept in the later years of his regime. According to Robey, Lundy spent a great deal of money in the early years with the intention of being the best in the business, but his power and his inability to manage finances had conspired by 1987 to "bring on the money troubles." When he began to run out of cash, he made "pacts with people who promised bags of gold that were filled with dirt."

Bob Fox was another defender of the man he once called "Chief." Even though Lundy and Fox now rarely spoke, Fox believed Lundy was an innocent victim in a situation that careened out of control. Lundy was a simple man with simple tastes who never lived extravagantly. Fox said he even had to urge Lundy not to buy suitcases at J. C. Penney. He once took Lundy to a fine leather-goods store in New York where Lundy refused to spend thousands of dollars on suitcases he could get at Penney's for a hundred dollars. Fox, sitting in his New Jersey office suite one day in early 1992, whipped out a photo album and pointed to a picture of Lundy standing on a boat. He's wearing Top-Siders, a T-shirt with a black and white design, and flowered shorts that don't in any way match the shirt. He has on a sun hat and is squinting from the brightness of the South Pacific sun. "Now is this a man who steals millions?" asked Fox, who recalled how Lundy used to take his own pillow with him on trips. "He's just a farmboy who wanted to bring Calumet back to its glory and wiped the place out in the process. I'm not saying somebody shouldn't have stopped him from some of the loans; somebody should have explained to him that he couldn't afford all that interest, but nobody did."

A common argument on Lundy's behalf was that he was a generous person whom others took advantage of and that he bought the friendship and respect of a coterie of smart, smooth deal makers and advisers who didn't have Calumet's interests at heart. The so-called hidden millions were in the pockets of these people, according to this defense. "No one knows how many fees here and there were paid out to people who helped Calumet. . . . Not even J.T. kept track of this, and this is where you'd find any missing money," said one Lundy friend. "Though I'm not saying it's legal or ethical, the missing money everyone is looking for is not in J.T.'s backyard. Little bits and pieces of it are in the pockets of everyone he did business with. And no way could anyone prove anything against anyone. Boom, it's gone forever in the most convoluted bunch of transactions in history."

Many people meanwhile said the fault lay with the lawyers and bankers who were paid to oversee the Wright assets and advise farm officials. Lundy had only one vote on the three-member executive committee of Calumet's board; the bank that managed the Warren Wright, Jr., Trust and Robey had the other two, and, hence, the power to stop Lundy. But they apparently never exercised their control. Every piece of paper documenting every deal supposedly ended up either on the desk of Robey, as the head of Wright Enterprises, or on the boardroom table as a matter for the Calumet directors to consider. And while the board met infrequently, the executive committee was supposed to regularly oversee proposals. But then it only met quarterly, and according to an individual knowledgeable about such matters, Lundy, though questioned on several occasions about what he was doing, never experienced any opposition. Lundy's watchdogs at the bank and at the family partnership were off duty, according to this theory; Lundy hadn't the experience of running such a huge enterprise and so needed advice that he just wasn't getting.

Lundy, too, apparently took this view. In one of his few depositions, Lundy said that Robey or Gary Matthews typically negotiated loans for the farm and drafted legal papers. Then they asked Lundy to sign his name. The deposition, taken on December 30, 1991, was part of IBJ Schroder's case against the Wright heirs and Lundy.

Q (LAWYER): And they [Matthews and Robey] would be the two individuals charged with reviewing the legal documents to determine their legal sufficiency and the correctness of them?

A (LUNDY): That or some attorney they would have selected to do it. I don't—

Q: Within their law firm?

A: With their law firms or with somebody they were dealing with.

Q: Well, in terms of the primary responsibility, that would lie either with Gary Matthews or Lyle Robey?

A: Yes, and then we would be required to sign.

Q: So if either Robey or Matthews said, "J.T., I've reviewed this, this document is all right, sign it," then you would accept their advice?

A: Yes. . . . You know, they—I have faith in them and, you know, they would have taken care of it. . . .

Q: You would not exercise your independent judgment as to whether the document was right or not right?

A: Well, I would probably glance at it to see that it wasn't something that I didn't like or didn't—but as far as the technicalities of it, I don't consider myself to really be on a par with them to, you know, review it.

In other testimony Lundy made it sound as if Robey was also doing all the talking. In a case involving the stallion Wild Again, Lundy was asked whether the Calumet board knew about the four Wild Again lifetime breeding rights he had taken as compensation for managing the stallion. Lundy responded that he hadn't informed the board, but he was "sure Lyle explained it." And did the board convene to discuss and approve the Wild Again purchase and all accompanying arrangements? Lundy couldn't recall a

meeting, but "the way it was done" was that "Mr. Robey usually would talk
to them."

Most of the time, in public documents and sworn statements, Lundy
couldn't remember much about the deals at Calumet. His comments were
often as follows:

"I see I signed it, but I don't remember anything about it."
"I don't remember exactly."
"I really don't know."
"I don't know that either. Now, which are we talking about now?"
"I just don't know."

Lundy's critics found holes in every defense. Lundy may have dressed
simply and carried cheap luggage, but he traveled worldwide on his private
jets and stayed in lavish hotels. While on the road, he often rode in limousines and ate in the finest restaurants in Paris, London, Hong Kong, or
wherever he went. And in Robin Hood fashion, he treated his friends and
cohorts to the same. Once he and several friends went on an African safari
that cost at least $35,000. Another time in Sydney, Australia, he rented a
white Rolls-Royce and chauffeur to transport friends to the zoo. In Hong
Kong, he was in the habit of staying at the priciest of hotels. And he had a
palatial estate in Marathon just down the road from his Key West condo. His
was not a humble lifestyle.

Lundy allegedly had taken at least $6 million in commissions for himself,
plus numerous free breeding rights to Calumet stallions. His critics firmly
believed there were countless sweetheart deals and kickbacks that resulted
in losses to the farm and gains for Lundy. Many of the farm's loans weren't
paid back, so Calumet probably didn't pay $7 million in debt service each
year. It didn't pay cash for all purchases, and there were millions of dollars
unaccounted for in assets such as oil investments in Wright Enterprises.

Besides, Lundy wasn't exactly putty in the hands of his advisers; he didn't
always follow Robey's or Matthews's suggestions. Occasionally he would call
Matthews to talk about a purchase or sale he wanted to put together and
how he had heard that it was possible to do this or that regarding taxes and
the law. He'd insist that that's the way he wanted it done, period. Once
Matthews called Robey in a panic about such a conversation. Robey told
him to ignore it. "Maybe it'll just go away," Robey said, referring to the deal.

Robey and Matthews were Lundy's friends but they also were frustrated with him because they believed they were not privy to all the deals in which Lundy was involved or all the arrangements he had made with his business partners. "He kept his power over everyone, his control, because of selective information," said one insider.

The family, meanwhile, was tight-lipped. In 1992, Bertha's loyalty in the face of increasing aggravation and mounting legal fees was remarkable. Courtenay was praying hard to learn to forgive Lundy, she told friends. The money, Courtenay believed, had been a curse for her and her family. "If God came down now and said you can have it all back, I'd say, Please no, just let me live in peace," she told a close friend.

Lundy's wife, Cindy, who from the day of the bankruptcy was rumored to be planning a divorce, didn't talk much. But she did tell one of her lawyers, "It was a wild ride, but I wouldn't have missed it for anything."

In 1992, the only indisputable fact regarding the Calumet disaster was that everyone who had previously avoided or failed to understand the legal papers they had signed during the past decade suddenly was forced to read the fine print of dozens of lawsuits regarding those papers and the millions of dollars owed to creditors. And no one—neither the creditors nor the family—was willing to fund an investigation to find out whether or not there was a missing treasure. Was it possible, as Bertha Wright had said, that no one would ever know the truth?

By spring, about eighteen months after the death of Alydar, there wasn't time enough nor money enough to get the kind of answers needed to save the farm. Judge Lee signed an order giving Mutual Benefit permission to go to state court and foreclose on Calumet. And so in mid-March four men carried a large white billboard with red trim through the Calumet gates. They pounded the posts of the sign into the ground behind the white fences near the farm's entrance. At the same time, at the opposite end of the farm, a bright yellow billboard was afixed to the grounds. Both read: ABSOLUTE AUCTION. CALUMET FARM. MARCH 26TH.

PART V

PHOENIX

1 Shortly before noon on March 22, 1992, a line of cars, jeeps, vans, and pickup trucks began to form at Calumet's main entrance. At 1:00 P.M. when the devil's-red gates swung open, the caravan, now nearly a mile long, moved onto the farm's main roads following the crowd to roped-off pastures designated as parking lots. They had come for Calumet's open house, arranged to give prospective bidders a chance to look over the land and the hundreds of items listed in the auction catalog.

It was a wet, dreary day, with a light drizzle that always seemed about to stop but never did. Spring rains had intensified the deteriorating condition of Calumet's land, turning brown spots into thick puddles of mud and water. A sharp wind, colder than usual for late March, blew across empty fields, accenting the atmosphere of desolation. About 5,000 people braved the weather to visit Calumet, some to ogle, some just to say they had been there, and some to decide on which items they would bid. Their presence helped create a carnival atmosphere. At strategic points across the farm, vendors sold red-trimmed white T-shirts that displayed a horse's head and the caption "Calumet, A Legend that will live FOREVER." An artist, crouching in corners of crowded barns, sketched their interiors and the faces in the crowd. In the stallion barn directly across from the stalls where Alydar, Affirmed, Secreto, Mogambo, Wild Again, and Criminal Type had lived were long tables where people could register for the March 26 auction and receive an official paddle to signify bidder registration.

Buses carried people from building to building to view the items on sale. These were items that had the power to retrieve moments and memories from the past. Among them: the horse van made exclusively for Calumet by General Motors in 1939; oil paintings of Alydar, Secreto, and fifteen other Calumet stallions and mares; cast-iron jockey hitching posts; one of the first cans of Calumet Baking Powder; cherry, mahogany, and maple furniture; silver julep cups and an array of silver and gold trophies won during the Lundy years; a cast-iron boot scraper with equine sculptures flanking the scraper; and the everyday necessities of a working farm such as mop buckets, feed buckets, saddles, bridles, footlockers, brooms, pitchforks, blankets, tractors, trucks, plows, and even spires from the tops of two Calumet buildings. A piece of Calumet, like fairy dust, brought the promise of magic into a person's life.

A mass of humanity pressed against one another as dozens of people climbed the exterior stairway to the second floor of the Calumet office. There paintings, sketches, sculptures, trophies, and all sorts of knickknacks were stacked against walls, on tables, in corners. No room and no item was spared inspection. Some people even ventured into the attic storage room where Calumet staffers found them rummaging through boxes of papers and Calumet jackets. One woman was heard saying she had found some Calumet envelopes and proudly displayed a handful. Another pocketed a Calumet ashtray from a table in Lundy's former office.

As dark clouds moved swiftly across the gray sky, some visitors hiked across the fields talking among themselves about the farm's legendary feats, showing off their knowledge of the Calumet athletes and race earnings, and telling their children stories from their own youth about Mrs. Markey or Ben Jones, Citation or Tim Tam. They pointed to the signs of spring such as blossoms on dogwood trees, and, of course, they discussed the possibilities for Calumet's future. A few visitors had more enterprising pursuits in mind, like the young man who spent part of the day scraping white paint off a barn and placing it in little plastic bags to sell as souvenirs for two dollars a bag.

In recent weeks the fate of Calumet had become a cause célèbre in the Bluegrass, engaging politicians, businessmen, philanthropists, creditors, and horse lovers in the challenge of saving the farm. Calumet was the showplace of the region and the biggest tourist attraction. Because of its location near the airport, its fields and fences were a visitor's first impression of Lexington and in some cases of the Bluegrass region. If its 847 acres were transformed into office parks, condos, or airport hotels, as many people feared, the impact on tourism could be dire. Acres and acres of former farmland in Lexington had already succumbed to developers of residential and commercial complexes, and though Calumet was added to the National Register of Historic Places in February 1991, thus protecting it from public projects, the bulldozers of private developers could still invade.

With the horse industry in a slump and equine businesses laying off workers, the region didn't need to lose its symbol of prosperity and reminder of better times. During the months after Ward and the Wright family announced to the world that Calumet was hanging by a thread, the public, through letters and phone calls, expressed grave concern. Most wrote nostalgically of their memories of the farm; others asked what they could do to help. One Michigan couple sent $15 to the cause. From midsummer 1991 through the winter, cars occasionally pulled up to the Calumet entrance, their passengers getting out to peer between the bars of the giant gates. They'd take pictures of one another against the backdrop of the eagle-topped columns or the nearby white fences.

Just as the Wrights and Lundy had wanted to believe the money was limitless, the public seemed to want to believe that Calumet was indestructible. But more than that, it was a fantasy, a Camelot in people's minds that wasn't even real enough to be destructible. For many, Calumet and the stories of William Monroe Wright and his son Warren were the evidence in life that hope and hard work could bring great success. Each time the public passed the undulating miles of white fences, they were reminded of hope. For this, they depended on Calumet and the trademark fences, which is why no one wanted to lose the farm and why everyone felt somehow a part of it, as if they each owned a tree, a fence post, or a stall door. No matter who bought the farm, it would always belong to the people.

On March 22 it was never clearer that the soul of Calumet was the people who had come to worship its beauty from miles around. Tony Leonard, a photographer who for thirty years had been taking pictures of Calumet, told a television reporter shortly before the open house, "It's God's gift to Kentucky is what I think Calumet is. . . . I love this place, I absolutely love it. I almost feel that I own part of it."

A "Talk of the Town" item in *The New Yorker* read:

> A young woman we know in Kentucky writes: Everybody in the
> Bluegrass has been a little blue this spring, with the news that the
> world-famous Calumet Farm, Lexington's premier thoroughbred-horse
> farm, was bankrupt and would be auctioned off. Calumet is so much a
> part of our landscape and our history here that it seemed impossible
> that it would end, or change.

In mid-March three elderly gentlemen from New York City had toured
the farm, taking pictures of one another in the cemetery, along the roads, by
the barns. "When they left," Ron Sladon recalled on the day of the open
house, "they were all crying. And this is the way it's been."

But by the end of March, despite the tears, tributes, and tentative offers,
no one had made a commitment to buy Calumet. The previous November,
after the dispersal of the horses, American International Bloodstock Agency,
a Lexington firm that had done some work for Calumet during the Lundy
years, including appraisals, filed a motion in Lexington bankruptcy court
offering $26.28 million for the farm and the farm's interests in the stallions,
which then had not been sold. The firm, owned by two brothers, Phil and
Norman Owens, was joined in the offer by a Maryland veterinarian, Dr.
D. Michael Cavey, who owned thoroughbred horses in partnership with
Mrs. Augustus Riggs, a wealthy Maryland horsewoman. It was unclear, however, where the money was coming from. A letter from the group said the
offer was from them "or an entity to be formed by them." Regardless of their
source of cash, the group was committed to preserving "the integrity of
Calumet," a representative told the Calumet management.

In December a higher bid came from another group of private investors
whose agent would not reveal their names. They wanted the land and the
stallion interests for $32.5 million. Their offer looked promising, but after
one member of the group slipped unnoticed into a bankruptcy court hearing one day and listened to hours of squabbling over who owned how much
of each stallion, the group dropped the horses from the bid and reduced its
offer to $27.5 million for the farm, the equipment, the name, and the tro-
phies. The group called itself Professional Sports Investments and though its
membership was never clear, it was advised by six men who called themselves Thoroughbred Executive Advisory Mentors. They were Lundy's Lexington attorney Montjoy Trimble; Washington, D.C., lawyer Herman
Braude; Harry Rosenblum, a securities dealer in Arkansas; New York horse

trainer Dick Dutrow; Robert Dooley, a financial consultant from San Jose, California; and Steve Wolfson, the Florida breeder who had recently sold a portion of his own farm in a foreclosure sale to Lundy and who now worked at the Mirage casino and resort in Las Vegas. Both Trimble and Wolfson had ties to Lundy, which set the local rumor mills churning over the possibility that such a deal might put Lundy back in the driver's seat. A spokesman for the group assured the Lexington paper there would be no role for Lundy at Calumet if the investors' bid was successful. Besides, the advisers were not necessarily the investors. The investors never revealed their identities.

Both offers were above Mutual Benefit's appraisal, which placed the value of the farm, without any stallion interests, at $24.59 million. That included $29,000 an acre for the land, $600,000 for the main house, $400,000 for the Calumet office, and $500,000 for Calumet's equine therapy facility. The stallion interests were estimated to be worth nearly $10 million. In outstanding mortgages on the land alone, Calumet owed a total of $53 million to Mutual Benefit and First City.

Politicians, recognizing the importance to the voting public of preserving Calumet, devised their own plans. Scotty Baesler pledged to "do everything in [his] power" as mayor of Lexington to block developers from taking over the farm. At a news conference in December, he announced the city was willing to buy approximately 250 acres and turn them into a buffer park with a four-mile scenic drive on elevated land along the perimeter of the farm. The park would give visitors panoramic views of a famous working horse farm. There would be a picnic area, visitors' center, exhibition hall, and two and a half miles of new road. The city would work with the private buyers and by offering to buy part of the land, lower the cost to buyers while controlling the use of the land. The plan would cost $5 million to $6 million, which the city hoped to obtain from donations, short-term loans, and grants.

Meanwhile a Florida developer considered buying the land and turning it into a resort. A financial consultant in New York City wanted to transform the main residence into an inn and create a combination spa and riding camp. His plan was to lease the farm for $1 a year and after one year, to take the company public, selling 10 million shares at $6 each. He had a network of 1,700 brokers who would buy whatever he suggested, he said. He could save the farm, he hoped, without a cent of bank debt. "We'll have patrons with big names, like General [Alexander] Haig and the ex-chairman of Mobil Oil to give it credibility, and we'll raise the money, all of it," the consultant, Donald Waugh, said.

Ric Redden, an equine podiatrist who first toured Calumet when he was six years old, also had a plan. He wanted the citizens of Kentucky to buy the farm themselves. In a lengthy column with the headline "Memories Drive Effort to Save Calumet Farm," local reporter Jacalyn Carfagno outlined the details, helping to spread the word throughout the state. Redden believed that Kentuckians cared enough about the farm that he could raise $25 million to buy it. If horsemen contributed $100 to $500 each and school-children donated $1 apiece, the people could do so, he said. They would then give the deed to the city of Lexington, and the city could appoint a board of horsemen to run it. "We can't allow Calumet to become a golf course and ten years from now say we wish we'd done something about it," Redden said.

But by the day of the open house, on March 22, no one with a plan or a dream had made a commitment to buy. In late December Calumet had received a letter from the agents for the investors offering the $26.28 million saying they were no longer considering the property, just the stallion interests. And representatives of the group whose offer was $27.5 million had yet to submit the necessary financial information. Others who had promised documents and written proposals hadn't come through.

In the Calumet offices the day of the open house, as streams of visitors left clumps of mud on the red and blue carpet, the newest rumor was that Issam Fares might buy the farm. Such speculation made sense because Fares Farm was adjacent to Calumet, which would be simply an extension to Fares's domain. It was easy to distinguish the two because Fares Farm had black fences. This was how the Calumet staff had picked up on his potential plans to buy the farm. A local retailer supposedly had received a call asking for an estimate on enough black paint to cover thirty miles of fences. Regardless of the high respect local horsemen held for their neighbor Fares, painting Calumet's fences black seemed almost as bad as developing the land.

2 J. P. King Auction Company of New York and
Swinebroad-Denton of Lexington spent nearly $300,000 to promote the Ab-
solute Auction of Calumet Farm. Ads appeared in the *Wall Street Journal*, *The
New York Times*, the *Financial Times* of London, and various Japanese and
European publications. At least 25,000 brochures were mailed to prospective buyers, including Queen Elizabeth II, who had visited the farm in 1984
and whose mares had been bred to such Calumet celebrities as Alydar. A
glossy ninety-six-page auction catalog with the restored 1939 Calumet horse
van on the cover was an instant bestseller in Lexington. At $15.90 a copy,
the first thousand copies were sold out within two hours of arriving at the
Calumet office. The next four thousand copies were gone five days later.

The catalog displayed the 675 items visitors had viewed four days before
at the open house. Enclosed was a single sheet explaining that the real estate
would be sold in four pieces, one 767-acre lot, a 36-acre lot, a 44-acre lot,
and a 2,550-square-foot home adjacent to the farm. On the largest lot were
forty-three buildings, including the main residence, nine two- and three-
bedroom houses, numerous barns and equipment buildings, the vet clinic,
two racetracks, the equine swimming pool and underwater treadmill, a
swimming pool adjacent to the main house, tennis courts, a gazebo, and the
log cabin where Gene Markey wrote his favorite book, *Kentucky Pride*.

Serious bidders for the farm's main tract were required to post a
$500,000 cashier's check prior to bidding, which would count toward a 10
percent down payment for the winning bidder. The speculation about who
might come forward at any minute was the talk of the town. Queen Elizabeth II was still on the list, and so were rap singer M.C. Hammer, Sheik
Hamdan bin Rashid al Maktoum, Jack Kent Cooke (owner of the Washington Redskins and of nearby Elmendorf Farm), the sultan of Brunei, and New
York Yankees owner George Steinbrenner. News that a group of Arabs had
taken over an entire floor of the Hyatt Regency in Lexington for the week of
the auction caused a flurry of local intrigue.

Meanwhile, a tide of nostalgia and melancholia engulfed the Bluegrass.
On the eve of the big sale, a local NBC affiliate ran an hour-long tribute to
Calumet that was so moving one of the lawyers connected with the Calumet
bankruptcy said he had tears streaming down his cheeks as he watched it.
While everyone involved with Calumet knew the story all too well, the

show, with its historical perspective and camera shots of lush fields, forced people to realize what was about to happen. Suddenly it was clear that no matter who bought the farm, the next day would mark the official end of a nearly seventy-year-old dynasty.

3 By the morning of March 26, the carnival atmosphere had disappeared. Now the long lines of cars slowly passing under the gaze of the cast-iron eagles that flanked the entrance seemed as if they were coming to a funeral or visiting a dignitary lying in state. The rain continued to fall for the fourth straight day; the wind seemed colder than ever.

Nearly 3,000 people took trains or buses, drove or flew from all over the country to attend the auction. Some came to buy and some to have their pictures taken by Alydar's grave. Horse aficionado Jerry Grief drove all the way from Birmingham, Alabama, to bid Calumet farewell. "I'd feel like a vulture if I came to pick over the remains," said Grief, as he searched for an empty seat in the big tent. "If someone buys it and paints the fences black, I'll come back and blow the place up. Those white fences are a bit of heaven. . . . I don't cry at funerals, but I may here today."

Evan Landis and David Herndon drove up from Atlanta the night before. "It's the passing of a moment of glory in American history, so I just thought, wouldn't it be good to be there," said Landis, as he looked at a Calumet cap his friend had just purchased. "This was the last cap they sold, the last Calumet cap ever, just think of that," said Herndon, placing the cap on his head.

Margaret Glass came in her self-styled devil's-red pants suit with the blue trim, modeled after the Calumet racing silks. Hershel Lathery, who was in charge of the Calumet grounds and had worked at the farm since 1948, was also there. So were John Ward, Ron Sladon, and David Switzer, numerous lawyers, local bank presidents, and representatives of Calumet creditors. Bertha Wright appeared too, holding her head high, though her spirits were low.

In recent months, the Wright heirs had taken as much heat from the public as Lundy had for letting the farm fall apart. Their crime, in the public eye, was passivity and a laissez-faire approach to the most cherished dynasty in racing. Horsemen who worked hard just to own one or two horses and felt honored to set foot on the Calumet land were critical of a family that seemed uninvolved in racing and appeared to take for granted its barns full of blueblood thoroughbreds.

Bertha, whose wide, ingenuous face was taut with the energy it took to fight back tears, was the only Wright to attend the auction. She nodded to a few acquaintances and reporters as she entered the big red-and-white striped tent, occasionally smiling as she moved on to a smaller tent where prospective bidders for the real estate were seated. Six rows ahead of Bertha sat a man who would soon help to divert the public eye from her problems. He was a small man with a deep tan and thick gray hair who held a wooden cane with a sterling handle. His name was Henryk de Kwiatkowski.

4 The auction opened with another sentimental video in homage to the farm, pushing the emotional tide almost to the point of melodrama. Half the audience were wiping their eyes as Ryan Mahan of Swinebroad-Denton stepped to the podium and proclaimed: "Those of us who have witnessed the various stages that have led to this moment have regarded what we have seen as a sad thing. Now, however, the sad part has been played out, it is over." He thundered, "The business we are about to conduct does not represent the end of something but the beginning. A new dawn, you might call it. The buyer of Calumet Farm will become the immediate hero of the thoroughbred world, from Santa Anita to Belmont, from Longchamps to Ascot. He or she will also be taking on both the privilege and the responsibility that goes with the stewardship of any great institution and, make no mistake, Calumet Farm is a great institution. . . . Time and fortune have brought us to this moment. If history surrounds the past, it also beckons from the future, and now, ladies and gentlemen, we are pleased to offer at Absolute Auction, Calumet Farm."

Next, tuxedo-clad auctioneer Walt Robertson moved onto the platform, taking one last look over his right shoulder to the part of the audience he cared about most: the bidders' tent. It was crowded now, with curious onlookers, members of the news media, and the six individuals, or their agents, who had put down the required $500,000 to bid on the main tract. Among them: de Kwiatkowski; Fares; a local bloodstock agent representing an unidentified foreign buyer; Dinwiddie Lampton, a Louisville insurance executive; and Jack Hecker, a Las Vegas businessman who said he had sold hundreds of acres in Ohio, Florida, and Virginia to pay for his planned purchase of Calumet. None of the famous prospects touted during the pre-auction days were part of this final group.

Robertson began the bidding for the main tract, 767 acres of land, at $30 million, quickly moving to $20 million. Within seconds, one of fifty professional auction spotters signaled Robertson that he had a bid for $10 million. The bidder was the man with the cane: Henryk de Kwiatkowski.

The bidding continued, slowly climbing to $12 million with a bid by Nijad Fares, the son of Issam Fares, the owner of adjoining Fares Farm. After $12 million, the only two bidders were Fares and de Kwiatkowski. Robertson pushed higher—"$13 million, $13 million, do I hear $13 million?" The atmosphere suddenly changed from morose to breathtaking—as enthralling as the Kentucky Derby, though instead of two minutes, this race would last twelve minutes. The auctioneer, like a racing commentator, shouted the progress of the competition. The audience chanted, "Yes, yes, higher, higher," as if they themselves would be the recipients of the proceeds. $12.5 million. $13 million. $13.5 million. $14.5 million. $15.5 million. $16 million. And then the pace began to slow.

"Do I hear $16.5 million? $16.5 million?"

After long seconds, the answer, from Fares: "$16.2 million." But de Kwiatkowski quickly came back with $16.5 million. Perched on the edge of his chair, he leaned on his cane with both hands cupped over its engraved silver top.

Fares countered with $16.7 million. Another pause. Silence. Was the man with the black fences going to win the farm?

Then de Kwiatkowski, with a broad, confident grin, as if he knew he had won the battle, came back with $17 million.

"$18 million, $18 million, do I hear $18 million? Let's go, let's go, to $18 million," urged the auctioneer.

"Hold tight!" a spotter in the bidders' tent shouted to the auctioneer.

"Doesn't take long to hold a minute," the auctioneer shouted back. Pause, then: "I have $17 million. Do I hear $18 million? I have $17 million. $17 million. Going, going, gone. Sold for $17 million!"

The gavel fell. And suddenly the red and white stripes of the auction tent shimmered with light. After days of rain, shafts of sunlight broke through the clouds, as if Pegasus, the messenger of the gods, would appear at any moment to approve what had just transpired. Spectators strained their necks to see who had bid the $17 million. The small man with the broad grin showing a mouthful of bright white teeth walked into the auction tent, saying to the person next to him, "I love it so much. I love this farm." As the audience cheered, many standing and clapping in unison, de Kwiatkowski adjusted the microphone to his height.

"We're very glad to have you as our neighbor," said Ryan Mahan.

"If I knew that this reception would have been part of my bid, I would have gone higher," said Calumet's new owner.

Then, raising his arms to quiet the audience, he said, "I would like to assure all you neighbors that I love horses and that most of the people who know me know how involved I am with horses. . . . I was very fortunate to buy many horses here. . . . When I saw this place being dismantled, it was a personal offense to me, and I assure you that no grass will be changed, it will remain in perpetuity, as it is."

The audience roared its approval for fifteen minutes. Many cried with the joy and relief of knowing that someone had saved their beloved monument. Bertha Wright, too, seemed relieved, though she later admitted she had hoped the farm would bring more than $17 million.

De Kwiatkowski, who owned more than two hundred horses boarded at farms throughout the world, also bought the forty-four-acre tract adjacent to the main tract for $175,000, and he outbid First City Bancorporation of Texas at $210,000 for the name Calumet Farm. Mutual Benefit paid $525,000 for a thirty-six-acre tract cut off from the main farm years ago by U.S. Highway 60. The Calumet colors went for $12,000 to a Brazilian horse breeder. The Kentucky Derby Museum in Louisville paid $72,000 for the 1939 horse van; a painting of Alydar sold for $22,000; devil's-red and blue footlockers emblazoned with the Calumet name went for as much as $3,000; silver-plated mint julep cups, won at various races, brought in $900 to $1,400. The wall plaque awarded to Alydar when he was inducted into the Racing Hall of Fame in 1989 went for $2,700 and Criminal Type's 1990 Horse of the Year award, a bronze horse on a wooden base, for $4,500. Water buckets sold for $15, Calumet jackets for $65, and feather dusters for $30. Proceeds of the auction, which went to Mutual Benefit and First City, totaled a little more than $19 million.

At a press conference later that day, the man who would soon write a cashier's check for more than $17 million leaned on his cane and announced: "The fences will be painted white as long as I live!"

5 Throughout the many months that Ward, the creditors, and the public had hoped for a buyer, Henryk de Kwiatkowski was never mentioned as a possibility. But just as it seemed an American landmark might soon be eaten up by bulldozers, this spirited, elfin man arrived on the scene, like a heroic character on the last page of a fairy tale. When he flew into Lexington from the Bahamas at 10:30 on the morning of the auction, it was as if he had suddenly swooped down from the clouds on the back of a winged, white steed. No matter what might surface later about who he was or wasn't, this man was truly a hero. He was the new king of the Bluegrass, anointed by the press and public as the "count of Calumet."

There was much about de Kwiatkowski that was reminiscent of past regimes at Calumet. He had homes in New York, Connecticut, Paris, Monaco, Buenos Aires, and Nassau, all decorated with paintings by Monet, Degas, and others. Like Warren Wright, Sr., he knew how to make a lot of money, and like Gene Markey, he knew how to spend it in style. His love for life and a good time was infectious, just as Markey's had been. Like Markey, de Kwiatkowski seemed to glow with an inner light that drew in and mesmerized those who met him. British novelist Jeffrey Archer modeled a character after de Kwiatkowski in his novel *Kane and Abel,* just as a character in the John Wayne movie *In Harm's Way* was modeled after Markey. His flyaway eyebrows reminded people of Markey, who also collected silver-tipped canes; and like Markey, he was a storyteller, though de Kwiatkowski's subject was often himself. Like J. T. Lundy, he had a passionate interest in airplanes, and like Lucille Markey, he was in the habit of dodging the question of age. De Kwiatkowski seemed to have his secrets, in keeping with a now well-established tradition at Calumet.

At the press conference in March, a reporter asked him his age, and he smiled that big, radiant smile, showing teeth as white as the fences he now owned. In a thick Polish accent, he answered, "What do you think I look like?"

The reporter asked again.

De Kwiatkowski said, "You can guess."

The reporter said, "Twenty-four."

De Kwiatkowski replied, "I'll settle for that. That's fine."

In private he told a reporter he was sixty-six years old, but his driving record in New York placed his birthdate two years earlier, and his military record showed a birthdate two years earlier still, establishing his age at seventy in the year 1992.

It was soon evident that de Kwiatkowski was something of an enigma. Though a lovely, charming man, he had a habit of embellishing his past and rearranging details with each new account—for example, his story of what he was doing the day before the Calumet auction.

There was the version in which his first wife, knowing how much he cared about the farm, called him the day before the auction at his home in Lyford Cay, in the Bahamas, after she had read a story about the auction. She told him he should buy it, and so he decided to go for it.

Another version was more dramatic. In this scenario he received a call, also at his Bahamian home, from a friend in Beirut who was the head of a big Middle Eastern company and asked de Kwiatkowski to entertain his cousin who was in the United States.

"Where is your cousin now?" asked de Kwiatkowski.

"He's in Kentucky," replied his friend. "He's going to buy a farm called Calumet with a group of friends."

At this point, de Kwiatkowski, who was talking on the phone in the master bedroom, was so stunned he slid off the satin bedspread onto the floor. "And is the plan to go into racing?" he asked.

"No," said his friend. "The plan is for a shopping center. The land is so fine for that."

De Kwiatkowski was so shocked he said simply, "Thank you very much," and hung up. He then quickly called a friend in Lexington to find out the conditions of the sale. After learning about the $500,000 requirement, he got a check at Lloyds Bank in Nassau, packed his bags, and flew to Lexington on his private jet.

There were also conflicting stories about his past, but despite the question of veracity, the details were always compelling and sometimes heart-wrenching.

He was born on February 22, 1924, according to his passport. His birthplace was Poznan, a town in western Poland. The youngest of seven children, he grew up on a farm that raised horses for the cavalry. His father died fighting the Nazis in 1939, and though they captured and killed his mother and sister, de Kwiatkowski escaped harm by hiding in a haystack on the farm. With their bayonets, the Germans cut his legs as they slashed through the hay in search of a body. In one version de Kwiatkowski escaped by hopping into a cattle car on a train going east but was captured by the Soviets, who held him in a labor camp for more than two years. In another version he joined a youth underground movement in an effort to stop the invading Russians and was captured and put in a camp. But in every version he lost his mother and his sisters and spent time in a Soviet camp.

He survived the camp partly through his own industry; he worked in the kitchen where he could keep warm and scavenge. He has said that he escaped in 1942 and fled to Iran, where in 1943 he boarded the *Empress of Canada,* a ship bound for England. But German submarines torpedoed the ship off the coast of Sierra Leone. When he finally made it to England, he joined the Polish squadron of the Royal Air Force, where he stayed for four years and where he says he won several medals. He has said on several occasions that he lied about his age so he could enlist, accounting for the discrepancy between the birthdate of February 22, 1922, on military records and other dates he has given. In the RAF he fought side by side with two of his brothers, who were both killed. At the end of the war, he was the lone survivor of his family.

After the war, he somehow ended up in Pakistan, where he helped the government put together a national airline. And after meditating at a Buddhist monastery for several months, acting in a few English films such as *A Matter of Life and Death* and *The Wooden Horse,* he studied aeronautical engineering in England, supposedly at Kings College.

His next stop was Canada, where he obtained citizenship, though he has also said he first spent time in Florence studying sculpture. Soon thereafter he worked at Pratt and Whitney Aircraft Company, the engineering division of United Technologies. It was about this time that the U.S. airline industry was converting from prop planes to jets. This opened new business opportunities such as selling parts of U.S. aircraft and used planes to foreign countries.

In 1962, with a few thousand dollars, de Kwiatkowski opened a small office at Rockefeller Center in New York for his new aircraft brokerage firm, Kwiatkowski Aircraft, incorporated in Nassau. Over the years, he would sell more than $2 billion in used planes and parts, mainly for Boeing and Trans World Airlines, throughout the world. This was a big business. A used 747 could sell for as much as $60 million, and de Kwiatkowski, typically charging a 7 percent fee, might make $4 million on such a deal.

His business made use of his language skills—he was fluent in six—and expanded his already sizable network of foreign connections. Perhaps his biggest deal came in 1975 when he sold nine TWA 747s to the Shah of Iran for $150 million. Press reports at the time claimed the deal saved TWA from bankruptcy. Later, de Kwiatkowski said he arranged the deal through a network of acquaintances in Pakistan. There he had met Princess Ashraf, the shah's twin, who eventually introduced de Kwiatkowski to her brother. The shah apparently liked de Kwiatkowski so much that he would talk to no one else about the purchase of the planes. He trusted de Kwiatkowski to the extent that he supposedly wrote a check to him for the down payment of $90 million, which de Kwiatkowski had to endorse before TWA could get its money. De Kwiatkowski made $15 million on the transaction. Other deals included the sale of 707 planes from Boeing and TWA to Saudi Arabia in the early 1980s. *Fortune* reported that he sold close to two hundred 707s in 1982; his commission on each was about $70,000.

In the mid-1970s, de Kwiatkowski, now among the superrich, was able to indulge his lifelong love for horses. His first purchase was a filly named Kennelot, for which he paid $280,000. Although she wasn't much at the track, her progeny were, and for good luck he named his stable after her. His horses won two Eclipse Awards, including Horse of the Year in 1982 for Conquistador Cielo, one of his two winners of the prestigious Belmont Stakes. His horse Stephan's Odyssey was runner-up to Spend A Buck in the 1985 Kentucky Derby. Like many owners and breeders, including Warren Wright and the Markeys, de Kwiatkowski named his horses for people and places close to him. There are horses named for each of his ten children. Croydon was named for a place outside London where de Kwiatkowski was stationed during World War II, and Danzig, his first stallion, was named after the city in Poland where his mother was born. Danzig was also the pre–World War II name for Gdansk, the center of Poland's Solidarity movement in which de Kwiatkowski has said he was involved.

In an article splashing some inconsistencies in de Kwiatkowski's stories across the front page of the local newspaper, Lexington reporter Robert Kaiser called de Kwiatkowski to task two months after the Calumet auction. Kaiser was critical of de Kwiatkowski's inability to tell the same story twice the same way. "It doesn't help that some of his claims cannot be verified and that others contain historical inaccuracies," he wrote. Kaiser pointed out the various versions of de Kwiatkowski's age and that Kings College had no record of his degree in engineering. De Kwiatkowski's response to the attack on his credibility was that "only 10 percent of what I have done has ever been written about."

Still, de Kwiatkowski was a hero, a passionate, charismatic man who seemed committed to carrying on the Calumet tradition, and that's the only way he would be judged in the Bluegrass. A few months after the article, he announced at a Keeneland luncheon that he had changed his will to include the stipulation "that my children, my grandchildren will not be able to sell it [Calumet]." Soon he would donate a bronze sculpture of Citation to the city of Lexington, and he would hire Sister Parish, the doyenne of designers, to redo the interior of Calumet's main residence. To celebrate the reopening of Calumet, he threw a black-tie dinner dance for 250 guests, including many bluebloods. He brought back former Calumet workers—including Alton Stone—who had lost their jobs in 1991. He also reinstated public tours of the farm. His wife, former model Barbara Allen, would tour the Paris fashion shows in a limo displaying the Calumet Farm logo.

In a television interview de Kwiatkowski told his local audience, "I never loved anything like I love Calumet." He recalled one rainy night during the renovation of the house when he spent the night there alone. The house was mostly empty except for a bed, a few tables, workers' equipment, and a little radio. He was so taken with the aura, he said, and so in love with the place that that night when he turned on the radio and heard a waltz playing, he danced around the vacant rooms holding his pillow. It was corny, he admitted with a mischievous giggle; anyone who saw him might have thought he was "around the bend." Members of his audience, having been informed by the local press of his habits of embellishment, wondered about the veracity of this whimsical tale, but it was a story that conveyed how he felt and people loved to hear positive things about their land, especially from someone with such regal style.

De Kwiatkowski could say he was a Polish king if he wanted to, or revise every detail of his past five times, and no one would care. This man had the money, the power, and the imagination to bring back the Calumet magic. Because of him, the dew covering Calumet's pastures would seem to glisten once again like a blanket of diamonds as it caught the light of the morning sun, though the innocence would never be completely restored.

6   What was left of the old Calumet was now called
Phoenix Corporation, four rooms in the basement of an office complex two
miles from the farm. Phoenix consisted of two desks, two phones, a Xerox
machine, and about 175 boxes with labels such as "Invoices 1982, 1983,
etc.," "Foals of 1989," "Last broodmares bred at Calumet in 1991,"
"Calumet-Gussin-Riggs," "First City loan docs.," "Schroder loan docs.," and
"Foyt."

Ron Sladon, knowing the name Calumet would be auctioned off, came
up with the new name. Positive thinking, he decided, might indeed help
Calumet rise from the ashes like the mythological bird. But he knew that
such a feat would require help from a few mythic gods as well, for the fate
of Phoenix would be held in the Lexington courts for a long, long time.
Perhaps it was appropriate that Calumet was no longer called Calumet, the
French word for the Indian "peace pipe." There was little peace in sight.

There were disputes over everything, it seemed, even the Calumet devil's-
red and blue racing silks. De Kwiatkowski's horse Al Sabin wore the silks in
the Kentucky Derby in May 1992, but Brazilian businessman Goncalo Torrealba bought them for $12,000 at the March auction and his horses were
racing in them, too, though, so far, only in Brazil. And then there was
Warren Wright III in whose name the silks were registered in New York,
making it difficult for de Kwiatkowski's horse to wear them at the Belmont
Stakes that year.

At Phoenix, Sladon, John Ward, Dave Switzer, and accountant Todd
Wright were the only employees left. They spent much of their time in
depositions, testifying at hearings, sorting through file cabinets and piles of
papers searching for documents requested by lawyers for the bankrupt farm,
lawyers for the family, lawyers for the banks, and lawyers for owners of
stallion seasons, as well as accommodating the requests of some persistent
reporters. By June there were about 10,000 pages of documents in the
Calumet bankruptcy file, not counting those in the bankruptcy file of the
Calumet-Gussin partnership on the shelf next to Calumet's. In the eleven
months since the filing, Judge Lee had presided over nearly seventy hearings.

During the summer of 1992, disputes over two Calumet stallions were
finally settled, allowing Phoenix to sell them and chip away at the debt.

Japanese veterinarian Teizo Aida bought Calumet's 50 percent stake in Secreto for $650,000, an interest Calumet had purchased in 1984 for $25 million. The Thoroughbred Breeders Club Company of Japan purchased the farm's half interest in Criminal Type for $1.9 million.

The breeders and investors who had purchased a right to breed to the stallions, or to whom Lundy had given seasons in exchange for Alydar seasons in the fall of 1990, were not pleased. Sending a mare to Japan was costly, and Secreto had failed so far as a sire. Those who didn't send mares would have to find someone in Japan to buy their seasons or just consider it one more loss connected to the fall of Calumet.

By summer, Phoenix was about as far from living up to its name as Calumet was, and the only possible association with birds taking flight was an image of vultures. Auctions and bankruptcies had become a way of life among the players in the Calumet saga. And a sense of loss weighed down any possibility of rising from the ashes. Bertha knew this perhaps more than anyone. Six weeks after the Calumet auction, boxes of books, paintings, antique furniture, and fine china filled a room at the Fasig-Tipton sales pavilion in Lexington. At the top of one of the boxes was Warren Wright, Jr.'s 1941 college yearbook. "Raise another Whirlaway," a friend had written on the flyleaf. Now, more than fifty years later, someone Warren Jr. had never met would soon place the yearbook on his or her shelves.

On May 10, 1992, Bertha Wright auctioned off hundreds of her personal belongings, including some of the best Warren Wright and Calumet memorabilia, items that belonged not to the farm but to the family and were therefore spared from the earlier auction. But with legal bills mounting and millions of dollars in judgments against her and her family, Bertha had no choice but to continue liquidating the Wright legacy.

There were framed photographs of Bull Lea, Whirlaway, Blenheim II, and others; sculptures of the champions of the 1940s and 1950s; nineteenth-century engravings of horses; and family portraits, including the painting of William Monroe Wright that had hung for so many years at the original Calumet homestead. A five-foot steamer trunk with the initials "LPW" (for Lucille Parker Wright) stood near a set of luggage bearing the initials "LM" (for Lucille Markey).

Bertha never intended to sell parts of her personal Wright family archive, but one creditor, CommerceNational Bank, the trustee for the Warren Wright, Jr., Trust, had insisted. "I'd hate people to think that I personally sold the Warren Wright memorabilia," she told the *Lexington Herald-Leader.* "Warren Wright's name meant more to me than that."

Later, in a private interview, she commented on letting go of the portrait of William Monroe Wright. "Well, Courtenay kept the portrait of Warren and his mother. But the other one, the one of Warren's grandfather, well, no one knew him. Poor man didn't have anyone who remembered him at all. I'm not sure who bought it. But if Warren were alive, he would have wanted it. He liked his grandfather very much."

The items brought good prices, such as $1,000 for a single photograph of Whirlaway, $1,800 for the cherry chest from Bertha's childhood, and $900 for the portrait of William Monroe Wright. She made $96,622 from the sale of more than four hundred items, hardly enough to pay even half her legal fees so far. She also sold privately a 1986 Jaguar for $13,500. Bertha would now drive a leased 1992 Oldsmobile Calais.

With the farm and many family possessions gone, there were only two sources of funds remaining: the Warren Wright, Jr., Trust and the Calumet trophy collection. Whether or not the principal in the trust could be invaded to pay legal fees and creditors was an issue for the courts to decide. The trophy collection, which was on display at the Kentucky Horse Park Museum north of Lexington, might be more accessible. Several days after Bertha's auction, one of her lawyers met with Horse Park officials to talk about the possibility of yet another auction.

No one really knew who owned what was supposedly the largest private collection of gold and silver trophies in the world. Neither Warren Wright, Sr., nor Warren Wright, Jr., had in his will defined the trophies as personal property (such as furniture and Viennese crystal) or as part of the farm. If the collection was part of the farm, it belonged to the heirs, but if it was considered personal property, it would likely belong to Mrs. Markey's estate.

Margaret Glass, Chicago lawyer Bill Sutter, an appraiser from Sotheby's, and others had spent two days in Mrs. Markey's basement shortly after her death examining and photographing the silver platters, silver punch bowls, silver pitchers with scalloped rims, fourteen-karat-gold vases on marble bases, fourteen-karat-gold urns studded with diamonds, Baccarat crystal bowls, silver-plated urns from the eighteenth and nineteenth centuries, and dozens of silver and pewter mint julep cups. Glass listed 541 items; they were valued at $2.9 million.

Mrs. Markey apparently assumed they were hers to give away. In the wills she wrote during the 1950s, she bequeathed the entire collection to the Keeneland Foundation, but after the 1968 Derby, the Kentucky racing establishment was on Mrs. Markey's blacklist. That was the Derby that Calumet's Forward Pass won, but only after Dancer's Image was disqualified for being administered a then-illegal drug before the race. Mrs. Markey was irate about the way Churchill Downs and the Kentucky State Racing Commission treated her as the new winner of the Derby. She was especially peeved at their tardiness in sending her the several hundred thousand dollars of purse money—five years after the victory. Mrs. Markey swore she'd never race in Kentucky again, and in 1969 she altered her will. This time she left the trophies to the National Museum of Racing in Saratoga Springs. But in her 1973 and 1975 wills, she changed her mind again and left them to the Churchill Downs museum, though it's unclear why she had a change of heart.

In 1976, she did another flip, revising her will to send the trophies again to the racing museum at Saratoga. Confirming this, she sent a letter in March 1977 to the museum president saying she had left the collection to the museum as well as $100,000 for its care.

Two years later, the museum president, worried that Mrs. Markey might again change her mind, sent a letter to the Markeys outlining plans to build a large display for the collection. Margaret forwarded it to the Markeys in Florida, and almost immediately the admiral ordered her to box up the trophies and send them to the Saratoga Springs museum. When Glass asked why the trophies would be taken away from Calumet while Mrs. Markey was still alive, he replied, "To prevent that b——— [J. T. Lundy] from Midway from getting his hands on them."

But before any boxes were packed, Mrs. Markey rejected the museum's design for the display and dispatched Margaret to send a letter saying nothing would be done with the trophies at that time. Eventually, the trustees running Mrs. Markey's affairs, when she was no longer able to, agreed to loan the trophies to the Horse Park. The Wright heirs approved.

Not long after Mrs. Markey's death, the ownership of the multimillion-dollar trophies became an issue, with both the Saratoga museum, as a benefactor of her will, and the Wright heirs claiming ownership rights. In the spring of 1983, the Markey estate trustees filed a suit against the heirs for the purpose of getting a judge to rule on the question of who owned the trophies.

The suit dragged on for two years, when finally in December 1985 the presiding judge said at a hearing that if he were to rule on the issue—which he never did—he would probably say that the trophies won up to Warren Wright's death in 1950 belonged to the Wright heirs. Those won after 1950 and before 1982 were Mrs. Markey's and therefore should end up in Saratoga as she specified in her will.

The matter remained unresolved, though everyone agreed the collection shouldn't be divided and should remain on loan to the Horse Park. In 1988, the Markey trustees dismissed the claims against the Wright heirs, thus ending the 1983 case.

But in 1992, as everyone picked over the remains of the Wright empire, the question of ownership resurfaced. The dismissal of the 1983 case meant there was still nothing in writing about who owned the trophies or where they permanently belonged. Bertha's lawyer had hoped the trophies might provide a proverbial pot of gold for his client, but he soon discovered that like everything else connected with the Calumet debacle, the trophies were entangled in legal complications. The Wright heirs and a bank trustee for Bertha had signed a renewal contract in 1988 agreeing to loan the trophies to the Horse Park until 1997.

Meanwhile, at the beginning of the summer, a state judge ruled that the Wright heirs had to pay $7.3 million to Mutual Benefit Life Insurance Company. This was the difference between what Mutual Benefit had received as a result of the March auction and what it was owed on the farm's 1986 mortgage. It was a depressing decision for the family, whose lawyers argued that the heirs had not been the recipients of the loan. Calumet had borrowed the money, and the family had signed papers guaranteeing the loan. Courtenay's lawyer claimed she did not remember ever signing the note.

7 A few minutes before ten o'clock on an autumn morning in 1992, bankers, reporters, curious townsfolk, and Lundy seekers gathered at a side entrance to the Scott County Courthouse in Georgetown. Workers leaned out of second-story windows as television cameras moved in on one of the bankers who announced he was about to auction Lundy Farm.

This wasn't as big an event as the Calumet auction or even Bertha's sale, but there was an intriguing element: J. T. Lundy might be watching. By all accounts he loved his farm, and no one thought he would let it go. Some people believed he would march right up to the courthouse steps to buy his own farm back.

This was the farm Lucille Markey had questioned Lundy about many years ago at lunch in Hialeah, wondering where he had gotten the money for such a vast spread. Known as the Patterson Farm before the Lundys purchased it in early 1977, it was a fine piece of land, 318 acres with a beautiful stream, Elkhorn Creek, running through parts of it, and top-notch facilities. It had two 160-year-old hemp barns made of hand-hewn walnut logs that the Lundys had been careful to preserve by building stallion barns around them. The farm itself had three twenty-stall horse barns, one twenty-eight-stall barn, a ten-stallion breeding barn, a big tobacco barn, an office, a machine shop, two log-and-stone residences, and a stone residence. Former Calumet employees claimed that Lundy used Calumet resources, in the form of their colleagues' labor, to fix it up even more in the mid-1980s.

Lundy and his wife used the farm along with the St. Thomas house to secure a December 1988 loan for $6.65 million from Citizen's Fidelity Bank in Louisville. When the Lundys defaulted on the loan, the bank sued in May of 1992 for the balance due, and a Scott County judge ordered the sale of the farm. On this day, the amount due, plus daily accruing interest, was more than $5 million.

The day before the auction Lundy's lawyers filed a chapter 11 bankruptcy petition for the reorganization of Farm, Inc., the company that owned Lundy Farm and whose major shareholders were the Lundys. Because of the filing, the auction could take place only if the bankruptcy judge approved. Judge Lee called an emergency hearing for 9:30 A.M., a half hour before the auction was to begin.

At the hearing, Lundy's lawyers argued that the farm was necessary for a successful reorganization of Farm, Inc. The company deserved the right to have a chance to reorganize and revive itself.

Judge Lee questioned the lawyer about the company: What were the financial details, earnings, and other assets? How did it operate?

The lawyer responded that Farm, Inc. "operated the same way as Calumet."

This did not endear the judge or anyone else to the plight of Farm, Inc. Judge Lee approved the auction, and the crowd moved in a caravan of cars and TV news trucks from the federal bankruptcy courtroom in Lexington to the courthouse steps in nearby Georgetown.

Within about a minute, Citizen's Fidelity bought the farm for $1.05 million. Lundy didn't appear, disappointing the small crowd that had gathered like townsfolk coming to the public square for a hanging. One man seemed particularly frustrated. He had come from Tennessee for a client in Florida, to "serve papers on Lundy," he said. "It's okay. It was a long shot, and I'll find him soon enough," he added as he picked up his briefcase and walked to his car.

Reporters and lawyers headed up the main street in town to a diner where a sign above the soda fountain announced, "If I can't take it with me, I'm not going." The lawyers sat at the back of the room and the reporters near the window at the front, but the topics were likely the same. There was a collective instinct that Lundy was moving to Florida, though at that very second he was probably somewhere near Lexington putting his affairs in order. One reporter claimed to know for a fact that Lundy and Janice Heinz had broken up, which raised a question from another reporter about whether in fact there had been a relationship to break up.

When Robey's name came up, eyes closed and heads shook, as if in disbelief. Robey was having a tough time; there was more stress in his life than at the center of a twister. He had just lost a $50,000 libel suit and at the same time was dragged into messy litigation involving a state veterinarian who claimed Robey, as chairman of the racing commission, had wrongfully dismissed her. The veterinarian alleged she was fired because she had refused to continue a relationship with Alex Harthill, another vet and friend of Robey's. Harthill, now in his sixties, wasn't a defendant in the case and claimed he had nothing to do with her dismissal. The case had been going on for nearly two years when in September a state judge ordered that the woman's job be restored.

In addition to these two cases, there was, of course, the Calumet mess. Robey knew some people suspected him of taking advantage of the Wrights. And on top of all that, the FBI had just completed a sting operation exposing certain lobbyists for the racing community who had bribed lawmakers for legislation favorable to thoroughbred racing. Robey, as chairman of the racing commission, had been called several times to testify before a grand jury. Two of his closest friends were nabbed; one was sentenced to several years in prison, and the other was awaiting sentence.

During an interview in March 1992, Robey stated that maybe it was time for him to leave the Bluegrass. "Allergies're getting to me," he said, sitting in a big leather chair at his racing commission office as he turned around to face the window. His view was a creek and a fenced-in pasture of the Kentucky Horse Park. "Maybe it's just time to go."

Where would he go?

"Don't know," he said, as if he wasn't listening anymore. Gazing out at the park's white plank fences, he fiddled with a paper clip, twisting it back and forth until one part broke off and fell into the puffy palm of his right hand. "Probably nowhere."

The stress of legal disputes may have been something Robey could handle. He was tough and seemed to revel in challenges related to the law. He knew too that, despite the current discomfort and inconvenience, the conflicts in his professional life would be resolved. But what happened next was insurmountable for Robey: on April 15, Dow, the younger of his two boys, was killed when an earthen wall collapsed on him while he was helping a friend construct the foundation of a house. The shock and sorrow swept over Robey like a firestorm.

Then on September 1, Robey's brother-in-law, who practiced law in Georgetown, Kentucky, and was a longtime friend, died of cancer. A week later Robey called his sister. "I'm comin' out there to practice law," he said. He seemed genuinely enthusiastic about returning to Georgetown and running a small-town practice. He moved his law books into a small, homey office on a side street in the center of town and positioned a big oil painting of Alydar on the wall behind his new desk. But the slump of his shoulders and the forced smile gave away his true condition. By October he had drifted again into a sort of void. Depression came in waves, mainly when he tried to fulfill his obligations as the appointed administrator of his son's estate. He just couldn't do it.

8 Growing up in Scott County, Lundy was known as "John Thomas," but after marrying into a prominent Fayette County family and going out on his own, he had preferred "J.T." and signed his name "J. T. Lundy." Yet in December of 1992, for some reason, perhaps a subconscious desire to go back in time, Lundy signed "John Thomas Lundy" to his declaration of bankruptcy.

He filed the papers in Miami on December 16, giving his street address as 9701 Biscayne Avenue in Miami Shores, Florida, which was the address of his good friend and former partner Bill Allen. He stated the value of his personal property as $418,185.65, which included $400,000 that he claimed Calumet owed him, a 50 percent interest in some oil and gas leases in Illinois, a 50 percent interest in two colts, some furniture at Lundy Farm, $100 worth of clothes, one pistol, and one "old shotgun." His only real estate asset was a $350,000 condo in Key West that had $284,401 in liens against it.

His earnings over the past two years were significantly less than those during his tenure as Calumet's chief. In 1992, Lundy earned $44,000 in commissions, $20,000 from the sale of a horse, and a $5,000 consultation fee. The year before, he brought in $5,000 from gambling, more than $37,000 from interest and dividends, and $249,508 from the sale of un-specified property. But some things hadn't changed. After leaving Calumet, he continued to borrow money. His most recent loan appeared to be on August 10, 1992, from ITT Capital Finance in St. Louis; whatever the principal might have been, he now owed $224,868.

His liabilities amounted to $77 million but could go up or down depend-ing on the outcomes of the seventeen lawsuits he listed. As the guarantor of notes from Farm, Inc., Wright Enterprises, and a personal loan, he owed Citizen's Fidelity nearly $8 million. To Equine Capital Corporation, he owed over $3 million. As a guarantor on the First City loan to Calumet, he owed $34 million and another $6.1 million on the personal loan to buy the Picasso and Miró paintings. Citibank was owed $175,000; First National Bank of Georgetown, over $500,000; North Florida Farm Credit Service, $1.6 million; and as a guarantor on a Calumet loan, Lundy was one of several people who owed $7.3 million to Mutual Benefit as well as $2.6 million to Midlantic.

Lundy owed the Golden Steer Steak House in Las Vegas $624.87. He owed $1,085.53 on his MasterCard from First National Bank of Louisville, but much more on his MasterCard from Liberty National Bank in Lexing-ton—$7,076.48—and $3,135.38 on his Liberty National Visa.

There were nearly one hundred creditors from all over the world, includ-ing France, Spain, Hong Kong, Canada, New York, Massachusetts, Missouri, California, Pennsylvania, Texas, Florida, Connecticut, Maryland, North Car-olina, Oklahoma, and, of course, Kentucky. Three creditors had secured claims and were first in line for payment: the Prudential Home Mortgage Company, which held a mortgage for the Key West condo and was owed

$284,000; the Monroe County tax collector, whom Lundy owed $5,014 in property taxes on the Key West property; and the Key West Beach Club, which he owed $2,879.12 in condo fees. Next in line to be paid were the unsecured priority claims, which consisted of taxes owed to the state of Kentucky, listed as "unknown," and $2,338.56 that Lundy owed in taxes to the sheriff in Scott County. All the rest were unsecured claims, and the people involved, like the creditors in Calumet or any other bankruptcy, would have to fight it out in court and hope for the best.

Bertha Wright, Courtenay Wright Lancaster, Warren Wright III, Calumet Farm, Inc., Wright Enterprises, Thomas C. Wright, the Warren Wright, Jr., Trust, and Lundy's wife, Lucille W. Lundy, were all listed as creditors, but in the column listing the amount owed was typed "unknown."

Lundy's bankruptcy was not a surprise to people following the Calumet saga. He was, after all, entangled in reams of litigation, and a bankruptcy filing creates an automatic stay against any further action in pending lawsuits unless approved by the bankruptcy judge. Lundy was now a defendant in suits filed by Citizen's Fidelity; ECC; Mutual Benefit; Bank One, Lexington; Sun Bank, N.A.; IBJ Schroder; Midlantic National Bank; and Axmar, among others. The scariest of them all was a result of the master paintings scheme he had engaged in with Frank Cihak in 1990. In the spring of 1992, members of the Coca family of Madrid named First City, Cihak, former bank chairman Robert Abboud, and various others including Lundy and lawyer Gary Matthews as defendants in one of the largest lender liability cases in history. Claiming $185 million in actual damages and $1 billion in punitive damages, the Cocas alleged the defendants had used "economic duress and coercion" to obtain control of the family's assets and then damaged them through self-dealing and mismanagement.

Lundy's inability to sell the paintings to pay back his multimillion-dollar debt to First City was intensely frustrating. Commenting on the situation in a deposition during the summer of 1991, he said, "I don't care about getting the cheese; I just want out of the trap."

Worse still, by November it was clear, and Lundy must have known, that a grand jury had convened in Houston to investigate First City, apparently focusing on two of the bank's bad credits: the $120 million loan to the Cocas back in 1989 and the $44 million in loans to Calumet Farm, Inc. The probe was exploring alleged "corner of the office" deals, that is, loans that were not part of the normal committee process at First City. A junior officer in First City's credit department told the *Houston Post,* "We were doing things that were just crazy. We were wiring money to fund loans before we got any of the paperwork. They were approving loans without any due diligence at all."

What was surprising about Lundy's bankruptcy was to see in print his claim that his assets amounted to not much more than an old shotgun, a pistol, and $100 in clothing. This was a man who had had breeding rights each year to several Calumet stallions, including Alydar, Wild Again, Secreto, and Talinum. He could sell them or keep them and sell the foals from the breedings—whatever, he made money. He had his commissions, totaling more than $6 million. He had proceeds from personal bank loans and mortgages yet he had a list of unpaid bills including his personal credit cards. What was going on here? Was he a big gambler, like his friend Libutti? Had he been paying off a boss? Was it possible that to keep the colts and fillies of Calumet's stallions selling at high prices, he was forced to pay off certain deal makers? Did he give it all away? Or did he, as so many people loved to believe, stash it away in the Cayman Islands?

The bankruptcy papers amounted to a financial and legal map of Lundy's life in recent years, and they revealed what everyone wanted to know: where he lived. Until February 1992, the papers divulged, he had resided at Lundy Farm. From March to May, he was in Venice, Florida, and now he appeared to be living with Bill Allen in Miami Shores, an affluent Florida community. Most Lundy watchers believed he had made a cunning move. If he had filed his bankruptcy papers in Kentucky, he'd have to face hordes of reporters and the curious masses at every court hearing. With his farm gone, there was little reason now to go to Kentucky. Friends could visit him in Florida.

But that's not the way things turned out. The federal bankruptcy judge in Miami, at the request of Calumet creditors, ordered that the case be moved to Judge Lee's court in Lexington with the rest of the Calumet-related litigation.

Then, a few days before Christmas, Robey fell into a coma, and on New Year's Eve he died at age fifty-one. While the official cause was viral hepatitis, his close friends said he died from a combination of drinking, depression, and a broken heart.

Lundy went home to Kentucky for the funeral of his childhood friend. He kept a low profile at the visitation, standing in remote corners away from the familiar faces of one or two reporters who mingled in the crowd. He apparently stayed to see Robey lowered into the ground, then departed.

About ten days later he reappeared. His farm was on the auction block again, and he was apparently trying to work out a way to repurchase it.

Citizen's Fidelity had tried for four months to sell the property but couldn't, so the bank hired Swinebroad-Denton, the auctioneers who handled the Calumet sale, to orchestrate the deal. The sale was held in the breeding shed at Lundy Farm and attracted a crowd of about one hundred. A Lexington dermatologist, Ira P. Mersack, won the contest with a bid of $3,410 an acre, or $1.08 million. Mersack knew Lundy and spoke highly of him, saying after the sale that he would not change the name for a while, "out of respect for the Lundys." He also didn't plan to move to the farm, but he would move the four horses he owned to it.

Rumors were rampant that Lundy tried to keep buyers away while he searched for someone to front for him in purchasing the farm, but Mersack denied that he had anything to do with such a scheme. No one could believe Lundy would actually let go of this fine piece of land, that he would allow himself to be landless in the Bluegrass. Now his only tie to Fayette County would be the courthouse.

9

Seventy years after William Monroe Wright bought his first four hundred acres in the Bluegrass, few of his descendants remained on Kentucky's high plateau. Circumstances had evolved in such a way that it was impractical for the Wright heirs to remain there, especially considering the legal advantages of living in another state, such as Florida.

Because of Florida's Homestead Law, property was protected from creditors and bankers. By putting their money into Florida real estate the Wrights, like many other well-to-do debtors, could shield their remaining funds from creditors. In a bankruptcy the size of Calumet's the rush of creditors in search of money was like the force of a flood seeking the path of least resistance—they'd pursue the unprotected debtors. For the Wrights, the key was to protect as many assets as possible.

Cindy Wright Lundy was the first to move to Florida, where she bought a home in Palm Beach County. She paid $675,000 in cash for the house, drawing on the $850,000 in proceeds she received from selling her stake in Waddell Ranch. Later, Tommy Wright moved to Tampa, Florida, and Warren Wright III settled in Alachua County, in the town of Newberry near

Gainesville. Only Bertha and her daughter Courtenay would remain in the Bluegrass.

Remaining in Kentucky seemed a brave move, especially after Judge Lee, early in 1993, announced that an attorney would soon be hired to compile a list of entities and individuals for creditors to pursue in a quest to recoup more money. Former members of the Calumet management and board were on the short list of people who might be sued for lost funds. It was possible, too, considering the oral and written allegations throughout court testimony that pointed to rampant self-dealing and fraudulent practices, that a federal investigation could follow.

Courtenay insisted on keeping her home in Kentucky, despite the financial risks. A friend said Courtenay "had a feeling for the Wright name; Calumet meant a lot to her and so did family honor." Courtenay vowed, "If it takes the rest of my life, I'll bring honor to the Wrights, not the glory, not the past glory of Calumet. What I mean is honor."

Bertha stayed, too. She didn't harbor any resentment toward the Florida Wrights. "Everybody's hurting in their own way, and they have to do what they have to do. But this is my home, and so I want to be here. I'll survive." But just to be safe, in February she filed for bankruptcy, creating an automatic stay against any new litigation, though it was only a matter of time before the creditors and their lawyers would try to invade the Warren Wright, Jr., Trust, the source of Bertha's income.

Bertha's assets of about $307,000 included $123,203 worth of antique furniture and household goods; $100 in cash on hand; $5 on deposit at a local bank; $90.20 in a checking account at another bank; $990 at a third bank; $1,700 worth of clothes including a mink jacket and a beaver jacket; $3,000 in jewelry; and two apartments in Lexington. One of the apartments was occupied by a former Calumet staffer who lived there rent free.

The filing revealed hints of a luxurious lifestyle, such as the pricey antiques, Persian rugs, and mention of the 1986 Jaguar she had recently sold. But it also showed her generosity. In 1992, Bertha had given $36,300 to various church groups, mainly the Episcopal Christ Church Cathedral, and for Christmas each of her children had received $5,000; her grandchildren, $1,000; and her great-grandchildren, $500.

Bertha's income from the Warren Wright, Jr., Trust was still considerable, ranging from $45,000 to $80,000 a month, according to the filing. In 1992, income from the trust plus the sale of furnishings and royalties from certain oil and gas leases had given her $600,000, up from 1991 when the trust and royalties and dividends totaled about $221,000. So far in 1993, her trust income had been $73,176. According to an individual with knowledge of the trust, there was nearly $6 million left.

But Bertha's liabilities were nearly $70 million. Secured creditors held $6.6 million in claims against Bertha; the unsecured creditors, a total of $62.9 million. Whatever happened now, the revenue-producing assets in her trust, including some oil and gas properties, couldn't generate enough money to pay off creditors and attorneys. Once again it was clear that the Wright fortune was gone.

While the bankruptcy appeared to be an admittance of failure, almost a surrender to the evils that had befallen the farm and the family, buried in the fifty or so pages were signs that the family might fight back. Like most bankruptcy filings, this one had a list of contingent and unliquidated claims that might eventually bring in some money. Regarding the case of First City in which Bertha, as one of the guarantors, was liable for $31 million, her lawyers noted a possible claim for damages "for fraudulent inducement of [Bertha's] guarantee of Calumet Farm, Inc., and various federal law violations including National Bank Act, the federal racketeering act known as RICO, mail fraud and others; other possible co-conspirators or aides and abettors: Frank Cihak, J. T. Lundy, and others unknown."

Cindy, too, filed for bankruptcy a few months after her mother. She listed $1.5 million in assets, including the $675,000 home, and $330,000 worth of insurance annuities she had purchased with some of the Waddell Ranch proceeds, three dogs, nine parrots, two lovebirds, six parakeets, eight conures, six cockatiels, and two finches. In the category of wearing apparel, she noted "Used clothes, costume jewelry. . . . No value." No furs, cars, boats, farm equipment, airplanes, or firearms. She listed $83.1 million in liabilities, and among the one hundred or so creditors were fifteen banks in Florida, New Jersey, Texas, New York, Alabama, Colorado, and Kentucky. There were also small creditors such as the workers who had cleaned the pool in her Florida home in early January 1992 and the Eagle County treasurer in Colorado, where she had lived after St. Thomas and before Florida. She owed them $1,076.69 and $3,293.53, respectively. Numerous creditors had also appeared on her husband's earlier filing, because she had co-guaranteed loans with him. Creditors were about all they seemed to share now.

10

On July 14, 1993, almost two years to the day after Calumet's bankruptcy and eleven years after Mrs. Markey's death, the divorce of Cindy Wright and John Thomas Lundy was finalized in Dade County, Florida. Cindy had filed for divorce on January 28, 1993; in May, her lawyer hired an investigator to find Lundy and serve him with the papers. But Lundy didn't respond, so a month later a default judgment was entered against Lundy "for failure to serve or file any papers required by law." Two weeks later the court granted Cindy her divorce.

On that same day Lundy's whereabouts were still something of a mystery, though lawyers in the Calumet-related suits weren't as worried anymore. They knew his bankruptcy filing would pull him back to Kentucky whenever the judge or creditors demanded his presence. Then the lawyers involved with matters in the Calumet bankruptcy would be all over him, like the birds outside the courthouse.

Wherever he was, he wasn't seeing many of his old cronies, having fallen out with some and losing others when he lost the status of Calumet. Some, too, were up to their necks in problems and likely didn't have time for late-night phone conversations with Lundy, as was his habit.

In April, for example, a federal grand jury had indicted Frank Cihak on thirty-four criminal counts, including bank fraud, wire fraud, laundering millions of dollars, and making false statements to obtain loans. The government claimed he paid certain consultants, including Lloyd Swift, hefty fees in exchange for kickbacks and then approved fraudulent loans for them. Swift was also indicted on ten counts of conspiracy and other charges. In addition, the government alleged, Cihak made false entries in First City's financial records and pledged false collateral at Citibank in New York to obtain a $1.6 million loan, illegally using funds from First City to pay down the loan.

The government described the indictment as the first of several in a continuing investigation into the failure of First City Bancorporation. Prosecutors claimed Cihak had used First City as his "personal piggy bank," but Cihak pleaded not guilty to all charges and his friends claimed the government was using him as a scapegoat for First City's failure. He was released on a $200,000 bond awaiting his trial, set for fall. If convicted, Cihak faced a maximum sentence of 391 years' imprisonment and fines totaling $11 million.

Lundy's friend Bob Libutti was also entangled in legal processes. He had been indicted in Newark federal court during the fall of 1992 on five counts charging bank fraud, conspiracy to commit bank fraud, and tax evasion, and because he was already a convicted felon, he was also charged with illegal possession of firearms—fourteen handguns and a rifle. If convicted, Libutti, whose trial was set for early 1994, faced a maximum sentence of thirty-five years.

Bob Fox was still in the horse business, though he no longer published clever ads from exotic locales and he and Lundy rarely, if ever, spoke to one another. Jan Heinz remained in Kentucky, while Susan McGee was in Florida, supposedly spending a lot of time with Lundy. Marc Rash was out of the horse business; Gary Matthews was practicing law in Lexington where he shared office space with Montjoy Trimble's firm.

Peter Brant, Lundy's former partner in Fasig-Tipton, the auction house, and in the racehorse Mogambo, was nowhere near Lundy. They hadn't seen much of each other since they'd sold their Fasig-Tipton stock, but both had been busy. Brant, along with his cousin and former partner Joseph Allen, had spent a brief stint in jail after pleading guilty to defrauding the government of $1.5 million. They were accused of charging substantial personal expenses to their companies, then reporting the expenses as business deductions. Calumet still owed Brant millions of dollars on the Mogambo deal, though he wasn't bitter toward Lundy. His White Birch Farms had sued Calumet, but Calumet had countersued White Birch, claiming the Connecticut farm had damaged and depreciated Mogambo's value through "secret sales" of shares and breeding rights at less than the stud fee established by Calumet. Calumet also sued White Birch for the $693,000 it said was mistakenly transferred to the Connecticut farm when the Georgetown bank sent it $770,301 instead of $77,301. But their distance had less to do with the money owed than with their separate social spheres. Brant had always traveled in highbrow East Coast circles and now, more than ever perhaps, was spending his money on art-related enterprises. Shortly after Andy Warhol died, Brant's company, Brant Publications, repurchased *Interview* magazine. Old friends of both men said it was the lure of Calumet that originally had brought Brant into Lundy's world.

Meanwhile, the latest "J.T. sightings" were in Florida. Many people claimed they'd seen him in Miami, a logical choice considering his address in the bankruptcy file was Bill Allen's home in the sedate, conservative neighborhood of Miami Shores.

But he was actually spending most of his time at Lou-Roe Farms, which the feds had attacked with helicopters and SWAT teams the year before because of their suspicions that the luxurious spread was used by a colleague of John Gotti's to launder money.

Early in 1993, around the time the farm's founder Anthony Gurino pleaded guilty to charges of money laundering, his son, Louis, was in the parking lot of a local shopping mall and saw Lundy walking out of a real estate office. By then the government, in exchange for Anthony Gurino's plea, had dropped charges of money laundering and fraud against twenty-seven-year-old Louis and his mother. Louis Gurino had always been grateful to Lundy, who in his dealings with Lou-Roe had sent numerous Calumet-bred horses for Louis to train, so he asked Lundy to come to the farm. Now, though the two men lived only twenty yards apart, Louis would receive phone calls from Lundy at 2:30 A.M. Some things hadn't changed at all.

11

On chilly nights in late autumn, an unlikely sound, like that of waves crashing against a shore, can be heard in Bluegrass fields. It is the rush of horses galloping across rolling savannas, their hooves crushing icy blades of frost-laden grass. By the autumn of 1993, as Calumet's new owner continued to fill his pastures with dozens of fine thoroughbreds, this sound had returned. It was a sign that three years after Alydar's death all was again normal on the land that bore the name Calumet. But the saga of Warren Wright's Calumet continued through lawsuits and allegations, and everyone wondered whether there would be an official probe into the stable's collapse.

There were numerous investigations swirling around the Calumet tragedy, but none targeted it. Litigation involving deal makers or banks with past ties to Calumet revealed titillating details that inspired federal investigators to visit Phoenix Corporation and the bankruptcy court files on several occasions. The Federal Deposit Insurance Corporation was interested in

Calumet's link with First City in its larger investigation of the Houston bank. IRS agents, too, spent time looking at the Calumet bankruptcy files, but their purpose in doing so was not specified. An FBI agent in western Kentucky was inquiring, mainly among litigants in Calumet-related civil cases, about who knew what about hidden assets. Some people still ardently believed Lundy was hiding money. And some creditors who didn't have the money to fund a private investigation complained about injustices. In the impoverished regions of eastern Kentucky, someone could steal $100 from a filling station and end up in prison, while over the mountains on the high plateau it seemed as if people could steal millions and get away with it.

Lloyd's appeared to have no intention of reexamining the death of Alydar, though questions and suspicions cropped up now and then like clumps of dandelions on the once-perfect Calumet pastures. A Lloyd's spokesperson was asked more than once about what Lloyd's planned to do about such suspicions, and the response was that an extensive investigation had been conducted at the time of Alydar's death and if the firm believed it was important to reexamine the incident, then of course that would happen. So far Lloyd's apparently saw no need to do so, though clearly it had been living with doubts and questions for several years.

From that hot July day in 1991 when Calumet filed for bankruptcy and its troubles spilled into public view, Alydar's death had assumed an aura of suspicion. Recollections of things that seemed unusual or mysterious about the tragedy began to slip into conversations at Keeneland and Saratoga Springs during the summer and fall of 1991. A few observers of the Calumet debacle suspected then that Alydar might not have been worth more alive than dead.

Thereafter, concern about Alydar would ebb and flow with the intensity surrounding the farm's collapse, rising to a high pitch at times like the dispersal sale when the procession of Calumet horses brought emotions to the surface. As events of the years leading up to November 1990 trickled into the court files, with one case revealing details unexplained in yet another case, it was possible to see the horse's death as more than just bad luck, more than just a bizarre set of coincidences.

Around the time of the second anniversary of Alydar's death, news reports about federal investigations of plots nationwide to murder showhorses and thoroughbred racehorses for insurance money brought the fear and suspicions back. The FBI was looking into cases of insurance fraud in eight states involving at least forty owners, trainers, riders, and vets. One hit man was known as "The Sandman" because he killed or "put to sleep" so many horses. In another case, the code word for slaying a horse was "doing a Friars Club."

Particularly haunting was a case in Miami federal court involving Lawrence Lombardo, a thoroughbred owner from Bayside, Queens, New York, with alleged connections to the Colombo organized crime family. The case was part of an ongoing Justice Department investigation into allegations that the Colombo family was killing horses for insurance money and laundering the proceeds by investing in real estate. Lombardo, who ran New York Thoroughbred Productions, based in Elmont, New York, was accused of killing a horse named Fins, a son of Triple Crown winner Seattle Slew. Lombardo had purchased the horse for $7,500, hyped the value to $400,000 through the sale of shares at $10,000 each, insured the horse at its new value, and allegedly ordered it killed. What sent chills through horse country and the insurance community was that the horse's death looked so natural. Fins developed a fatal case of colic, induced by an injection of parasitic bloodworms. When Lombardo boasted on FBI wiretaps about the killing, he talked about how it had taken the horse five hours to die, on September 9, 1990.

Lombardo pleaded guilty in the spring of 1993 to mail fraud, loan sharking, and conspiracy in connection with the death of Fins, but he adamantly denied he had killed the horse himself. He was sentenced to four and a half years in prison.

The Lombardo case was evidence of the greed and evil that had gripped segments of the horse industry during the 1980s. When tax laws changed and prices fell from their pinnacles, the unthinkable began to occur: the killing of magnificent animals that for centuries had devoted their lives to serving the interests of those who fed and bred them. For those familiar with the Calumet tragedy, the case was perhaps more unnerving. The government's research into the relationships and deals of Lombardo's world revealed a name familiar to Calumet insiders: Bob Libutti. Libutti wasn't involved in the Fins case, but he had had dealings with Lombardo. One such deal involved a dispute concerning a racehorse that Libutti had sold to Lombardo and his associate Howard Crash, a New York securities dealer. To settle the dispute, the government was told, there was a "sit-down" between Lombardo's alleged buddy Victor Orena, the reputed head of the Colombo crime family, and Libutti's alleged pal John Gotti.

In the clubby world of horse trading, it wasn't surprising that Lombardo and Libutti supposedly knew each other. But the mere mention of a man tied to Calumet having ties to a man connected with the killing of a thor-

oughbred horse was troubling to those who still fretted over the death of
Alydar. Most unsettling, however, was the talk about parasitic worms and
induced colic. The government had tapes from the investigations surrounding the Lombardo case in which various individuals bragged about their
skillfully executed murders. While certain prosecutors were aware of
Alydar's death and some seemed familiar with details of the night Alton
Stone had discovered the horse sweating profusely in his stall, what was on
those tapes was still unknown. Was it possible that Alydar had received such
an injection and had hurt his leg during his frantic attempts to relieve his
extreme discomfort, flailing about on the stall floor and then accidentally
plunging his leg into the crevice between the stall door and the wall? As the
conditions of colic began to set in, were the symptoms thwarted by painkillers he was given by the crew who tried desperately to save his life hours
later? Or was this simply another theory provoked by the intensity surrounding the Lombardo case?

At the November 1993 auction at Keeneland, the last two Calumet stallions
were sold. Talinum, once valued at $3.6 million, went for $160,000, and
Calumet's 50 percent stake in Wild Again, which the farm had purchased
for $6 million in 1985, sold for $1.5 million. As always, the sale was a time
for breeders and horsemen nationwide to congregate. In restaurants and
taverns, in barns and farm offices, they'd talk about the equine economy,
which was showing signs of recovery, and on this the third anniversary of
Alydar's death it was inevitable that some conversations would focus on the
mystery surrounding the event.

Now it seemed there were more theories than ever about what had happened that November night. Some horsemen firmly believed that the
bracket at the base of the stall door had been filed off before the horse was
discovered just to fit the official story that the horse had kicked the door so
hard he broke his leg. Calumet insiders who knew about Lundy's skill in
filing the hood ornaments off cars thought perhaps he had done this, simply
out of panic after discovering that someone had tried to hurt or kill the
horse. Lundy was moving with a fast crowd and was perhaps no longer in
control of the fate of Calumet or Alydar. While some people would always
believe that Lundy had known exactly what was planned for the highly
leveraged stallion, others felt he appeared much too upset during Alydar's
struggle to have been the one to order the horse's murder. And some people
related stories from Calumet grooms who swore they had seen bruises on

Alydar's injured leg. These horsemen still envisioned an assassin ramming a crowbar into Alydar's cannon bone, though vets had discounted that possibility long ago.

At the Calumet cemetery on November 15, a sudden gust of wind blew clusters of leaves against Alydar's tombstone. There were no red roses as there had been on previous anniversaries of his death. All that remained were the secrets surrounding his demise and the mysteries, sinking ever deeper into the darkness, becoming part of the soul of Calumet.

Notes

General Sources

- *Horse stats and sales prices:* Statistics on Calumet horses, their earnings, and their trainers prior to 1982, mostly from Margaret Glass's eighteen-page booklet, "The Calumet Story."

    Sales prices for horses sold at public auction, from "Keeneland Sales Summaries" or sales reports in *The Blood-Horse* magazine, unless otherwise noted.

    Sales prices for stallion seasons, from the Lexington firm Stallion Access, from bloodstock agents, or from Calumet records.

    Stats on the performance of Alydar's progeny, from The Jockey Club in Lexington, Ky.

- *Descriptions of events and scenes:* From the summer of 1991 forward, according to the author's own observations, unless otherwise noted. Events prior to that, from individuals who attended, unless otherwise noted.

- *Name changes:* Some commercial banks and investment banks mentioned in this book changed their names during the period portrayed.

The Second National Bank and Trust Co., the trustees of the Warren Wright, Jr., Trust, became the CommerceNational Bank in 1986 after being acquired by First Kentucky National Corp. and then merging with Bank of Commerce and Trust Co. CommerceNational then became National City Bank in 1992, four years after National City of Cleveland acquired First Kentucky National Corp.

First City Bancorp. was taken over by Texas Commerce Bank. Citizen's Fidelity Corp. of Louisville became PNC Bank in 1992.

Bank One of Lexington was once Citizens Union National Bank and Trust Co. until Bank One Corp. of Columbus, Ohio, acquired it and renamed it Bank One. And Prudential-Bache became Prudential Securities.

- *Interviews:* Individuals interviewed for this book are not included in these notes. Whatever information is not documented here was provided by individuals knowledgeable about the particular topic.
- *Other writers:* Especially helpful in understanding the Bluegrass Bubble and its consequences were the insightful writings of Andrew Beyer, David Heckerman, Kent Hollingsworth, Deirdre Biles, Steven Crist, Jackie Duke, Billy Reed, and Jacalyn Carfagno among others. Writings about horses that were particularly inspiring included pieces by William Nack at *Sports Illustrated* and Bill Barich's outstanding book *Laughing in the Hills* (New York: Viking Press, 1980).

Part I: Mystery

ALYDAR

- *Temperament and achievements:* As easygoing, from individuals who worked with him and from " 'Glory Days' of 1940s and 1950s," by Frank Phelps, *Lexington Leader*, Aug. 17, 1977.

    Laz Barrera's comment, from "Season of Heartbreaks," by Mike Smith, *National Sports Daily*, Nov. 16, 1990.
- *Breeding:* From Jockey Club records and individuals who had worked with the horse. Southern Hemisphere breeding, from Jockey Club records and sources in Australia.
- *Income:* From financial statements in Calumet records.
- *Injury:* Calumet press release, from the files of *The Blood-Horse* magazine.

    Dr. Bramlage quoted as saying Alydar was "in as good a shape for this type of fracture as he could be," in the *Lexington Herald-Leader*, Nov. 15, 1990.

J. T. LUNDY

• *Ulcer:* description according to his lawyer Montjoy Trimble in a 1991 interview.

Part II: Dynasty

Chapter 1

GENERAL SOURCES

• *Individuals:* Prof. A. J. Powell, Agronomy Dept., University of Kentucky; Prof. David G. Powell at the Gluck Equine Research Center, University of Kentucky; Prof. Frank Ettensohn, Dept. of Geological Sciences, University of Kentucky; Lexington residents Neil Chethik, Stanley Petter, Jr., Porter McRoberts, and Mary Jane Gallaher.
• *Books:*

Alvey, R. Gerald. *Kentucky Bluegrass Country.* Folklife in the South Series. Jackson, Miss.: University Press of Mississippi, 1992.

Beall, Wilma. *Horse Farms and Horse Tales of the Bluegrass.* Nicholasville, Ky.: Sunshine Publications, 1992.

Buchanon, Lamont. *The Kentucky Derby Story.* New York: Dutton, 1953.

Clark, Thomas D. *A History of Kentucky.* Lexington, Ky.: John Bradford Press, 1950.

————, ed. *Bluegrass Cavalcade.* Lexington, Ky.: University of Kentucky Press, 1956.

Estes, J. A., and Palmer, Joe H. *An Introduction to the Thoroughbred Horse.* Lexington, Ky.: Blood-Horse, 1942.

Hollingsworth, Kent. *The Great Ones.* Lexington, Ky.: Blood-Horse, 1970.

————. *The Kentucky Thoroughbred.* Lexington, Ky.: University of Kentucky Press, 1976.

Longrigg, Roger. *The History of Horse Racing.* New York: Stein and Day, 1972.

National Museum of Racing and Hall of Fame Guidebook. Saratoga Springs, N.Y.: Tempus, 1989.

Patent, Dorothy Hinshaw. *Thoroughbred Horses.* New York: Holiday House, 1985.

Racing in America. New York: Jockey Club of New York; vols. 1 and 2, 1665–1865, by John Hervey; vol. 3, 1865–1922, by W. S. Vosburgh; vol. 4, 1922–36, by John Hervey; vol. 5, 1937–59, by Robert F. Kelly.

Roberts, Peter, ed. *The Complete Book of the Horse.* New York: Smith Publishers, Gallery Books, 1989.

Thompson, Lawrence. *Kentucky Tradition.* Hamden, Conn.: Shoe String Press, 1956.

Wharton, Mary E., and Barbour, Roger W. *Bluegrass Land and Life: Land Character, Plants, and Animals of the Inner Bluegrass Region of Kentucky: Past, Present and Future.* Lexington, Ky.: University Press of Kentucky, 1991.

White, Dan. *Kentucky Bred.* Dallas: Mountain Lion, 1986.

Wright, Jr., John D. *Lexington: Heart of the Bluegrass.* Lexington, Ky.: Lexington–Fayette County Historic Commission, 1982.

Chapter 2

WILLIAM MONROE WRIGHT

- *Snubbed by Bluegrass elite:* Anecdote about Rolls-Royce, from son of "the prominent horseman."

    Wright's purchase of Balgowan Farm, from "Wright, Chicago Turfman, Buys Henry Clay Farm," *Chicago Tribune,* Dec. 19, 1926.

    Wright's "lofty aspirations" as a breeder viewed as "an old man's plaything," from "William Monroe Wright: Improver of the Breed," by Tom White, *Hoof Beats,* June 1978.

- *Details of his life and character:* In part from interviews with Mary McElroy, an elderly relative who remembered the "Uncle Will" of her childhood; from Warren Wright, Sr.'s comments about his father in published interviews; from nineteenth-century city directories and census records; from published genealogies; from Calumet Baking Powder Co. archives; from Anita Beaver, librarian at the Springfield Sun newspapers in Ohio.

    As "the best salesman to ever carry a grip" and as "the old man . . . in the office," from "Boss of Calumet Farm," by Hambla Bauer, *Saturday Evening Post,* Sept. 11, 1948.

- *Parents:* Death dates from "Robinson's History of Greene County," Greene County Public Library in Xenia, Ohio, and from Alfred S. Andrews, *Andrews, Clapp, Stokes, Wright, Van Cleef* (Cleveland: Andrews, 1984).

- *Siblings:* Handwritten census records for Xenia, Ohio, 1860, listed the nine-year-old WMW and two male siblings, three-year-old Edgar S. and five-year-old C.F. In the Andrews book, C.F. is also referred to as Calumet Wright. There is no record of when brother Calumet died, and Andrews could not be found for further details.

- *Wives:* WMW married Clara Lee Morrison in 1875, according to Ohio records for Greene County and Clark County. Her origins are hazy. She was Warren Wright, Sr.'s mother—he was born in 1875—and in interviews through the years, WW said his mother was a Vassar College graduate. But Vassar has no records for a Clara Lee or Clara Lee Morrison. Other references to her in the Calumet company literature and early stories refer to her having been college educated but do not name the college. It's unclear when she died. However, the WMW obituary, Aug. 29, 1931, in *The New York Times* stated that he married his second wife, Georgia Daniel, five years after Clara died. And one of the codicils of WMW's will reveals an "ante-nuptial" agreement in 1897, which likely means that he got married that year. A reasonably accurate date for the death of Clara, WW's mother, is therefore about 1892.

• *Rumored relatives:* The Wright brothers, inventors of the airplane, are occasionally mentioned as WMW's relations. One relative described the famous brothers as WMW's first cousins. But no record of any familial connection was found in relevant genealogical records in Dayton, Ohio.

• *Portrait of WMW:* Details from "Warren Wright Farm Reflects Love of Horses," by Rose Cour, *Chicago Sun,* April 23, 1944.

WARREN WRIGHT

• *Chickens anecdote:* From "Chickens Killed by Pet Dogs; All Pass as Fresh Killed," *Chicago Tribune,* June 25, 1910.

• *Relationship with father:* "Warren was always fighting the old man about his extravagance with the horses," from Hambla Bauer's profiles of Warren Wright. Bauer wrote two articles about Calumet: one was published in the *Saturday Evening Post* in September 1948, and the other—largely a profile of WW—appeared in various versions alongside WW's Dec. 29, 1950, obituaries in the *Springfield Sun,* the *Dayton Daily News,* and the *Miami Daily News.* Bauer, through extensive interviews with WW, was able to fill her articles with rich details about WW's management style on the farm, his personality, and his struggle to succeed as a thoroughbred breeder. These are the most detailed published interviews with WW. Because of that, chapters 2 and 4 of Part II contain some details and quotes from Bauer's work, about WW's relationship with his father, WW's officious style, and his vitamin regimens for the horses. Bauer also is the source for the anecdote about the conversation in which a farm employee told WW about the difference between raising trotters and thoroughbreds.

In addition to Bauer and individuals with good memories, other helpful sources for WW's demeanor and the ambience at Calumet Farm during the early days were: "Blue Grass Bonanza," by Maurice Shevlin, *Chicago Tribune,* June 4, 1948; "Can Calumet Do It Again?" by Peter Bolter, *American Legion Magazine,* Jan. 1950; and several *Chicago Tribune* profiles during the 1930s and 1940s.

CALUMET BAKING POWDER COMPANY

- *Meaning of word "calumet":* According to the General Foods "Family Album."
- *Company growth:* From "Little Stories of Success: Warren Wright," by Drury Underwood, *Chicago Tribune,* Nov. 4, 1918; "The Door to the Calumet Plant," in "Salesgrams," published by General Foods, Sept. 1937; "Calumet . . ." from the General Foods "Family Album"; and "Calumet Leads Its Field," *Postum Magazine,* Dec. 1928.
- *Sales practices and federal investigation:* From the files of the Federal Trade Commission on the 1920s investigations. Most details from: *In the Matter of Calumet Baking Powder Company,* complaint synopsis F.T.C. Docket 868, Feb. 8, 1926; also *The Royal Baking Powder Co.* v. *F.T.C.,* Equity No. 47284 (S.Ct., D.C., Nov. 7, 1927); *The Royal Baking Powder Co.* v. *F.T.C.,* Equity No. 4740 (App.Ct., D.C., 1929); *In the Matter of Calumet Baking Powder Company,* 1127 (F.T.C.), June 12, 1929.

  Industrial espionage details, also from "Burns Men Linked to Trade Inquiry: Calumet Baking Powder Co. Charging Espionage," *New York Times,* Nov. 18, 1927, and "Calumet Says Rival Company Hired Detective Spies," *New York Times,* Dec. 17, 1927.
- *Calumet and Postum Company:* Description of merger, from Postum Co. Annual Report, 1928.
- *$32 million merger:* From "Movies, Baking Powder, Postum Vie in Mergers," *Chicago Tribune,* Sept. 13, 1928, and "Calumet Merger," *New York Times,* Sept. 14, 1928.

Chapter 3

WARREN WRIGHT AS CHICAGO POLITICIAN

- *Contender for political appointments, and views on Chicago gangsters:* Quote, "the mayor must be fit morally," according to "From Office Boy to President Is Wright's Record: Head of Lincoln Park Board Mentioned as Mayor Possibility," by Paul R. Leach, *Chicago Tribune,* Dec. 5, 1930.

- *The Park Commission:* "Wright Reports $361,000 Saving in Lincoln Park," *Chicago Tribune,* Dec. 12, 1930; "Retire Lincoln Park Bond Issue; Finances 'Excellent,' " *Chicago Tribune,* July 16, 1932; "Lincoln Park's Costs to Be Cut Nearly Million," *Chicago Tribune,* Sept. 2, 1932; and other articles in *Chicago Tribune* throughout 1932.

  Quote, "Idle and unnecessary employees have been eliminated from the payroll," from *Chicago Tribune,* Dec. 12, 1930.

  Quote, "This has been one of the biggest years in our history, with unemployment adding thousands daily to the number of park visitors," from *Chicago Tribune,* Sept. 2, 1931.

  Quote, WW as "the despair of certain politicians" because he'd cut the payroll "with outrageous disregard for the political affiliations of those who were dropped," in "From Office Boy . . ." by Paul R. Leach, *Chicago Tribune,* Dec. 5, 1930.
- *Winter house:* Announcement of $350,000 home in Miami, Fla., from *Chicago Tribune,* April 11, 1932.
- *Probe into commission finances:* "Friends of the [new] governor" claim the board "had switched cash from fund," from "Horner Finds Lincoln Park Shy $400,000," *Chicago Tribune,* Jan. 18, 1933.
- *Resignation:* Letter, from "Warren Wright Resigns," *Chicago Tribune,* Jan. 11, 1933.

Chapter 4

WILLIAM MONROE WRIGHT

- *Last will and testament:* Filed in Cook County Probate Court and in Fayette County Probate Court. Also reported in news stories nationwide: "Will Disposes of $59,000,000," *Chicago Tribune,* Nov. 28, 1931; "W. M. Wright Left $60,000,000 to Kin," *New York Times,* Sept. 10, 1931.

WARREN WRIGHT

- *Club memberships:* From Edward F. Dunne, *Illinois: The Heart of the Nation,* vol. 3 (Chicago and New York: Lewis Publishing, 1933).
- *Quotes:* "The setup in harness racing is such that" and "I made up my mind that," from Bauer, *Saturday Evening Post,* Sept. 11, 1948.

  "My father did better than anyone else" and "made a fortune saving money," in Bauer, *Miami Daily News, Dayton Daily News,* and *Springfield Sun,* Dec. 29, 1950.

- *Success as breeder:* His winning theory, "the person who puts in the most money deserves to win the most races," according to Margaret Glass.

     His "will to win," from, among other sources, the Warren Wright Associated Press obituary, Dec. 29, 1950.

     "Warren Wright Stable Headed for No. 1 Ranking: Chicagoan Draws Interest of Turf World," *Chicago Tribune* headline, 1938.

     "Warren Wright Honored as 'Man of the Year' in Turf World at Thoroughbred Club Dinner," *Lexington Herald,* Oct. 11, 1940.

- *Aging and illness:* Losing his way to winner's circle, from *Chicago Tribune,* May 9, 1949.

     "I feel 57, instead of 75," from *Townsfolk: Society, Sports, Travel, and the Fine Arts,* vol. 27, no. 2 (January 1951).

- *Eulogy:* "His rimless glasses and gray homburg hat," from obituary by Haden Kirkpatrick, *Thoroughbred Record,* Jan. 6, 1951.

HORSES

- *Foals:* Percentage of mares each year with healthy foals, and stats on odds of horses winning races, according to Nick Nicholson at the Jockey Club in Lexington, Ky.
- *Allure:* "There is something about the outside of a horse," from "The Boss of Calumet Farm: Kentucky Profiles," by Rena Niles, *Courier-Journal Magazine,* May 6, 1951.

BEN JONES

- *At Calumet:* According to his son, Jimmy Jones, author Kent Hollingsworth, turf writer Joe Hirsch, and numerous other individuals, as well as Steven Crist's *The Horse Traders* (New York: Norton, 1986), and Jim Bolus's *Kentucky Derby Stories* (Gretna, La.: Pelican Publishing, 1993).

     "Why didn't you take the ducks, too?" from "Calumet Farm Off to Another Record Season," *Chicago Tribune,* Mar. 14, 1953.

HORSE RACING

- *As number one spectator sport:* Attendance nationwide for thirty successive years, according to a study published by the *Daily Racing Form,* Jan. 1982.

Chapter 5

WARREN WRIGHT

- *Estate:* From his will and from various attorneys connected with the estate. The same attorneys disclosed WW's intentions and concerns regarding his estate and Mrs. Wright's income from the oil investments and the trusts.
- *First wife:* WW had a wife before LPW, but no trace of this first wife could be found in court records or *Chicago Tribune* news clippings. The divorce must have occurred long before his business achievements placed him in the Chicago spotlight; or it was hushed up.

LUCILLE PARKER WRIGHT

- *Before meeting WW:* Information is scant. LPW told Lexington friends through the years that she was from the prominent Parker family of Maysville, Ky. Some Maysville Parkers were told as children that LPW, the famous matriarch of Calumet Farm, was a relative, although they were unclear about the exact connection. The Maysville Historical Society has no record of LPW's father, John Winslow Parker, or of Lucille Parker.

In nearby Lewis County, in the town of Tollesboro, there is a record of a "John Win. Parker"; *History of Lewis County, Kentucky,* by Rev. O. G. Ragan (Cincinnati: Jennings and Graham, 1880). This book says that School District No. 30 owed Parker $81.06 for teaching. Elderly residents of Tollesboro knowledgeable about town history are certain LPW was from there, not Maysville. Some believed her father was a Baptist minister, although there are no records to substantiate this belief. The census records for this period, which would have indicated his occupation, were destroyed in a fire in 1911.

LPW's longtime friends believe that it's possible her prominence required an equally prominent pedigree, and so she put a twist on her past, moving her homeland a few miles away to Maysville. At the same time, a new generation of Parkers grew up, proudly believing that the now-famous LPW was in fact from the Maysville Parker line.

It is unclear what LPW was doing when she met WW. Some Lexingtonians claim she was a Chicago call girl. Others say she met WW at a party in Chicago. Another story was that she served as his secretary or as a clerk at Calumet Baking Powder Co., but there is no record of LPW having worked there.

Margaret Glass, Bertha Wright, and researcher Porter McRoberts helped piece together LPW's background. For an understanding of the impact of new money becoming old, including the phenomenon of fabricating biographical details, I consulted several books, the best of which was Nelson W. Aldrich, Jr., *Old Money: The Mythology of America's Upper Class* (New York: Knopf, 1988).

- *Love of eagles:* From "Warren Wright Farm Reflects Love of Horses," by Rose Cour, *Chicago Sun,* Apr. 23, 1944.
- *Emergence:* The "exceptionally well-bred" LPW, from *Enchanted Bluegrass,* by Elizabeth Simpson (Lexington, Ky.: Transylvania Press, 1938).

"The newest entry in sportdom's most glamorous field [racing] is Mrs. Warren Wright," from "Women Owners Win, Place in the Turf Earnings Race," *Chicago Tribune,* Jan. 23, 1951.

Chapters 6 and 7

GENE MARKEY

- *General information:* From dozens of interviews with individuals who knew GM, including former Calumet staff members, horsemen, socialites, and Lexington residents.
- *Life with Myrna Loy:* From Loy autobiography, *Myrna Loy: Being and Becoming,* by James Kotsilibas-Davis and Myrna Loy (New York: Knopf, 1987), and "Myrna Loy, Markey Wed," *Los Angeles Examiner,* Jan. 4, 1946.
- *Ladies' man:* The article "Other Men Say: What's Gene Markey Got That We Haven't Got?" has an accompanying photograph of the famous actor Rudolph Valentino with a caption reading: "NOT SO HOT—By comparison. Though all American womanhood swooned over him in his day, Rudolph Valentino was no Markey," *Washington Times Herald,* Jan. 6, 1946.
- *Films:* List, from the National Film Information Service in Beverly Hills, Calif.
- *Upbringing:* Concept of "social antiquing," as part of blueblood mystique, from Nelson Aldrich, Jr.'s book *Old Money: The Mythology of America's Upper Class* (New York: Knopf, 1988).
- *Recitations with Sonny Whitney:* Sonny Whitney's wife, Marylou, was kind enough to write out "The Ballad of Yukon Jake," by Edward E. Paramore, Jr., copying it from the edition that Sonny Whitney and GM shared for their late-night dramatizations of the poem.

- *Love for Kentucky:* "I cannot restrain my ardor for the place and its people. . . . No duck ever took to water as I have taken to Kentucky," from "Adm. Markey, Horseman and Writer, Dies at 84," *The Courier-Journal,* May 2, 1980.
- *As a writer:* Details about GM's research for the book *That Far Paradise,* as well as description of interior of log cabin, from "Log Cabin Is Calumet Retreat," by Rena Niles and Mary Jane Gallaher, *The Courier-Journal,* Apr. 21, 1957.

  His love of writing is taken from a questionnaire filled out by GM and found in his files at *The Saratogian* in Saratoga Springs, N.Y.
- *Love of booze:* "The Kentucky Jug," by Gene Markey (Lexington, Ky.: Kentucky Jug Society, no date). Dedicated "To the Lady of Calumet Farm—'I raise my glass!' "
- *Names Alydar:* The account in this book of how Alydar was named is according to Charles Rankin, the Markeys' butler, who walked into the room the moment GM decided on the name.
- *Loved by Lucille:* "I never knew what love was until I married [Markey]," from "Horseracing and Calumet: Thoroughbreds from the Start," by Beverly Fortune, *Lexington Herald-Leader,* May 6, 1978.

Chapters 8 and 9

WARREN WRIGHT, JR.

- *Birth:* Date he celebrated his birthday, according to his wife, Bertha Wright, and his Northwestern University transcript.
- *Schooldays:* From the records of Riverside Military Academy in Gainesville, Georgia, from conversations with professors who remembered WW, Jr., and from general Northwestern University records. At Northwestern, WW, Jr., lived at Lindgren House, which no longer exists. The fact that his parents attended his college graduation is from a longtime college friend of Warren Jr.'s. Details about his involvement with the university radio station come from friends and a former employee of Associated Dispatch.
- *Adulthood:* Recollections of WW, Jr.'s hobbies and interests are from friends. Stories about his helping the police come from a former police officer and the son of a deceased Lexington policeman.
- *Rift with mother:* Information on the mid-1950s rift with Lucille Parker Wright that caused WW, Jr., and BW to move off of Calumet Farm,

according to individuals close to the incident and knowledgeable about the details.

- *Homes away from Calumet:* Description of BW and WW, Jr.'s first house and price, according to BW. In 1961, they built a new nine-room house, with five baths, costing $80,000, according to the *Lexington Herald,* Aug. 17, 1961.

- *Tax problems:* Three-count indictment for failure to pay taxes, *U.S. v. Warren Wright Jr.,* 27509 (W.D., Ky.), Nov. 6, 1970.

  Summons to appear to answer charges of failure to file income tax returns, *U.S. v. Warren Wright Jr.,* 24924 (W.D., Ky.), mailed Nov. 12, 1970.

  Receipt of summons signed by WW, Jr., Nov. 16, 1970. Order detailing arraignment and WW, Jr.'s plea of not guilty to all three counts, *U.S. v. Warren Wright Jr.,* 27509 (W.D., Ky.), Mar. 18, 1971. Order detailing his withdrawal of previous "not guilty" plea and his entering a plea of "guilty," *U.S. v. Wright,* 27509 (W.D., Ky.), filed Apr. 15, 1971.

  Sentence to three months on each of three counts to run concurrently and a fine totaling $15,000, *U.S. v. Wright,* 27509 (W.D., Ky.), Apr. 15, 1981. Order directing Wright to surrender himself to the U.S. marshal in Montgomery, Ala., at 9:30 A.M. on Apr. 30, 1971, *U.S. v. Wright,* 27509 (W.D., Ky.), filed Apr. 30, 1971.

LUCILLE PARKER WRIGHT MARKEY

- *Quotes:* Comment on son two weeks before his death, "I didn't leave [the farm] to him, but my former husband did," "Horseracing and Calumet: Thoroughbreds from the Start," by Beverly Fortune, *Lexington Herald-Leader,* May 6, 1978.

  Comment on Calumet horses, "They knew me and knew my voice," from "The Lady of Calumet," by Irene Nolan, *Courier-Journal,* May 1, 1971.

GEORGIA WRIGHT

- *Death:* William Monroe Wright's widow dies, *Chicago Tribune* obituary, Sept. 11, 1936.

Chapters 10–16

LUCILLE PARKER WRIGHT MARKEY

- *Death:* "She was an inspiration," from obituary by Steven Crist, *New York Times,* July 26, 1982.

  Veitch's praise, according to *New York Times* obituary and "Lucille Markey, Owner of Calumet Farm, Dies," by Billy Reed, *Courier-Journal,* July 26, 1982.

  She "greatly enhanced the luster that surrounds Kentucky's name as an international center of Thoroughbred racing," editorial, *Courier-Journal,* July 26, 1982.

  "They were applauding a great and courageous lady," from "Late Mrs. Lucille Markey, Exemplary 'One of a Kind,' " by Joe Hirsch, *Daily Racing Form,* July 26, 1982.

- *Personal estate:* "Even among America's gleaming pantheon," from "Mrs. Markey's Money: She Willed Her Wealth to Science," by Margaria Fichtner, *Miami Herald,* Dec. 2, 1990.

- *Assets:* Information on the value of the Wright assets, oil properties, trusts, etc., that were distributed upon the death of Lucille Markey and details about Waddell Ranch and the Gulf litigation, from William Sutter, Hopkins and Sutter in Chicago, and from Calumet Farm records.

- *Handwritten notes:* From Margaret Glass's scrapbook.

J. T. LUNDY

- *Efforts to control Calumet before LPWM's death:* Information about all letters and meetings, according to Lyle Robey and the letters themselves.

- *Bluegrass property values:* From "The Bluegrass Stakes," by John Ed Pearce and Richard Nugent, *Courier-Journal,* Dec. 1981.

LESLIE COMBS II

- *Description:* According to his friends and enemies and from journalists such as Mary Jane Gallaher, who wrote about him and traveled in his circle during the 1940s and 1950s.

CHARLES ENGELHARD

- *The man and his era:* From "The Late, the Great Charles Engelhard," by Gerald Stine, *Horsemen's Journal,* July 1980; Engelhard obituary, *The*

Blood-Horse, Mar. 8, 1971; and "Playing the Horse Market," by Whitney Tower, *Sports Illustrated,* Apr. 28, 1969.

BLUEGRASS BUBBLE

- *The need to modernize horse business:* "Automation in Racing: 'The Sign Is Right,' " transcript of Joe Estes's talk reprinted in *The Blood-Horse,* Oct. 27, 1962. The idea that the boom years subtly began with Estes's talk in the 1960s came from bloodstock agent Stanley Petter, Jr., during a conversation at the Saratoga races in Aug. 1992.
- *Horse bidders as "Sangster's gangsters":* Nickname from local horsemen and from Steve Crist's *The Horse Traders* (New York: Norton, 1986).

Part III: King of Calumet

Chapter 1

CINDY WRIGHT LUNDY

- Quote: "I thought we should work," from her deposition in *IBJ Schroder Bank & Trust Company* v. *Wright et al.,* 91-354 (E.D., Ky.), Dec. 23, 1991.

WARREN WRIGHT III

- *Property:* According to Deed Book 1326, p. 519, and Mortgage Book 1380, p. 697, in the Fayette County Clerk's office.
- *Biographical information:* About WW III and brother Thomas C. Wright, according to their depositions in *IBJ Schroder Bank & Trust Company* v. *Wright et al.,* 91-354 (E.D., Ky.), depositions filed Dec. 17 and Dec. 27, 1991. From affidavit of Bertha Wright, dated December 14, 1993, submitted in conjunction with *Re: Bertha Wright,* Debtor, 93-50224, Adv. 53-5102, *CommerceNational Bank* v. *Bertha Wright et al.* (Bankr., E.D., Ky.)
- *Calumet finances:* WW III wouldn't know what Calumet financial statements said, from transcripts of hearings related to *In Re: Calumet Farm, Inc.,* Debtor, 91-51414, *J.T. Lundy, William M. Allen, et al.* v. *Calumet Farm, Inc.,* Adv. 91-0179 (Bankr., E.D., Ky.).

COURTENAY WRIGHT LANCASTER

- *Biography:* In part from her deposition in *IBJ Schroder Bank & Trust Company* v. *Wright et al.,* 91-354 (E.D., Ky.). And from Bertha Wright affidavit, noted above, of December 14, 1993.

FINANCIAL PROFILE OF WRIGHT HEIRS

- *Trusts and assets:* After 1982, according to letter dated Sept. 6, 1983, to Second National Bank and Trust Co. of Lexington, Ky., Wright Enterprises.

Chapter 2

J. T. LUNDY

- *Description:* Habit of eating ice cream out of cartons and quote, "If they weren't picking on me," from "A Different Breed: Calumet's Lundy Is a Racing Maverick," by Jennie Rees, *Courier-Journal*, Aug. 19, 1990.
- *New regime at Calumet:* "Calumet will stay" and "Business will continue as usual," from "Hopeful Signs for Calumet Tradition," by Steven Crist, *New York Times*, July 27, 1982.

  "There's no way this place is going to be houses," from "Calumet Aims for Heights of Its Heyday," by Maryjean Wall, *Lexington Herald*, Sept. 9, 1982.

  "I've been watching it [the farm] ever since I've been in the family," from "With Mrs. Markey Gone, It's a Whole New Show at Calumet Farm," by Jim Bolus, *Courier-Journal*, Oct. 11, 1982.

  "Quintessential small-mindedness," from a column by Art Grace in the *Miami News*, as noted in "The New Order at Calumet," by John Ed Pearce, *Courier-Journal*, May 8, 1983.

  "He [Foyt] must have gotten a real good buy," from "Calumet Farm Discovers a New Way to Get Some Horsepower," by Dave Koerner, *Louisville Times*, May 19, 1983.

Chapter 4

J. T. LUNDY

- *Education:* According to his deposition taken in *IBJ Schroder Bank & Trust Co.* v. *Wright et al.,* 91-354 (E.D., Ky.), Dec. 30, 1991, filed Jan. 23, 1992.
- *Aspirations:* Dream of winning both the Kentucky Derby and Indy 500, from "Calumet Farm Discovers a New Way to Get Some Horsepower," by Dave Koerner, *Louisville Times*, May 19, 1983.

Harry Ranier

• *Contribution:* To Tammy and Jim Bakker, according to "He's No Blue Blood, But His Coal Money Is Pretty Well Bred," by Robert T. Garrett, *Courier-Journal,* Apr. 26, 1981.

Chapter 5

J. T. Lundy

• *President of Calumet Farm, Inc.:* From "Corporate Resolution" signed by Lundy and by Robey, Sept. 20, 1982, in Calumet records.
• *"Hold-harmless" agreement:* From copy of agreement.

Chapter 6

Racecars

• *1983 Indy 500:* Lundy quote, "This gives us a world of exposure," from "Calumet Farm Discovers a New Way to Get Some Horsepower," by Dave Koerner, *Louisville Times,* May 19, 1983.
• *Valvoline letter:* Dated May 13, 1983, from Calumet records.

J. T. Lundy

• *Image:* Quote, "While there has been some criticism," *The Blood-Horse,* July 1983.

Calumet Farm, Inc.

• *Second National Bank bills:* To Calumet Farm, according to memo to Wright family from Lyle G. Robey, dated June 22, 1983.
• *Jet planes:* Expenses, according to Calumet monthly statements, May 31, 1983.
      Other details, in part from *Re: Sun Bank, N.A. v. Southeastern Aircraft Holding Corp., J.T. Lundy, et al.,* 91-10704 (Cir. Crt., 15th Jud. Cir.), filed Sept. 16, 1991, in Palm Beach Co., Fl.
• *Memo about debt:* According to letter dated Sept. 6, 1983, to Second National Bank and Trust Co. of Lexington, Ky., from Wright Enterprises.
• *Calumet debt by 1984:* From the Calumet records.

Chapter 7

KEENELAND SALES

- *July 1984:* As the most extravagant in the history of the industry, from "Those Yearling Sales Riches, It's Fools' Gold," by Andrew Beyer, *Washington Post,* July 25, 1984.
- *Sky-high:* Prices up 918 percent, from *Wall Street Journal,* Oct. 25, 1989.
- *Number of yearlings auctioned:* From the Jockey Club's "1993 Fact Book."
- *Equine studies:* From the studies themselves; from "Understanding the Impact of the Equine Industry in Kentucky and the Central Bluegrass," a report by the Center for Business and Economic Research, College of Business and Economics, University of Kentucky, Lexington, Ky., 1991; and from "The Economic Impact of the U.S. Horse Industry," by Policy Economics Group of Peat, Marwick, Mitchell and Co., Jan. 1987.

BOILER ROOMS

- *Breeding industry schemes:* The Miami company that bilked investors was International Thoroughbred Bloodstock Agency of Broward County, Fla., according to Securities and Exchange Commission records. Additional details are contained in a 1985 series of articles by Bob Lowe for the *Miami Herald;* and from "Investors Fret as Horse Firm Runs Out of Money, Closes," by Peter Vilbig and Sarah Oates, *Miami Herald,* May 22, 1986.

DAN LASATER

- *Federal case:* Indicted on October 24, 1986, with eight others on cocaine-related charges following a three-year investigation by the Organized Crime Drug Enforcement Task Force and sentenced to two and a half years in prison by U.S. District Judge G. Thomas Eisele, from series of articles in the *Arkansas Democrat,* during the fall and winter of 1986, including "Judge Hands Lasater, Locke Prison Terms on Drug Counts," by Patrick Casey, Dec. 19, 1986. Served six months in prison, four months in a halfway house, and two months under house arrest. Then–Arkansas governor Bill Clinton pardoned him in Nov. 1990. Roger Clinton pleaded guilty in Jan. 1985 to separate federal cocaine-distribution charges and was named as an unindicted co-conspirator when Lasater was indicted. He testified against Lasater during grand jury proceedings. Clinton-Lasater connection, in part from "Clinton Disputes Report He Aided

Wealthy Backer," by William C. Rempel and Ralph Fammolino, *Los Angeles Times,* Mar. 24, 1992.

J. E. JUMONVILLE, JR.

- *Quote:* "My purpose was to get the quality," from "Super Sprinter?" by the Associated Press, *Courier-Journal,* Dec. 30, 1984.
- *Loan:* Louisiana National Bank of Baton Rouge, La. (later renamed Premier Bank), loaned Jumonville $5 million for the Alydar venture on Aug. 30, 1984. The bank sued him for payment of the note on Nov. 13, 1986, in state court. Judge Paul B. Landry ordered Jumonville to repay the bank. He appealed, and on Nov. 17, 1988, the state appeals court upheld the $5.5 million judgment against him. The appeals court reaffirmed the judgment in May 1990.

SECRETO

- *Purchase:* Details from copy of July 10, 1984, "Secreto Agreement of Purchase and Sale," signed by J. T. Lundy and Luigi Miglietti on July 2, 1984.
- *Commission:* On the deal, according to Calumet records.

J. T. LUNDY

- *Quote:* "Not as much fun," from "Calumet Rebuilding Itself," by Woodson Emmons, *Lexington Herald-Leader,* Oct. 14, 1984.

Chapter 8
CALUMET OVERPAYS

- *Kinderhill colt:* According to letter from Kinderhill, Mar. 26, 1985, stating desired price of $200,000 and copy of Calumet Farm canceled $300,000 check to Kinderhill for "purchase 1984 Green Dancer–Baby Diamonds Colt."

J. T. LUNDY

- *Drive:* Early views of J. T. Lundy's single-minded determination compared with WW, Sr.'s, from individuals and from "Calumet Rebuilding Itself," by Woodson Emmons, *Lexington Herald-Leader,* Oct. 14, 1984.

- *Guns:* Two versions of the gun under the sofa. Some staffers said it was a submachine gun, while one of Lundy's former associates said it was a collector's item that Lundy just liked to look at and show to guests.
- *Equus:* Lundy's sister later said, in a deposition regarding another matter, that she had paid back the loan to Calumet.
- *Fence expenses:* From Calumet records.

ROBERT LIBUTTI

- *Calumet tie:* From individuals knowledgeable about it.
- *Exclusion from New Jersey casino gambling:* Petition to place Libutti on N.J. casino gambling exclusion list, Feb. 19, 1991. Orders excluding Libutti from N.J. gambling industry on the basis of his ties to organized crime, according to *State of New Jersey Department of Law & Public Safety Division of Gaming Enforcement* v. *Libutti,* 91-11-6 dated Mar. 18, 1991, and 91-25-15 dated Sept. 10, 1991.
- *Indictment:* On thirteen counts for bank fraud and other charges, *U.S.* v. *Kruckel and Libutti,* U.S.A. No. 9003996 (United States Dist. Ct., Newark, N.J.), filed Oct. 29, 1992.
- *Quote:* "Malicious conspiracy," etc., from "Odd Tale of Colt Kept from Races," by Steve Cady, *New York Times,* Nov. 12, 1976.
- *Boasts Gotti tie:* Note, at least one such proclamation was taped by the then CEO of Trump. Among other things, Libutti said Gotti wanted him to find out if he could play at the casinos and told the executive that Trump could make a lot of money from Gotti and other organized crime figures. From petition filed Feb. 20, 1991, by the New Jersey Division of Gaming Enforcement at N.J.'s Casino Control Commission. Other details, from articles in the *Newark Star-Ledger* through the years.
- *Car deals:* Note that Trump Plaza was fined $450,000 for the car deals related to Libutti's gambling.
- *Heavy tipper and childhood details:* From an account in *Temples of Chance,* by David Johnston (New York: Doubleday, 1992), pp. 244–248.

JANICE HEINZ AND SUSAN MCGEE

- *Heinz's compensation:* And job description, and quote, "I was paid a flat amount whenever I would ask for it," from her deposition in *In Re: Calumet Farm, Inc.,* Debtor, 91-51414, *Black Chip Stables* v. *Calumet Farm, Inc.,* Adv. 91-5226 (Bankr., E.D., Ky.), and from Kimberly Dawn Day's testimony in *In Re: Calumet Farm, Inc.*, Debtor, 91-51414, Adv. 91-0179 (Bankr., E.D., Ky.), May 28, 1993.

- *Lifetime breeding rights:* For both women, according to "Agreed Order," *In Re: Calumet Farm Inc.*, Debtor, 91-51414 (Bankr., E.D., Ky.), Mar. 25, 1992.
- *Ties to Heinz family:* From Frank Kurtik, curator, Heinz Family Office, Pittsburgh, Pa.
- *Heinz's right to sign Lundy's name:* From Lundy's deposition in *Axmar Stable* v. *Calumet Farm Inc.*, 91-212 (E.D., Ky.), June 25, 1991.

WILLIAM M. ALLEN

- *Introduction to J. T. Lundy:* According to decision by bankruptcy judge Joe Lee, *In Re: Calumet Farm, Inc.*, Debtor, 91-51414, *J.T. Lundy, William M. Allen, et al.* v. *Calumet Farm, Inc.*, Adv. 91-0179 (Bankr., E.D., Ky.), May 28, 1993.
- *Businesses:* According to Allen's deposition, taken in *Allen* v. *Smith* v. *Perez*, 91-424 (E.D., Ky.), Mar. 12, 1992.
- *Conviction:* For conspiracy and mail fraud, called "country-club fraud" by the media, from *Post* v. *U.S.*, 407 F.2d 319, 132 U.S.App.D.C. 189, 1967. Sentenced at age thirty-nine to twelve to thirty-six months with four months in prison and the remainder on probation, according to the *Montgomery County Sentinel*, Jan. 1, 1967.
- *Pardon:* By President Richard M. Nixon in December 1972, according to U.S. Department of Justice, pardon attorney.

WILD AGAIN, STALLION

- *Purchase, breeding rights, and management:* From decision by Chief Judge Joe Lee, *In Re: Calumet Farm, Inc.*, Debtor, 91-51414, *J. T. Lundy, William M. Allen, et al.* v. *Calumet Farm, Inc.*, Adv. 91-0179 (Bankr., E.D., Ky.), May 28, 1993.
- *Lundy's earnings from breeding rights:* From testimony of Todd Wright, Calumet's accountant, in the above Adv. 91-0179.

WRIGHT FAMILY

- *Claiming ignorance:* Family's alleged limited knowledge of business transactions, and their quotes, according to trial hearings and decision by

Chief Judge Joe Lee, *In Re: Calumet Farm, Inc.,* Debtor, 91-51414, *J. T. Lundy* v. *Calumet Farm, Inc.,* Adv. 91-0179 (Bankr., E.D., Ky.), May 28, 1993. Years later lawyers for Calumet alleged Lundy had defrauded the corporation by concealing the terms of the Wild Again syndicate agreement, but Judge Lee said, in the May 28, 1993, opinion noted above, that the lawyers didn't prove this sufficiently. Part of the problem in the case was that the corporation board included Robey, who had drafted the syndicate agreement, and so concealment, no matter what the family knew or didn't know, was tough to prove. Also, the family did have access to records such as this agreement. The judge suggested, however, that the lawyers had gathered enough proof to allege that Lundy had defrauded the corporation by switching seasons to his own advantage and shuffling breeding records, among other things.

- *Courtenay's claim:* From her affidavit in *Mutual Benefit Life Insurance Co.* v. *Lundy et al.* (Cir. Ct., Fayette Co., Ky.).

CALUMET FARM, INC.

- *Board meetings:* Details according to hearings in Adv. 91-0179 in Debtor 91-51414 (Bankr., E.D., Ky.) and the May 28, 1993, decision in that case.
- *Management practices:* Extended book described as "dumping ground," by Chief Judge Joe Lee, in same May 28, 1993, decision in Adv. 91-0179.

VACA CUT (LATER KNOWN AS VACA BLOODSTOCK)

- *J. T. Lundy corporate holdings:* According to records of the Florida secretary of state.
- *Property:* Verification of estate built on property owned by Vaca, according to *Reed* v. *Vaca,* 88-10063-CA-09 (Cir. Ct., 16th Jud. Cir.) and other documents filed in Monroe County, Fla., Court, including "Notice of Federal Tax Lien," filed Apr. 24, 1992.

THE FAMILY AND THE BANK

- *Buying the bank:* From five-page general report, with thirty-four pages of financial analysis, of then Second National Bank and Trust Co.
- *Family terminates trust and bank sues:* Details from *The Second National Bank & Trust Co. of Lexington* v. *Bertha C. Wright, et al.,* 85-CI-3222 (Cir. Ct., 3rd Div., Fayette County, Ky.), filed Sept. 26, 1985. Later, "Opinion

and Order," in same case, filed Aug. 5, 1987; "Agreed Order and Judgment of Dismissal," filed Sept. 4, 1987. And more details, from affidavits
of Bertha Wright, dated December 14, 1993, and Timothy Cone submitted in conjunction with *In Re Bertha Wright*, Debtor, 93-50224, Adv. 93-
5102, *CommerceNational Bank* v. *Bertha Wright et al.* (Bankr., E.D., Ky.).

HORSE INDUSTRY

• *Forebodings:* Quote, "When this is over," from "Those Yearling Sales
Riches, It's Fools' Gold," by Andrew Beyer, *Washington Post,* July 25,
1984.

Chapter 9

BREEDERS' LOSSES

• "The cost of bringing the 2,377 horses," stats from a study by the *Washington Post.*

LOANS FROM CALUMET TO WRIGHT PARTNERS

• Loans to the partners of Wright Enterprises (who were Bertha C. Wright,
her children, and J. T. Lundy), according to *In Re: Bertha C. Wright,*
Debtor, 93-50224, *National City Bank of Lexington, Kentucky* v. *Bertha C.
Wright,* Adv. 93-5065 (Bankr., E.D., Ky.), May 21, 1993. And from various documents filed in conjunction with the bank's counterclaims in *In
Re: Wright* v. *CommerceNational Bank & Trust Company of Lexington, Ky.,*
91-CI-3076 (Cir. Ct., Fayette Co., Ky.), Aug. 15, 1991. Note that the
loans totaled $17.6 million and were made from Sept. 30, 1985, to
Oct. 1, 1988.

MOGAMBO

• *Lundy's quotes:* "He reminds me of Alydar," from "Calumet's Lundy Buys,"
by Dave Koerner, *Lexington Herald-Leader,* 1986.
• *Purchase price:* Undisclosed at the time, revealed in later years, and in
same article noted above he says, "It's kind of hard to put a price on it,
but [$10 million] is not too far off. The whole horse would be worth
more than $20 million."

Courtenay Wright Lancaster

• *Quote about pressure to sign promissory note:* "Misrepresented the nature of the document," from her affidavit in *Mutual Benefit Life Insurance Co. v. Lundy et al.* (Cir. Ct., Fayette Co., Ky.).

Calumet Debt

• From Calumet records.

Luigi Miglietti

• *Death:* He suffered a massive heart attack while traveling in his private jet from Miami to Lexington. The fifty-five-year-old Venezuelan millionaire died before he could reach a hospital.

Robert Perez

• *Sentenced:* Apr. 28, 1967, in Queens County, N.Y., Supreme Court for, in 1964, defrauding Astoria Medical Group and Nationwide Mutual Insurance Company by making fraudulent claims regarding injuries, according to New York State Department of Correction–Inmate Record Card, Sing Sing Prison.
• *Other career details:* From "The Powerful Paver," *New York Daily News,* Nov. 18, 1990.
• *His connection with Robert deFilippis:* Note that deFilippis later pleaded guilty to interstate travel to promote extortion.
• *His relationship with Calumet:* In part from his July 8, 1992, deposition in *Allen v. Smith v. Perez,* 91-424 (E.D., Ky.).
• *Racehorse success:* Quote, "After the Acorn," from " 'Joy' Wins Acorn," by Steven Crist, *New York Times,* May 23, 1982.

Chapter 10

Calumet Farm, Inc.

• *Borrowing heavily:* Amounts from Calumet records.
• *Lundy profiting:* Beshear quote, "Any time a choice came," from Wild Again trial proceedings, on October 11, 1991, regarding case *Calumet Farm, Inc.,* Debtor, 91-51414, *J. T. Lundy, William M. Allen, et al. v. Calumet Farm Inc.,* Adv. 91-0179 (Bankr., E.D., Ky.).

LUCILLE "CINDY" WRIGHT LUNDY

- *Power of attorney:* Document dated Jan. 6, 1987, signed by "principal," Lucille W. Lundy. Note, from document, "To draw checks and drafts upon any and all checking or savings accounts in the principal's name in any bank or savings institution, and for the purpose to sign the principal (Cindy Lundy's) name thereon; to invest and reinvest any property owned or due the principal." Document filed in *Sun Bank, N.A.* v. *Southeastern Aircraft Holding Corp., J. T. Lundy, et al.,* No. 91-10704 (15th Jud. Cir., Palm Beach Co., Fla.), September 16, 1991. Lundy did have this right but it's unclear when he used it. At least he did not sign documents using it in the conventional manner, which would be to sign her name and then below it sign his, followed by the initials AIF, for attorney-in-fact. In this particular case regarding Southeastern Air, Cindy, according to one of her lawyers, denied the liability of Southeastern because she said she had not signed the documents related to Southeastern. The implication was that her name had been forged.

LUNDY ASSETS

- From exhibits in *IBJ Schroder Bank & Trust Company* v. *Wright et al.,* 91-354 (E.D., Ky.). Net worth of Wright heirs, from memo dated Mar. 5, 1987, to Schroder's private banking credit committee.

1987 AUCTIONS

- *Scent of scandal:* From interviews, and hint of it from "Shifting into High Gear," by David Heckerman, *Thoroughbred Record,* Sept. 1987.
- *Partnership with Axmar:* In part from Betty G. Marcus's deposition, June 12, 1991, in West Palm Beach, Fla., *Axmar* v. *Calumet,* 91-212 (E.D., Ky.), vols. 1 and 2. And from *Calumet Farm, Inc.,* Debtor No. 91-51414, Adv. 91-5231, *Axmar Stable* v. *IBJ Schroder Bank & Trust Co. and Calumet Farm, Inc.* (Bankr., E.D., Ky.), July 29, 1993.
- *Sales tickets:* From Keeneland records.
- *Marcus:* Quotes, "I had advisers," and "That's a value," from Marcus's deposition.

EQUINE CAPITAL CORPORATION

- *Background:* In part from Michael Lischin's deposition in *Axmar Stable* v. *Executive Bloodstock Management Corp., Barry Weisbord, and Marc S. Rash,* 90-300 (E.D., Ky.), taken Oct. 19, 1990, and May 29, 1991.
- *Memo from Rash to Matthews:* Dated July 2, 1990, from Calumet records.

CALUMET DEBT

- *New loans and total debt:* From Calumet records.

Chapter 11

MELVIN CINNAMON

- *Quote:* On breeding, from "Calumet Memories," by Deirdre B. Biles, *The Blood-Horse,* Sept. 6, 1986.

J. T. LUNDY

- *Quote:* To breed often was "like shooting," from "A Different Breed: Calumet's Lundy Is a Racing Maverick," by Jennie Rees, *Courier-Journal,* Aug. 19, 1990.

HORSE STATISTICS

- *Nationwide:* 5,696 foals in 1938, according to the Jockey Club records.

Chapter 12

IBJ SCHRODER BANK AND TRUST COMPANY

- *Loan:* 1988 loan to Calumet, details in part from *Calumet Farm, Inc.,* Debtor No. 91-51414, Adv. 91-5231, *Axmar Stable* v. *IBJ Schroder Bank & Trust Co. and Calumet Farm, Inc.* (Bankr., E.D., Ky.), July 29, 1993. And from Marcus's deposition, June 12, 1991, in West Palm Beach, Fla., *Axmar* v. *Calumet,* 91-212 (E.D., Ky.), vols. 1 and 2.
- *Officer's comment:* "It was one of the premier farms," from Deborah White's deposition, Feb. 14, 1992, in *IBJ Schroder Bank & Trust Company* v. *Wright,* 91-354 (E.D., Ky.).
- *Value of farm:* From Mar. 5, 1987, memo to Schroder credit committee, regarding a potential $3.2 million loan. This loan eventually went

through, with the family as guarantors rather than the oil property itself as security.

Lloyd Swift

- *Horse partnerships:* Information comes, in part, from court records regarding a class action suit filed against him and the Bank of East Tennessee, *Gramlich et al.* v. *Swift and the Bank of East Tennessee, Bank of East Tennessee* v. *Pankey, Levinson and Fithian,* 90-5768, 90-5217-19 (6th U.S. Cir. Ct.).
- *Letter:* Written by Swift, alias "Spud," allegedly sent to Cihak.

Frank Cihak

- *Description:* Likening Cihak to a Chicago Bears lineman and revealing Robert Abboud's jobs prior to First City Bancorp., in "Houston Highflier: Abboud's 1988 Rescue of First City Bancorp Looks Less Heroic Now," by Michael Allen, *Wall Street Journal,* Jan. 24, 1991.
- *At First City:* Dealings with Lloyd Swift after arriving at First City Bancorp. of Houston, Texas, according to *U.S.* v. *Cihak,* Indictment H-93-119 (S.D., Tex.), Apr. 21, 1993.

Allen Deal

- *About Matthews:* From his deposition in *Allen* v. *Smith* v. *Perez,* 91-424 (E.D., Ky.). Lawyer refers to him as a "clean-up man," and he agrees that that is what he was. Note that Matthews eventually resigned his post as a Calumet officer because of a conflict of interest between being on the board, and handling bank matters and giving legal advice.

Lou-Roe Farms

- *Anthony Gurino:* Ties to Arc Plumbing and Heating Corp. as well as Hi-Tech Mechanical, various other New York corporations, and Lou-Roe Farms, according to indictment, *U.S.* v. *Gurino,* 92-01007 (N.D., Fla.), Feb. 27, 1992.
- *Louis Gurino:* Record as a trainer, according to *American Racing Manual* (Lexington, Ky.: Daily Racing Form, 1986–92 editions). *Note:* Gurino is first mentioned in the 1990 and 1991 editions of the manual.
- *Calumet bills:* From Calumet records.

CALUMET PHILANTHROPY

- *Special Olympics:* Press release dated Nov. 15, 1988, announcing Kentucky Special Olympics event to be held at Calumet Farm Nov. 16, 1988.

SPENDTHRIFT FARM

- *Collapse:* Leslie Combs II quote taken from " 'Kind of Inevitable' Spendthrift's Action Saddens, But Doesn't Surprise Horse Industry," by Judith Egerton, *Courier-Journal,* Dec. 23, 1988.

Chapter 13

BERTHA WRIGHT

- *Dealings with Ricco Antonio:* Lawsuit and Wright's counterclaim, in *Ricco Antonio v. Bertha Wright and Ricco Antonio, Inc.,* C660-323 (S.Ct., L.A. Cty., Calif.). Filed Sept. 1987, the suit claimed $30 million. The case ended in a settlement.

FIRST CITY

- *As money store:* Amounts borrowed, from financial statements in the Calumet records.

CALUMET FARM, INC.

- *Back taxes owed on breeding rights:* Note that sales of shares in horses are exempt from taxes under Kentucky laws, "provided the purchase or use is made for breeding purposes only." The state said the exemption didn't apply because rights, sold for the lifetime of the horse, are in fact breeding fees, not ownership interests in the horse. A judge in Fayette Circuit Court agreed.
- *Travel expenses and logs:* From Calumet records.
- *Salaries:* Note that Robey also took a percentage of gross receipts coming into the farm and Wright Enterprises.
- *Robey:* Drunk driving, from *Lexington Herald-Leader,* Aug. 17, 1989, and Dec. 5, 1989.
- *More deals:* Sales prices for yearlings and mares, according to *In Re: Calumet Farm, Inc.,* Debtor, 91-51414, *J. T. Lundy v. Calumet Farm, Inc.,* Adv. 91-0179 (Bankr., E.D., Ky.), May 28, 1993; and from files of *Allen v. Smith v. Perez,* 91-424 (E.D., Ky.). Destinies of mares and yearlings that

Allen sold to Calumet, from Allen's letters to Calumet Farm, dated 1991, Oct. 29, May 1, and June 12.

- *Lucinda Lea:* Mare's fate, from records in *Allen* v. *Smith* v. *Perez,* 91-424 (E.D., Ky.).
- *And more deals:* Another way the farm was getting money was through the vehicle of Gray Cliff, Inc., incorporated in August 1988 in Kentucky by attorney Matthews. He was also director and sole member of the Gray Cliff board, while Rash owned 100 percent of the company. In early 1989, Matthews resigned from the board and Rash took his place, becoming Gray Cliff's vice president and treasurer. Lundy was company president. Gray Cliff was created for the sole purpose of selling horses, partly because of the credibility problem that the farm seemed to have after the 1987 Saratoga auction. That was when most of the Calumet horses that appeared to be sold didn't really change hands. There was the idea, too, that a separate sales unit would create tax advantages for Calumet. But it was never used in this manner. Instead, the new company served to suck more funds from the American banking community. In early May 1989 Gray Cliff borrowed $2 million from Citizen's Fidelity using ECC. With the money, Gray Cliff bought $2 million worth of Calumet horses, bringing $2 million into the Calumet coffers. The collateral for the loan consisted of the horses Gray Cliff was buying. Also, Calumet guaranteed the loan. It was a perfect deal for Calumet, because it allowed the farm to get $2 million from Citizen's Fidelity, except that Lundy worried about letting go of such a pricey group of horses whose value might increase over time. So he asked Matthews to add an option that allowed Calumet to purchase Rash's shares in Gray Cliff for $25,000. Lundy exercised the option one year later, thus allowing Calumet to receive the $2 million loan and to get the horses back. After the option was exercised, in 1990, Gray Cliff became a subsidiary of Calumet. In late July 1989, while Gray Cliff was still a separate entity and not yet part of Calumet, it borrowed another $650,000 from ECC out of Citizen's Fidelity. Calumet Farm guaranteed the promissory note and the collateral for the loan consisted of the horses Gray Cliff was buying from Calumet. But this time, though Gray Cliff paid the money to Calumet for the horses, the horses never changed owners. Their ownership papers were never transferred to Gray Cliff's name. This meant that Gray Cliff had used collateral belonging to another company to get a loan, a questionable way of doing business. In this deal, too, nearly $50,000 of the money that came from Citizen's Fidelity to ECC to Gray Cliff to purchase horses from Calumet was diverted to pay

interest on loans to two entities that had nothing directly to do with Calumet or with Gray Cliff. One was Maricopa Ranch, a company 100 percent owned by J. T. Lundy.

FINANCIAL PORTRAITS

- From "Accountants' Compilation Report," signed by Deloitte Haskins and Sells, July 7, 1989. The firm also did another report, signed by Deloitte and Touche, Aug. 6, 1990.

DOOMSDAY MEMO

- Dated Sept. 20, 1989, from Calumet records.

AXMAR STABLES

- *Partnership with Calumet:* Official dissolution of the Axmar-Calumet partnership, terms of redemption agreement, from the agreement; from Betty G. Marcus's deposition, June 12, 1991, in West Palm Beach, Fla., *Axmar* v. *Calumet,* 91-212 (E.D., Ky.), Dec. 19, 1991; from *Calumet Farm, Inc.,* Debtor No. 91-51414, Adv. 91-5231, *Axmar Stable* v. *IBJ Schroder Bank & Trust Co. and Calumet Farm, Inc.* (Bankr., E.D., Ky.), July 29, 1993.
- *Versus Rash:* Lawsuit, *Axmar Stable* v. *Executive Bloodstock Management, Corp., Barry Weisbord, and Marc S. Rash,* 90-300 (E.D., Ky.), filed July 24, 1990. Note that although trial dates were set, the case eventually ended in a settlement in 1992.

Chapter 14

CRIMINAL TYPE

- *Wins Pimlico Special:* J. T. Lundy's quote, "That's the way racing is," from "Return of the Devil's Red," by Milton C. Toby, *The Blood-Horse,* May 19, 1990.

CALUMET'S RETURN TO GLORY

- *J. T. Lundy as authority:* Opinions on all sorts of topics, including taxes, "When they [the federal government] took away many of the advantages," from "On Pedigrees, Racing, and the Fun of It All," by Deirdre B. Biles, *The Blood-Horse,* June 30, 1990.

- *Quote:* "Why live in the past," from "New Days at Calumet: The Famed Lexington Farm Again Is Turning Out Major Winners, under the Direction of J. T. Lundy," by Deirdre B. Biles, *The Blood-Horse,* June 30, 1990.
- *Expenses:* Jet costs exceed payroll during August, from Calumet records.

ALYDAR

- *Income from breedings:* From financial statements in Calumet records.

FIRST CITY BANCORPORATION

- *Loan for J. T. Lundy's purchases in Spain:* Copy of "Sale and Purchase Agreement," dated Feb. 7, 1990, between J. T. Lundy and Silvia Moroder Leon y Castillo and Inigo Coca Moroder, for Pablo Picasso's *L'Araignée de Mer* and Joan Miró's *Femme et Oiseau dans la Nuit.*
- *Paintings:* Market value of paintings bought by J. T. Lundy in Spain, according to memorandum, note no. 4780800, dated Mar. 13, 1990, in files of E. Kevin Hart, who, according to *The Wall Street Journal* ("Spanish Family Sues First City Bancorp., Potentially Snarling Bank's Rescue Plan," Apr. 1, 1992), was a "close aide to Mr. [Frank] Cihak" and head of Pelican Group, a Texas corporation. Evidence of efforts to sell the Picasso and Miró at Sotheby's and Christie's, from two letters to the auction houses, both from Kevin Hart and dated Sept. 24, 1990.
- *Lawsuit:* $1.18 billion lender liability case, *Moroder v. First City Bancorp.,* 92-014367 (Harris Cty., Tex.), Mar. 31, 1992. *Note:* In 1992, defendants J. T. Lundy and Gary Matthews, a Lexington, Ky., attorney, settled the claims in this case against them, according to Matthews, who declined to disclose details of the agreement. According to individuals knowledgeable about the case, Lundy returned the Coca assets as part of the settlement, leaving him with the First City debt. Lundy and Matthews settled in July 1992.
- *Trips to Houston:* From Calumet records.
- *Terms of restructured loan:* From loan agreement dated Oct. 25, 1990, filed in *Calumet Farm, Inc.,* Debtor, No. 91-51414 (Bankr., E.D., Ky.).

MOUNTING DEBTS OF CALUMET AND LUNDY

- Pieced together from documents in *Calumet Farm, Inc.,* Debtor, 91-51414 (Bankr., E.D., Ky.), Oct. 25, 1990, and Calumet records.

Chapter 15

INSURANCE PREMIUMS

- *Calumet misses payments:* Quote, "It began to get harder at that time," from Kathy Lundy Jones's deposition, in *Midlantic National Bank* v. *Calumet Farm, Inc., Triple C Thorostock et al.,* 91-2277 (Cir. Ct., Fayette Co., Ky.), filed June 19, 1991.
- *Expiration dates for policies:* From "Alydar Coverage in Effect as of Feb. 2, 1990," in exhibits of Jones's deposition.
- *Alydar's mortality coverage:* From "Calumet Farm, Inc., Mortality Policies in Effect at Alydar's Death," in exhibits, also in Jones's deposition.

Part IV: Frenzy

Chapters 1–4

ALYDAR EULOGIES

- *Charlie Rose:* "I feel like you'd feel," from *Los Angeles Times,* Nov. 16, 1990.
- *John Veitch:* "I was on the phone at an airport," quote from "Alydar's Death . . ." by Mike Smith, *National Sports Daily,* Nov. 23, 1990.
- *Flowers:* Note that flowers continued to appear on Alydar's grave periodically until the spring of 1993.

ALYDAR AFTERMATH

- *Dixon's investigation:* Interview with Stone, from "Transcribed Recorded Conversation of Calumet Farm Night Watchman, Alton Stone on 19 November 1990," in Calumet files.
- *Replacement of Alydar seasons:* Prepledged seasons, from Calumet records, though exact numbers impossible to determine because records are incomplete. Giveaway breeding rights, also from Calumet records. Wild Again breedings, from decision by bankruptcy judge Joe Lee, *In Re: Calumet Farm, Inc., Debtor,* 91-51414, *J.T. Lundy, William M. Allen, et al.* v. *Calumet Farm, Inc.,* Adv. 91-0179 (Bankr., E.D., Ky.), May 28, 1993. Farm owed Black Chip $1.2 million, from Calumet records.
- *First City and Criminal Type:* From Calumet records.
- *Manganaro Stables:* Transactions according to Amendment to Exchange Agreement dated Jan. 9, 1991, signed by J. T. Lundy and John Manga-

naro; also, *J.M.J. Stables Corporation* v. *Calumet Farm Inc.,* 91-CI-1757
(Cir. Ct., Fayette Co., Ky.), May 10, 1991.
- *Fred Gussin's Alydar breeding rights:* In signed letter from Lundy to Gussin
dated Nov. 21, 1990, Exhibit 3, *In Re: Calumet-Gussin* No. 1 91-5-01413,
Calumet Farm Inc., Debtor, 91-51414 (Bankr., E.D., Ky.), Sept. 6, 1991.

Chapters 5–7

EFFORTS TO GET MONEY

- *From Craig Singer:* According to Singer's affidavit dated Aug. 6, 1991, in
his later case trying to reclaim losses from Calumet.
- *Deals using season buybacks as lures:* From Calumet records.

THE JANUARY 1991 SALE

- *And First City:* Letters regarding First City and the question of reserves,
from Calumet records.
- *Lundy public statements about reasons for sale:* "Nowhere to put them,"
from "Calumet Farm to Sell 100 Horses for Space, Business Reasons," by
Jacqueline Duke, *Lexington Herald-Leader,* Nov. 22, 1990.
    "It's just horses and horses," from "Calumet Sells 62 Horses Despite
What Lundy Calls 'Weak' Market," by Jennie Rees, *Courier-Journal,* Jan.
16, 1991.

LAST DAYS OF LUNDY REGIME

- *Austin Mittler:* Details on attorney Mittler and Axmar Stables and the
March 27 meeting, according to Mittler's deposition in *Axmar Stable* v.
Calumet Farm Inc., 91-212 (E.D., Ky.), June 26, 1991.

Chapter 8

LUNDY RESIGNS

- *New Lundy loans:* From Citizen's Fidelity Bank, according to "Modification
Agreement," J. T. Lundy, dated June 27, 1991, regarding promissory note
dated April 1, 1991, filed in Scott County Court, May 1, 1992. Also *In Re
John Thomas Lundy,* 92-17096 (Bankr., S.D., Fla.), Dec. 16, 1992.
- *April 3 board meeting:* From Lyle Robey and other individuals who were
there.

- *Marathon mortgage:* From documents filed in Monroe County Court regarding federal tax liens and including copy of May 3, 1991, mortgage document, which was originally filed on July 11, 1991.
- *Calumet office staff told to leave:* From affidavits of Heinz and McGee, in *Equus Unlimited, Inc.* v. *Calumet Farm, Inc.,* 91-CI-1907 (Cir. Ct., Fayette Co., Ky.), filed July 10, 1991.
- *Reflections on Lundy's resignation:* Bertha Wright's quote, "J.T. has done what he set out to do," and J. T. Lundy's quote, "time to quit," both from "Lundy Resigns as President at Calumet," by the Associated Press, published in the *Courier-Journal,* Apr. 5, 1991.

Chapter 9

TALINUM PURCHASE

- *Terms and other details:* From *In Re: Northern Equine Thoroughbred Productions, Ltd. and 724334 Ontario, Ltd.* v. *Calumet Farm, Inc.* (Cir. Ct., Fayette Co., Ky.), filed Jan. 11, 1991, later Adv. 91-5224 in Calumet Farm, Inc., 91-51414 (Bankr., E.D., Ky.). Includes copy of Talinum agreement of purchase and sale, dated Dec. 15, 1988, including list of recipients of breeding rights, the "Limited Price Call Option Agreement." And the deposition of John Sikura, Jan. 14, 1992.

CALUMET BANKRUPTCY

- *In Re: Calumet Farm, Inc.,* 91-51414 (Bankr., E.D., Ky.), July 7, 1991. Final registry of claims, *In Re: Calumet Farm, Inc.,* 91-51414 (Bankr., E.D., Ky.), Feb. 2, 1992.

Chapter 10

NOVEMBER 1991 SALE

- *Lewis Burrell:* Quote of M. C. Hammer's father, from "Matriarch Says She Feels She Let Family Down," by Joseph S. Stroud, Jim Jordan, and Hiawatha Bray, *Lexington Herald-Leader,* July 12, 1991.
- *Seattle agent:* Name of Seattle bloodstock agent leaning against barn 9 was Ron Ratcliff.

Chapter 11

THE BLAME GAME

- *Calumet Farm, Inc.'s loans to family:* According to *In Re: Bertha C. Wright, Debtor,* 93-50224, *National City Bank of Lexington, Kentucky* v. *Bertha C. Wright,* 93-5065 (Bankr., E.D., Ky.), May 21, 1993.
- *The family blames the bank:* Wright v. *CommerceNational Bank & Trust Company of Lexington, Ky.,* 91-CI-3076 (Cir. Ct., Fayette Co., Ky.), Aug. 15, 1991.
- *The bank blames the family:* In counterclaims of above case 91-CI-3076. And, CommerceNational, which changed its name to National City Bank of Lexington, Ky., sued members of the family, *In Re: Bertha C. Wright, Debtor,* 93-50224, *National City Bank of Lexington, Kentucky* v. *Bertha C. Wright,* Adv. 93-5065 (Bankr., E.D., Ky.), May 21, 1993.
- *The unsecured creditors blame Robey:* Filed July 8, 1993, against the estate of Lyle Robey in (E.D., Ky.) 93-291, *Phoenix Corp.* v. *Karen Compton, Executrix of the estate of Lyle Robey, deceased.* Robey's sister denied the allegations in an answer to the complaint filed in federal court on July 29, 1993.
- *Bertha Wright:* Quote, "He does things his way: 'I'm the leader. You follow,'" from "A Search for Answers as Calumet Crumbles," by Joseph Durso, *New York Times,* July 15, 1991.

    Quote, "I'm the last of the four," from "Matriarch Says She Feels She Let Family Down," by Joseph S. Stroud, Jim Jordan, and Hiawatha Bray, *Lexington Herald-Leader,* July 12, 1991.

Chapters 12 and 13

BERTHA WRIGHT

- *On television:* Interview with Sue Wylie, from videotape of show.

SUSPICIONS IN THE BLUEGRASS

- *Libutti indictment:* Thirteen-count indictment for bank fraud and other charges, *U.S.* v. *Kruckel and Libutti,* U.S.A. No. 9003996 (U.S. Dist. Ct., Newark, N.J.), filed Oct. 29, 1992.
- *Gurino indictment:* Gurino and Lou-Roe, *U.S.* v. *Gurino,* 92-01007 (N.D., Fla.), Feb. 27, 1992.

- *John Gotti link:* Quote from Lieutenant Frank Alioto of the Marion County Sheriff's Department linking Lou-Roe Farms to reputed Mafia kingpin John Gotti is taken from Charles Bartels, "Arrests Link Marion Farm to Mobsters," *Ocala Star-Banner,* Feb. 28, 1992.
- *Elusive Lundy:* Report of warning order attorney, filed in *Bertha C. Wright v. CommerceNational Bank,* 91-CI-3076 (Cir. Ct., Fayette Co., Ky.), May 14, 1992. Local interest in J.T.'s whereabouts, according to Don Edwards's column, "Buffy Reads the Future in Her Crystal Horseshoe," *Lexington Herald-Leader,* Jan. 3, 1993.
- *Responsibility:* Robey's quote, "[Lundy] did everything," from *In Re: Calumet Farm, Inc., Debtor,* 91-51414, *J.T. Lundy v. Calumet Farm, Inc.,* 91-0179 (Bankr., E.D., Ky.), May 28, 1993. "I don't know," etc., quotes from Lundy, taken from his depositions in *Axmar Stable v. Calumet Farm Inc.,* 91-212 (E.D., Ky.), June 25, 1991, and in *IBJ Schroder Bank & Trust Company,* 91-354 (E.D., Ky.), Dec. 30, 1991.

Part V: Phoenix

Chapter 5

HENRYK DE KWIATKOWSKI

- *Biographical details:* From interviews and from various articles including: "Henryk de Kwiatkowski: The Man and the Myth," by Robert Kaiser, *Lexington Herald-Leader,* May 31, 1992; "The Man Who Makes the Market in Used Planes," by Eleanor Johnson Tracy, *Fortune,* July 12, 1982; "Sentimental Journey: From Poland to Polo," by Cornelia Bernard, *Spur,* July/ Aug. 1990; and "The Knight Who Saved Calumet's Day," by Jacqueline Duke, *Louisville Magazine,* Apr. 1993.

Chapter 6

BERTHA WRIGHT'S SALE

- *Auction:* Details gleaned in part from "Wright Belongings Lure 300 to Auction," by Jacalyn Carfagno, *Lexington Herald-Leader,* May 10, 1992; from auction catalog: "Auction Featuring Household Furnishings of Bertha Wright and Others," Swinebroad-Denton, Inc., Lexington, Ky.; from interviews with Bertha Wright and others several months after the sale.

- *Trophies:* Details gleaned from Margaret Glass's fifteen-page account, with twenty-five exhibits, for all interested in the value and ownership, dated Apr. 15, 1993. Quote, "To prevent that b—— [J. T. Lundy] from Midway from getting his hands on them," from Margaret Glass's recollections.

Chapters 7–9

BANKRUPTCIES AND STRESS

- *Robey's stress:* Libel suit involving Robey, on appeal as of fall of 1993.
- *Lundy files bankruptcy: In Re John Thomas Lundy,* 92-17096 (Bankr., S.D., Fla.), Dec. 16, 1992.
- *Lundy and the paintings:* From his deposition in *Axmar Stable* v. *Calumet Farm Inc.,* 91-212 (E.D., Ky.), June 25, 1991.
- *Bertha Wright:* Details regarding Bertha's finances, according to her bankruptcy petition, Bertha Wright, debtor, 93-50224 (Bankr., E.D., Ky.), February 12, 1993.
- *Lucille "Cindy" Wright:* Finances regarding the purchase of her home in Palm Beach County, according to her deposition taken Dec. 10, 1992, in *IBJ Schroder Bank & Trust Co.* v. *Wright et al.,* 92-6502 (Cir. Ct., 15th Jud. Cir.). With the rest of the money from her oil property sales, she purchased two annuities from Canada Life Assurance Co., also from deposition.

    Her bankruptcy filing, *In Re: Lucille Wright Lundy,* 93-31460 (Bankr., S.D., Fla.), May 3, 1993. Monies owed and assets, according to "Statement of Financial Affairs," *In Re: Lucille Wright Lundy,* Debtor (Bankr., S.D., Fla.), May 18, 1993.

    Her divorce, *In Re: The Marriage of Lucille Lundy* v. *John Thomas Lundy,* 93-1939 (Cir. Ct., 11th Jud. Cir.), Jan. 28, 1993. Divorce finalized, "Final Order as to All Parties," *In Re: The Marriage of Lucille Lundy* v. *John Thomas Lundy,* 93-1939 (Cir. Ct., 11th Jud. Cir.), July 19, 1993.

FIRST CITY

- *Probes, etc.:* Quote, "We were doing things that were just crazy," from "First City Probe Looks at Bad Deals: $180 Million Worth of Loans Questioned," by Daniel Fisher, *Houston Post,* Nov. 21, 1992.

Chapter 10

FRANK CIHAK

- *Indicted:* Thirty-four-count indictment, *U.S.* v. *Cihak,* H-93-119 (S.D., Tex.; Houston div.), Apr. 21, 1993.
- *Convicted:* Convicted on thirty-two counts, including money laundering, wire fraud, bank fraud, and conspiracy, Nov. 19, 1993.

LLOYD SWIFT

- *Indicted:* On ten counts along with Cihak, *U.S.* v. *Cihak,* H-93-119 (S.D., Tex.; Houston div.), Apr. 21, 1993.
- *Convicted:* On ten counts, Nov. 19, 1993, including fraud and money laundering. Also convicted in the same case, Wilma Allen on eight counts for various charges of bank fraud and money laundering.

ROBERT LIBUTTI

- *Indicted:* In thirteen-count indictment for bank fraud and other charges, *U.S.* v. *Kruckel and Libutti,* U.S.A. No. 9003996 (U.S. Dist. Ct., Newark, N.J.), filed Oct. 29, 1992.
- *Update:* Convicted Feb. 18, 1994, of attempting to avoid paying $3.5 million in income taxes and of defrauding a New Jersey bank of $1.25 million. Separate trial pending on possession of firearm.

PETER BRANT

- *Update on Brant:* From *Wall Street Journal,* "Legal Beat" column, Apr. 13, 1990, June 11, 1990, Mar. 19, 1993, and Marketing and Media Column, May 9, 1989, Mar. 16, 1992.

ANTHONY GURINO

- *Guilty pleas:* From plea agreement, Money Laundering Section, Criminal Division, U.S. Department of Justice, *U.S.* v. *Gurino,* 92-01007 (N.D., Fla.), Feb. 8, 1993. Statement of compliance with plea agreement reveals that charges were dropped against Louis Gurino.

Chapter 11

Horse Killers

- *Numerous cases:* Some details from "Blood Money," by William Nack and Lester Munson, *Sports Illustrated,* Nov. 16, 1992.
- *Lawrence Lombardo:* Some details from twenty-one-count indictment for criminal activity in connection with the thoroughbred Fins, *U.S.* v. *Lombardo,* 92-0483 (S.D., Fla.), Aug. 4, 1992. Government response to defendant's objections to presentence report, *U.S.* v. *Lombardo,* 92-0483 (S.D., Fla.), June 14, 1993. Transcript of proceedings before U.S. District Judge Shelby Highsmith of Miami, Dade County, Fla., Apr. 9, 1993. Note that Lombardo's lawyer, in "Objections to the Presentence Report," "objected to the reference of organized crime intercession to settle a dispute between Howard Crash and Robert Libutti. . . . It is counsel's belief that this 'sit-down' never occurred."

Acknowledgments

To thank everyone who helped nurture this book would be impossible. I must extend my deepest thanks to my husband, John, a fellow writer, who understood my devotion to the book and always was supportive; to super-agent Alice Martell whose upbeat spirit and endless energy are what every writer seeks in an agent; to Bill Strachan, my editor, who recognized from the start the universal scope of the human tragedy in the Calumet story and whose enthusiasm and talent are simply heaven-sent; to Neil Chethik whose contributions were brilliant; and to Rorie Sherman, for her wisdom. Very special thanks to Paul Steiger, managing editor of *The Wall Street Journal*, and to Margaret Glass, Todd Wright, Paula Cline, Sari Levin, Stanley Petter, Jr., Mary Jane Gallaher, Ilyce R. Glink, Dan Kelly, Charlie Carberry, Darcy Tromanhauser, Harriet Gold, Marylou Whitney, and Priscilla Loeb for their generosity at various stages of reporting and writing this story.

Before I began my research, everyone who knew anything about the horse industry warned me that it was such a clubby business I'd be lucky to interview a dozen insiders. As it turned out, hundreds of people were willing to talk to me and I am grateful to them all. I would like to thank especially: Melinda Bena, Jimmy Jones, Robbie Lantz and Myrna Loy, Pam Michul, Ron Sladon, Alton Stone, William P. Sutter, David Switzer, Whitney Tower, John Veitch, John Ward, and Sissy Woolums.

Several people were willing to speak to me about such sensitive topics as the questionable practices of their industry during the 1980s. Some did so at the risk of being implicated and yet they came forward, they said, because they believed the greed and excesses of the Bluegrass Bubble nearly destroyed the horse industry in this country. They felt that if they didn't reveal what had happened during that era, it could occur again. I am very grateful to those who opened up to me.

At the same time, numerous people declined interviews. I understand their reticence and harbor no resentments. In most cases, their lawyers advised them not to talk because of pending litigation. Bertha Wright was willing to speak with me on a few occasions regarding matters prior to 1982 that had nothing to do with her immediate family or the bank that managed her trust. I thank her for the time she was able to spend with me.

Interviewing so many people whose collective experiences in the horse industry spanned nearly fifty years taught me that despite the corruption and fraud revealed in this book, the business is filled with hardworking and honorable people who love horses for what they are and can be—beautiful animals and great athletes. However, this is clearly a "buyer beware" business. Anyone who buys a piece of a horse for the sole purpose of making money and who has no desire to watch the enthralling process of a yearling becoming a racehorse should invest in something else. In the horse industry, there are no guarantees except perhaps a shiver of excitement as the crowd sings "My Old Kentucky Home" at the Derby each May and the feeling of hope as a newborn foal takes its first wobbly steps.

In addition to interviews, I relied heavily on primary source material. This required a tremendous amount of research, in courthouses, libraries, historical societies, and archives nationwide. My adept researchers Ilyce R. Glink, Kristin Svingen, and Porter McRoberts doggedly pursued details that seemed at first impossible to find. My thanks also to Bruce Levy at *The Wall Street Journal*, to both Hylind InfoQuest and Decision Strategies, as well as Beverly M. Burden and Donna Famularo in Judge Lee's chamber at the Federal Bankruptcy Court in Lexington, Anita Beaver at the Springfield *Sun* newspaper, Theresa Fitzgerald at *The Blood-Horse*, Marianne Kane at the Greene County Public Library, Nick Nicholson at the Jockey Club, and Doris Warren at the Keeneland Library.

Also thanks to those who helped me at: The Australian Jockey Club,

Chicago Historical Society, Chicago Public Library, *Chicago Tribune,* Dayton Public Library, Fayette Circuit Court, Georgetown Public Library, the Kentucky Room at the Lexington Public Library, Kraft General Foods Archives, Los Angeles Superior Court, Louisville Federal Court, Louisville Public Library, Manhattan Federal Court, Maysville Public Library, Miami Federal Court, *Miami Herald,* Miami Public Library, National Film Information Services, the *New York Daily News,* the Newark *Star-Ledger,* Palm Beach Federal Court, Saratoga Public Library, Scott Circuit Court, Springfield Public Library, Stallion Access, Tallahassee Federal Court, U.S. Federal Trade Commission, U.S. Department of Justice, and Xenia Public Library. I'm especially grateful to the staffs of the county and federal courts in Lexington whose files are better organized than any I've ever used.

Special thanks to fellow reporters Jacalyn Carfagno and Jacqueline Duke who graciously accepted me into the inner circle of the local press for the nearly two years that I attended events related to the Calumet debacle. Beat reporters often resent book writers who swoop into their territory, grab their sources, and ask a million questions for an opus that isn't due for at least a year. I've been on both sides of this situation now and I must say that the courtesy and tolerance of these reporters as well as turf writers Joe Durso and Joe Hirsch and business writer Bill Quinn was quite refreshing.

I also owe a debt of gratitude to my parents, my sister Sarah, and Harry and Eunice Landis who taught me many years ago to respect the power and beauty of horses. When I was six years old, my mother and father took me to Calumet Farm for the first time. We toured the barns, visited Tim Tam in his stall, and photographed Citation rolling in the grass. In spring and sometimes summer for the next five years, we made the trip to the Bluegrass from our home in Dayton, Ohio. I never asked why we did it year after year, taking the same pictures of famous racehorses and the white fences and watching foals test their spindly legs across Calumet fields. But it's clear to me now that besides the sheer beauty of the land and the horses, my parents wanted us to witness the tradition of achievement and excellence that Calumet then represented. And so my last note of thanks is to Henryk de Kwiatkowski for his vision of resurrecting that tradition and for opening the farm to the public once again.

Index